Anti-Racism as Communism

Anti-Racism as Communism

Paul Gomberg

BLOOMSBURY ACADEMIC
LONDON · NEW YORK · OXFORD · NEW DELHI · SYDNEY

BLOOMSBURY ACADEMIC
Bloomsbury Publishing Plc, 50 Bedford Square, London, WC1B 3DP, UK
Bloomsbury Publishing Inc, 1359 Broadway, New York, NY 10018, USA
Bloomsbury Publishing Ireland, 29 Earlsfort Terrace, Dublin 2, D02 AY28, Ireland

BLOOMSBURY, BLOOMSBURY ACADEMIC and the Diana logo are trademarks
of Bloomsbury Publishing Plc

First published in Great Britain 2024
Paperback edition published 2025

Copyright © Paul Gomberg, 2024

Paul Gomberg has asserted his right under the Copyright, Designs and Patents Act,
1988, to be identified as Author of this work.

Series design by Adriana Brioso
Cover image (c) AleFron/Adobe Stock

For legal purposes the Acknowledgements on p. xii constitute an extension
of this copyright page.

All rights reserved. No part of this publication may be: i) reproduced or transmitted
in any form, electronic or mechanical, including photocopying, recording or by means
of any information storage or retrieval system without prior permission in writing from the
publishers; or ii) used or reproduced in any way for the training, development or operation
of artificial intelligence (AI) technologies, including generative AI technologies. The rights
holders expressly reserve this publication from the text and data mining exception as
per Article 4(3) of the Digital Single Market Directive (EU) 2019/790.

Bloomsbury Publishing Plc does not have any control over, or responsibility
for, any third-party websites referred to or in this book. All internet addresses
given in this book were correct at the time of going to press. The author and
publisher regret any inconvenience caused if addresses have changed or sites
have ceased to exist, but can accept no responsibility for any such changes.

A catalogue record for this book is available from the British Library.

Library of Congress Cataloging-in-Publication Data
Names: Gomberg, Paul, author.
Title: Anti-racism as communism / Paul Gomberg.
Description: London; New York, NY : Bloomsbury Academic/Bloomsbury Publishing Plc, 2023. |
Includes bibliographical references and index. | Summary: "Anti-racism is a necessary part of modern
political discourse, but too often it excludes the Marxist analysis of class and labor. Paul Gomberg
argues that any anti-racism platform must discuss the entrenched inequality created by the capitalist
system of exploitative labor relations. In this book, Gomberg re-orientates the history of modern
America, to show how racism was built upon the exploitation of slave labor, and how this developed in
the modern American polity as entrenched class and race-based discrimination. In particular, the history
of the American Communist Party is studied as an example of how without anti-capitalism, racial
injustice is reconstructed even through anti-racism campaigning. In this analysis, the only lasting way to
establish an anti-racist society is to undo the capitalist system which has entrenched wealth in the
hands of white settlers" — Provided by publisher.
Identifiers: LCCN 2023010846 | ISBN 9781350257979 (hardback) | ISBN 9781350258013 (paperback) |
ISBN 9781350257993 (pdf) | ISBN 9781350257986 (epub) | ISBN 9781350258006
Subjects: LCSH: Anti-racism—United States. | Communism—United States. |
United States—Race relations. | Equality—United States. | Income distribution—United States.
Classification: LCC HT1521 .G565 2024 | DDC 305.800973—dc23/eng/20230323
LC record available at https://lccn.loc.gov/2023010846

ISBN:	HB:	978-1-3502-5797-9
	PB:	978-1-3502-5801-3
	ePDF:	978-1-350-25799-3
	eBook:	978-1-350-25798-6

Typeset by RefineCatch Limited, Bungay, Suffolk

For product safety related questions contact productsafety@bloomsbury.com.

To find out more about our authors and books visit www.bloomsbury.com
and sign up for our newsletters.

Contents

List of Illustrations	viii
List of Abbreviations	ix
Credits	xi
Acknowledgements	xii
A Personal Introduction	1

Part One Origin and Persistence of Racism

1 The Origin and Meaning of Race in English North America 11
- European slavery before conquest of the Americas — 11
- European invasion — 11
- The English Colony of Virginia — 12
- White benefit? — 21
- Regional variations — 23
- The meaning of race — 25
- Slavery, race, and the rise of capitalist society — 26

2 Race in the American Revolution through the Civil War 29
- Race and the revolution of 1776 — 29
- Racism becomes American — 31
- The expansion of racist society — 33
- Racism in northern cities — 36
- Resistance to slavery and racism — 38
- Black fighters in the Civil War — 40

3 Black Workers in Southern Agriculture: From Reconstruction to World War II 45
- Reconstruction and its aftermath in the South — 45
- The new racial injustice: plantation agriculture, cotton production, and resistance — 49
- Jim Crow laws — 54
- Agriculture under Jim Crow — 55
- Southern agriculture, black labor, and capitalism — 58

4	**Race and Anti-Racism in Industry: Coal Miners 1870–1921**	61
	Overview	61
	Background: industrial slavery	61
	Some lessons from the life and thought of Richard L. Davis	62
	Anti-racist lessons from battles of Alabama coal miners 1870–1921	66
	The United Mine Workers of America (UMWA) in Alabama 1890–1921	67
	Communist lessons	73
5	**Race and Anti-Racism in Industry: The Communist Party Fights Racism**	75
	Overview	75
	Lessons from the life of Hosea Hudson and Alabama communists	76
	The Communist Party becomes anti-racist	84
	The Unemployed Councils (UCs)	86
	The Scottsboro Campaign and the International Labor Defense	88
	More communist anti-racist practice	90
	Some lessons of the CP's practice in the early 1930s	91
	The CP's anti-racist understanding	92
	Reform and revolution	93
	Communist work in the CIO	93
	The anti-racism of red-led CIO unions	94
	Repression and reversal	109
	Lessons of communist anti-racism	112
6	**The Creation of Today's Racism**	117
	Overview	117
	The New Deal: deepening racial inequality	117
	The rise and fall of civil rights	122
	Workers without rights: recreating racial injustice	126
	Function and social change	127
	The relative decline of the United States	128
	The recreation of state-centered racial injustice	130
	Cheap food, cheap chicken	137
	What goes around comes around	140
	The year 2020 and thereafter	141

Part Two Fighting and Ending Racism

7	**Is Racism Interracial?**	145
	Two models of racism	145

	The interracial model of racism	146
	A racial harms model of racism	153
	Racism is not interracial	157
8	**Alienating Race and Fighting Racism**	159
	The social psychology of group identity	159
	"Othering" people and racist social thought	163
	Seeing and fighting racism when black people are in charge	164
	Seeing and fighting racism when non-black people are in charge	168
	Alienating race	169
	The paradox of this chapter	175
9	**Race-Centered Marxism**	177
	Introduction	177
	Du Bois and Cox: pioneers of race-centered Marxism	177
	Race-centered aracial Marxism	183
	Who are my people? Whose oppression is my oppression?	185
	Some objections and replies	193
	Summary of race-centered Marxism	195
10	**A Society Without Race**	197
	What vision of a society without race can inspire anti-racists?	197
	Why proposed remedies to racism would not correct it	199
	Only communism can end racism	206
11	**Reasonable Hope?**	209
	An objection	209
	Urban uprisings and revolutionary situations	209
	How people are transformed through struggle	211
	How might a large group of communists develop?	214
	Communists, non-communists, and communist revolution	215
	Communism and workers' empowerment	218
	Revolution and state power	227
	We should prefer reasonable hope to reasonable despair	227
References		229
Index		243

Illustrations

5.1	UPWA logo.	105
9.1	January 27, 2007 anti-war demonstration Washington, DC.	188
9.2	May 1, 2007 demonstration Los Angeles, California.	188
9.3	September 15, 2007 in Jena, Louisiana protesting prosecutorial racism against black youth.	189

Abbreviations

ACTU	Association of Catholic Trade Unionists
AFL	American Federation of Labor
AMC	Amalgamated Meat Cutters
ANLC	American Negro Labor Congress
ARU	American Railway Union
BTC	Birmingham Trades Council
CCP	Chinese Communist Party
CIO	Committee for Industrial Organization, after 1938 Congress of Industrial Organizations
Comintern	Third (Communist) International
CORE	Congress of Racial Equality
CP	Communist Party of the United States of America
CR	Cultural Revolution, Great Proletarian Cultural Revolution
CRC	Combahee River Collective
FHA	Federal Housing Administration
FTA	Food, Tobacco, and Agricultural, and Allied Workers Union
GLF	Great Leap Forward
GLP	Greenback Labor Party
HOLC	Home Owners Loan Corporation
IFLWU	International Fur and Leather Workers Union
ILA	International Longshoremen's Association
ILD	International Labor Defense
ILWU	International Longshoremen's and Warehousemen's Union
Journal	*Journal of the United Mine Workers of America*
Knights	Knights of Labor
KUTV	University of the Toilers of the East
LSNR	League of Struggle for Negro Rights
Mine Mill	International Union of Mine, Mill, and Smelter Workers
NAACP	National Association for the Advancement of Colored People
NIRA	National Industrial Recovery Act
NLRA	National Labor Relations Act
NLRB	National Labor Relations Board
NMU	National Maritime Union
NNC	National Negro Congress
NTWIU	Needle Trade Workers Industrial Union
NUMCS	National Union of Marine Cooks and Stewards
PHWIU	Packing House Workers Industrial Union
PLP	Progressive Labor Party

PWOC	Packinghouse Workers Organizing Committee
SIU	Seafarers International Union
SUP	Sailor's Union of the Pacific
TCI	Tennessee Coal and Iron
TUUL	Trade Union Unity League
UAW	United Auto Workers
UC	Unemployed Council
UCAPAWA	United Cannery, Agricultural, Packing, and Allied Workers of America
UE	United Electrical, Radio, and Machine Workers of America
UFCW	United Food and Commercial Workers
UMWA	United Mine Workers of America
UPWA	United Packinghouse Workers of America
US	United States
USSR	Union of Soviet Socialist Republics
USWA	United Steelworkers of America
VA	Veterans Administration

Credits

Parts of Chapter 5 appeared in *Symposion: Theoretical and Applied Inquiries in Philosophy and the Social Sciences* 4(1) May 2017, pp. 49–76.

The epigraph to Chapter 8 is from the film *James Baldwin: The Price of the Ticket*, directed by Karen Thorsen, www.jamesbaldwinproject.org.

The Epigraph to Chapter 11 is from Meisner 1999, p. 35.

Acknowledgements

A project that has taken over thirteen years, in consultation with many people, acquires a lot of debts. In fact, so many have helped me that I am certain that I will not mention everyone. I will do my best. I apologize in advance to anyone who helped me whom I have left out.

At Chicago State Lionel Kimble, Roland Wulbert, Phillip Beverly, and Mark Johnson all were stimulating interlocutors. Pancho McFarland, Ann Kuzdale, and Emmett Bradbury read chapter drafts and offered useful comments and advice. I read some material at meetings of the Association for Political Theory and the Midwest Political Science Association. I thank my critics and commentators. The Department of Philosophy at University of Illinois Chicago organized a colloquium where I presented a chapter. I presented a chapter in 2015 to a colloquium at UIC, organized by Stephen Engelman. In the fall of 2014 I discussed alienating race at University of California at Davis, Portland State University, and University of Washington, again receiving much useful criticism.

Later at Davis I presented more material to the Davis Group on Ethics and Related Subjects (DaGERS). Tina Rulli, who disagrees deeply with some arguments, was more helpful to me than (I suspect) she knows. David Copp, Marina Oshana, and Adam Sennet all offered criticism which affected what appears. Many others in that wonderful group gave helpful criticism and suggestions.

Jillian Wilkowski has listened, encouraged me, and offered criticisms that have occasioned changes. Richard David has long discussed the issues and guided me to his and James Collins' contributions to issues of infant mortality and racism. Caro Brighouse helped me to understand important points.

Various chapters have been read by Miriam Golomb, David Lyons, Charles Mills, Justin Holt, and Sheldon Jones. Lucas Stanczyk, Alex Gourevitch, Jeppe von Platz, and Sam Arnold read a chapter, gave criticism, and offered encouragement, deeply appreciated. Inayah Baaqee, Maricarmen Suarez, and Edwin Ortega discussed a chapter draft, leading to improvement. Kathy Dahlgren has read and guided revision of the last chapter. Caleb Ward helped me with Chapter 9.

Chris Rudd, Floyd Banks, Carol Caref, the late John Boelter, and many other Chicago friends listened to and argued with me for many years. Carol read a chapter and gave enthusiastic encouragement. Jim Griesemer, department chair my first five years at Davis, encouraged me and showed respect for the project.

Anthony O'Brien, Greg Meyerson, Steve Rosenthal, Miriam Rosenthal, and Barbara Foley read one of the early drafts and showed me how to express simultaneously the severity of class oppression and the extra oppression of race. Ellen Isaacs read a draft and offered help.

Bill Sacks read most of the manuscript and corrected me on numerous points. I am extremely grateful. Rose Lenehan, representing a new generation of Marxist philosophers of race, has done the same and taught me so much. Barbara Foley again read the entire draft and offered many helpful criticisms, as did Finley Campbell. Andrew Chitty read two chapters with the sharp eye of an excellent philosopher and saved me from errors and unclarity. Adam Sennet read much of the book and challenged me in ways that led to further revision. I benefitted from two anonymous reviews from Bloomsbury and editorial support from David Avital, Tomasz Hoskins, Atifa Jiwa, Nayiri Kendir, Nadine Staes-Polet and Tamsin Ballard.

Terry Rudd has been my political mentor and instructor about racism for the past thirty-five years. She has taught me so much that appears on page after page of the book.

My daughter Ruth Gomberg-Muñoz has encouraged this project from the start and has helpfully read and criticized several chapters. The discussion of workers without rights in Chapter 6 grew out of our conversations many years ago.

I love the title of the book, but I didn't think of it. It emerged from a conversation between Rose Lenehan and A. J. Julius. Rose was telling A. J. about the argument of the book, and he replied, "Oh, anti-racism as communism! He should call it that." Rose conveyed that suggestion to me, and, while I rejected it at first, I finally wised up.

The main person who has kept this project going is Mary Conklin Gomberg, who heroically read the book three times to help me make it better. She was right on so many points and got me to make many changes that have helped the work. More than anyone else, she believed in the project (despite her political skepticism) and insisted that I must complete it. Not least, she has been my marital companion for fifty-eight years, giving my life daily joy and laughter.

The ideas in the book are due to instruction from two collectives. Students I have known in my twenty-nine years at Chicago State taught me more about racism than I taught them. My comrades in Progressive Labor Party have shown me how to end it. I dedicate the book to these two collectives.

A Personal Introduction

I don't know enough to write this book. But if I wait until I know enough, the book will never be written. I believe I have learned enough to write something useful to others.

The problem with "knowing enough" is the breadth of my topic. Part 1 is a narrative of the origins and persistence of racism in the United States (US). I was trained as a philosopher. The narrative covers history, sociology, social psychology, and political economy. In order to fight and end racism (the topics of Part 2) we need to understand its history and persistence. Thus the reason I don't know enough is not that I am especially ignorant—I am ignorant enough but not remarkably so; I don't know enough because the topic is immense: how to end racism. No one knows enough. Most academics concentrate on narrower problems where they can become expert. We urgently need to know how to end racism. If I have come to understand anything helpful to others, I need to share it now.

In 1970 I participated in several demonstrations against a particular racial injustice. Charlie McNeil, a black electrician's apprentice at Harvard University, was trying to make the transition from the custodial staff (for which black workers were typically hired) to a skilled trade, where workers were almost exclusively white. Harvard had threatened to drop Charlie from the electrician's apprenticeship program. Students for a Democratic Society and some graduate students and faculty were supporting Charlie's effort to stay in and complete the program. I became more aware of anti-black racism.

I had grown up "white" and am perceived socially as white. As a young person I had little awareness of racism affecting people identified as black. Moreover, typically for people ambitious to have an academic career, my friends did not include those called "black." So 1970 also marked the year when I first made an effort to form friendships across the divides created by racist society. These two processes—anti-racist activism and changing the "color" of my circle of intimates—are related; the first is pretty limited without the second. For more than fifty years now I have tried to fight racism and defeat racial divisions in my social world. This book grows out of and is intended to be part of this life.

* * *

I have used scare quotes—so-called "black" people, so-called "white" people—to express alienation from racial categories: we are called by these names, but the categories were invented and are sustained to exploit and oppress. The racial categories in which we are placed affect what we are likely to experience. Still, I do not accept them because I oppose and seek to end racist society. However, racial harms and categories are my topic. If, instead of talking about black and white people, I always wrote "people called 'black' in racist society" and "people called 'white' in racist society" readers would, I judge, find it distracting and annoying. So I won't do that. But that is what I mean.

About the racial terms I will use: I will not capitalize words for races. Except for capitalization at the beginning of a sentence, the first letters of racial terms will be lower case. That allows me to mark some useful distinctions. John was born and grew up in Los Angeles where he went to public schools; his parents spoke English at home and cooked meals typical of people in LA; yet his face displays features stereotypical of people from East Asia. He is racially asian, but he is not from Asia. Susan, on the other hand was born, raised, and now lives in China, having gone to schools there; she speaks only Chinese. Her parents migrated as a childless couple in the late 1940s from the United States to China to participate in the revolution. She is Chinese and Asian, but she is not asian. So, as I will use the terms, many asian people in the US are not Asian and a few Asian people are not asian. The word "asian" (as I use it) refers to people fitting a racial category in racist US society; it does not say anything about a person's relationship to Asia.

"But, Paul, that reasoning doesn't work for Black people. The word 'black' (lower case) names a color. 'Black' names a race of people. Black people are not black; they are various shades of brown. To use 'black' (lower case) for Black people is to speak nonsense." In reply, yes, black people are not black and white people are not white. There are no good terms for categories invented as instruments of exploitation and oppression; it is better not to try to make any other sense of them. "African-American" does not fit the US racial category. Many Africans who are not American are nevertheless black on the streets of any US city and will be treated accordingly. Don't try to make sense out of categories invented to exploit and oppress.

"Paul, you are erasing Black people's agency. We have taken a category invented to oppress and given it a positive meaning as representing the history, language styles, manners of dress, and other culture of our people. That is why we capitalize 'Black,' to represent our cultural or national identity." In reply, people who are racially black do not represent a unique culture or a single language style. There are white people who are code switchers, totally fluent in Black English Vernacular (BEV). Some white people adopt dress styles and music common among urban black youth but are not racially black. Some black people do not speak BEV and buy clothes at Brooks Brothers. Who is black? The people racist US culture identifies as black.

"Paul, this reply equates the way Black people are *racialized* by others with the meaning Black people themselves give to their Blackness. That equation erases our agency, autonomy, and authority. We take a negative and demeaning thing and turn it into something positive, representing our subjective experience of Blackness, webs of meaning tying us to others. Our Blackness sustains us and gives us dignity."

In reply: no doubt that many black people give blackness a positive meaning. But the category is still the enemy's category. If racism was no longer a social reality, if the racist categories of racist society in no way limited what people could be or do, where they could live or go to school, whom they could associate with, befriend or love, then blackness would no longer have a meaning. The webs of subjective meaning that black people give to their blackness would disappear along with racism. The ways that black people give blackness a positive meaning are helpful to *enduring* racism. Accepting racial categories is not helpful to *ending* racist society—or so I will try to show.

"Latino" leaves out women and insists on gendering people, as does "latina." "Latinx" is a word made up to deal with this problem. I came to political consciousness in the 1960s, and we used the word "latin" for people perceived as latin. "Latin" is the name of an ancient language. As I will use the words, latin people don't (often) speak Latin. "latin" (lower case) is just the name of a racial ascription in racist US society. So for me the racial terms will be black, white, latin, and asian. In the western US latin people are commonly called mexican. For indigenous peoples of the Americas I use the term "indigenous."

There are other ways of using racial language, equally justified. This way of using the language of race makes sense to me: let racial language be obvious nonsense.

* * *

Mostly I use the word "racism" but sometimes the phrase "racial injustice." These refer to social organization where some people are systematically harmed because of how they are identified racially. "Racism" primarily refers to racist society. Racist social organization consists of particular acts or events, which I also call racist when they target the racially oppressed. "Racism" often refers to individual bigotry, a suggestion I seek to avoid. Calling racist society an "injustice" expresses opposition to it, nothing more (I have no "theory of justice"). I write for an anti-racist audience. People unbothered by racist social organization need read no further.

The anti-racism developed here is grounded in a working-class interest in fighting for a world without race, where we flourish together by contributing to one another's flourishing. There is no appeal to abstract justice independent of class.

This book displays Marxism's resources for understanding, opposing, and ending racism. Racism is here explained in the context of capitalist society and its need for labor that produces commodities and services at a profit for the capitalist. Black workers (and latin, indigenous, and others racially stigmatized) are a segment of the working class which has been and still is typically employed in jobs that pay less, require less formal schooling or other training, are more dangerous, dirty, and difficult, and are less secure. Black workers experience high unemployment and are disproportionately casual workers. They are more likely to be abused and killed by cops and to be incarcerated. Many black children are especially abused by racism, confined in schools which create greater opportunity to go to jail than to college. This worse treatment is part of their being treated as black. Because black people are treated worse, some stigmatize them as inferior to justify oppression; stigma is an extra burden. Inequalities in exploitation and oppression marked by racial identity divide the working class. Divisions undermine common collective action, making it hard for workers to attain decent conditions, much less improve them.

That much is common to much Marxist thought about race. However, for me—as for W.E.B. Du Bois in *Black Reconstruction* (1962 [1935])—capitalism itself and the modern world develop from the exploitation of workers of color in Asia, Africa, the

Americas, and other regions. This exploitation grounds the development of industry in the global "north." While Marx recognized some of this in the last section of *Capital* (1976 [1867]), on primitive accumulation, that understanding did not inform his account of the norms of capitalist production. What happened in the US—my focus—should be understood as part of this worldwide development. We need race-centered Marxism.

The Marxism here is at the revolutionary pole of the Marxist tradition: racism can be ended only in a society without race and class, where the opportunity to develop and contribute abilities for the good of all is unlimited—in short, a communist society. Karl Marx and Friedrich Engels closed *The Communist Manifesto* (1974 [1848]: 98) with these words:

> The Communists disdain to conceal their views and aims. They openly declare that their ends can be attained only by the forcible overthrow of all existing conditions. Let the ruling classes tremble at a communistic revolution. The proletarians have nothing to lose but their chains. They have a world to win.

I am partisan: I oppose racism. I am a partisan of the working class in its struggles with the capitalist class. For a revolutionary communist, struggle culminates in a revolution that destroys capitalist society and the state power that sustains it. I am a partisan of that revolution. So I use the language of partisanship, often calling the capitalists "the enemy." In using that language I am *not* trying to persuade the reader that capitalists are the enemy. The burden of persuasion is carried by facts and arguments. In using the language of "enemy" I am displaying a partisan attitude. To refrain from such language is to distort revolutionary Marxism, to convey neutrality in the class struggle rather than partisanship. So while I strive to persuade the reader of the Marxist views that follow, I also display Marxist revolutionary partisanship.

I strive for objectivity in understanding racism. Objectivity and partisanship are compatible. The opposite of "partisan" is "neutral" not "subjective" or "biased."

* * *

I must limit my topic somehow, but limitations create distortions. I emphasize anti-black racism in the US for two reasons. The United States was, for the second half of the twentieth century, the leading capitalist power in the world (as I write, it is being overtaken by China). So anything central to US social organization is important to the world. In the US there were two foundational and continuing horrors: the four-hundred-year physical and cultural genocide of indigenes and appropriation of their lands and the enslavement and then super-exploitation of African-descended labor (so-called "black" people). The story of the first of these horrors is dealt with only tangentially here. It needs more, but I can't do it. The story here is of how anti-black injustice helped the US become a world economic power and how it continues to make US capitalism more profitable. However, black people are far from the only group whose labor has benefitted US capitalists: immigrants, Mexicans and mexicans in the Southwest and West, Chinese and chinese, Filipinos and filipinos in the Pacific West, indigenous peoples, immigrants from many countries, and many so-called "white" people who are not racially targeted. Still, anti-black racism is foundational and is the focus here.

Racism is tightly woven with sexism, the use of women as low paid workers who can be demeaned, brutalized, and exploited with impunity. Often women workers are also people with demeaned racial identities, but not always. Sexism is a form of exploitation and oppression by capitalist society in its own right. (Non-capitalist societies also often exploit and brutalize women. Capitalist society modifies the sexism it inherits and uses it for the purposes of the capitalist class.) I explore it only tangentially. It deserves its own treatment in the spirit of the account of anti-black injustice here.

My focus on the US may suggest that I adhere to some form of US nationalism or patriotism. I am neither a patriot nor a nationalist. The limitation is purely to make the scope—already too ambitious—narrow enough that I can say something useful.

* * *

Part 1 develops a *materialist* history of race in the US in contrast to *idealist* histories. Let me express the contrast simply and crudely. Idealist histories of race argue that black people in the US were viewed from the beginning as inferior, condemned by long-held European assumptions about racial inferiority (Robinson 2000 [1983]). Social and economic subordination of black people were *consequences* of these assumptions. First the idea, then the deed.

Materialist history starts with material life, the production of the means of life and—in the emerging capitalist society I write about—commodities for trade. People decide what to do for practical reasons. Capitalists seek profit. An example developed in Chapter 1: when indentured servants were cheaper, planters preferred them to enslaved Africans; when enslaved people were cheaper, planters preferred them. Racist thought is the *consequence* of material life, developed to rationalize and justify it. First the deed, then the idea.

Idealist anti-racism says we must change people's ideas, their ways of thinking (or, pessimistically, that they can't change). Then racist social practice would end. Capitalism as a system is exonerated. Materialist anti-racism says that capitalists profit from racism. To end it we must end capitalism. Anti-racist thought develops in the struggle against material racism and in the struggle to end capitalism. The reader will see some of this at work in Chapter 5, where we study the anti-racist practice of the Communist Party.

The history here is *selective* and thematic: I focus on key episodes in the construction and reconstruction of racist society and on anti-racist movements that offer the most helpful examples to today's anti-racists. Most of the story of anti-black racism in the US is omitted.

Emerging capitalists in English North American colonies profited from exploiting Africa-descended enslaved people on lands taken by violence from indigenous people. Enslaved people produced cash crops which were exported. The wealth of capitalists in Britain and the US came from expropriating indigenous land, enslaving Africans and their descendants and, after the Civil War, the labor of other workers driven down by racism.

Racism is central both to profitability of capitalist production and to racial divisions in the working class. These divisions make unions weak and wages low for US workers. They weaken their shop floor power over production and make working lives often barely tolerable.

Yet where there is oppression and exploitation, there is also resistance. I stress episodes of workers' resistance: maroon escapes and settlements, running away, slave uprisings, and especially those historical moments, exceptional as they were, where white workers abandoned the lie of whiteness to unite with their black (and other racially oppressed) co-workers to fight the capitalists. Accordingly, I emphasize the organizing of the Communist Party (CP) in the US, particularly at the height of its anti-racist influence in the 1930s through the 1950s. We have much to learn from studying what communists were able to achieve.

A common phrase used to describe racial oppression is "white privilege." This term is, at best, highly misleading. I stress evidence that when whatever privileges white people may have that black people lack, many white people are harmed as a consequence of those privileges, a point Du Bois (1962 [1935]) also emphasized. This argument is related to anti-racist strategy: far from benefitting from anti-black oppression, a large segment of the non-black working class has a material need to fight against and end the oppression of black (and other racially oppressed) workers.

Finally—related to struggles resisting racism—the US was founded on appropriation of land occupied by other people, killing or driving off those others whenever that land and its mineral resources were of use to the capitalists' profits (a continuing process). Every square inch of the US was appropriated in these ways. Moreover, the country itself was founded to maintain the slavery so profitable to its ruling class. The struggle to end slavery succeeded, but the capitalists regrouped. A sharecropping system was enforced by seizing workers and selling them as convicts if they did not work for a landowner. When black and white farmers fought back in the Farmers Alliances, Jim Crow developed as a new system of racist terror, disciplining black workers and driving down white and mexican as well. The end of Jim Crow was followed by the rise of mass incarceration. *Whenever* racism is defeated in one form, it re-emerges in a new form. This fact is evidence that racism profits the ruling capitalist class. Race divides and weakens the working class, providing vulnerable workers. The greater oppression and exploitation of these workers leads to worse conditions even for workers who are not the most *direct* targets of racism.

My history of racism is not an all-sided story of the history of racist society in the US or of people identified as black. It does not emphasize racist thought and culture. Instead it presents the core material meaning of the history and persistence of race: profits for capitalists. This history sets the stage for the practical arguments of Part 2.

* * *

The late Charles Chastain arranged a luncheon in the fall of 1990 so that I could meet Charles Mills, especially given our shared interest in Marxism. Sometime after this I sent Charles a paper I had written about racism; he pointed out that it was not ready for prime time. Later in the 1990s I was part of a reading group with Charles and others where Charles presented a draft of what became his book *The Racial Contract* (1997). I disagreed at the time; I believed Charles had underestimated Marxist resources for addressing racism and gave insufficient emphasis to the profitability of racism in capitalist economies.

For thirty years Charles and I argued back and forth. As his work gained renown, he supported me in many ways, especially by his presence at forums where we presented our disagreements. He read much that I wrote, including drafts of chapters here.

His recent death was a great loss, not just to many others, but to me as well. He congratulated me in March 2021 about my contract with Bloomsbury. The book that follows here was meant to extend our conversation. I had anticipated Charles's response. I have not attempted to change the text even though the person to whom much of this is directed is not here with us to read it and respond.

* * *

When I started graduate school in philosophy in 1964 my ambition was to have an academic career teaching and writing philosophy. Then the events of the mid and late 1960s caught hold of me, changed my philosophical interests, called me to anti-war and then anti-racist activism and eventually to communism. This book is a partial report of what I have learned along the way. It is meant to be a helpful word, not the last word.

Part One

Origin and Persistence of Racism

1

The Origin and Meaning of Race in English North America

This chapter explores several themes: How and why did race arise? Why was slavery adopted? Did non-slave owners benefit from slavery?

European slavery before conquest of the Americas

We can't understand race as it came to exist in the United States without understanding slavery because people of African descent came to be uniquely identified as slaves. Slavery was common in ancient societies of Egypt, Mesopotamia, Greece, and Rome, but not based on race. The Roman Empire depended on an imperial military to control people enslaved on plantations. With the end of the Empire the imperial state was replaced by small local semi-states consisting of local lords and their armed thugs (knights) who could coerce grain and labor from serfs, who had some rights. Slavery declined.

Enslaved Africans first entered Europe through Islamic slave trade. In the 1440s Portuguese ships raided the west African coast for hostages, then slaves. Before the decade was over the Portuguese, rather than raiding, traded with African rulers for people. Trading was easier and more profitable. The African people thus obtained were sold as servants in Europe or for labor on Atlantic islands such as Madeira or the Canaries, often to produce sugar. Slavery, which had been in decline, began to grow again (Blackburn 1997).

European invasion

European invasion of the Americas from 1492 onward changed the world Europeans entered; two continents with cities and agriculture were depopulated. At the time of European entry 100 million or more people—more than lived in Europe—may have lived in the Americas. Diseases and deliberate massacre may have killed 95 percent or more of indigenous people in the centuries that followed (Mann 2005; numbers are speculative and disputed).

As Europeans, particularly the Spanish, conquered indigenous societies, they enslaved indigenous people in mines, extracting wealth and shipping it to Europe. That transfer of wealth, begun in the sixteenth century, continues to the present day in both mining and agriculture—bananas, coffee, and tin, for example. Jack Weatherford writes, "Between 1500 and 1650 the gold of the Americas added at least 180 to 200 tons to the European treasure," worth at least $2.8 billion (Weatherford 1988: 10). One mountain, the Cerro Rico in Bolivia, produced 85 percent of the silver that came from the central Andes; now it is mined for tin. This silver made silver coins common in Europe, facilitating growth of commerce.

Mining of gold, silver, and other metals was complemented by plantation agriculture on the Brazilian coast by Portuguese and Dutch and on Caribbean islands by Portuguese, Dutch, Spanish, French, and English. Workers were increasingly enslaved Africans. The Spanish, Portuguese, French, and Dutch jumped right into enslaving Africans (slavery had survived through the Middle Ages in Spain and Portugal). The English were slower. In 1638 there were ten times as many European bondservants as enslaved Africans in Barbados, but by 1653 there were 2.25 enslaved people for every indentured servant. Barbados was by then a major exporter of sugar to England (Blackburn 1997: 231–2).

The important point is this: when European powers financed voyages of exploration and conquest, when they established colonies, when they organized the digging of mines and the planting of sugar, they sought wealth. The colonies were profit-seeking ventures.

The English Colony of Virginia[1]

To explain how race developed I concentrate on Virginia. The "founding fathers" Washington, Jefferson, Madison, and Monroe were Virginians. All owned human beings. Washington, Jefferson, and Madison articulated racist views (Feagin 2006: 87–116). All were presidents of the United States. In 1800 39 percent of US enslaved people were in Virginia (US Department of State 1801: 2). Focusing on how slavery and race developed in Virginia, we understand much of how they developed in the US.

The colony at Jamestown (in the Chesapeake Bay area) was founded in 1607. The worst atrocities against indigenous people did not occur in the first two years, but after the starving winter of 1609–10. A new administration imposed military discipline on colonists (one man who stole some oatmeal had a needle driven through his tongue and was chained to a tree until he died) and tried to subjugate the neighboring indigenous people, unleashing atrocities. Later, when indigenous retaliation in 1622 killed 347 English, the atrocities worsened: William Tucker, concluding a peace treaty with indigenes, offered them poisoned wine in celebration, then set upon them, claiming to kill 200 with poison and another 50 with swords and guns.

---

[1] Except where noted, this section is based on Morgan (1975).

The worst crime an Englishman at Jamestown could commit was "going native." The punishment for Englishmen who defected to the local people was breaking on the wheel, hanging, shooting, and burning to death.

Indigenous people were said to be savages and heathens, but white, black and red people did not yet exist. These categories emerged toward the end of the century. For a while English brutality toward indigenous peoples was matched by indigenes toward the invaders: a 1609–10 siege of Jamestown by indigenous people caused starvation and most settlers to die (Fausz 1990: Appendix); the 1622 raid killed many more. These early conflicts are very different from nineteenth-century removal and genocidal wars against indigenes, acts of an imperial power, and full-blown racism. Racist society develops a coherent *social system* of either super-exploitation and oppression or extermination and elimination—or both (but usually directed toward different people) (Wolfe 2016).

At this early stage we have group-centrism: the division of people into groups so that there is an "us" and "our people" and there is a "them" and "those people." There can be one set of norms of behavior toward "our people" and another set toward "those people." Out-group attitudes can be as brutal as you can imagine, including wanton killing and torture of members of the out-group. We see in the English behavior toward indigenous peoples an out-group norm where any behavior is allowed toward the out-group; no moral standards apply. Similarly indigenes came to regard the English as invaders and enemies.

In the colony at Jamestown most settlers died of hunger or disease. Most did not know how to grow food, and what food they grew was poorly distributed. They abused local indigenous people, who then would not trade with them. High mortality continued for decades. New arrivals died during the hot summers from disease. Eventually cattle and pigs became common. Colonists grew corn and orchards produced staples. The death rate declined in the 1640s and 1650s.

In 1616 colonist John Rolfe planted tobacco. The results were good. The following year colonists grew tobacco in quantity and shipped it to England where it sold for three shillings a pound, a lot of money. So despite high mortality Virginians could make money growing tobacco. The economy developed primarily on that basis. But that created a problem for the rulers: to produce tobacco you needed labor. Use enslaved Africans? That solution was not adopted, for at least three reasons.

First, the English did not have a status of slave written into English law. This inhibited the development of slavery by a little, not by a lot. A more important reason is that in the middle of this century slaves were twice as expensive as indentured English servants. Investors will not pay a lot of money for someone who might die before they get their money's worth. Indentured servants were a better bargain. Related to this was a third reason: from 1500 to 1650 the population of England and Scotland together had grown from three million to five million people. Population growth was not matched by economic growth. England was swimming in poor people. The rulers shipped them to Virginia, solving two problems at once: they provided plantation labor to Virginia, and they relieved population pressure in England. Poor people were encouraged to go to Virginia or were seized. While two-thirds chose to go, the other third were kidnapped, conned, seized as street children, or otherwise forcibly transported, particularly Irish but poor English as well (Jordan and Walsh 2007). The cost of transportation was covered by the Virginia Company or by a sponsor in Virginia. In return they would work as a servant-slave for the company or the sponsor, usually for five or seven years. (Given high mortality as well as penalties extending the term of service, this was often lifetime servitude.) Plantation agriculture developed based on English bondsmen, not African slaves.

The 1620s experienced a tobacco boom. The price of tobacco was high, between one and three shillings per pound, and Virginia tobacco was popular in England. In 1630 the price went to a penny a pound (twelve pence to a shilling, a steep drop). Tobacco's price never returned to 1620s levels, but when the price was high, there was a huge demand for labor. Even after 1630 the price was often between 2 and 3 pence per pound, and serious money could be made from tobacco at that price. The more servants a grower could obtain, the greater the profits. This did not lead to treating the servants well, just the opposite. In Virginia a servant was "a machine to make money for someone else" (Morgan 1975: 129). Planter-masters often did not adequately provision them. So servants arrived in Virginia without enough food to survive the year to come. Eager for tobacco profits, capitalist planters did not plant enough food crops. So people arriving were destined to die, partly from inadequate nutrition. The profits were so great that the planters were not concerned. They worked servants to death, then paid for more.

In a book about racial injustice, why do I elaborate on brutalities done to English and Irish? It is important to understand racial injustice in the context of other injustice. English servants were not really people to their masters. Barbara Fields writes:

> Indentured servants ... could be bought and sold like livestock, kidnapped, stolen, put up as stakes in card games, and awarded—even before their arrival in America—to the victors in lawsuits. Greedy magnates ... stinted the servants' food and cheated them out of their freedom dues, and often out of their freedom itself, when they had served their time. Servants were beaten, maimed, and even killed with impunity.
>
> 1990: 102

There are other ways to write a history of racial injustice. One is to concentrate on the unique injustices and brutalities done to Africans and their descendants. Another is to emphasize the similarities between the treatment of Africans and working-class people who are not African. I attempt a third way: to see how racial injustice continues and intensifies what was done to others. About the period where the plantation labor force was primarily English bond-servants, Lerone Bennett, Jr. (1993: 40) writes, "The plantation pass system, the slave trade, the sexual exploitation of servant women, the whipping-post and slave chain and branding iron, the overseer, the house servant, the Uncle Tom: all these mechanisms were tried out and perfected on white men and women." There is great similarity between the oppression of disadvantaged workers and racial injustice. Still, racial injustice—as it developed in English North America—is something more vicious: permission to brutalize people is *signaled by the appearance of a person's body*. We must keep in mind both similarities and differences in how the English rulers treated English (or Scottish or Irish) servants and enslaved Africans.

Virginia was ruled by its governor and governor's council—the biggest planters who owned the most servants, using government to increase the number of servants they owned.

The first people of African descent came to Jamestown in 1619 on a Dutch ship (the Dutch were challenging the Portuguese as traffickers in human cargo, eventually supplanting them, only to be replaced later by English and New England slavers). Unlike people who came later from Africa, these first generations were what Ira Berlin (1998) calls "Atlantic creoles," people of African (or Euro-African) descent who may have lived in African port cities, Europe, the Caribbean, or New Amsterdam (New York), spoken a European language, and been capable of defending their legal rights. Two presumptions worked against them: Africans were assumed to be heathen (not Christian) and assumed to be slaves for life. But these assumptions do not mean that we were dealing with racial discrimination. What they mean is, first, that they usually had been non-Christian and, second, that, unlike Europeans, they had been enslaved prior to their arrival in Virginia.

Many in this first generation of arrivals were treated as indentured servants and freed after a period of servitude. Others purchased freedom for themselves and their families. Virginia came to have many free people of African, Afro-European, or Afro-indigenous descent.

Africans were definitely assumed to be a different nationality. In court records they were often (but not always) identified as "negro." Other bond-servants were identified as Irish, Scottish, or Dutch, as opposed to English. There was definitely English group-centrism; Irish, Scots, Dutch, and Negroes were regarded as "other," not English. They were often subject to different, more severe norms than were English; for example, Irish bondsmen served a six year term when the standard for English was four years. The norms for Africans were more severe than those for Irish, often lifetime servitude or, where limited, a term of indenture might be ten years for an African.

I will not call people of African descent "black," nor will I use the word "negro." At that time "negro" (or spelled "negroe") was used in contrast to "English" or "Christian" not in contrast to "white." It seemed to denote a non-Christian nationality—not what we would call a race. (At that time "race" was used for what we would call nationality: the English race.) Irish, being Catholic, were not non-Christian but not really Christian either, in English eyes. Races had not yet been invented. So, for now, I use the word "African" to mean people who later came to be called "black" in the US and the words "English" or "European" to refer to people from England or elsewhere in Europe or descended from such people.

The tobacco plantation economy in Virginia developed off the labor of English bond-servants. As late as 1650 there were only about 500 Africans in Virginia out of a total Virginia population estimated at roughly 14,000—about 3.6 percent. Some were undoubtedly enslaved in our sense; others were servants for a term, and a significant portion were free, particularly on Virginia's Eastern shore, where in some counties as much as thirty percent of the small African population were free. Enslaved Africans might work for hire during free time or keep livestock, earning money to purchase their freedom and that of family members. Many went to court to defend themselves against unjust treatment. Some had Portuguese surnames (Breen and Innes 2005, Berlin 1998).

When John Punch ran away along with two other servants (one Dutch, the other Scottish) in 1640, the other two received one-year extensions of their service; Punch was punished with lifetime servitude. Was this racism? It could be a practical decision: to enslave Scots or Dutch (who chose to board ships) could create problems if word got back home. No similar issue existed for Africans (who had no choice), and planters wanted to get as much service as possible from people. It likely was influenced by the awareness that Africans were enslaved elsewhere. The history of Africans in Virginia can show how slavery and race can emerge from an initial situation where race (in our sense) did not exist and slavery was more flexible than it later became. The John Punch case certainly shows that some who controlled Virginia took advantage of an opportunity to impose slavery-for-life on an African where it would not otherwise have existed.

Other legal cases reveal another side of the story. Africans owned land, owned servants (including in some instances Europeans), married Europeans, and were able to pass their property on to their heirs. All of these appear in court records into the 1650s and seem regarded as unremarkable. But in the 1640s and 1650s there is also clear court evidence that some Africans are held as slaves for life (Morgan 1975: 154, n. 69).

Still even at this time, the overwhelming majority of plantation laborers were European. We should not assume that European servants had the same attitude as planter-rulers. Servants and enslaved people, European and African, ran away together, stole and enjoyed pigs together (to supplement a meager diet), got drunk together, and had sexual relations. These are the activities that made it into the court records because they were illegal ("fornication" was a crime). We should assume an even greater variety of unremarkable, day-to-day activities through which African and European servants developed friendship and solidarity: telling jokes and stories together, instructing and helping one another in day-to-day labor, covering for one another to the master, sharing food, wrestling and teasing, and other activities that only the weakness of our imaginations makes it hard to name. While masters are developing a status of slave for people vulnerable to it (they contemplated enslaving Europeans but never tried to do it, probably for fear of the consequences [Morgan 1975: 296–7]), servants are enjoying one another's company and developing friendship.

Why didn't the big planters, who were desperate for more labor, bring in more enslaved Africans? One reason is the higher price of the enslaved. Blackburn (1997: 319) asserts that for the half century after 1624 English servants (preferred because of their knowledge of the language and farm implements) were cheaper than slaves. By the 1650s some things had begun to change. Growing labor demand in England was raising the price for English servants and curtailing the kidnapping of poor English. Life expectancy in the colony was improving. By the 1660s and 1670s enslaved Africans had become a sensible economic investment. Servants were outliving their indenture and gaining their freedom. Planters tried to prevent this, extending servitude when possible. To force freedmen back onto their plantations planters seized tidewater land with access to ocean ships, tracts that they did not cultivate. Many freedmen had insufficient or inaccessible land or no land at all. Without land they could not live except by working for the master. There was a class struggle: the big planters enacting laws, seizing land, and extending terms of servitude, the servants and freedmen struggling to free themselves and become self-sufficient as farmers, often moving to the frontier or squatting on unused land owned by a big planter. They rioted and rebelled.

In 1676 rebellion led to civil war. The leader of the rebellion was Nathaniel Bacon, a prominent member of Virginia's planter class. Frontier farmers were coming into conflict with some indigenous people. Bacon proposed vigorous and vicious war against indigenes. He assembled an armed force and carried out some raids. Governor Berkeley disagreed with Bacon's specific tactics (though they shared brutality toward indigenous peoples). Bacon directed the anger of landless freedmen and small farmers against indigenous people rather than big planters who had seized land and imposed taxes. He pointed this out to Berkeley but did not prevent his men from appearing before the statehouse demanding "no taxes!" When Bacon threatened force against the governor, Berkeley gave Bacon a military commission to fight indigenous people, then rescinded the commission, essentially declaring Bacon an outlaw.

War ensued. Berkeley retreated to the Eastern Shore. Bacon and Berkeley both promised freedom to servants and enslaved people who joined their cause. What had started as a conflict over Indian policy and an attempt to divert mass anger away from the big planters had become a civil war where each side appealed for support to the most oppressed. Many more flocked to Bacon's cause than to Berkeley's. Bacon's army showed that freedmen, servants, and enslaved people would unite in struggle against the ruling class.

Bacon died of dysentery in October. In November English warships and Redcoats arrived from England, intimidating many rebels to surrender. The English promised rebels that enslaved people and servants would be free. Thomas Grantham, commander of the thirty-gun ship the *Concord*, made "never to be performed" promises of freedom to twenty English servants and eighty enslaved Africans (Allen 1997: 214). They were later tricked into allowing themselves to be drawn into the range of warship guns, whereupon they surrendered and were returned to their owners (Jordan and Walsh 2007, Morgan 1975).

Bacon's Rebellion was only the largest of many arsons, poisonings, conspiracies, disorders, and riots before and after. Along with the other disorders it showed that servants and the enslaved would unite and take up arms against their masters.

Virginia's ruling class needed labor for their plantations, and they needed to prevent servile insurrection. Slavery was their solution to the first problem, race to the second. While the two solutions are related, they are not the same. Over the next thirty years laws were passed that strengthened the status of slave and further degraded Africans, elevating even European servants above them. These laws developed central elements of racial injustice.

By the 1660s Virginia's ruling planters are putting into law a status of slave-for-life, including progeny. The laws eventually reserve this status for Africans.[2] In 1659–60 Virginia's lawmakers eliminated the longer period of service for Irish. A 1662 law

---

[2] The details of Virginia colonial law that follow are taken from Hening 1823. Allen (1997: 249–53) and Morgan (1975: Chapter 16) have guided my efforts.

reversed the English common-law tradition that the status of children was determined by the status of the father, prescribing instead that children of an enslaved woman would have the status of their mother; masters could augment their human property by impregnating enslaved women. A 1667 law stated that being baptized does not cause a slave to be free (prior to that enslaved Christians had sued for and won their freedom), a 1669 law that masters who killed slaves were exempt from felony charges, a 1670 law that African immigrants (non-Christian servants entering the colony by water) would be enslaved for life while indigenes (non-Christian servants entering by land) would be enslaved only until thirty. These laws created a status of slave for Africans only. In the 1680s import of enslaved Africans increased.

None of this implies that Virginia's rulers believed that Africans are somehow fundamentally different. All of it can be understood as actions of practical businessmen securing a labor force. With enslaved people living longer, big planters enhanced profits by creating a legal status of slave. It is possible or even likely that the reason why they did not enslave English or especially Irish was the practical consideration that to do so would jeopardize their ability to obtain servants in the future.

Other laws move in the direction of creating race—of dividing workers by race and creating racial contempt. Virginians had a problem with runaway servants, and when running away, servants paid little attention to distinctions between servants for a term and servants for life. Servants for a term could be punished by extending their term. But how could you punish servants for life? Instead they punished indentured bondsmen who run away with enslaved people by making bondsmen serve a longer term for accompanying enslaved people. Laws passed in 1661 and 1662 did that and also discouraged cooperation between servants and slaves. Still, these laws were not designed to create racial contempt.

A law passed in 1680—after Bacon's Rebellion—seems designed for just that effect. Entitled "An act for preventing Negroes Insurrections" [sic], the law forbade any "negroe or other slave" from carrying any sort of arms, from leaving his master's land without permission, and from "lift[ing] up his hand in opposition against any christian." (It also provided that runaway Africans may be killed.) The law was to be read aloud in church every six months (Hening 1823: Part 2, 481–2).

Imagine the effects of such provisions on European servants. Imagine you are European and I African. We get in a disagreement, words lead to blows or wrestling, and then our friends pull us apart. That could have been the end of it. But now you can report me to the master, and, for fighting with you, I am liable to "thirty lashes on [my] bare back well laid on" (481). What *psychological* effect will that have on you? How could you avoid a feeling of superiority, of having rights against me, of impunity in any conflict between us? Unless you reject the law as unjust, you would have to be a saint to escape feelings of superiority.

Is this racial superiority? The Virginians did not yet have the biological concept of races articulated by Thomas Jefferson one hundred years later. They were struggling toward racial categories but did not typically frame these issues in terms of "black" (or "negro") and "white." In a 1705 law, prohibiting testimony in court, the category excluded is "negroes, mulattoes and Indian servants, and others, not being christians" (Hening 1823: Volume 3, 298). In the 1705 law reaffirming the prohibition of Africans striking Europeans, the prohibition is presented in this way: if "any negro, mulatto, or Indian, bond or free, shall at any time, lift his or her hand, in opposition against any christian, not being negro, mulatto, or Indian," he shall be liable to thirty lashes. (459) There is a sense in which the racial categories "black" and "white" are present; they are used in language in the law as early as 1691 in a law that requires that any "English or other white man or woman" who marries any "negroe, mulatto, or Indian man or woman bond or free" must leave colony forever within three months (87). But note that above, in the 1705 law, "white" people are referred to as "any christian, not being negro, mulatto, or Indian" (459). The laws do not escape framing in terms of Christian and heathen. But in a 1732 law any "negro, mulatto, or indian, either a slave or free" was prohibited from testifying in court (Hening 1823: Volume 4, 327). The religious reference is dropped. What does it mean to be white? It means that you are not black or indigenous. Racial categories are emerging.

These laws tend to promote ideas of racial superiority in people who came to be thought of as white at least to the extent to which they were observed (laws prohibiting sex between black and white were widely ignored). As the laws developed in the late seventeenth and early eighteenth centuries, they prohibited the whipping of European bondsmen (1705), specified freedom dues for European servants at the end of their term (1705), prohibited enslaved Africans from owning livestock (which had enabled enslaved people to purchase freedom) (1692, 1705), prohibited free Africans from voting in elections (1723), from owning Christian servants (though allowed to own servants "of their own nation") (1670), from holding public office with any power (Africans barred along with criminals) (1705), from bearing arms (1723), and from participating in the militia except as drummers and trumpeters (1723).

The laws of 1705 and 1723 were to be read aloud twice every year from every pulpit in Virginia. These laws were passed and implemented by Virginia's ruling class, the capitalist planters. Their goal was to render white servants and freedmen socially safe accustoming them to this new system of racial injustice. So they demanded the repeated readings of these laws from the pulpits. We should not assume that European servants and freedmen leaped to embrace this new system. They resisted through their behavior—through friendship, running away together, having sex and marrying together—and they resisted through petition to the Assembly: Lerone Bennett, Jr. (1993: 75) writes, "The minutes of the Council of Virginia, May 11, 1699, contain 'the petition of George Ivie and others for the repeal of the Act of the Assembly, Against English peoples marrying with Negroes, Indians or Mulattoes....'"

Solidarity and friendship between Africans and Europeans become less frequent further into the eighteenth century. In Bennett's (77) estimate, "by the middle of the eighteenth century a solid white front was developing." The white race, as well as the black race, was being created. To the extent to which these laws were accepted and obeyed, people were accustoming themselves to a social order where "white Christians" had rights denied to "negroes, mulattoes, and Indians." It is hard to imagine living inside and *accepting* such a social order without developing a consciousness which rationalized why some may be denied rights that are granted to others. (More about rationalization later.) From these laws emerged *a social order organized along categories of race*—a racist society.

People increasingly came to think of themselves through racial categories, to accept racial identities grounded in laws prescribing unequal treatment. Interracial conflict became more common. Today many people identify racism with interpersonal instances of bigotry, prejudice, and racial slights and insults. These are *consequences* of the laws and institutional practices which are the core of racism. As people adapt themselves to such laws and institutions, they adopt appropriate attitudes. These attitudes do not cause the laws but are intended consequences of racist laws.

Virginia's ruling class knew what it was doing. When the English Attorney-General questioned the justification for the 1723 law depriving "negro, mulattos, and indians" of the right to vote in any election, purely on the ground of race or nationality (whichever it was at that time—it was surely becoming race if it was not there already), Governor William Gooch replied that the purpose of the law was to "fix a perpetual Brand upon Free Negros and Mulattos" (Allen 1997: 242). Then Gooch explains why such a "perpetual Brand" is necessary: fear of servile insurrection with enslaved Africans joined by free black people; in addition Gooch argued that it was necessary to create a large distance between the social status of free black people and Englishmen (other related reasons were also given).

Virginia's rulers created racism to ensure control of their labor force. Use of English servants had led to increasing problems, culminating in a rebellion that united free and bonded, English and African, in an attack on the colonial order. This was unacceptable. The strategy adopted by Virginia's rulers after 1676 was to consolidate slavery, use Africans rather than Europeans, and create a division that would prevent unity. As Morgan puts it "the numbers [of poor freemen] ... were ... sufficient to keep the threat of another Bacon in everyone's mind.... The answer to the problem ... was racism, to separate dangerous free whites from dangerous slave blacks by a screen of racial contempt" (1975: 328). That required that *all* Africans, not just the enslaved, carry the same stigma—to prevent unity of the oppressed. "Free black people lost the right to employ white indentured servants, hold office, bear arms, muster in the militia, and vote" (Berlin 1998: 123). Fear of servile insurrection became fear of black people.

Increasingly English freedmen were asked to surrender their dream of independence as farmers and homesteaders in the tidewater. Many moved westward to the Piedmont and then the hills of western Virginia. Many worked as tenants in relative poverty. Some (about one-third) had farms substantial enough to require help from servants or enslaved people. A few took positions overseeing and disciplining enslaved African labor (Allen 1997).

In the late 1600s and early 1700s, as the plantation labor force became increasingly enslaved people, violence rose against the enslaved—now Africans who spoke no European language rather than Atlantic creoles—people facing "the pillory, the whipping post, and the gallows more frequently and in far larger numbers" as well as the rod and lash and other violent and humiliating means of control (Berlin 1998: 115–16). The number and length of workdays increased; quality of food and shelter declined. The independent economy of enslaved people shrank, owners seizing their livestock. In response enslaved people developed their own forms of resistance:

conspiracies to rebel, feigning ignorance of how to carry out tasks, truancy, particularly at crucial times in the agricultural season, and running away and sometimes establishing communities of runaways (called maroon communities).

Some enslaved people, especially those born in the Chesapeake (by 1750 eighty percent of the enslaved were American-born), acquired language and social skill to elevate their status. They strove, often successfully, to establish domestic life, name their children, have their own cabins, have some privacy, establish free time on Sunday and often on part of Saturday as a right, and limit planters' control over their work, often using as leverage their understanding of the production process. A slave economy re-emerged, including independent production and barter—although planters tried to limit these. After the mid-1750s enslaved people increasingly entered skilled trades, sometimes competing with white artisans. In the emerging cities enslaved people gained even more freedoms as workers and in how they lived. However, racial slavery provided labor for agricultural production. The dominant story of the eighteenth century is the development of a slave society based on deeper exploitation (Berlin 1998).

White benefit?

Did non-elite white people benefit from the new racial order? This question is thematic in the present book: the evidence is that *anti-black racial injustice oppresses non-elite white people*. The common phrase "white privilege" seems to suggest that white people benefit from having privileges that black people lack. It is not hard to understand why white workers do not: racism creates unequal oppression grounded in racial identity. However, unequal oppression creates divisions among workers that drive them all down. The *purpose* of creating race was to divide, weaken and oppress workers, but *unequally*. In the 1930s W.E.B. Du Bois (1962 [1935]) argued that the poverty of southern white people was due to the even greater poverty of southern black people, combined with anti-black terror and division between natural allies. (We meet Du Bois' argument in Chapter 9.) Did racism harm non-elite white people? Historians of Virginia divide on this question, Morgan arguing that white freedmen benefitted, Allen that they did not.

Morgan (1975: Chapter 17) argues that both the economic condition and the political status of non-elite white people in Virginia rose in the new racist slave society. The laws elevated the legal status of non-elite white people relative to black. About economic oppression Morgan (338) writes, "The status of poor whites rose not merely in relation to blacks but also in relation to their white superiors. ... as Indians and Africans began to man the large plantations ... , the economic prospects of the paleface poor began to improve" and later "as the rich grew richer so did the [white] poor" 341.

Morgan acknowledges the continuing presence of rootless poor single white men in Virginia and the substantial use of white convict-slave plantation labor through the mid-eighteenth century. His evidence that conditions for poor white people improved is that the percentage of single male households in *eastern Virginia counties* dropped between 1675 and the middle of the next century and that the percentage of small estates grew during the early and middle eighteenth century (342–3).

Morgan's evidence that the percentage of very poor men in these eastern counties declined does not show that "the economic prospects of the paleface poor began to improve." We don't know *why* the percentage declined. It could be a result of *upward mobility*, where people and their children did better. Alternatively, it could be the result of *outward migration* of single poor white men westward from those counties. Which is correct?

Allan Kulikoff (1986) gives relevant data from Prince Georges County, Maryland (also in the Chesapeake region, bordering the Potomac River, near Chesapeake Bay). Kulikoff points out that enslaved artisans tended to supplant white artisans in the eighteenth century (12). As slavery developed, the conditions of free white men without property seemed to decline: he writes, "About half the men who finished a term of service in Charles County, Maryland, during the 1690s left the county in search of employment, and more than three-quarters of those who stayed lived precariously as laborers or tenants" (40). More white men left than entered. By 1700 most bond laborers in the Chesapeake were enslaved black people.

By the second quarter of the eighteenth century upward mobility was becoming difficult for poor white men and downward mobility quite common for men whose fathers owned both land and slaves. In Prince George's County around 1733 if a tenant owned neither land nor slaves, then his sons likewise owned neither. Half of those who owned both could not pass both on to their sons. (87). Between 1733 and 1743 75 percent of all men without kin left the county; 58 percent of recent migrants who owned neither land nor slaves left; 39 percent of both county natives living with kin and long-term residents who owned neither land nor slaves left.

Now consider Morgan's observation about eastern Virginia during roughly the same period that the percentage of single male households had declined. If conditions in eastern Virginia counties are similar to those in Prince George's County, Maryland, this is what we should expect: finding little opportunity for a better life in the Chesapeake tidewater region, poor single white men headed for frontier areas in hope of better prospects. If that is true, decline of single-male households is no evidence that economic conditions of poor white men improved. Still the growth of small estates may show that *some* white men benefitted from racial slavery.

The emigration of poor single white men from the Chesapeake does not show that the increasing use of enslaved Africans as plantation labor *caused* a deterioration of conditions for poor white men. Causation is hard to establish in contemporary phenomena, harder still when considering unique historical events. Still, it is an article of faith among many activists and anti-racists today that white people benefit from racism. So that article of faith implies that the rise of racial injustice should cause the situation of white people generally to improve. But there is no evidence of this. Logically (no proof, just plausible conjecture), competition between white labor and more oppressed and deeply exploited enslaved black labor should cause the conditions of white workers to decline, as happened when slave artisans displaced white artisans (Wertenbaker 1959: 137–9).

Chesapeake societies become more unequal as the eighteenth century progressed, poor white people increasingly locked into a hopeless situation. By 1776, again in Prince George's County, Kulikoff finds that 90 percent of the sons of tenants who owned no slaves are also tenants owning no slaves (138). In Middlesex County in Virginia, studied by Darrett and Anita Rutman (1984b), they found that in the year 1700 property holdings were concentrated (the top 8 percent of families owning 62 percent of the property [154–5]) and, fifty years later even more concentrated: while in the second half of the seventeenth century the wealth of the wealthiest group was forty-six times that of the poorest, by the second quarter of the eighteenth century it was one-hundred-seventeen times that of the poorest (189). It was hard for tenants, sharecroppers, and wage laborers to compete with enslaved people without impoverishing themselves.

In the early to mid-eighteenth century, race in the Chesapeake begins to assume its typical form in the US. Ira Berlin (1998: 113–14) describes the changes:

> the ties between black enslaved people and white servants atrophied, as blacks sank deeper into slavery while whites rose in aspiration if not in fact. The strivings of white servants necessitated their distinguishing themselves from enslaved Africans, who were the recipients of harsh treatment that white laborers would no longer accept. No matter how low the status of white servants their pale skin distinguished them from society's designated mudsill, and that small difference became the foundation upon which the entire social structure rested. . . . Whiteness and blackness took on new meanings.

Tenancy and wage labor became the fate of former servants who did not move to the frontier.

Regional variations

I have focused on the origin of racial slavery in Virginia and the Chesapeake because racist Virginia slaveholders were "founding fathers" of the US. However, as Ira Berlin (1998) points out, racism and slavery are not single and constant but vary by region and time. I summarize very briefly.

In the Lowcountry coastal areas of the far Southeast, there was, at first, a rough equality between bond and free—bondspeople traveling and working a variety of jobs, being armed to fight indigenes and Spanish and earning their freedom in battle. But slavery developed faster, and oppression was greater. By 1700 planters held large rice and indigo plantations, using "the lash, the faggot, and the noose to discipline slaves" (150). Torture facilitated exploitation. Until the latter half of the eighteenth century, the enslaved did not reproduce themselves (a measure of brutal exploitation of women). Caribbean slaveholders fled rebellions there, bringing those they enslaved with them, thus reproducing in the Lowcountry danger they sought to escape (Horne 2018, 2014).

In 1720 there were twice as many enslaved black people as white people in Lowcountry South Carolina. The same process is repeated later in Lowcountry Georgia and, later yet, in northern Florida.

Enslaved people resisted: truancy, tool-breaking, slowdowns, and the unpunished killing of an overseer. People escaped to hinterlands and swamps to form maroon communities and to the west, where free black and white frontiersmen might welcome them. Conflict between English and Spanish created opportunity. Some fought on the winning side and won their freedom; others escaped to Spanish Florida. In contrast to Bacon's Rebellion of 1676, which united bondspeople and landless people, resistance now became slave resistance. White workers, embracing white identity became less militant. Slavery was more profitable, exploitation more severe, resistance more sustained than in Virginia.

The North provides another variation. There were considerable numbers of enslaved people in Pennsylvania and especially New York (some doing agricultural work). In 1700 the city of New York had the largest black population of any city in English mainland colonies (Foner 2015: 30). Rivalries developed between white artisans and their enslaved counterparts.

More important, capital accumulated in New York, Boston, Newport, and Philadelphia derived from trading in enslaved people, slave-produced crops, or in food to feed enslaved people. New England supplied food—as well as timber—to Caribbean sugar islands, so that land there could be devoted exclusively to profitable slave-produced crops (Warren 2016). Newport and Manhattan became slave-trading centers. By the mid-eighteenth century Manhattan sent food, timber, and linseed to the Caribbean. Philadelphia was a larger city and, as Peter Kalm observed in 1749, "reaps the greatest profits from its trade to the West Indies," trading flour, butter, meat, and timber for sugar, molasses, rum, indigo, and mahogany (Callender 1909: 20). Finance capital in the North developed from trade for slave-produced goods.

French settled in the Lower Mississippi Valley, including New Orleans, in the early eighteenth century.[3] With little interest in agriculture, many poor Europeans lived in forests and swamps, foraged for food, and intermarried with indigenous people. People in bondage included indigenous, European indentured servants, and Atlantic creoles, who also intermarried where possible, particularly with indigenous women. By 1731 the population was majority black people, and most enslaved people worked in New Orleans, becoming artisans as well as maintaining levees.

Slave plantations produced tobacco and some indigo, underfeeding and intensely exploiting enslaved Africans. The 1729 Natchez uprising of African and indigenous people killed 200 Europeans. With importation of African people virtually ending, planters had to choose: abandon slavery altogether or ease up on conditions so that people reproduce themselves. They chose the latter, giving the enslaved free time to produce their own food and a surplus, which they sold, leading to a vigorous slave economy. Enslaved people hired out their labor, the planter getting a cut, enabling them to move about and earn money as lumberjacks and woodcutters, and in New Orleans as carpenters and blacksmiths. Enslaved women were everywhere in New Orleans'

---

[3] Review of this region is based on Berlin 1998: Chapters 4 and 8.

markets selling their produce and even their bodies. A predominantly male European population in New Orleans led to voluntary sexual, marital, and quasi-marital alliances between European men and African-descended women. A polyglot population developed throughout the colony, a mixture, both in physical appearance and language. Efforts to build a plantation slave economy led to something else: a relatively freewheeling society with enslaved people, free black people, and people of mixed biological heritage and unique speech—alongside a European minority.

The meaning of race

A project of defining race may seem doomed from the start not just because "race" and "racism" are contested terms understood differently by different people but also because what race is changes over time. Nevertheless, I will *define* "race" as organization of social inequality based on a person's bodily appearance as supposedly revealing ancestry—combined with the rationalization of that organization.[4] What is racist in the primary sense is a *society*, not an individual, action, policy, or institution. Nonetheless, individual acts which harm racially oppressed people at least partly on account of their ascribed race help create racist society and will also be called racist. The definition assimilates race to racism (or racial injustice). That is intended. It is wrong to regard racism as bad but race as neutral: race arose and persists as a physical mark of social inequality. Our definition does not acknowledge racism or semi-racism that may be grounded in the culture of a people, their dress, their style of speech, their national origin or their religion; this is a limitation. The virtues of the definition are that it focuses on social inequality rather than prejudice or bigotry and that it articulates the uniqueness and viciousness of *anti-black* racism.

It is less adequate where physical appearance is less decisive. The definition of race changes as racial organization is applied where people's bodies are not reliably different in appearance: "That's funny—you don't *look* [mexican, jewish, etc.]." Here we could say categories are *racialized*. There is a continuum between "racial" (in the narrow sense I have suggested) and "non-racial" phenomena.

Indigenous people had a different experience of racism. As Patrick Wolfe (2016) points out, US rulers sought to take their land more than they sought to appropriate their labor. They are often pushed *out* rather than being brought *in* in an inferior status (but both occur).

Race was different things—even for people who came to be called "black"—at different moments in colonial history. Earlier "black people were defined as cosmopolitan cultural brokers, familiar with the languages, religions, jurisprudence, and trading etiquette of the Atlantic" (Berlin 1998: 92). Instead they became society's "designated mudsill." We live in that racial world, of racial slavery, Jim Crow, and now mass incarceration.

---

[4] Haslanger (2000) distinguishes race from gender, which also focuses on the appearance of a person's body, but based on a person's supposed reproductive role.

A *definition* of race does not say what it *means*. A definition gives a verbal formula that is supposed to apply to all and only the thing defined. The definition given here is intended to mark out anti-black racism. The *meaning* of race is its function or role in capitalist society. Its meaning helps to explain its persistence.

To understand the meaning of race consider how Virginia's rulers viewed their *English* servants: they were "filth and scum," female servants were prostitutes and "shameless creatures," and men "the boldest and most insolent young scoundrels in all England" (Rutman and Rutman 1984a: 130).

Where do such attitudes come from? Ruling classes try to justify why they may rule over others. If Virginia society was fundamentally just yet some were not motivated to work, then their lack of motivation is a flaw within them. They should be controlled and labor extracted from them. Race *transfers* the contempt for and control of the poor *onto a human body with a certain appearance*. Race arises from class and from a class attitude of contempt for the poor but makes it more vicious. Race creates an attitude of social contempt that people cannot escape by changing their last name, behavior, language, religion, or style of dress. Social contempt is attached to who I physically *am*. This is the peculiar viciousness of race and racism.

I define *racism* as the organization of social inequality based on the racial identity of a person's body *combined with* this racial contempt that arises to rationalize racist social organization. But the *meaning* of race and racism cannot be understood except as a form of class oppression and exploitation focused on a person's appearance.

Race (as a mode of domestic social organization) was *invented* in Anglo North America within a rising capitalist society in late seventeenth-century and eighteenth-century Virginia. Virginia changed from a society without race to a society with race. Race was *created* by Virginia's ruling class and *taught* from the pulpits to Virginia's masses. (Virginia's invention—or re-invention—of race is preceded by similar inventions in the Caribbean and by pre-existing color prejudice in Europe [Horne 2018, Jordan 1968, Sweet 1997].) As English laborers accepted these laws, they participated in the new system of race. They became white, seeing themselves as having a stake in racial injustice. That stake may be small potatoes or "chump change." It need only be enough to suck a person into the system of oppression. It created a group that experienced *markedly greater oppression*. It created contempt—attached to physical appearance—toward that more oppressed group, even among those who were themselves exploited and oppressed, but not racially. Those less oppressed often—*not always*—aligned themselves against workers identified as black. To the extent that "white" workers in Virginia adopted that attitude of racial contempt, Virginia's planter elite controlled how they thought and acted. "White" workers were locked into their own demeaned status. Essentially they accepted *our enemy's* way of understanding the world.

Slavery, race, and the rise of capitalist society

At the beginning of this chapter I cited Jack Weatherford's conclusion that the rise of mercantile capitalism in sixteenth- and seventeenth-century Europe presupposed a currency (gold and silver) extracted from mines in the Americas by enslaved indigenous people (as well as metals directly appropriated from indigenous ruling classes). That represents a broader view of the meaning of racial slavery than the one I have taken in most of this chapter—one focused on the function of race in the *world* economy rather than in a single society. However, if we are to fully appreciate the connection between New World slavery, race, and the rise of capitalist society we need to step back and look beyond the colonies of English North America (the ones that became the US) to understand that connection.

Eric Williams (1944: vii) called his book, "an economic study of the role of Negro slavery and the slave trade in providing the capital which financed the Industrial Revolution in England." Immanuel Wallerstein argued that the capitalist world-economy develops in "the long sixteenth century," depending largely on "the harvest of bullion [gold and silver], wood, leather, and sugar from the New World" (Wallerstein 1974: 337), much of that harvest the product of enslaved people, indigenous and then African. Concerning the period of colonial North American (and English Caribbean) racial slavery, Wallerstein (2011 [1980]: 163–7) emphasizes the central role of sugar in the continued development of the capitalist world-system, becoming (along with tobacco) a mass consumption crop. Brazilian gold production greatly expanded. Capitalists enriched themselves trading in New World commodities and enslaved human beings transported from Africa. While the center of the developing world economy shifts from the Iberian peninsula to The Netherlands, then England, then the US, and now China, its origin is in New World slavery.

Capitalism arises with enslavement and expropriation of indigenous peoples in the Americas, then enslavement of Africans. Racial categories, theories of racial difference and ranking of "races," and racist social thought generally rationalizes the social order. The rise of capitalism and the rise of racist social organization are *the same process*.

Most of Marx's *Capital* is an explanation of the bourgeois norms that weave profit-making into the norms of daily life. Primitive accumulation, introduced in Part Eight, is extra-legal seizure by force. Sailors are impressed for service on ships, children stolen from workhouses for factory labor, their labor essential to the efficient operation of the cotton mills. Children work twelve-hour shifts, sleeping in beds still warm from the bodies of the children coming in to replace them on the next shift; beds never get cold. Marx writes:

> While the cotton industry introduced child-slavery into England, in the United States it gave the impulse for the transformation of the earlier, more or less patriarchal slavery into a system of commercial exploitation. In fact the veiled slavery of the wage-labourers in Europe needed the unqualified slavery of the New World as its pedestal.
>
> Marx 1976 [1867]: 925

Capitalism works continuously on the norms implicit in capitalist social relations (the rules of the capitalist game) *and* on seizure by force. These work in conjunction as part of the *ordinary* if not the *normal* (in the sense, according to social norms) workings of capitalist society.

Marx *connects* New World slavery with capitalism in Europe. As Wallerstein argues, we have one world-wide economic system. The Atlantic Ocean becomes less a barrier than a highway where the labor of sailors carries commodities—including human beings treated as commodities—back and forth to create profits for various capitalists. This is not a pre-capitalist system. The enslavement of human beings is integral to the rising capitalist system.

In the seventeenth and eighteenth centuries English North America was a less important source of profits for British capitalists than the Caribbean sugar islands. Still, it was integrated into a single *system*: enslaved African labor (supplanting European bond labor) extracted the products that lay the basis for the continued development of the world capitalist economy. Moreover, English North America pioneered the development of racist capitalism in domestic social organization: it was the first globally important society where the racially oppressed were a *minority* of the exploited and oppressed workers, where the racial oppression of a minority was used to deepen and extend the oppression and exploitation of all workers, and where this was accomplished by persuading those workers who were not *racially* oppressed to adopt racist attitudes toward the racially oppressed, in this way dividing and weakening the working class. *Internal* division of the working class—marked by racial or semi-racial categories—now exists in capitalist societies around the globe, not just the US.

Racial organization of labor took two forms: super-exploited dark-skinned workers around the world produced raw materials, minerals, and crops transported to industrial areas; in the US and increasingly elsewhere the racially diverse domestic working class is divided by race, super-exploitation of the racially oppressed adding to exploitation of other workers. These forms of racial oppression and exploitation are even today the source of much wealth for the capitalist class. Racial slavery and racism were, from the beginning, central to what capitalism is.

2

Race in the American Revolution through the Civil War

Race and the revolution of 1776[1]

Why did the thirteen colonies rebel against the English crown, establishing the United States of America? The more common account is that they fought against the imposition of taxes, without consultation, that they fought for liberty and enlightenment ideals. A materialist explanation is different: interests of rising colonial capitalists conflicted with those of the British bourgeoisie—especially concerning westward expansion and exploitation of enslaved people.

The British were managing a world empire and recruiting black soldiers for wars. Conflict with North American indigenous peoples and slave resistance hampered these tasks. Hence, they sought to limit aggression against indigenes and compromise with the enslaved.

North American capitalists were building an integrated economy, accumulating capital from export of slave-produced crops and from intense exploitation of enslaved people, enforced by terror. Free white people with disappointed hopes rioted and rebelled. Westward expansion was a safety valve for them. As small farmers, those who moved west (New York and Pennsylvania, eventually Ohio, Indiana, and Illinois) supplied food to urban and rural (especially enslaved) workers. Westward expansion in the South increased wealth from slave-produced crops. Predatory wars against indigenes seized land for expansion.

Eighty-eight years earlier England's so-called "Glorious Revolution" had cast aside fetters on English mercantile capitalists; trade in enslaved human beings expanded along with catastrophic mortality. Slavery in the Caribbean and North America increased profits and danger. Masters' diaries, letters, and legislative records reveal pervasive fear of the people who created their wealth. Fearing alliance between enslaved and free black people, they fixed a "perpetual brand" on free black people. Fear was especially intense in southern Carolina, where enslaved people were a great majority.

---

[1] This section is based primarily on Horne 2014; also on Takaki 1979, Nash 2005, and Parkinson 2016.

In Jamaica the British made a peace deal with maroons in 1738, maroons agreeing not to provide refuge to people escaping slavery (Genovese 1979).[2] The British developed an intermediate stratum of free people of color, who were 72 percent of free persons in the emancipation year of 1834 and owned 23 percent of enslaved people (Allen 1997: 233, 235). Managing a global empire extending to South Asia and Africa as well as the Americas, the British confronted Spanish colonial competitors who used black people as soldiers, making the British vulnerable in combat where they oppressed large numbers in slavery.

These problems emerged during war with Spain 1739–1748. In September 1739 at Stono Creek near Charles Town, South Carolina enslaved people rose up, killed twenty-nine settlers, and fled southward to Florida, where the Spanish promised freedom. While most of the rebels were killed or captured, some made it to Florida and became part of the Spanish military force at Fort Mose near St. Augustine. The Spanish were widely thought to have incited or even organized the rebellion, infiltrating at Charles Town (Berlin 1998; Horne 2014). In 1741, to punish a Manhattan plot, four white people and thirty-one enslaved people were executed for conspiring to burn the town, kill white settlers, and overthrow the colonial government (Foote 2004, Linebaugh and Rediker 2012). "White" conspirators were likely Catholics, that is, "papists," thought to be agents of the Spanish enemy.

The Seven Years War of 1756–1763 against the Spanish, the French, and their indigenous allies left the British with a large debt. The main beneficiaries were South Carolina and Georgia slaveholders. Florida was ceded to the British, cutting off a path to freedom; slavery expanded. Shaken by innumerable stories of real and imagined rebellions, poisonings, and arsons by the enslaved, rulers lived in fear, responding with terror.

Two trials alarmed colonial rulers. In 1772 English courts freed James Somerset, an Africa-born man transported to London by his "owner." Since England had no law authorizing slavery, Somerset was free. The ruling stimulated English abolitionism. In June 1772 the British schooner *Gaspee*—patrolling to stop smuggling and illegal slave trade—ran aground off Newport, Rhode Island and was burned by a mob led by John Brown, a wealthy slave-trader. The British accepted testimony from Aaron Briggs, a black apprentice, that Brown had shot the ship's captain. Appalled by acceptance of Briggs's testimony against a wealthy slave merchant, colonists as far away as Virginia (including Thomas Jefferson and Patrick Henry) formed Committees of Correspondence and later the Continental Congress, crucial steps toward separation from Britain. In November 1775 Virginia's governor Dunmore, representing the British, offered freedom and arms to people enslaved by rebel colonists, confirming the separation.

These conflicts concerning expansion and slavery are exhibited in the Declaration of Independence, which complains that the British king has "excited domestic insurrections" as well as "merciless Indian Savages." The first would be most widely understood to refer to slave uprisings. Robert Parkinson (2016) documents how these

---

[2] The deal broke the alliance between the enslaved and the maroons, leading later to their defeat.

images of enslaved black people and indigenes became increasingly important in patriotic propaganda in the course of the war.

In splitting from the mother country, the founders, under the influence of aggressive slave-owners in the South and merchants who profited from selling and shipping plantation crops, created a republic that would expand and intensify racist brutality.

Racism becomes American

My historical narrative emphasizes how slavery and race arose and persisted because they helped to secure labor under conditions favorable to capitalists' profits. Still, any stable class society generates rationalizations favoring the ruling class and reconciling the rest of us to things we seem unable to change. So it is helpful, even to a Marxist materialist narrative, to describe the racist culture which racial social organization spawned.

The revolution disrupted things. Appeals to enslaved people by military commanders on both sides to fight in exchange for freedom, massive slave escapes in the chaos of war, religious and moral opposition to slavery among Quakers, Methodists, Presbyterians, and others, and the effort to justify the war on universal moral principles of equal liberty put pressure on the institution of slavery, continuing for a quarter century or so before abating. Constitutions prohibiting slavery were adopted in Vermont and Massachusetts. Slavery was eventually abolished in all the states of the North, though some provisions did not complete this task for another fifty years after the beginning of the revolution. Manumission laws were passed in some southern states—most notably Virginia—empowering masters to free their own enslaved people. In some states free black people gained the right to vote. So there was definitely, for a time, a movement in the direction of applying universal principles to black people too (Davis 1975, Evans 2009, Gilbert 2012, Harris 2003, Horne 2014, Klinkner and Smith 1999).

However, that was not the permanent and lasting difference the revolution made to race in America. Race had been introduced into a society ruled by the King of England. He ruled by royal privilege. Privileges were attached to status. Most people lacked privileges, being "commoners," a lower status than their lords and king. Society was divided into social grades; at the top stood the king, below the king the nobility, below the nobility the free commoners, and then below them lower orders of society, serfs and vagabonds. To strive to rise above one's place was to violate God's divine plan for the universe. When Europeans encountered non-European peoples, hierarchical thought was extended to include a hierarchy of humans from civilized to barbarian to savage. Virginia's rulers brought this idea to the new world, believing they ruled by royal authority (Morgan 1975). Slavery for Africans could be understood within the framework of this medieval worldview: Africans were descended from Ham and carried the curse that they serve the descendants of Ham's brothers, their rightful place in a divinely ordered social world.

The American revolution abolished royal and lordly privileges in favor of republican citizenship. Republicanism involved several related ideas (this definition emphasizes the republicanism of Thomas Jefferson 1954 [1787]): it implies an active self-governing citizenry; it embraces liberty; it emphasizes rule of law over arbitrary power. Republican citizens must be free and independent; enslaved people, servants, wage workers, and women are dependent on others and thus are ineligible for republican citizenship. Citizens are self-governing in two senses: the obvious sense is that they at least consent to their government, as justice requires; less obviously, republican government, which breaks the hierarchical chain of authority, requires that, not being governed by a lord, citizens must now govern themselves, use their reason to restrain their (especially sexual) passions.

How is race related to this development? With extension of rights to the "common man," racial injustice becomes more intense and more intensely defended. Barbara Fields (1990: 101) writes:

> During the revolutionary era, people who favoured slavery and people who opposed it collaborated in identifying the racial incapacity of Afro-Americans as the explanation for enslavement. [Fields here cites Davis 1975 chapters 4, 6, and 7.] American racial ideology is as original an invention of the Founders as is the United States itself. Those holding liberty to be inalienable and holding Afro-Americans as enslaved people were bound to end by holding [racial inferiority] to be a self-evident truth.

The new rationalization of race arose on the foundation of science, from biological classifications by Linnaeus: species are divided into local populations, or races, that breed within the race more frequently than outside it, thus creating significant biological properties of the race. Jefferson (1954 [1787]: 62, 274) footnotes his use of the term "homo sapiens europaeus" to the *System of Nature* where Linnaeus divides humanity into four subspecies. Linnaeus characterizes "homo sapiens europaeus" as active, very smart, inventive, and ruled by laws; Africans were classified as "homo sapiens afer," characterized as impassive, lazy, crafty, slow, foolish, and ruled by caprice (Lassiter 2009: 25).

Starting as early as the fifteenth century, light-hued mercenaries—serving European monarchs—dominated, enslaved, or colonized darker-hued peoples wherever the latter were militarily too weak to resist conquest. Africans increasingly entered European society as enslaved; indigenous Americans were enslaved in mines or killed. Other non-Europeans succumbed to conquest. Accepted as just and correct, conquest was rationalized. Linnaeus' opinions about race were echoed by David Hume and Immanuel Kant, by Jefferson and countless others. They were "all the rage." They rationalized the already-accomplished conquest, enslavement, and subordination of people of darker complexion.

Generally there is a time lag between the invention of an idea and its popularization. So it was especially at the end of the eighteenth century that European and Euro-American elites framed the emerging racial worldview in more scientific language and associated negative stereotypes with demeaned races.

Both elements—republicanism and framing race in the language of science—come together in the thought of Thomas Jefferson, though he declines to endorse slavery. His views on race are most fully developed in his *Notes on the State of Virginia*, composed originally in 1781 and published in 1787. Philip Klinkner and Rogers Smith (1999: 23) call it "probably the most influential American book of the 1780s" and point out (26) that by 1790, at the first Congress held under the newly adopted Constitution, opposing an anti-slavery petition by Benjamin Franklin and others, "William Smith of South Carolina cited Jefferson's *Notes* as proof that 'negroes were by nature an inferior race of beings.'"

Jefferson's influential views of race contain virtually all of the worst, most vicious and enduring anti-black thoughts: ugly, sweaty, smelly, oversexed, good at music, not too bright, and lack sensitivity and feeling. Black people are identified with the passions, while white people are identified with reason, which must rule over our passions. Black people are identified with the body, which must be ruled by spirit or mind (Jefferson 1954 [1787], Takaki 1979). Thus for the republican white over black echoes the rule of reason over the passions and the rule of mind over body. While these ideas are similar to common stereotypes of the lower classes by those above them, in anti-black racial ideology the negative stereotypes become attached to a racialized body. These ideas explained to a generation of republicans why, if black and white people are to live together, black people must be enslaved.

Other "founding fathers" agreed but did not elaborate as much. George Washington thought that the contradiction between equal liberty and black servitude was reconciled by the fact that "we do not include madmen or idiots; liberty in their hands would be a scourge" (quoted in Feagin 2006: 111). James Madison defended slavery in the *Federalist Papers*. He too advanced the stereotype of black people as "idle and depraved" (104; for more on the "founding fathers": Chapter 3) The "founding fathers"—Washington, Jefferson, and Madison—all Virginians, all owners of human beings, all believers in racial inferiority and racial separation—set the nation on its course, shouting in unison, "We are white America."

In the first section of this chapter we saw the racial foundations of US society, how the economy and social control were based on exploitation and terror. In this section we have seen how the "founding fathers" rationalized racist society.

The expansion of racist society

The chaos of the Revolutionary War—the British promising freedom to any who rallied to the crown—made it possible for many people to escape slavery, at least for a time. As many as 20,000 may have fled to the British, 4,000 of them permanently resettled by the British at the end of the war. Possibly as many as 100,000 may have either gone over to the British, fled to the western frontier or to Florida (which was still British until the end of the war, when it reverted to Spain), or passed as free people (Klinkner and Smith 1999). In order to compete with the British the "patriots" allowed some black people to serve, promising those enslaved their freedom, a promise sometimes kept. All of this, combined with the revolutionary rhetoric of liberty, put pressure on the institution of slavery.

In 1782 Virginia passed a law making it possible for slaveholders to emancipate the people they enslaved, and in that decade about ten thousand people received their freedom (Takaki 1979). Where did the law come from? Quakers fought for its passage. Probably many Virginians were troubled by the contradiction between the principles of the republic and the institution of slavery. Some black people had fought in the revolution when manpower was needed. Yet these explanations seem incomplete: people usually bend morality to coincide with their interests. Enslaved people did not produce high profits in late eighteenth century Virginia. There was a glut of tobacco and a surplus of enslaved people. The land was less productive after one hundred years of tobacco cultivation. Many planters switched to grains such as wheat, which require less labor and where enslaved people were of less use (Kolchin 2003).

At the Constitutional Convention Virginians opposed the slave trade from Africa. They wanted to export surplus enslaved people to South Carolina and Georgia where slavery was expanding. Slave-trading merchants and South Carolina and Georgia slave-hungry capitalists mostly prevailed. The African slave trade was extended for another twenty years. The banning of the slave trade in 1808, the result of an alliance of Virginia planters and moral opponents of the slave trade, was a partial victory for Virginia planters. They made huge profits selling enslaved people, who went initially to Georgia and South Carolina, eventually to the western South: Alabama, Mississippi, Louisiana, Texas, and Arkansas (Baptist 2014).

By the 1840s slavery was expanding and more strongly defended than ever. What changed? In 1793 the cotton gin was invented. While in 1800 39 percent of enslaved people were in Virginia, in 1860 it held only 12 percent. While it was still the largest single slave state—nearly 491,000 enslaved people—Alabama, Georgia, Mississippi, and South Carolina each had more than 400,000 and North Carolina and Louisiana had more than 300,000. The US government under Andrew Jackson's presidency launched an onslaught on indigenous peoples to clear them from the western south—western Georgia, Alabama, Mississippi, and Louisiana. A catastrophe for indigenes was a disaster for black enslaved people. A new generation of entrepreneurial planters became wealthy by acquiring and exploiting slave labor. They were deeply committed to slavery and to racism as rationalization of that slave system (Oakes 1982, Takaki 1979).The profitability of cotton made exploitation more intense. Owners worked enslaved people to death and then bought more. Despite the end of the African slave trade in 1808, the number of enslaved people in the US increased from less than 890,000 in 1800 to 3,950,000 in 1860. Virginia slave owners became rich by encouraging human beings to have children, whom the owners sold (Gibson and Jung 2002, Takaki 1979).

The labor of the enslaved grew increasingly productive up to 1860 based on masters' sharing effective methods of labor control. Edward Baptist (2014: 114–18) details one method: a lead enslaved person or "captain" sets the pace of labor carrying out a particular task (for example, chopping weeds) down a row between cotton plants. Other enslaved people work in rows parallel to the captain's and are expected to match his pace. This method enables the overseer to sit on horseback off to the side, with a whip and gun, observing whether any enslaved person is falling behind the captain's pace. The consequence for that is whipping or, if someone resists that, to be shot down in the field. Racist terror increased productivity while using supervision efficiently. Planters shared these methods in economic journals.

Did *white* people in the Deep South (the territory opened up by the expansion of slavery in the first half of the nineteenth century) benefit from this expansion of slave society? This is the wrong question: it lumps people together by race not class. We should ask whether *non-slaveholding* white people benefited, for it is clear that many slave-owning entrepreneurs became wealthy; even yeomen (farmers who physically worked their own land) holding a single person in slavery probably benefited from that person's labor. Keri Leigh Merritt (2017) estimates conservatively that a third of the free people of the Deep South were poor, owning neither land nor other human beings. What effect did slavery have on those landless free people of the Deep South? Merritt summarizes (338):

> Pushed off the land, and having to compete with the unpaid, brutalized slave labor, a significant portion of whites wallowed in extreme poverty, too, and the vestiges of this impoverishment are still evident today. The stain of slavery, it seems, is much more widespread and lasting than many scholars have admitted.

It was primarily in the Deep South that a human being could be called "trash." This was—almost literally—the capitalists' view of human beings whom they could not employ at a profit. Enslaved people created profits. Moving from place to place in search of land, poor white people found repeatedly that the best land had already been taken by northern capitalist investors or entrepreneurs with access to these investors' capital (Bolton 1996; for efforts to develop alternatives to northern capital see Baptist 2014: Chapter 7). They moved to remote deep woods areas and squatted on land they did not own (Merritt 2017).

Enslaved people could recognize the humanity and common plight of poor white people. In South Carolina some enslaved people took pity on the wife and eight or ten children of a very poor neighborhood *slave-catcher* (work that was available to him); they brought food stolen from their master to help feed his large family. His wife soon turned against her husband's cruelty toward the enslaved (Forret 2006). This story is only the tip of an iceberg of daily social ties between enslaved and poor white people, who sometimes played together as children and worked together in fields, tobacco processing, railroad and other construction, coal mines, and cotton mills. They often attended church or camp meetings together, gambled at cards or cock fights together, drank together in grog shops or at a corn shucking, traded together in the underground economy, and even made love together (Forret 2006). All this is not to deny the reality that many white people were contemptuous of enslaved people (a contempt that was often returned in kind) nor that poor white people in some situations, particularly sexual, had a power and immunity that black people lacked. Those ideas are often repeated to the exclusion of this other side: the simple fact that black and white people were under the thumb of the plantation masters meant that many (not all) developed a class sympathy and solidarity—within the limits of what the racist southern social order would allow.

Southern racial slavery—particularly the slavery of the Deep South—victimized poor white people and created brutal exploitation—even torture—for enslaved black people. Racism does not benefit white workers. The capitalist *system* drove down the enslaved and the poor white farmers, but *differently*.

The US economy grew from black labor. By 1860 the value of cotton exports from the US was $191,806,555 or 58 percent of total US exports; all slave-produced plantation crops together—including cotton and others—formed two-thirds of exports. Northern merchants, bankers, and railroad magnates derived their profits from these crops as well as from direct ownership of plantations. Cotton traders earned as much as a 40 percent profit on sales (Harris 2003). Northern industry processed southern cotton into cloth and clothing. Not just the new class of southern plantation owners but northern bankers and traders in cotton and textiles were determined to defend it. Northern industrialists, despite the protests of abolitionists, were not about to kill the goose that was laying those golden eggs every year (Baptist 2014, Evans 2009, Steinberg 2001, Takaki 1979). When, for a variety of reasons, the end of slavery became the central aim of the Union in the Civil War, northern capitalists had the task of making sure that the profits from black (and other) labor would continue in the aftermath of Union victory.

Racism in northern cities

The urban working class was growing in cities of the North and West (what is now called the Midwest, the Great Lakes states). From Jefferson's presidency until the Civil War, racist rationalizations of social inequality or slavery spread. Political writing, in newspaper articles and cartoons, minstrel shows, jokes and offhand remarks popularized ideas of black inferiority and racial separation. Scientific racists developed the doctrine of separate creations and of biological superiority of the Anglo-Saxon race, with Louis Agassiz of Harvard joining the chorus. Slavery was said to be the best way of bringing together races with very different capacities. Meanwhile from the pulpits preachers who rejected separate creations explained slavery as the curse of Ham (Evans 2009, Jefferson 1954 [1787], Klinkner and Smith 1999, Takaki 1979).

Jefferson's Democratic-Republican and later Jackson's Democratic Party and popular media (newspapers, minstrelsy) associated with them made their appeal to the common worker, particularly in the North. They popularized stereotypes of the white worker-artisan as skilled, self-reliant, and disciplined. These stereotypes of white workers were used to modify Jefferson's republican ideal so that not just yeoman farmers but also big-city workers could be included. The stereotypes criticized the big-shot bankers and merchants and, at the same time, disparaged black people, who were stereotyped as dependent, lazy, oversexed, and criminal. In this view black people were either enslaved people or servants (maids, butlers, waiters) and hence dependent or else pimps, prostitutes, or thieves (Litwack 1961, Takaki 1979).

The Democratic-Republicans' appeal to the common man was extraordinarily racist. By elevating the common man in rhetoric but not in actuality, the Democratic-Republicans brought more ordinary white people into the electorate on a basis that asked them to distinguish themselves from black people. Already many white workers blamed black workers for undermining their economic position, the blame itself a racist reaction to labor competition. The rhetorical elevation of white labor by Democratic-Republicans intensified anti-black racism, both in practice and in popular attitudes and stereotypes. City newspapers popularized racism. Politicians appealed to anti-black racism in elections. Legislation reinforced it. In July 1834 a three-day riot in New York City attacked abolitionists for advocating "racial amalgamation." This was assumed to be a terrible crime and was associated not only with abolitionism but with prostitution, dance halls, and the lowest of the lower classes. The white population of the US became overwhelmingly racist in its outlook. Even the abolitionist movement contained only a few white people who sought complete social equality and integration of black folk (Evans 2009, Harris 2003, Litwack 1961, Steinberg 2001).

White artisans were a declining group, their labor increasingly replaced by capitalist manufacture, where wages were low. Instead of good wages and self-direction in a small shop, workers were increasingly part of larger shops controlled by a boss (Fredrickson 1981, Jones 1998). Perhaps they voted, but they had no power. They were to satisfy themselves with thoughts of racial superiority. "The white group of laborers, while they received a low wage, were compensated in part by a sort of public and psychological wage." (Du Bois 1962 [1935]: 700). While Du Bois is writing of the South after the end of Reconstruction, this applies to white workers in the antebellum North as well.

In the 1840s minstrel shows with white actors in blackface became the dominant popular culture of the urban and small-town masses, popularizing negative stereotypes of black people. But black people were only two percent of the northern and western population. What purpose did racist culture serve in the North? One possible answer is that white workers were frustrated and angry at their own declining position. Racism gave a convenient target for that frustration. In fact, George Fredrickson (1981: 153) proposes a similar explanation of white participation in anti-black riots: "the participation of lower-class whites in these disorders was induced to a great extent by the status anxieties generated by a competitive society." The idea that they were superior to black people is a "crumb" of superiority that redirects their frustration toward black people and away from their employer.

There is another possible explanation that supplements the first. Consider the stereotypes of white people: self-reliant, disciplined, hard-working, industrious, inventive, intelligent. Consider the stereotypes of black people: lazy, stupid, drunken, unreliable, oversexed. Now consider the value of anti-black racism to an employer with a white labor force. If white workers internalize the white stereotype and regard as the deepest insult to be told "you are acting like a nigger," all of this enhances control and discipline of *white* labor (Takaki 1979). The white worker is working in a large shop for low wages controlled by a boss. By working hard, he strives to prove he is "white." The boss benefits.

The "white" stereotype is of the self-made man. Today this stereotype is still central to racist culture. Black and immigrant people are stereotyped as mooching off the state. In Chapter 9 we return to this link between individualism and racism.

In our earlier discussion of colonial Virginia we discussed how this process of becoming habituated to racial injustice created a sense of superiority as white people accustomed themselves to laws that did not allow a black person to strike a white person. In the North and West the most important laws probably had to do with suffrage. In the early to mid-nineteenth century many property qualifications for voting were weakened or dropped, but simultaneously *different rules* were applied to black men, limiting their eligibility to vote (Harris 2003). Once the law is implemented and poor white men now vote, they will naturally tend to rationalize why they may vote while black men may not—unless they reject the suffrage laws as unjust. The rationalization is racist: something is wrong with black people. Rationalization popularizes racist thought. Suffrage laws assisted this process, as did other racist laws.

To this argument it might be objected that racist suffrage laws were preceded by informal methods of preventing black people from voting—threats, intimidation, and harassment (Litwack 1961). These were common throughout northern states where the laws allowed black people to vote. Nevertheless, the laws, when passed, gave legal sanction to what had been extra-legal methods and strengthened racist thought.

The social order that developed in the North before the civil war was thoroughly racist with black people in the lowest paying and most disrespected jobs and in jail and prisons at a rate roughly ten times the rate for white people. Segregation was everywhere—in modes of transportation, in theaters, in hotels, restaurants, and resorts, in churches, in schools, prisons, hospitals, and cemeteries (Litwack 1961: 97). Black labor was demeaned labor. Black people typically couldn't vote, serve on juries, or testify in court. This social order arose from prior prejudice and stigma, but, even more, it cemented in the popular white mind the idea that black people were an inferior race. It disciplined white workers striving to show they were not black, contributing to their own exploitation while making their employers rich. But that is not the whole story; where there is injustice, there is resistance to it.

Resistance to slavery and racism

"Men make their own history but … not under circumstances they themselves have chosen," Karl Marx wrote (1973 [1852]: 146). Historical narrative should capture both the choices people make (history is made by people) and the limits that circumstances create for those choices. The ruling classes of the planter-controlled South and of the US had more choice and fewer limits, the white working classes less choice and more limits, free black folk even less choice and even greater limits, and enslaved people least and most. Yet all acted, and all influenced why the US had a Civil War from 1860–1865. Those with the least freedom did a lot.

Enslaved people resisted relentlessly. The Gabriel conspiracy of 1800 and that of Denmark Vesey in 1822 did not come to fruition. Remarkably Nat Turner's 1831 revolt in Virginia killed 59 white people before being suppressed (Aptheker 1993, Genovese 1979, Kolchin 2003). Most enslaved people must have suspected that it would be hard to succeed militarily (absent war among white people), and after Turner's revolt, there was more severe repression. However, running away, usually carried out individually or by a small group such as a family or couple, was incessant throughout most of the South but especially in areas close to free states, in remote sparsely inhabited regions, or near indigenous people friendly to the enslaved. But even where prospects of successful escape were remote, enslaved people ran away and hid out for days or longer and occasionally made it to a city or remote region where they became free. And besides escape, there were the everyday forms of resistance, shirking work, feigning illness, breaking tools, and countless other forms of evading work that people can invent when pressed. It was also fairly common for enslaved people to strike or kill masters or overseers who oppressed them (Franklin and Schweninger 1999).

Incessant newspaper ads for return of runaways, slave patrols, slave catchers, dogs bred to hunt for runaways all testify to the pervasive violence and terror of southern life. Guns were everywhere as weapons, initially against indigenous people. By the end of the seventeenth century anti-black racism is aiming those guns at black slaves and their free allies. After the Civil War, the freed people no longer had cash value, making them *more* vulnerable to being killed. Violence testifies to people's will to resist oppression and exploitation (Dunbar-Ortiz 2018, Horne 2014, 2018).

The related evils of expropriation of indigenes and enslavement of black people were resisted in the Second Seminole War of 1835–1842. There was close military alliance of black maroon communities and nearby Seminole villages. Many black soldiers viewed their struggle in the context of the Haitian revolution (1791–1804) as an effort to overthrow slavery. US Army commander Thomas Sidney Jesup said it was "a negro, not an Indian war," calling black fighters "the most active and determined warriors" that he had ever encountered. Burning crops, US forces, though defeated at first, starved out their opponents. However, US commanders allowed many to move West rather than be returned to slavery locally, regarding them as too accustomed to freedom (Rivers 2012: 136–45, quotes from 143 and 142).

The abolitionists were the largest movement against slavery and racial injustice and included both black and white. Generally black abolitionists opposed racial injustice. White abolitionists were often anti-black, leading to somewhat separate movements. Anti-racist abolitionists won significant reforms in Massachusetts, including virtually all citizenship rights. But Massachusetts was an outlier, and New England generally had only about 6 percent of the North's free black population. Elsewhere citizenship rights, voting for example, were limited.

In the 1850s things began to change. Organized networks of people aiding escaped people—the so-called "Underground Railroad"—undermined slavery, not by seriously depleting numbers but by giving enslaved people hope of freedom. Slave-owners counter-attacked. In 1850 Congress passed the Fugitive Slave Law to facilitate the return of enslaved people. *Requiring* bystanders to assist in the apprehension of people, the law provoked mass meetings where people denounced the law and vowed to resist. In Boston and Milwaukee people who had been apprehended under the law were freed, escaping to Canada. In Christiana, Pennsylvania a slave-owner was shot and killed and his son badly injured in a failed attempt to seize someone (and three freedom fighters were killed). Only two minor and temporary convictions were obtained in these incidents. In Ripon, Wisconsin at a meeting of opponents of the law, a federal marshal, when identified, was forcibly attacked by attendees. Many states, for example Michigan, passed laws making it harder for slave catchers to do their work. Slave-owners felt threatened by the North's sympathy with runaways (Campbell 1972).

By the mid-nineteenth century many northerners, the majority of white folk, were simultaneously racist yet hostile to slavery and sympathetic to runaways. They did not want to work with black folk, let them vote, serve on juries, or live near them. But they were hostile to slavery and willing to oppose attempts to repossess runaways (Litwack 1961).

So escaping enslaved people, those who assisted them on the Underground Railroad, and even ordinary northerners who thwarted slave catchers all made the southern ruling class feel insecure in the Union. Then a small group of committed abolitionists led by John Brown helped put anti-slavery forces on the offensive. Brown went to Kansas in 1855 and helped to turn the tide of the civil war there toward the free-state settlers through liberal use of terror to counter the terror of the pro-slavery settlers and Border Ruffians. Kansas entered the Union as a free state, frustrating southerners' plans.

Brown turned his attention to a plan for a guerrilla war against slavery: to take guns from the federal arsenal at Harpers Ferry, Virginia, to go to the hills to launch raids on slave plantations, to free enslaved people, and to build an ever-larger anti-slavery army in the Appalachian and Smokey Mountains. Harriett Tubman agreed to participate but became ill and could not join them. In October 1859 he and twenty others raided the arsenal but waited too long before leaving. Most were captured, and those captured were soon hung. But the deeds of this relatively small group, in Kansas and especially at Harpers Ferry, sparked unrest among enslaved people and helped to galvanize abolitionists toward more forceful action against slavery, further disturbing slaveholder confidence in their continued place in the Union (Anonymous 1979, Du Bois 1962 [1909], Nelson 1960, 1973, Quarles 1972, Reynolds 2005, Ruchames 1969).

Southern slave-owners and allied northern capitalists had controlled the federal government through the Democratic-Republican and Democratic Parties up to 1860. Then the Republican Party, with a platform opposing the expansion of slavery in the territories (but not proposing to end slavery in the South), won the 1860 presidential election. By December the first secessions—which had been contemplated for a while—had begun. Secessions led to a Civil War, the Union initially aiming only to preserve the Union, but rebel victories led eventually to the Emancipation Proclamation. This proclamation declared free only enslaved people in rebel states. Enslaved people secured their own freedom, once that was a war aim, refusing to serve the master, many joining Union forces. Roughly 180,000 free black and formerly enslaved people joined the Union army and navy, a decisive military force.

Black fighters in the Civil War[3]

When the first shots were fired on Fort Sumter in South Carolina in April 1861, many free black people in the North responded by drilling and volunteering to fight, but they were turned away with the response that this was a "white man's war," echoing Chief Justice Taney's sentiment in the 1857 Dred Scott decision that the US was a white man's republic. This response summarized 85 years of US development: anti-black racism and anti-indigenous predatory racist wars were central to the national project and national identity. It was only after a year and a half of largely unsuccessful military

---

[3] Unless otherwise noted, this section is based on McPherson 1965.

struggle that Lincoln in September 1862 issued the preliminary Emancipation Proclamation—making it a war aim to end slavery in the Confederate States—and the government opened the question of black people serving in the military and navy. When given the opportunity black people fought: 178,985 black soldiers entered service, "nearly 10 percent of the Union Army," fighting "in 449 engagements, of which thirty-nine were major battles. Approximately 37,300 Negroes lost their lives while serving in the Union Army. Seventeen black soldiers and four Negro sailors were awarded Congressional Medals of Honor" (McPherson 1965: 241).

Early in the war black people were already making contributions. In June 1861 the schooner *S. J. Waring* was captured by secessionists, retaining on board William Tillman, a black steward and cook, and keeping a white crewman in irons. Sailing to Charleston, where Tillman would be enslaved, he used a hatchet to club to death the captain and two other officers, the second of whom sounded an alarm before the fatal blow. Tillman took the second officer's gun, used it to subdue the crew and place them in irons, freed the captured white sailor, and took control of the ship, delivering it back to New York.

Robert Smalls was an enslaved assistant pilot on the side-wheel Confederate steamer *Planter*, used to ferry war supplies where needed around Charleston. Often left alone on the *Planter* overnight, Smalls hatched a plan. In May 1862 he and his brother John, an enslaved sailor—joined by their families—fired up the engines and, very early in the morning, left their berth, whistle-signaled their departure, and proceeded past Fort Sumter, where they gave a loud salute with their whistle, toward the Union naval blockade, now going full steam ahead. Approaching the blockade, they raised a white flag, avoided being blown out of the water by friendly fire, and turned *Planter* over to Union forces.

In January 1863, soon after black enlistment in the army had been authorized, abolitionist Thomas Wentworth Higginson led part of his regiment in a raid along the St. Mary's river which forms the border between Florida and Georgia. Former slaves from the region had intimate knowledge of the terrain and waterways and could provide excellent tactical leadership and guidance (Rivers 2012). The force decisively defeated Confederate troops they encountered. In March Higginson and James Montgomery led two regiments into the same region capturing Jacksonville. Military successes by black units further swayed white opinion in favor of further use of black soldiers, defeated anti-black stereotypes of cowardice, and led to formation of a Bureau of Colored Troops in May. Soon many black units were formed—in Louisiana alone nearly 15,000 new soldiers were recruited by late August—creating black fighting forces, bolstering Union military power.

Three battles of mid-1863 reinforced the reputation of black soldiers for courage. The May assault on the Confederates at Port Hudson ended in defeat, but black soldiers from Louisiana, led by free black line officers, made six charges into blistering enemy fire, despite huge casualties. A white Union officer reported that black soldiers had "behaved magnificently and fought splendidly; could not have done better. They are far superior in discipline to the white troops, and just as brave" (McPherson 1965: 189). At Milliken's Bend near Vicksburg, Mississippi on June 7 two regiments of black soldiers recruited from people recently freed from bondage repelled a Confederate assault, ultimately in hand-to-hand combat. Confederate General Henry McCullough, while disparaging the courage of white Union soldiers, wrote that black soldiers fought with "considerable obstinacy" (190). In July at Charleston's Fort Wagner the Fifty-fourth Massachusetts regiment (free black people recruited from the North) led the assault, despite withering fire, and breached the fort, but supporting troops failed to show up. The Fifty-fourth, forced to retreat as enemy fire intensified, suffered many casualties. Thus black soldiers proved their mettle, and the development of black military forces accelerated. By the last year of the war black soldiers fought in every major campaign, excepting Sherman's conquest of Georgia; they fought fiercely in the last major battle at Fort Blakely on April 9, 1865 (shortly after Lee's surrender in the East), leading to the conquest of Mobile.

Despite these contributions black soldiers were—with rare exceptions—not permitted to be officers. Up to mid-June 1864 black soldiers were primarily assigned to "fatigue duty," that is, menial labor rather than combat; then that practice was officially ended. Also in mid-June, after more than three years of war, black soldiers were given equal pay.

There was widespread anti-Confederate, anti-slavery, and even anti-racist sentiment among non-elite white people. "John Brown's Body" was a popular marching song of the war, displaying feeling antagonistic to slavery, and Brown was a strong believer in human equality. There were many anti-Confederate, pro-Union rebels within Confederate states. In a remote area of southeast Mississippi's Piney Woods a community formed called "the Free State of Jones." It included at least one enslaved person—Rachel was leader Newt Knight's partner and mother of several of his children. These people fought and often defeated Confederate troops—Confederates never subdued the area—and members of the community made it to New Orleans to enlist in the Union army. They hated the slave owners and had considerable sympathy for enslaved persons. Most appalling to Mississippi racists was their—and their descendants—forming "interracial" marriages (Bynum 2016).

David Williams (2008) details extensive resistance to the Confederacy among white southerners who knew that they did not benefit from the slave system. A Lexington, Kentucky meeting of mechanics and other workers issued a resolution opposing slavery, saying that "the institution of slavery is prejudicial to every interest of the state ... it degrades labor ... [and] interferes with the occupations of free laboring citizens" (21). Formerly enslaved Frederick Douglass wrote:

> slaveholders ..., by encouraging the enmity of the poor, laboring white man against the blacks, succeeds [sic] in making the said white man almost as much a slave as the black slave himself.... Both are plundered, and by the same plunderers. The slave is robbed, by his master, of all his earnings, above what is required for his bare physical necessities; and the white man is robbed by the slave system, of the just results of his labor, because he is flung into open competition with a class of laborers who work without wages.
>
> 24

This shared understanding by Lexington mechanics and Douglass presents the basis for a united interracial working-class movement against slavery. That movement never emerged.

Still, southern resistance to the Confederacy was extensive and not just among those enslaved. It mushroomed among non-elite white people after the "twenty-slave" law was passed by the Confederate congress in April 1862. The law allowed wealthy people to buy their way out of military service; it exempted anyone who "owned" twenty or more other human beings. Many called it "a rich man's war but a poor man's fight." The war was brutal, killing over a quarter-million Confederate soldiers and wounding nearly as many additional people. Poor people in the South began to resist as they became aware of the deaths of friends and kin. Throughout the South, including in the Deep South, bands of deserters and resistors fought Confederate forces and killed or terrorized agents of the state who tried to enforce conscription. These bands of white anti-Confederates, while not forming a single community with their indigenous and black allies—in fact, they were usually local movements—often cooperated with indigenous and enslaved people in resisting and fighting the Confederacy and aiding the forces of the Union. By September 1864 two-thirds of Confederate soldiers were absent, with or without leave (Williams 2008). Williams writes (157), "In spring 1864, Major James Hamilton, quartermaster for taxation in Mississippi, wrote his superiors that in the state's Seventh District, covering most of southern Mississippi, deserters had 'overrun and taken possession of the country.'" Williams adds that in the summer of 1863 there were "ten thousand deserters and conscripts in the Alabama hill country formed into armed bands."

The Free State of Jones was unusual but not unique in forming a community neither black nor white. Virginia Bynum (2016: 192) has learned since the 2001 publication of *The Free State of Jones* that there were a number of such communities, even in the Deep South. The memory of anti-Confederate struggle and the existence of non-racial communities were erased from popular consciousness by the southern racist elite and their thugs who engaged in widespread murder of opponents, later developed Jim Crow segregation, promulgated the myth of the Lost Cause, and erected statues and memorials honoring the Confederacy, a state that had been hated by many southerners of all "races."

3

Black Workers in Southern Agriculture

From Reconstruction to World War II

Reconstruction and its aftermath in the South[1]

Reconstruction unleashed social and political activism. It replaced the slave labor system with sharecropping. It gave freed people rights never entirely erased by the so-called "Redemption"[2] and later rise of Jim Crow. But, most important, it never severed the link between black labor and southern agriculture. An interpretation of Reconstruction can emphasize—at the extremes—either the unleashing of activism and permanent changes or the maintenance of the southern labor system in an altered form. I emphasize the latter because that system caused continued racial oppression.

The anti-slavery momentum of the war settled some questions: on paper at least, black people were citizens and entitled to vote; no state could deny them equal protection under law (the thirteenth, fourteenth, and fifteenth amendments to the Constitution, passed in 1865, 1868 and 1870). In reality, informal violence and organized terror (the Ku Klux Klan, similar regional groups, and vigilantes hired by planters and others) limited voting; exercising that legal right often led to injury or death. With the rise of Jim Crow laws around the turn of the twentieth century southern black people were almost entirely disfranchised.

After the preliminary Emancipation Proclamation of September 22, 1862, Democrats encouraged white fear of labor competition from free black people, calling the Republican Party:

> ...the party of fanaticism ... that seeks to turn the slaves of the Southern states loose to overrun the North and enter into competition with the white laboring masses, thus degrading and insulting their manhood by placing them on an equality with Negroes....
>
> Steinberg 2001: 179

---

[1] Unless otherwise noted this section is based on Du Bois 1962 [1935], Kolchin 2003, Steinberg 2001, Evans 2009, Blackmon 2008, and Beckert 2014.

[2] Called this by the southern ruling class; it refers to the return to power of Democratic Party forces (the power behind the Confederacy) after withdrawal of federal troops in 1877.

In Ohio the 1862 Democratic campaign slogan was "The Constitution as it is, the Union as it was, and the Niggers where they are." In Illinois, Democrats said they would "prevent the State from being overrun by free niggers, and the labor of white man being reduced to free nigger prices" (Klinkner and Smith 1999: 61). The Democrats made gains in the 1862 elections.

Throughout US history white workers have often embraced two racist ideas: never allow yourself to be lowered to the same level as black workers, and competition from black labor threatens to lower you to their level. These prejudices were concentrated in states such as Indiana and Illinois and among immigrants, who felt more threat of labor competition. These attitudes created a problem: where would freed people work and for whom?

Black soldiers who killed for freedom were unlikely to return meekly to their former status. Nevertheless, they did return to the plantations. An initial flurry of political and social activism was gradually suppressed, by vigilante violence or through law. Still, freed people could marry and form families, create their own churches, and send their children to school if one was available. Terms of labor were set by sharecropping contracts. Labor gangs—prevalent in the slave system—mostly disappeared. Freedmen felt more autonomous, not being closely supervised, but they forced themselves and their families to work long and hard to avoid debt. They produced cotton as well as tobacco, rice, and sugar.

The greatest concentration of wealth in the US before the Civil War was in the Southern planter class; their wealth derived from the people they enslaved, human beings whose monetary value is estimated at over $3 billion in 1860 value (Ransom and Sutch 1988). Human beings could be worth so much money because they produced even greater wealth. Formerly enslaved people did not lose that ability simply because they had won their freedom. Their potential as sources of wealth was recognized by Radical Republicans such as Charles Sumner. At the 1865 Massachusetts Republican Party State Convention he opposed colonization of freed people outside the US:

> You ought not to do it because, besides its intrinsic and fatal injustice, you will deprive the country of what it most needs, which is labor. These freedmen on the spot are better than mineral wealth. Each is a mine, out of whom riches can be drawn, provided that you let him share the product.
>
> Sumner 1875: 466

Sumner believed freed people in the South could recreate the wealth created by slavery. He also believed that the dignity and well-being of the worker could be respected. He was mostly right on the first point, wrong on the second: he failed to appreciate capitalism's intrinsic and necessary brutality.

The idea that freed people were a source of wealth appealed alike to northern capitalists and southern planters. Slave production of cotton and other crops had made northern capitalists wealthy. These crops were either shipped overseas or worked into products in growing northern industries. The key to understanding the aftermath of emancipation is to see how southern agricultural production—source of so much wealth—was recreated using "free" labor.

Three things cooperated to cause freed men and women to return to the plantations: (1) control of fertile southern lands by the planter class; (2) discouragement of black emigration from the South; (3) development of coercive institutions to replace slavery.

There was near-unanimity among those with power (and many without power) that freed people should return to the plantations. The victors in the war were the US government and the people it represented. It represented northern capitalists, in finance (banking), in commerce and transportation, and in manufacturing and industry. Much northern wealth came from southern crops, especially cotton. Banking, merchant, and transportation moguls favored restoring the southern agricultural machine devastated by the war. Owners of growing textile and garment industries in the North (though most cotton was still exported to England) also gained from resumption of cotton agriculture in the South. Moreover, politically active northern workers, immigrant and native born, feared competition with free black labor.

So northern capitalists needed southern black labor and northern workers did not want black labor competition. The most powerful losers in the war, the southern planter class, also had an interest in freed people returning to labor for them.

Did anyone in power speak for freed people? Radical Republican Thaddeus Stevens proposed seizing 400 million acres of southern land from planters, distributing 40 million acres to freed people in 40 acre plots, auctioning the rest (Foner 1993). This proposal had no large base of support in the politically active northern population and was defeated in Congress. No political group advocated incorporating freed people into the northern labor force.

The southern system of land tenure—fertile land owned by a wealthy few—was recreated with diminished concentration. Radical Reconstruction created voting rights, democratic state legislatures, and schools. However, the old planter class—controlling extra-legal armed force—seized cropland and forests. Many northern states had laws barring black immigration or requiring black immigrants to post a high cash bond. With freed people barred from northern states and land tenure in the South mostly unchanged, the plantation system was reconstructed with "free" black labor—now joined by poor white people.

At first many freed people believed they had rights and could choose to work on terms that suited them. Planters complained of "impudence" and disinclination to work. To recreate the plantation system based on "free labor," terror was needed, supplied by the Ku Klux Klan and similar racist organizations, often with participation of local government officials. Government-organized terror came from Black Codes—particularly vagrancy laws making it a crime for a black man not to be employed by a white man. The Fourteenth Amendment to the Constitution voided laws with explicit reference to race; still, a penal system developed in the South, where vagrancy could be punished by more than a year of labor. When there was a labor shortage, arrests were made, and labor agents funneled workers to where they were needed. Many never returned from the southern penal labor system.

There were two consequences. First, the convict labor system provided labor in mines, factories, plantations, and quarries. Second, arrests and forced labor terrorized black people into accepting plantation contracts, particularly with active "encouragement" of the Freedmen's Bureau. Semi-slavery was reconstituted on plantations. Laws enacted by planters' political representatives guaranteed labor. As Adolph Reed, Jr. puts the point, "The post-Emancipation criminal code was thus established as a vehicle of racial subordination, a device for ... stabilizing a cheap, tractable labor supply" (Klinkner and Smith 1999: 91).

These sources of terror are better known. The role of the federal government in securing freed people for plantation labor is less well known. The chapter on reconstruction in Stephen Steinberg's *The Ethnic Myth* (2001) fills this gap. Steinberg writes:

> ... the freedmen had to cope with the northern capitalist as well as the southern planter.... the North's legacy of racism and its own stake in the exploitation of black labor would deal a devastating blow to the hope of the ex-enslaved people for economic and social redemption.
>
> 190

More specifically, Steinberg writes, "the North was an active agent in the development of the sharecropping system that functioned as an economic surrogate for slavery" (191). How was this done? In school, history books tell us that the federal government's Freedmen's Bureau helped freed people. To be fair, the Bureau did create schools, offer health care, and administer justice more fairly than southern courts. However, its most important work was reconstituting the southern plantation economy. This work limited prospects for millions of freed people and their descendants for more than eighty years. Steinberg: "From its inception the bureau was designed to facilitate the transition from slavery to freedom in a manner that would not disrupt the southern economy or jeopardize the North's supply of cheap and abundant cotton" (191). It negotiated labor contracts that bound the worker for usually a year to work on a plantation. Typically the sharecropper is advanced food, tools, use of a mule, and seed; at the end of the year he returns a cotton crop. A share of that crop goes to the plantation owner as rent; then (the landlord usually setting the price for the crop), the sharecropper is paid for the rest, minus deductions for what was advanced and any additional living expenses (especially food) he incurred. This often left the sharecropper in debt to "the man" at the end of the year.

Still, freed people and poor white people, notably in South Carolina but throughout the South, participated in Reconstruction governments. Black suffrage was enforced. Public schools opened for black and white children. The US government—servant of the largest capitalists—made possible these inspiring actions of freed people and their comrades among oppressed white workers and farmers (Du Bois 1962 [1935]).

However, before long northern capitalists rebuilt their alliance with the southern planter class. The gains and activism of Reconstruction were eroded and reversed. In the 1870s a series of Supreme Court decisions rejected federal intervention to protect black rights in the South. Republican congressmen and senators in the North, increasingly rejected at the polls, backed off enforcement of Reconstruction. At the same time (the early 1870s) militias controlled by the planter class became the predominant organized force. Black people, no longer valued as property of some powerful owner, were killed for voting or exercising other rights. White Republicans in the South—the racists called them scalawags because they believed in black citizenship—were terrorized or killed if they challenged the planter class. The planter class was able to reassert its power for several reasons: black soldiers had surrendered their arms; armed opponents of the Confederacy had not formed a military alliance uniting indigenous, black, and white opponents of the Confederate war effort; poor white people, no matter their hatred of Confederate government, did not regard themselves as part of the same working class as freed people. Therefore, armed bands such as the Ku Klux Klan and similar groups—often directly led by the planter class— reasserted state power; the few remaining Federal troops in the South could not challenge that power. The planter terrorists, murdering, beating, torturing any who would oppose them, restored a kind of slavery for freed people (Evans 2009; on Mississippi see Jenkins and Stauffer 2009: Chapter 7). Northern capitalists and their southern allies reaped wealth from the cotton economy. They sold out the black soldiers and others who fought, killed, and died to end slavery. They disarmed them, exposing them to the armed power of their local capitalist masters, a disaster for the entire working class.

In the aftermath of the "Wormley bargain" of 1877—a deal to install the Republican Rutherford B. Hayes as President in a disputed election in exchange for the withdrawal of federal troops from the South—Reconstruction reforms were legally reversed by so-called "Redemption" governments. Convict-leasing expanded to coal mines, turpentine farms, factories, construction of roads and railroads (Blackmon 2008). Lynchings of black people were more common than legal executions between 1882 and 1930, creating further terror (Tolnay and Beck 1995). Other rights—voting, racially mixed schools, rights to hold government office—were eroded more gradually, many lasting until the early twentieth century when Jim Crow laws erased them.

To summarize: southern planters and northern capitalists would profit from resuming plantation agriculture. By private and government force, land was restored to planters. Northern workers did not want freed people in the North competing for jobs. Racist culture, North and South, viewed black people with contempt. With little opportunity to migrate to the North to work in industry or westward to homestead[3], freed people mostly stayed in the South. With the threat of penal servitude for vagrancy in the background, freed people returned to the plantations as sharecroppers—where most remained until the mid-twentieth century.

The new racial injustice: plantation agriculture, cotton production, and resistance

Edward Baptist argues that the 400 percent increase in cotton picked per worker between 1800 and 1860—without any innovations in productive technology—was the result of systematic practices of torture developed and shared among cotton planters. In Chapter 2 I described one method; another was an accounting log for picking; the

---

[3] There were many exceptions, mostly small. For one see Painter 1977.

workers had to meet a standard set by the boss; bringing the cotton picked that day for weighing, the worker received one lash from the bull whip for every pound short of the standard, an incentive system "whose bottom gear was torture." A measure of the price enslaved people paid for this system is the infant mortality for children of enslaved people in cotton areas, which could reach forty percent and averaged twenty-five percent. After the end of slavery this labor productivity was never matched until the invention of the mechanical cotton picker; even as late as the 1930s efficient hand pickers were picking only half or a bit more what enslaved people were picking in the 1850s (Baptist 2014: 126–39).

Total cotton production in the US did not again reach its 1860 peak until 1875, but then it grew rapidly. The US produced nearly 5.4 million bales of cotton in 1860 (Beckert 2014: 352). Production was 6.6 million bales for 1880, growing steadily to over seventeen million bales by 1931. Cotton was the highest value export commodity until 1937; for example, in 1911 the value of cotton exports was $639 million compared with $144 million for copper manufactures, the next highest valued commodity (Dattel 2009). Racism in cotton production—dependent on southern black sharecroppers as well as exploitation of many non-black sharecroppers—underpinned the US as a capitalist power for seventy-five years after the end of the Civil War.

Cotton production expanded dramatically while labor productivity declined. How is that possible? From 1880 to 1931 the number of acres in cotton production grew from almost sixteen million to slightly more than thirty-nine million with a corresponding expansion in the labor force producing cotton. Cotton lands expanded into the Southwest, initially Texas and Arkansas, eventually Arizona and California; many new sharecroppers and tenants were recruited to cotton production, including many poor white farmers in the South and Southwest as well as mexican in the Southwest. In 1940 forty-five percent of sharecroppers were either white or mexican (Kirby 1987: 237). US capitalists became wealthy from the ginning, transport, trade, and manufacture of agricultural commodities, from racist exploitation of black labor, from a growing force of white and mexican agricultural labor and the ways racism— against both black and mexican workers—undermined workers of all three identities.

Why did Jim Crow laws mandating racial separation only become prevalent at the end of the nineteenth and beginning of the twentieth centuries, not earlier? To understand this we should look at resistance in the 1880s and 1890s to the new system of agriculture.

In the Deep South yeomen farmers[4]—most of them white—were drawn into cotton production. Cotton production could raise cash, but to produce a crop, debt was necessary to supply food for humans, seed for crops, fodder for farm animals, and often tools. These were typically obtained from a local store-owner, who might also be a large local landlord (devoting some of his crop to food and selling surplus). Crop lien laws gave a creditor first claim on the crop. Yeoman farmers, as small producers, had to sell their crop to a local cotton buyer, who might be the merchant-landlord or his ally. The result was what Michael Schwartz (1976) calls the "tenantization" of yeomen, their

---

[4] A yeoman typically works land that he owns without significant hired help.

reduction to perpetual debt, mortgages, and dependence on their creditors. Already in debt at the end of the Civil War, many lost their land, becoming sharecroppers or tenants (Beckert 2014).[5]

In response to their declining position many white yeomen joined the Southern Farmers' Alliance during the 1880s, initially in Texas, eventually throughout the South. (Farmers' Alliances were also in the Midwest and in the plains.) The Arkansas Wheel was a similar group; it spread to Mississippi, Tennessee, and elsewhere. By 1888 the two organizations had merged, by 1890 having nearly one million members in the South.

Local Alliance chapters gave white yeomen and tenants leverage against merchants, buying from one supplier only in exchange for price reductions, or creating cooperative stores for supplies. Merchants and their banker allies counter-attacked, forming agreements among themselves not to work with the Alliance or depriving an Alliance store of credit.

To raise prices for their crop, Alliance chapters bulked members' crops to bargain for a higher price and even built warehouses, enabling them to wait until demand could command a higher price. Buyers counterattacked, working with railroads, banks, and manufacturers to boycott Alliance cotton and deprive members of credit.

The Alliance eventually developed state-wide grand exchanges, which attempted to combine the necessary borrowing and marketing of crops for all Alliance members in a single state. It worked; in a single year many farmers escaped liens. Again the planter-merchant-cotton-buyer oligarchy counter-attacked, particularly appealing to northern bankers to deny credit or charge higher interest to Alliance exchanges, to railroads to refuse shipments or raise rates, and to manufacturers to refuse to deal with the exchanges. The southern oligarchy—tasked with providing crops to northern merchants—had a long relationship with bankers and railroad magnates: northern capitalists supported their southern allies as long as the South supplied the goods. These counter-attacks, combined with internal weaknesses in the Alliance—management problems and rank-and-file failure to appreciate the need to develop counter-institutions—caused the exchanges to collapse.

The Alliance in Texas and elsewhere supported the Colored Farmers' Alliance—with a similar program—which by 1890 claimed to have a million members. Though separate, the two organizations were allied. White Alliance men recognized that their problems were similar and connected to the problems of black farmers. Still, there was no suggestion of black/white social equality nor any challenge to the power of the Democratic Party, representing the alliance of southern with northern capitalists.

There were important class divisions *within* the white Alliance. Pushed into debt, their prospects declining, yeomen were angry and desperate; tenants and sharecroppers were also being pushed deeper into debt. But local planter-landlord-merchants too were squeezed by declines in the price of cotton which often dropped below the costs of production (Fannin 2003); they were being squeezed between their tenants and the buyers, gin operators, and railroads. As with coffee buyers today, northern cotton merchants encouraged cotton production throughout the South and, for English

---

[5] The discussion of the Alliances is based on Schwartz 1976.

buyers, in Egypt and India, resulting in overproduction. This reduced prices and benefitted the buyers; it oppressed the producers and even squeezed the landlords, creating potential for some of them to rebel against the system.

Some planter-landlords (and their allies) joined the Alliance, bringing organizational and public speaking skills. With landlords leading, the Alliance might dominate at state and regional levels. Their interests were often antagonistic to those of poor farmers: they might be the merchant-landlords exploiting tenants and 'croppers or landowning creditors holding the mortgage on a yeoman's farm. They pushed programs to build agricultural colleges and reduce railroad shipping prices. This elite leadership favored politics at the state level where they could push for legislation. Moreover, their "respectability" was threatened by Alliance radicalism.

The Alliances (white and black) collapsed soon after the failure of exchanges. In the 1890s the People's Party (Populists) replaced the Alliances as the voice of southern discontent. It put out newspapers and other literature about the plight of the small farmer and oppression by the big capitalists and Wall Street boys. In 1890 Populist leader Mary Ellen Lease called for the government to provide to farmers the credit they needed and for abolishing the national banks (Zinn 2003). The Populist monetary program was to free up the money supply (abandon the gold standard), creating inflation, which aided landlords (and perhaps workers) in debt.

Populist success in elections tended to be incompatible with race hatred. So we hear a white Texas Populist saying of black farmers, "They are in the ditch just like we are." The 1891 convention of Texas Populists elected two black delegates to the party executive committee. Other states did likewise. The assistant secretary of the national body was black. An observer of populism in Georgia and Alabama expressed optimism that "the colour line seemed to have broken down" and that black people would soon have full political rights (Woodward 1971: 257). Tom Watson, a wealthy landowner and Populist politician in Georgia, addressed black and white farmers in 1892:

> You are kept apart that you may be separately fleeced of your earnings. You are made to hate each other because upon that hatred is rested the keystone of the arch of financial despotism which enslaves you both. You are deceived and blinded that you may not see how this race antagonism perpetuates a monetary system which beggars you both.
>
> Zinn 2003: 291

This passage does not exhibit anti-racism. Watson blames the *monetary system* for farmers' problems. He advocates printing money. To advance this program—which would benefit some dissident planter-capitalists at the expense of their banker-creditors—Populists needed both black and white votes. They had to defeat the stereotype of the Republican Party as the party supporting black people and the Democrats as representing white people. They formed a party that included both. They did not affirm racial equality. When black voters did not overwhelmingly support Populists, they turned against black people.

That racist turn is anticipated in white Populists' rhetoric. They explicitly rejected social equality of the races and competence of black people to serve in political office.

Nevertheless, they argued that economic interests of black and white farmers were inseparable, that what benefited one benefited the other, that black workers were an unavoidable part of the life of the South, and that only an electoral alliance—on the racist terms the Populists offered—could advance the interests of the "producing class" (a term used to lump together landlords, yeomen, tenants, 'croppers, and laborers) (Gerteis 2007: 157–70). It is understandable that under these conditions, black voters retained an attachment to a Republican Party under which black people had assumed leadership in government.

The 1890s were a volatile time: were white farmers and workers to ally with black farmers or were they to follow the Democratic Party? Did they ally with their black neighbors or did they participate in the lynchings of black people? *They could go either way*—or vacillate. In the end interracial alliances—direct action or electoral—collapsed under the weight of southern racism. The bankers and their allies won.

While Populist leaders too were capitalists, they wanted to shake the power of the Democrats. Like the Alliance, Populists were class divided, but capitalists were even more firmly in control: leaders such as Watson were often landowners whose wealth derived from exploiting black and white tenants—fleecing farmers while expressing outrage about their being fleeced by "a monetary system." Yet many white tenants and sharecroppers to whom the Populists wished to appeal were indeed "in the ditch" along with black people.

In North Carolina in 1896 the Fusion Party (fusing Republicans and Populists) ousted the Democrats, elected a governor, took control of the state legislature, improved education, and voided a contract giving J. P. Morgan control of the state-owned railroad.

The Democrats fought back. With Morgan's help, they intensified anti-black propaganda, intimidated voters with paramilitary organization, and, after a narrow victory in the 1898 election, seized Wilmington, the largest city whose majority was black, burned down the black-owned newspaper, killed as many as a hundred black residents, terrorizing the rest, and seized control of the city government. The Fusion governor did nothing. Wilmington, with black people fleeing, became majority white. With more paramilitary terror, Democrats overturned other local Fusion governments in black areas, then used control of the state legislature to reverse the gains the Fusionists had made. In 1900 the Democrats' gubernatorial candidate encouraged followers to kill any black person who tried to vote. Democrats won by a landslide (Evans 2009).

The Democratic Party would not tolerate threats to its power. They had the backing of their northern capitalist allies. They controlled more guns and used them. What happened in North Carolina was repeated elsewhere. They smashed the Populists. Evans summarizes this:

> [the Democrats] saw increase the fearful possibility of a white-black alliance of the poor against them. They sounded the alarm of "black domination." They promoted lynchings, which increased in frequency and ferocity as the agrarian crisis deepened, reaching an all-time high in the 1890s. More and more elections were decided by violence and fraud.
>
> 2009: 179

The Democratic Party had used bribery and threats to gain black votes. Populist effort to unite non-elite farmers threatened the Democrat's political control of the South. In 1892 the *Mobile Daily Register* threatened black voters who supported the populists: "the Alabama legislature" will "take negro suffrage by the throat and strangle the life out of it." If black voters sided with Populists, "they can expect nothing from us beyond the naked skeleton of the law" (Schwartz 1976: 283). The threat posed by the Populists led the Democrats to implement Jim Crow laws depriving black (and poor white) voters of the suffrage and prescribing a racial caste system.

Jim Crow laws

The Democrats called for Constitutional Conventions in southern states. Behind closed doors they were frank about their intentions. At the Virginia Constitutional Convention of 1902, William A. Anderson reminded the convention that its main purposes were to write a constitution to simplify and improve the government's work and, more important, to reform elections and suffrage. He then explained that by suffrage reform he meant to "eliminate the vicious and ignorant negro vote" putting government in control of "the voters of the Caucasian race" (State of Virginia 1906: 2399). In 1904 Eaton Bowers of Mississippi explained to Congress that the purpose of Jim Crow laws was "preservation of the purity and supremacy of the Caucasian race" and disfranchisement "not only the ignorant and vicious black, but the ignorant and vicious white as well" (Cong. Rec. 8 April 1904: 4536).

These statements by southern ruling class politicians nicely explain their view of the aims and accomplishments of laws disfranchising nearly all black people and many poor white people. These laws eliminated threats to the Democratic Party alliance of southern planter-landlords and the northern capitalists who controlled the cotton empire.

Other Jim Crow laws sought to make impossible social contact between black and white people on terms of equality. They prohibited marriage between people identified as black and white (usually called "anti-miscegenation"). While laws varied a little by state, they typically required separate sections or cars on trains or streetcars and separate sections on steamboats; some required bosses at factories where black and white workers labored together to separate black and white workers in different rooms and prohibit workers from using the same entrances, exits, pay windows, doorways, stairways and windows at the same time and from using the same "'lavatories, toilets, drinking water buckets, pails, cups, dippers, or glasses' at any time" (Woodward 1974: 98). They might require separate hospitals, nurses only of the same race as the patient or prohibit white nurses from caring for black men. Some required separation in penal institutions often in elaborate detail. They typically required separate schools, drinking fountains, rest rooms, and waiting rooms at train and bus depots, separate parks, separation at circuses, prohibition of meeting together or requirement of separate seating at public events such as lectures, political rallies, or movies. Some required residential segregation in cities and even in rural areas (Woodward 1974).

These laws sought to drive a wedge between black and white people, making unity in struggle against capitalists impossible. From 1988 until 2004 Mark Schultz interviewed older people in Hancock County, Georgia about their experiences in the Jim Crow South, mostly about the 1920s and 1930s. I use an incident Schultz describes (2005: 98–9) to show how contact between workers might lead to anti-racist class unity.

This incident occurred "a few years before World War I." When Mary Hunt was six or seven she played with a young white girl, also from a sharecropper family, who lived nearby. One day the white girl's father called the girls over to have some water, which they drank from the same dipper. After they were done, the father "threw out the water and washed the dipper." Mary was so hurt by his actions that she refused to play with the girl again and would not come out when she came over to play. One day Mary's mother spoke with the other girl's father. He asked why Mary no longer played with his daughter. Mary's mother said, "'Cause you insulted her. You made her feel bad." He replied, "Susie, I knew I was wrong, but I just wasn't used to drinking after them [that is, black children]." Eventually Mary Hunt relented and played with the white girl but only at her own house; Mary would not let her drink water from the family dipper and made her go home if she needed water, a kind of reciprocal insult.

What struck me was the father's admission that he *knew* he was wrong—even though he was only following Jim Crow norms. He seems to recognize Mary's humanity, that it was wrong to hurt a child unnecessarily and that in following that norm he was doing that. Still, it was the confrontation with Mary's *mother*—where a black person criticized the behavior of a white person—that induced him to acknowledge Mary's humanity and the harm he had done. In the context of Jim Crow laws that were becoming prevalent, this confrontation had no further meaning or consequence, as far as I know. However, in the context of class struggle by sharecroppers against landlords and merchants, such confrontations, if frequent, could spawn anti-racist egalitarian relations. Anti-racism could unite workers.

The purpose of the Jim Crow laws was to divide the working class by making it *normatively required* for white people—including the poor—to insult black people. Where people have contact as equals, racial hostility and hierarchy can break down.

Besides the passage of separation and disfranchisement laws the 1890s saw other vicious responses to interracial cooperation in the Populist and Fusionist movements: the Democratic Party encouraged lynchings of black people and others (roughly 80 percent of southern lynchings were of black people); terror was intensified, leading to the consolidation of a one-party Democratic South (which lasted until the 1970s when—an irony, given the history of the Republican Party—Republicans inherited the mantel of southern racism, as the two parties realigned). With the presidency of Woodrow Wilson, Jim Crow was extended to the federal bureaucracy, including segregated washrooms and downgrading or removal of black government workers (Klinkner and Smith 1999).

Agriculture under Jim Crow

Southern agriculture increasingly depended on *non*-black labor. Because freed people and their descendants shared a legal status of freedom with native born white people and mexicans, capitalists needed to drive a racial wedge between these workers. Essential to driving this wedge is unequal oppression and exploitation: racist thought by itself does not gain a grip unless it explains something that people can observe. When there is unequal oppression, racist thought rationalizes that inequality. The system of southern racism used laws and extra-legal terror to create unequal oppression. Terror turned people of African descent into semi-slaves and drove down white people who were not the *direct* objects of racist terror.

Jim Crow laws created not just segregation but also racial stigma. When black people were enslaved, the ruling class could be more tolerant of informal contacts between enslaved people and poor whites; contacts did not threaten slavery. However, with black and white people alike being legally free, norms of white-over-black induced white workers to identify with their white bosses not their co-workers, hampering class unity and subordinating the entire working class. Even informal contacts between workers became taboo. Still, in remote areas the racial divide might be inconsistently policed and segregation flouted: even common-law marriages between white men and black women could be tolerated (Schultz 2005).

If we look at this system up close, we can see that even under Jim Crow the oppression of black and white are linked. The vulnerability of black people to lynching, random murder, and conviction for any minor violation, created systematic terror and inhibited black people's self-assertion. However, subservience of black people in response to terror did not work to white workers' advantage. Here is how this worked (Kirby 1987: 238):

> White managers preferred the most powerless dependents when they could get them. Ned Cobb, a black Alabama farmer, recalled a telling incident from Tallapoosa County during the 1940s. A white landlord inquired of Cobb if he knew of a suitable family looking for land. Cobb recommended a white family, and the landlord responded (as Cobb quoted him), "Aw, hell ... I don't want no damn white man on my place." Cobb reflected, "That teached me fair that a white man always wants a nigger in preference.... How come that? How come it for God's sake? He don't want no damn white man on his place. He gets a nigger, that's his glory. He can do that nigger just like he wants to and that nigger better not say nothin against his rulins." Whites, on the other hand, "won't take that ... off another white man."

Cobb's views about preference for black sharecroppers were not unique. Pete Daniel (1985: 87) writes about New Deal rural relief programs of the mid-1930s in Leflore County, Mississippi in the Yazoo delta:

> ... landlords never liked to deal with whites. As blacks filtered back to the county, planters attempted to get rid of the whites.... When [New Deal programs] reached the county, landlords released white sharecroppers and retained blacks. The report quoted one landlord as saying, "I won't have any G—damned white 'cropper on my place. Get off and stay off. All I want to work are niggers who will do what I tell them to."

Daniels adds that white farmers were willing to use weapons against their landlords. So the oppression and terror directed at black people in the Jim Crow South indirectly harmed poor white farmers who may themselves have participated in it.

However, racist terror was functional for capitalists. A terrorized black labor force, being more vulnerable, drove down white labor as well. Profits for capitalist farm owners but especially for cotton buyers, merchants, and bankers in the East were enhanced by this arrangement. The tragedy was the failure of white labor to understand that the racist oppression of black labor was *their own* oppression, that the working class as a whole needed to fight racist oppression. Instead many white workers participated in the oppression of their black fellow workers, undermining them all.

Further west, particularly in Arkansas and Texas white 'croppers and tenants were far more prevalent and often were the majority of farm labor. From 1890 until the present Texas has been the largest producer of cotton, producing between twenty to twenty-five percent of the US crop. In the late nineteenth and early twentieth centuries Texas cotton production employed mostly black and white sharecroppers in East Texas and mostly white tenants (some hiring mexican labor) in Central Texas' Blackland Prairie, usually on smaller farms; in South Texas, mexican labor was primary.[6] Generally white tenants, who brought their own tools and farm animals to their tasks, rented land on shares of one-fourth their cotton crop while sharecroppers, who brought only their own labor (including that of family members), owed one-half the crop plus payment for anything else they used. Tenants often aspired to buy land and thought of themselves as businessmen-farmers, while sharecroppers were agricultural labor. Landowners engineered three-way competition between black, white and Mexican 'croppers and tenants. In Texas US-born mexicans and Mexican immigrants were poorer and more vulnerable than both black and white labor. Just as, in the Deep South, planters often preferred more vulnerable black labor to white, in Texas they may prefer mexicans. Views of white superiority were applied to mexicans. Land owners gave mexicans inferior housing and regarded them as more easily dominated. By 1915 white farmers had largely been pushed out of Central Texas. By mid-century cotton production was mechanized. White tenants moved to cities, most never realizing their aspirations to be yeoman farmers. While poor and middling white people might have "white capped" (terrorized) black and particularly mexican laborers competing with them for opportunity, this only added to the power of capitalists, who regarded them as "off white," as an inferior sort of white (Foley 1997).

There was also resistance against the capitalists. The Knights of Labor organized a strike of Louisiana sugar cane workers in the fall of 1887 (harvest time) after achieving enthusiastic acceptance from black workers. The strike was suppressed when the state militia forced one thousand cane cutters into the town of Thibodaux. Then, after the militia withdrew, a group of armed vigilantes massacred strikers from November 21–23. After the massacre shallow graves were discovered in the vicinity of the town for weeks (Gourevitch 2015).

---

[6] People who were racially mexican might be US-born or they might be from Mexico. See the Introduction for the difference between mexican and Mexican.

The Great Depression of the 1930s led to resistance despite Jim Crow. The Communist Party organized a mostly black Share Croppers Union (SCU) in Alabama. Union members shot it out with sheriff deputies in Camp Hill in 1931 and Reelville in 1932. By 1935 the union had 12,000 members and engaged in some successful strikes. The union was militant and made it possible for sharecroppers to assert their power. Nevertheless, it had little success in recruiting white 'croppers (Foley 1997, Kelley 1990).

The Southern Tenant Farmers Union (STFU) united black and white 'croppers and tenants, resisting some racial division. Black and white ate together at indoor dinners and outdoor picnics, violating a powerful Jim Crow norm. Still, most locals were monoracial or nearly so, and white farmers tended to retreat from activism as black 'croppers asserted themselves. There was racial tension, as some white members sought racially separate locals and some black 'croppers sought an all-black union (Kirby 1987).

The efforts by the Knights of Labor, the STFU, and the SCU were very brave. However, a powerful united movement of southern tenants and farm laborers never developed. Class division between tenants and sharecroppers (including wage laborers), the Jim Crow divisions and distrust between black and white southerners, and the virtually universal rejection by white farmers of "social equality" with black people (adherence to white supremacist norms) were too much to overcome. Only communists, starting in the late 1920s, openly embraced social equality and successfully united workers in the urban North and in Louisville around a program that fought racial injustice and fought for the immediate needs of workers.

Southern agriculture, black labor, and capitalism

In 1942 International Harvester had a workable mechanical cotton-picker, and soon so did other manufacturers. In the 1950s a chemical herbicide was developed that would make the hand weeding (chopping) of cotton unnecessary (Dattel 2009). Cotton production would no longer need millions of black, white, and mexican workers.

US wealth and power developed from the beginning from the hands of black people, enslaved or nominally free, subject to brutal oppression, and from the hands of many white and immigrant workers whose conditions were limited by competition with exceptionally oppressed and exploited black labor. Black workers were central to the development of southern agricultural crops which provided US bankers with the wealth to build up industry in the nineteenth century. From that industry and the continued export of southern agricultural crops, the US became a world power. The dominance of the US as a capitalist power after the Second World War was founded on racial injustice, on the appropriation of indigenous lands, the slaughter of indigenous peoples, the efforts to exterminate their culture and languages, and the labor of black and other workers.

Every successful effort to unite black and white workers was answered by armed terror, an indication of capitalism's dependence on racism. We cannot reform racial injustice out of capitalism. We need to put an end to racism or any comparable injustice forever. That is what at least some of the Knights of Labor, anarchists, activists in the Industrial Workers of the World (IWW), and socialists believed and fought for. But only the communists in the Communist Party of the United States of America (CP) made the fight against racism and for *social equality* central to working class struggle. In doing so, they transformed the lives of workers whom they led. We come to that story soon, in Chapter 5.

4

Race and Anti-Racism in Industry

Coal Miners 1870–1921

Overview

This and the next chapter are not a thorough account of either the role of black labor or of the effect of race on industry in the United States. I aim at something more limited: to mine the history of industrial struggles to find the greatest promise of a world without racial injustice and of the forces that might bring that world into being. Our best hope comes from the leadership of workers most oppressed by racial injustice, particularly black workers, particularly when workers simultaneously battle racial injustice and oppression of all workers.

In this chapter I sketch a working-class leader and a working-class anti-racist movement. Richard L. Davis was a black coal miner in Ohio and leader of the United Mine Workers of America in the 1880s and 1890s. He fought white miners' and union leaders' racism. He fought black miners' separatism. Most of all, he fought the coal operator/capitalists. His life adds a personal dimension to the story that follows of Alabama coal miners from the 1870s through the strike of 1920–1921. Davis's brief life and then the fight to build interracial unionism in Alabama illustrate the most promising working-class anti-racism of that period.

Background: industrial slavery[1]

Black enslaved labor helped build southern industry. Although its technology was poor compared with northern industry, southern industry was substantial and employed five percent of people enslaved in the South. Some industries were almost entirely staffed by slave labor, others by a mixture of enslaved and wage workers.

Many industries were closely tied to agriculture, in small towns, at a crossing accessible to farmers, or on large plantations: refining sugar, processing tobacco, cotton, and hemp, milling textiles, grain and cotton, and pressing cotton into bales. For lighter work bosses preferred women and children. Enslaved people mined salt, gold, lead,

---

[1] The discussion of southern industrial slavery is based on Starobin 1970a and 1970b.

iron, and coal and worked in iron foundries. With inferior coal seams, profitability in southern coal mining depended on enslaved people and low wages. The enslaved extracted turpentine, and harvested cypress, oak, and pine forests; worked in sawmills, doing back-labor; laid railroad track, dug canals, built plank roads, dredged rivers and harbors, built levees, maintained streets, and worked on rivers as boatmen. They built and rebuilt the US Capitol.

Southern industry was technologically backward because northern bankers "drained plantation profits northward.... [C]apital accumulated by northern merchants, bankers, and insurance brokers tended to be reinvested in northern industries" rather than southern (Starobin 1970a: 163). Capitalists invested in cotton, where torture and brutalization of enslaved people extracted maximum labor and profits.

Union victory in the Civil War ended slavery but not the South's reliance on black labor. In industry black people did as convicts or for wages work similar to the work they had done as enslaved. Southern industry remained technologically backward. Southern industrial capitalists needed cheap southern labor to compete on national markets. The key to cheap labor was racism. Terror directed against black labor held down all workers.

Some lessons from the life and thought of Richard L. Davis

Some people show us how to live and how to fight. Richard L. Davis was one. Born in 1862 in Virginia and almost certainly having some formal schooling, Davis was working in tobacco processing at age eight. He left for West Virginia coalfields after 1880 and then the Hocking Valley, Ohio coalfields in 1882. He settled in Rendville and worked in William P. Rend's Mine #3, where all miners were black. Other mines in the Sunday Creek Valley (region of Rendville and other mining towns) excluded black workers from the mines. By 1886 Davis had become an active member of the Knights of Labor, a group he supported because of its commitment to the cause of black labor.

In an 1892 letter to the *Journal of the United Mine Workers of America* (hereafter *Journal*; the union will be called UMWA) Davis recalled a struggle against racism of the mid-1880s under the auspices of the Knights. Here is Herbert Gutman's (1977: 133–4) description of that struggle:

> In the "Negro mine," Mine 3 ... the screens on which the coal was separated from dirt and rock permitted more wastage of coal than those in the other mines, and its men got no pay for dead work.[2] This means a lower weekly wage for the same quantity of work that whites performed.... The Negroes in Mine 3 protested first to the operator [Rend] and learned that their screens would be altered to conform

---

[2] Coal miners were paid by the tonnage of coal loaded on coal cars and removed from the coal face. Cutting the coal face and loading coal requires preliminary work—for example timbering the roof and laying track—and some clean up; all of this was considered dead work and was unpaid in Mine #3.

with the "white" screens but only if whites worked in "their" mine. The men told the operator, Davis remembered, "to put the white men in, as they wanted the screens changed. So the screens were changed, and this was the advent of the white men in mine No. 3." At about the same time, the local Knights, including Davis and other Negroes among their members agitated for wider Negro job opportunity in the entire valley, and succeeded in gaining entry for Negroes in other valley mines.

These struggles illustrate two principles: intolerance for inferior treatment of black workers—screens that cheat them or exclusion from mines—and rejection of racial division. In my mind—I suspect in Davis's—the two are linked. Unity between black and white miners is possible and desirable but depends on rejection of inferior treatment of black people. Davis fought for those principles consistently. They are the essence of his anti-racism.

In 1892 letters Davis opposed racial segregation of miners in a nearby Congo, Ohio mining camp's "model town" of houses leased from the company:

Congo ... sits on two hills or ridges with a deep ravine between, access to either side by means of a bridge. On one of these ridges or hills the white miners' houses are built. I don't know what they call this ridge, but on the other ridge the colored miners' houses are built; they call it Nigger Ridge, see? A distinction is made by the company, and if a colored man goes there seeking a house he is very courteously conducted over on the other ridge, you know. If he wants one on the white folks' ridge, why he is told that he can't get it, and if he insists he is called saucy, and is told that he can get neither house nor work; that's freedom, you know.

Now I will leave the houses alone and go down into the mine. Here we have another distinction. On one side all the white men work, on the other all the colored men work. This is called "over in Africa." how is that, eh? Don't suit me.

Gutman 1977: 138–9

Congo bosses also excluded local farmers from the miners' camps to insure a monopoly for the company store. Parodying the phrase "the land of the free and the home of the brave," Davis wrote that Congo was better called "the land of the rich and the home of the slave" (Doppen 2016: 122). Davis consistently opposed racial segregation. He believed that separation was introduced to split and weaken the workers, writing "employers ... keep up the distinction between men for the purpose of breeding strife and dissension in our ranks.... While we are fighting among ourselves, they wag away with the spoils, and what do we get—only the dregs" (Gutman 1977: 139). In 1897 Davis wrote that Congo was "the best mining camp in this part of the valley" after visiting and finding that the union had improved conditions.

While Davis fought hard for the UMWA, this depended on the union's commitment to racial equality and inclusion. Davis urged the American Railway Union (ARU) to drop its clause barring black membership and demanded black inclusion. He opposed affiliation between the inclusive UMWA and the ARU. In an article for the *Journal* in

1893 entitled "The Colored Race and Labor Organization" Davis acknowledged that in seeking work the black worker competed with white; still

> we find that the labor organizations, or rather some of them, did that which no other organization had done, the church not even excepted, [and] threw open their doors and admitted him as a full member with the same rights and privileges as a white brother. This, in our opinion, was the first or initiative step toward the equality of mankind, and we are sorry to say that until the present day the labor organizations are the only ones that recognize the negro as an equal and as a man.
> Gutman 1977: 154

This passage exhibits confidence in unions when in fact the UMWA may have been the only one that came close to observing that principle as this time. Davis extrapolated hopefully from his experience as a full member of UMWA but was aware of a contrary tendency:

> ... some of our people have not yet gained enough confidence in his white brother as to trust him very far. And yet, is this strange? When we notice the fact that in our midst we have some as bitter enemies as anywhere else. While we admit that our labor organizations are our best friends, it would be well to teach some of our white brothers that a man is a man no matter what the color of his skin may be. We have nothing but the best of words for labor organizations, and hope they may continue in the same line of actions, and we are confident that they will not only better the conditions of the working classes, but will also wipe out all class and race distinctions, and in the meantime the negro will be found as loyal to labor organizations as his white brother.
> 155

These remarkable passages express commitment to the UMWA, hope that unions bring about racial equality, but also a warning that racism among white workers must be expunged. Davis's commitment was unflagging because he retained that hope.

Davis opposed black separatism. In July 1892, when a black mine boss was installed at Mine 8, white workers walked out. As a district leader Davis called a meeting. Although both black and white miners were angry, Davis apparently got the miners to return (neither Gutman nor Doppen makes it clear). The anger simmered, and some black miners wanted to leave the UMWA. In his letters to the *Journal* Davis criticized both black and white miners, writing "a man is a man, no matter what the color of his skin is, and I don't care who thinks different" (135). He suggested that black miners should not be sensitive to verbal insults. He attacked the color line, writing that it was "high time" for it to be dropped, urging workers to fight the capitalists rather than one another. Then Rend offered to return Mine 3 to its former status as an all-black mine, and some black miners wanted to take him up on that, despite a warning from another black miner that Rend was trying to break up the union. Davis also responded, reminding workers of their inferior treatment in Mine 3 when it was an all-black mine in the 1880s, pointing out that Rend's purpose was "to keep up the race fighting among us." He wrote:

Does it stand to reason that he thinks any more of you or me because of our color? Not much. He is like the balance; he will get his coal where he can get it cheapest, no matter whether it be from white or black. Now, then, do you mean to say that you can produce coal cheaper under this plan?

136

Davis's stand against both the racism of white miners and the separatism of black miners made him unpopular with many of both races, at least in the short run. White miners' walkout at Mine 8 exacerbated racial antipathy. Davis sensed that the black miners who criticized him thought that "capital has a right to the reins of supremacy and that labor should bow submissively to the bidding of capital" (137). Davis understood that workers had power only if united. Both the racism of white miners and the separatist anger of black miners threatened that fragile power. It threatened to give capital unchecked dictatorship. Davis wrote several months later that things in the area were much better. He had weathered the storm and continued to be accepted as leader by all miners.

Davis visited Alabama coalfields as UMWA organizer in 1897-98. Appalled by southern segregation, he noted that some white as well as black miners did not like it. Davis responded to celebrations of Emancipation Day on January 1, "As our people [black people] are celebrating the emancipation proclamation, ... we need another proclamation of equal importance, and that one is to emancipate the wage slaves, both white and black" (148). Davis does not explain this criticism of the capitalist wage relation (being a slave to the boss) but was likely influenced by his participation in the Knights of Labor. The Knights, as labor republicans, criticized capitalism and wage slavery: the wealth of capitalists allowed them to dominate the worker in violation of the worker's republican freedom. A cooperative commonwealth of labor would do away with wage slavery (Gourevitch 2015).

Hope of such a cooperative commonwealth, alternative to the domination workers experienced daily, likely inspired Davis's activism. Davis seems to have hoped that the UMWA, to which he adhered as the Knights' organizational presence disappeared, could be such a vehicle of liberation and republican freedom. Davis was present at the UMWA founding convention in 1890 and served on the executive committee of Ohio's District 6 from 1890 through 1895. After several years of agitation and complaint in the *Journal* about the absence of black leadership at the national level Davis was elected to the national executive board in 1896, receiving the highest vote total among the fifteen candidates; he was re-elected the following year but not in 1898. In 1896 Davis, who already in 1891 had been branded an "agitator" by Rend, was dismissed from his position as checkweighman at Mine 3 and was blacklisted by the area's coal operators.[3] Unable to find work in the mines, he received small amounts from the union for his organizing work in Ohio, West Virginia, and Alabama (Doppen 2016). The repeated affirmations of his leadership within the UMWA were likely one source of Davis's hope that the union would lead workers to the end of wage slavery and give black workers equal respect.

---

[3] The checkweighman is responsible for supervising the weighing of miners' coal and giving them credit for what they mined, thus determining their pay; in union mines the checkweighman was selected by the workers, trusted to give them fair credit for their work.

Rendville of the 1880s and 1890s had enough racial egalitarianism in daily life to give substance to such a hope. It seems to have been extraordinary within its region and known for its bi-racial citizenry. The town was started in 1879 and 1880; that year's census listed its residents as all white. By August black miners came to Rendville but worked in the mines on a sliding scale that represented a lower pay rate. White miners saw this lower rate for black miners as a threat to their position and in September organized a large protest of regional miners demanding to meet with black miners. Protestors would not disperse. The national guard was called with a Gatling machine gun. By early October the troops were gone along with the sliding pay scale. Black miners were working for 80 cents per ton, as were whites. By 1882 a racially integrated public school opened with one black teacher among the three. The school continued to expand, and by 1887 two of three school board members were black. The company doctor, hotel keeper, the grocer, and by 1887 the mayor were black. Yet in 1900 the town was still majority white (Doppen 2016). So whatever racial tensions existed, Rendville seemed to show to some people that black and white people could live side by side as equals, an experience that might add to Davis's optimism.

Despite the racism that persisted inside the UMWA and eventually became dominant, the social environment of the UMWA and of some of these towns enabled a significant cadre of black miners to emerge in Ohio, West Virginia, and Alabama, take initiative, and become leaders among other workers. Davis was one of these, but there were many more.[4] This fact can inspire anti-racists as we seek precedents to justify optimism: it showed what was *possible*.

Anti-racist lessons from battles of Alabama coal miners 1870–1921[5]

While the letters of Richard Davis reveal the life and thoughts of an individual miner, a broader history of the miners of the Birmingham, Alabama region provides further lessons to anti-racists about opposing and ending racially unjust social organization. At the end of this section I discuss these practical lessons.

Capitalists of the "New South" strove to develop southern industry.[6] Birmingham was built from scratch in the early 1870s. It was near a junction of newly built rail lines and iron, coal, and limestone deposits at the southwestern end of Appalachia, seemingly the ideal location for a southern iron industry. Birmingham suffered from inferior iron ore, narrow, steep coal seams, and technologically inferior iron furnaces.

Because of inferior coal seams and technology, Birmingham iron could enter the market at competitive prices only if wages of miners and other workers were much lower than national averages. Birmingham capitalists had an advantage: intense southern racism, historical divisions of black and white labor, recruitable black

---

[4] For black leadership of West Virginia coal miners see Brier 1977, 1989.
[5] Unless otherwise noted the discussion of Alabama miners is based on Letwin 1998 and Kelly 2001.
[6] For "New South" thought as espoused by Henry Grady of the *Atlanta Constitution* see Takaki 1979.

agricultural labor, and impoverished white people. Racism intensified in the 1890s (in response to the threat of southern Populism); lynchings, beatings, and murders of black people grew along with more mundane abuses. Since white labor competed with black, racial injustice drove down wages for white labor also. The region was remote, population sparse, and coal settlements isolated and tightly controlled by operators who owned everything including workers' housing. Workers were often paid in company scrip, which could be spent only at the company store where high prices enhanced profits. Operators used convict labor, especially Tennessee Coal and Iron (TCI) at its Pratt Mines. (TCI, the largest coal operator in the region and iron producer in Birmingham, was incorporated into United States Steel in 1907.)

Under the contract system operators gave a contract to a "miner" who hired "laborers" at low wages. This had a racist edge: most but not all "miners" were white, and most but not all "laborers" were black (never a white "laborer" working for a black "miner"). A small farmer might show up with his black hired workers and be given a contract. Given racism and a compliant labor force, operators could make a profit.

Compliant labor was their problem. Workers organized and fought to improve their condition. In the 1870s the Greenback Labor Party (GLP) stressed the idea of a common class experience and common working class interests among miners. By the early 1880s the GLP had faded, but the larger Knights of Labor promoted interracial class cooperation. A paradox with the Knights was that they simultaneously *enabled* miners to stand up to operators and strive to improve conditions and *discouraged their militancy* when miners' activity threatened bourgeois social order. The Knights tended to oppose strikes. Their approach was practical, viewing racial divisions among workers as weakening their hand against operators. Rhetoric and actions had a *moral* dimension recognizing full humanity of all workers. This challenged the color line: a Knights funeral for a worker who died in the middle of an 1884–85 strike was attended by fifty-one white and twenty-six black miners.

Still, the Knights were limited. Writers often assumed a white audience, rather than a racially inclusive one. In 1887 a militant strike of 1,300 miners at Patton Mines in Walker County demanded a wage increase. The bosses evicted strikers and brought in strikebreakers (scabs) and guards. Miners responded with district-wide material assistance to strikers. Alabama Knights leader Nicholas Stack tried to arbitrate a settlement, but the miners wanted no part of that. Stack threw the Walker County chapter out of the Knights. This action only fed the strikers' determination to keep fighting. A much larger strike in 1888 led to the formation of a new miners organization. While labor mutuality and egalitarianism were popular among miners in the district, Stack's opposition to strikes was not.

The United Mine Workers of America (UMWA) in Alabama 1890–1921

In 1890 two national miners' organizations, one affiliated with the Knights, united to form UMWA and District 20 of UMWA in the Birmingham area. There were large strikes through 1898, a period of relative tranquility through 1904 with many mines working under UMWA contracts which recognized some miners' rights, then a major strike against the large iron producing companies in 1904 in which UMWA suffered a big defeat, a district-wide strike against other producers in 1908, where again UMWA was beaten. The operators had their way from 1908 until 1914, when labor shortages during World War I created alternatives for workers, pressured operators to raise wages and make other concessions. The government intervened in labor contracts. A large strike in 1920–21 led to another major defeat of UMWA.

The strength of UMWA was its struggle for miner unity and its real although inconsistent opposition to the color line, white supremacy, and racism.[7] In 1894 TCI brought many black strikebreakers to the coal district and made their mine at Blue Creek for black miners only, advertising it as "an 'Eden' for black workers" (Letwin 1998: 102). Miners resented the strikebreaking. UMWA appealed for unity and urged that resentment not take a racial form, writing, "Poverty is the odium here, no matter what the color" (103). Despite some white miners' distrust of black people generally, a Pinkerton agent sent to spy on miners in their saloons reported that black and white strikers continued to socialize together with (Letwin's paraphrase) a "remarkable, if casual camaraderie between black and white strikers." He observed them "'all talking together,' agreeing with stony determination that they would not return to work for 35 cents per ton" (104). Letwin observes that "the bonds of unionism submerged the racial divide," citing as evidence an interracial protest of the arrest of a black striker and a march of 2,000 strikers from Pratt City to Birmingham, equally black and white. Wives and children protested together, defying the color line and maintaining unity. Miner defiance of the color line was extensive across the district in union meetings and social gatherings. The miners at an all-black mine called a meeting on the eve of a strike; however, the meeting was "half painted black and the other half white" as miners from neighboring mines, both black and white, arrived to show support and were admitted by a unanimous vote of the black miners. Letwin writes: The event epitomized the textures of race relations in the strike district: the southern culture of segregation was not strong enough to prevent a joint meeting of black and white miners, but it *was* strong enough to compel 'quite a discussion' among them" about whether to hold a racially mixed meeting, leading to "a reaffirmation of interracial engagement at the initiative of black miners (104).

I have selected these incidents to illustrate interracial solidarity, camaraderie, and unity in this one strike, but Letwin's (1998) and Brian Kelly's (2001) books are filled with many other examples, remarkable in the Deep South in a period of rising Jim Crow laws and disfranchisement.

The imperative of interracial unity often was grounded in practical considerations of the harm that racial division and oppression creates for miners, including white miners. "Union leaders reminded white miners that the abuse of black miners affected all" and the *Journal* "detailed how the agents of 'a certain coal company' had taken to lashing with 'black snake' whips African Americans who refused to work. 'This may not

---

[7] I use "racism" for *organization* of inequality based on racial identification and "white supremacy" to refer to a *doctrine* of white superiority. The doctrine of white supremacy contributes to racism against black people and, as we will see, the social subordination of many white people.

cause the blood to boil in the veins of our Caucasian brothers in the South ... but ... the blows of the "black snake" fall indirectly on your shoulders'" (103 Letwin's elisions). White miners could recognize it too. "Shack rousters" were thugs sent to the cabins of black miners to force them to go to work. Brian Kelly explains that the "harsh treatment" of black workers was "not lost upon all whites in the coal camps." As one miner remarked, "The white miner is treated bad enough ... [but] the Negro as a general thing simply catches hell in the big way." He noted that bosses did not send shack rousters to the homes of white miners, but if white miners did not stand up for black, "we will be catching as much hell as the Negro." White miners must, he said, "lay aside prejudice" and "reorganize the UMWA on an interracial basis" (2001: 95–6). While not all white miners shared this miner's awareness of the linked oppression of black and white and of how black oppression prepared the same for white, he was surely not alone.

The UMWA often explicitly opposed white supremacist doctrines. Letwin notes that in an 1890 strike the union "took exception to the language of white supremacy" and attacked a coal boss for calling black workers "niggers" (93). Letwin quotes an article in the *Journal* that it was "preposterous" that any miner should not stand "on a plane of equality" with their brothers "because the man's face is black," condemning those who raised "the evil spirit of race prejudice" as "the most infernal" (100).

After an 1894 strike at Corona a white miner "likened 'our colored brothers' to a 'stone wall,' adding that 'any miner may well be proud to take a Corona darkey by the hand and acknowledge him to the world as a brother'" (100). In 1895, after the Birmingham Trades Council voted to admit unions with black membership, the *Labor Advocate* wrote that white workers had—until this vote—"assisted their enemy in its work by allowing race prejudice to discolor their judgment." Many miners recognized, in Letwin's words, that "the color line did not promote the supremacy of white miners as much as that of capital" (119). There was action, not just words: in 1901 Birmingham hotel owners would not rent space to the UMWA for their convention because black and white miners would be meeting in a common space; the union used their own facilities. The following year a black union vice president of the Alabama State Federation of Labor was to make the arrangements for the Selma meeting. The local press objected to the black leadership of an interracial organization and to black and white workers meeting together. The racially mixed union meeting went ahead when the United Confederate Veterans offered their hall for use "without regard to the color line" (Kelly 2001: 113).

However, it would be misleading to suggest that UMWA always rejected white supremacy. As Letwin stresses, the union walked a fine line of flouting the color line and fighting for class unity while at the same time conforming to Jim Crow norms. For example, ordinarily the president of any racially mixed union group would be white while the vice president would be black, never the reverse, which would too directly challenge racial norms. Union leaders would endorse white supremacy in words and affirm that they did not agree with social equality of the races. They would attack operators for violating white supremacy by preferably hiring black miners. During the 1920–21 strike, when all miners were suffering bitterly, a "Colord Union Woman" complained with justice that black miners had been slighted in distribution of what workers needed, and a union organizer reported that of 80 pairs of shoes distributed, only 13 went to the families of black miners (Kelly 2001: 188–9). Letters from white miners to union publications often expressed racist sentiments or condescendingly suggest that white miners should lift up black miners. The union was a mixed bag.

Whatever its weakness and ambivalence, the union created a social space where black miners asserted themselves and gave leadership to other miners and where white miners changed—at least for a while—as a result of their union experiences and activities.

Coal operators—and many miners—stereotyped black workers as docile, pliable workers favorable to owners. This stereotype was a result of Jim Crow terror and more intense black poverty. Both made black self-assertion dangerous, exposing people to beatings, lynching or economic harms. The coal district could change that. Even with the operators' tight control of coal towns, the massing of workers required by industrial work provided some protection against random violence, compared with isolated rural settings. The openness of the UMWA to black membership and initiative created an avenue for black miners to assert themselves against the operators and against racism from other workers. Many black miners took that road. In 1895 at TCI's all-black Blue Creek mine black miners—refusing to enter the mines—forced the disciplining of a blacksmith's helper who had mistreated a miner. At the height of Jim Crow racism, Birmingham's UMWA District 20 contracts in 1901 prohibited discrimination against black miners in assigning labor tasks. In 1900 the Birmingham Trades Council (BTC) asked District 20 to avoid businesses that did not have union contracts. Black miner delegates objected that some of the BTC unions and the BTC itself banned black membership. The BTC repealed its color bar.

Most remarkable were black miners' actions during strikes. Brian Kelly (2001) notes that black miners "were often the most militant defenders of the union" (86) and "the most determined strikers" (20). When, during the 1908 strike, operators brought in trainloads of black strikebreakers, black miners were waiting for them at the train depot, saying, "Get off and join us and we'll feed you and give you five dollars a week!" (86). Kelly writes, "Black strikers were 'armed to the teeth and everywhere in predominance,' warned Major G. B. Seals of the Alabama Guard." When deputies tried to stop black strikers from displaying guns, the strikers "stood up and gave the deputies a fight, firing at them with considerable precision" (22). Kelly notes, "The willingness of black and white strikers to join forces—frequently in arms—against the operators seemed to many to signal an unwelcome blurring of racial lines" (21).

The strike of 1920–21—by then seventy percent of the miners were black— especially revealed the anger and militancy of black miners, when a strike enabled them to express it. Kelly summarizes, "black miners ... proved unwilling to submit any longer to the old regime, placing themselves at the forefront in this new round of struggle" (163). When a black miner and a sheriff got into an "altercation" at Carbon Hill, William Hicks, a white miner killed both the sheriff and his deputy and was then himself killed. Kelly (181) writes:

> Similar violations of racial protocol occurred on a regular basis throughout the strike: black strikers attacked white and black strikebreakers; white strikers

broke with politicians of their own race and physically defended black union organizers against company and state repression; black UMWA members spurned appeals of "race leaders" in favor of those from UMWA organizers, both black and white.... [such actions] bore a ... troubling salience for the operators and their allies and seemed to portend the collapse of the foundations of southern society.

When strikers could gain access at train depots to people recruited to break the strike, they were, according to a report to UMWA leaders, "remarkably successful in convincing them to honor the strike" (181). Indeed, the oppression and exploitation of *strikebreakers* was so severe that these "docile" and "pliable" workers "launched a strike inside the stockade erected to seal them off from contact with the UMWA" (183). Even *convicts* went on strike!

The unity that was endorsed and sustained in struggle profoundly affected how people behaved and the persons they could become. In one remarkable meeting in 1900 as union miners waited for operators to arrive, a white miner started singing "The Honest Workingman," other white miners joining him in the chorus. District 20 president William Fairley requested a song from "one of the colored brethren." A black miner sang "We Are Marching to Canaan," with black delegates joining in the chorus. This was followed by more songs led by both black and white miners at the meeting. Letwin (1998: 133) writes that the "very frivolity suggests an atmosphere of interracial fellowship spilling beyond the purely expedient. Shared purpose inevitably fostered shared identity.... District 20 was very much the *joint* endeavor of black and white unionists, with all the commonality and difference implied in the term" [emphasis in Letwin]. Through experiences such as these and the camaraderie of a strike miners begin to develop a distinctive *miner* culture and identity; race becomes less salient.

Later Letwin points out that the union leadership, trying to deflect attacks by the Birmingham press and operators that the union was promoting social equality, affirmed its commitment to white supremacy and denied any advocacy of social equality between black and white. But Letwin (149) remarks that:

> Such defenses rang disingenuous. The UMWA was never, after all, a purely bread-and-butter or workplace-centered association.... The range of concerns the union addressed—from mine safety to company stores, wages to housing—inevitably engaged the wider community. So did the UMWA's almost evangelical promotion of mutualistic values—a sweeping moral vision that rendered it, in the phrase of Herbert Gutman, a "secular church." Never did the union emerge more fully as a community institution than during strikes. The mass evictions of miners' families, the provocative intrusion of troops and company guards, the vital roles of both women and men in confronting strikebreakers, supplementing livelihood, and sustaining morale—these developments turned labor battles into broad-based, social struggles.

Letwin is here alluding to a phenomenon of the 1908 strike, the encampments of evicted miners and their families, black and white together, eventually encompassing 70,000 people. Living together and helping one another to survive, surely a measure of social equality and sister-and-brotherhood developed between black and white families.

Some developed a radical rejection of capitalism. Kelly (2001: 113) writes,

> For a small minority of white workers the transparency of the employers' racial strategy and the barriers erected against defense of their basic economic interests led them to question the very foundations of southern society. For some attracted to a left-wing critique of southern racism, their experience led them to reject white supremacy as a crude hoax being perpetrated against the poor of both races in the interests of capital.

Though Kelly does not say it, what was true of white miners was also true of black, and what was true of miners was true of their families. Kelly tells this story: when a letter appeared in a Birmingham paper telling

> miners that their homes were their "castles," a striker's wife responded bitterly that the author "seems to forget that even our castles have been shot into by our noble soldiers.... We are going to get rid of these blood-suckers and put them to work and not let them live off the toiling masses."
>
> 193

However, radical anti-capitalist *leadership* was absent from the Alabama UMWA. It emerged soon with the work of the Communist Party (CP). We will soon see that a cadre of committed radicals with a revolutionary vision of an egalitarian collectivist society can transform anti-racist organizing among workers.

So far, we have said nothing about the actions of the operators and the Birmingham capitalists generally. Often operators prepared for and provoked strikes. The operators would not tolerate workers setting limits to the bosses' absolute authority. In 1904 TCI and the other large furnace companies (those who mined coal for their own iron product as opposed to those who sold coal on the market) went on the offensive to destroy union contracts. Operators demanded a longer work day and a reduction in wages, trying to induce a strike. TCI chairman Don Bacon explained to stockholders that operators needed to run the mines: "The authority of your representatives over the property in their charge, as to the manner in which the work should be done, as to what should constitute a fair day's work, and as to who should be employed, had to be restored and maintained." He explained that "the cost of a long strike is 'a necessary investment' if TCI were once again 'to fully control its own operations, untrammeled by union restrictions'" (Letwin 1998: 141–2 first quote Bacon's words, second Letwin's but quoting Bacon). A year later Bacon explained to *The Wall Street Journal* that bosses needed to control the workplace to make profits: "unless company officials succeeded in reestablishing 'control... over the business of the company... all hope of permanent, successful competition with the products of other districts must be abandoned'" (Kelly 2001: 28, Kelly paraphrasing and quoting Bacon). Absolute dictatorship in the mines was needed. Capitalism could not allow workers to work under conditions that recognized their humanity.

Every major strike was lost. Operators systematically used race to try to divide workers; they imported gunmen and private armies; they cultivated and financially supported "black leaders" (often Birmingham preachers) who would advise black miners to avoid UMWA, shun white workers, ally themselves with operators, and form a separate black union. During strikes operators and their allies used the Birmingham press to whip up racism among local people. The press attacked the union as tolerating free mixing of black and white people, including white women and black men. The operators encouraged and organized KKK and other vigilantes to terrorize striking workers; they evicted them from their houses; they removed local law enforcement officials who were not sufficiently anti-miner; their gun thugs shot up workers' houses; their "shack rousters" beat black workers and raped their wives; when all else failed to defeat the strikes of 1908 and 1920-21, they called in government troops to tear down workers' encampments on private land of local sympathetic farmers.

Efforts to divide workers by race failed. Unity among workers held strong. Even in defeat, racial recriminations were largely absent. However, capitalists' use of the press won public support for the armed attacks by state militia on the strikers. They had many more guns, including Gatling guns, firepower that miners could not match, and presumably state militia soldiers believed that miners' racial egalitarianism was something bad. They were not about to disobey orders and ally themselves with the miners.

Communist lessons

When strikes reached these climactic points—bosses using media and state power to smash a strike—UMWA leaders sought government help or a compromise. It didn't work. Victory was absolute. Miners in defeat were angry at their leaders for selling out.

I suggest a lesson for anti-racists. UMWA leaders had a better understanding of the capitalist system and its limits. They were *optimists about reform* but not revolutionaries. So when it became clear that the operators were adamant, that they would not compromise, UMWA leaders had no answer, nothing for miners to do but rely on a government over which the operators had much more influence than did the miners. Miners too probably were optimists about reform, but unlike their leaders they did not have a professional commitment to making reforms. They were miners, not labor union officials. They needed to understand that these battles prepared themselves for proletarian revolution.

The capitalists had to make profits. The operators judged (probably correctly) that reliable profits required defeat of the strike. Operators were able, when private armies failed, to mobilize the power of the state to defeat the strikers militarily. The same power was used at about the same time to defeat West Virginia miners in mine wars that culminated in the Battle of Blair Mountain. Unionization threatened the operators' control of production and their profits (Green 2015, Lewis 1987). The result of these defeats was years or decades of miserable conditions for pit miners, eventually replacement of most miners by machinery, continuing health problems in inadequately ventilated mines for those that remained, then the decline of the pit mining industry, and now widespread addiction and suicide among those who have remained in pit mining districts.

Can workers achieve a flourishing life when the capitalists hold state power? Some readers may think the answer is "yes." Consider this possibility (later I shall argue that it is a fact): given competition among capitalists, their need for profit tends to be incompatible with workers having good lives (see also Gomberg 2007). From this point of view, the most important thing that strikes accomplish is the preparation of workers for a seizure of state power that enables the reorganization of society so as to meet the needs of workers (Gomberg 2016, Lenin 1964c [1917]). Without state power workers generally cannot improve their lives. Gains for some workers are offset by losses to others. Only the seizure of state power makes a truly human society for workers possible.

5

Race and Anti-Racism in Industry

The Communist Party Fights Racism

Overview

This chapter sketches another working-class leader and the anti-racist party to which he belonged. Hosea Hudson was a Georgia sharecropper who moved with his wife and son to Birmingham in the 1920s. There he met, joined, and became a leader of the Communist Party (CP). Hudson's activism exemplifies the CP's commitment to social equality along with full inclusion and leadership of black workers. The CP escalated the fight against racial injustice, making the struggle for social equality a leading edge of class struggle—fighting directly against Jim Crow, an important advance on earlier anti-racism. CP-led struggles by autoworkers, meatpackers and farm equipment workers—among many others—introduced anti-racist principles to workers on the job and in the larger community, far in advance of anyone else at the time. During the period before and just after World War II a million people were in CP-led unions. Many others were in mass organizations influenced or led by the CP. Red-led unions fought against racism on the job and for civil rights off the job.[1]

At the end of the Second World War capitalists were losing control of the shop floor. They needed to defeat working-class anti-racism and shop-floor militancy. They did that. The Taft-Hartley amendment to federal labor legislation made it illegal for members of the CP to lead unions. As CP members resigned from the party, were expelled from union leadership, or had their unions taken over by anti-communist unions, unions ceased fighting racism. Few activists today are aware of the working-class anti-racism of the 1930s, 1940s, and early 1950s. There was some anti-racism in industry in the 1960s and thereafter, but radicals had a limited base there. The unions had become enforcers of racist social order.

Most important was the CP's abandonment of revolution. The early CP combined revolutionary optimism, proletarian internationalism, and practice that empowered workers who were otherwise powerless. The CP's work after 1935 shifted toward alliances with liberals, top-down organizing, and softening of revolutionary politics,

---

[1] "Red-led union" refers to unions whose leaders were deeply influenced by the CP's politics, whether or not they were formally in the party.

while preserving some work that empowered workers. When it came under government attack in the late 1940s it was proclaiming US patriotism and peaceful transition to socialism. The earlier revolutionary tradition was largely lost to anti-racists today.

Lessons from the life of Hosea Hudson and Alabama communists[2]

Hosea Hudson, born in 1898, married at 19 and began sharecropping in Georgia. Threatened by local racists, he moved to Atlanta and then Birmingham, along with his family. By 1925 he was working steadily at Stockham foundry molding iron pipe, becoming skilled enough that he could tell the bosses how he would do his work.

In March 1931 nine black young men and boys were arrested near Scottsboro, Alabama, charged with raping two white women, becoming known as "the Scottsboro Boys." Defendants' fate in such cases was usually legal or extra-legal murder. The International Labor Defense (ILD), a CP-led legal group, took up the case.[3] Birmingham was flooded with CP and ILD leaflets in their defense. Conversation on the streets caught Hudson's attention.

Hudson says, "Whenever Negroes was frame-up, I would always look for somebody else to say something about it. I wouldn't say nothing because I didn't think there was nothing I could say ... until the Scottsboro case, when these people from all over the world began to talk. Then I could see some hope" (Painter 1979: 83).

Hudson had known Al Murphy—his background similar to Hudson's but ten years younger—from the shop at Stockham. Murphy had joined the CP in 1930, shortly after it arrived in Birmingham. In September 1931 Hudson ran into Murphy on the street. Murphy explained that he had been fired from Stockham "because I was participating in that organization about the Scottsboro boys" (85) and that the organization held meetings in Birmingham. Later Murphy came by Hudson's house, gave him a communist newspaper and invited him to a meeting where Murphy explained about the party, the struggle for black self-determination, the economics of capitalist impoverishment, and the Scottsboro case. That night, September 8, Hudson joined the CP, an organization that made something that had seemed impossible—resistance to Jim Crow terror—possible.

At that same meeting Hudson assumed responsibility for leading a group. The workers from Stockham were divided into six units; he was the leader of Unit One and the unit organizer for all units. As the leader of party work at Stockham, he met on Friday with unit organizers from other areas of work. His job at these meetings was to report on the work at Stockham, the distribution of the CP newspaper *The Daily Worker* and other literature especially about the Scottsboro struggle, and recruitment of new party members. The meetings included political discussion. In reviewing their

---

[2] This section is based on Kelley 1990, Painter 1979, Hudson 1972, and Solomon 1998.
[3] Anti-communists call organizations such as ILD "communist fronts," but they are communist-led (or "red-led") groups; people who are not party members work under party leadership in causes with which they agree.

work, Hudson recalled, there was "a strict check-up and also collective criticism, where everybody had to take a part. Everybody had to say something on the subject." At his first meeting he had "wondered why they made such a miration over me that night." The answer was that the party had an industrial concentration, and he was responsible for that concentration. He didn't understand why his was the only industry represented, but "I would be on time to my meetings, I wouldn't give up. I'd go every Friday night, rain or shine. I'd come back and tell the unit guys, 'We done pretty good'" (89).

What explains Hudson's devotion to the party? The party stood for dignity of black workers—equal to that of any other human being. This was manifested both in the demand of social equality and in the call for black national self-determination, which identified black people as a nation equal to all other nations. The party did not ask black comrades to conform or assimilate to a white norm. On the contrary, black workers were to be leaders of the struggle for racial equality and vanguard of the entire working class, including white workers. Struggle against black exploitation and oppression was integral to workers' fight for the revolutionary dictatorship of the working class, the building of socialist society, and eventually a communist world. Black members, like white members, were expected to be active on their jobs, in their neighborhoods and churches, and elsewhere fighting for the party's line and building the party. In Birmingham black CP members planned and led their own activities. In meetings with white comrades, black members were expected to participate, criticize the work of white members, and accept criticism like anyone else. They were *active* participants in an egalitarian collective.

At least that was the ideal, and they came close enough to the ideal that perceptive, confident black men such as Murphy and Hudson were inspired to be loyal to the party. There were examples where Hudson thought black comrades were victims of "white chauvinism" (the CP's term for racist attitudes and behavior), but Hudson insisted that these were failings of individual comrades. Black comrades might claim white chauvinism to deflect criticism for shirking an assignment. White comrades might soft-pedal criticism of black comrades or slight the needs of black members. All these things happened. We should not expect that, after two and a half centuries of racist society, black and white people would come together without anyone carrying scars. The CP got what should have been expected: decent men and women with faults of people spawned by racist capitalism aspiring to build a world without racial oppression. That imperfect reality inspired loyalty to the CP in Murphy, Hudson, and others.

When Hudson joined the party in 1931, its work displayed the CP's commitment to racial egalitarianism in three ways: the party fought Jim Crow and for full racial equality; the party developed black workers as leaders; and programs and actions empowered black workers. The *linking* of these three racially egalitarian tendencies made the CP's early work powerful and attractive to many black workers.

In the South the CP fought against Jim Crow and advocated and practiced the taboo norm of racial social equality. In November 1932 Mary Leonard, a white Alabama communist, was part of a delegation sent from a demonstration of five to seven thousand at the city hall to meet with city commissioner Jimmie Jones. Jones asked her, "Do you believe in social equality for niggers?" She replied, "Yes, why not? They are just as good as you and I are. Why not?" (136–7). This answer caused the mayor to order immediate dispersal of demonstrators. The CP never wavered in its advocacy of racial equality, even if in practice it sometimes failed to treat black people equally. The party fought Jim Crow, violated segregation norms in secret and openly where they could, and fought to register black voters. Moreover, *internally* the party sought to build a racially egalitarian communist collective.

On January 1, 1934 Hudson and two other comrades jumped a train to hobo to New York for a ten-week communist training school. After a week of great difficulty, some minor but painful physical injury to Hudson, suffering from cold, and running out of money on the way, they arrived. Harry Haywood and James Ford were enraged that the district leader had not provided these black comrades adequate funds and complained to the national committee. The district leader, called to New York, faced considerable criticism.

There were thirty-seven students at the school, led by veteran communist Jacob "Pop" Mindel. A group of six students, Hudson among them, formed the leadership of the school. He was assigned to lead the "house committee," responsible to ensure order at the school and conformity with school rules of conduct concerning curfew, noise, conflicts and like issues. His roommate was Jim Gray, a young white minister from North Georgia, who spent 30–45 minutes with Hudson each night, helping him to read better (204–5).

An issue arose that Hudson "settled [him]self" without Mindel's help. Gray complained about a blatant sexual dalliance, a young man entering another student's (shared) room at night. Hudson assembled the house committee. He didn't want to identify Gray as the source of the complaint, concerned that Gray, a southern white person, would be attacked by northern white people who thought southern whites were backward. So he asked Hill, an eighteen-year-old black comrade from Camp Hill, Alabama to say *he* was raising the issue. At the meeting, when Hudson raised the issue, the comrade who was sneaking replied, "Nobody can tell me how to live my life, as long as it don't affect nobody else" and asked who was raising the issue. Here Hill responded, "I think we here to learn Marxism-Leninism, and the comrades at home have sent us here, sacrificing. I think we ought to lay all this personal stuff aside. . . . I know it's affecting me to see all this going on at night, and I'm the one raising the question" (206). Hill having complained, Gray added his criticism. Hudson took pride that he had used his "mother wit"—and a small deception—to force the couple to be more discrete (205–6).

A bigger issue was harder to resolve. A young man from Harlem—Miller—had borrowed scissors from Gloria (from Florida) and face cream from Gloria's roommate from Chicago. When Miller finally returned the cream, the Chicago comrade exclaimed that Miller "done used up half my cream out this jar!" Miller denied it. When the Chicago comrade turned to Gloria for support, Gloria said, "Now Miller, listen. You know you borrowed my scissors and hasn't brought them back. If you don't tell the truth about this cream, I'm going to call you a thief and a liar" (207). This phrase "a thief and a liar" was (trusting Hudson—it was a news to me) racial code used by white southerners to put black people "in their place." Used by a member and prospective leader of the CP, it was an appalling example of white chauvinism. Miller exploded in protest. Two white male comrades (Evans and Bogart) visiting the women (Evans often slipping in for sex with Gloria) sat silently. Mindel, hearing the hullaballoo, came to the women's room, sent everyone outside, then soon informed the bureau that it would meet.

Every evening for a week the school met to discuss this issue, bureau members sitting at the front. Mindel opened by explaining the white chauvinism of Gloria's phrase and the CP's position of not tolerating white chauvinism. Miller spoke next, explaining the insult to himself and his comrades, then the Chicago comrade, who did not understand that it was white chauvinism, then Gloria, who cried and said she was sorry. Then Bogart and Evans: Evans, a political orator, spoke first denouncing Gloria. Mindel asked what Evans had done "to try to develop Comrade Gloria." Evans gave a meaningless reply. Then Mindel said, "Do you think you was helping Comrade Gloria when you was slipping in her room at night when the other comrades supposed to been in their rooms asleep?" Hudson described the outcome, "[Evans] had been a big shot, been a big fish, but now he looking like a minnow" (210). Mindel asked him to resign from the bureau and moved him from the front of the room. Bogart was up next, saying he did not want to get involved. Mindel compared his silence to a southern landlord's silence during a racist whipping by another landlord, asking Hudson to testify about this.

The following evening Miller went again before the group, this time to tone down his criticism of his comrades. Mindel called on Hudson to comment. Hudson tore into Miller's retreat on the question of white chauvinism, endorsed Miller's account of the previous evening, saying about Miller's current retreat, "I consider that this is *capitulating* to white chauvinism" (212). Over the course of the week every member of the school had to say what they thought and listen to criticism of their views from others, including Mindel and Hudson. Miller had to write a self-criticism. Gloria was expelled from the school, but could attend lectures as an auditor. The comrade from Chicago was reprimanded. Reports on the incident were sent to Florida and Chicago.

What effect did this incident and the party's response have on Hudson? He said:

> But that one battle of how the Party handled discrimination, white chauvinism against Negroes, that give me double determination that I had somewhere that I could fight for against [sic] the oppression. That one thing in itself established great confidence in me. I surprised myself, when I was able to stand up there, when I spoke out. Comrade Mindel congratulated my remarks. And here I was from the South, I hadn't been talking. That was the first major speech [criticizing Miller] I made out in public. I had talked around among our people in the units, but not with no big top leaders like that before.
>
> 212–13

The CP's intolerance toward racist behavior and speech in their own ranks was new in US social life and influences us yet today. It inspired Hudson's commitment to the party. It explains why, when he encountered white comrades slighting black comrades, he attributed that to a failure of the comrade, not to a lack of commitment by the party to anti-racism. The CP's commitment to black workers as leaders helped Hudson to become a leader.

The third way the party displayed racial egalitarianism was in empowering many black people. Soon after Hudson joined, Birmingham passed a "criminal anarchy" law making the party's activities illegal, forcing it underground. However, underground work did not *lessen* the CP's activity but empowered many black workers to participate. Hudson describes the work that went into writing and distributing literature about Scottsboro and other CP campaigns. This work empowered black workers to fight on their own and others' behalf. They approached the work as if any worker could be a communist and had reason to be. In Hudson's words (to Nell Painter), "It's a whole lot of Hudson's around, you just haven't never met them."[4]

The CP organized in a communist spirit. Although the party was illegal, any grievance could occasion party organizing. For Hudson this started soon after he was recruited at Stockham. At a November 1931 meeting of Hudson's unit at Stockham, party members wrote down their grievances about their treatment at the hands of the bosses and gave the grievances to a party leader. They were written into a letter and published in the *Southern Worker* and the *Sunday Worker* (a CP national paper). These papers were distributed to Stockham workers, who were thrilled to see their grievances in print. The bosses corrected some of the conditions cited in the letter. However, the letter identified the plant. Stockham bosses investigated the source of the letter, recruiting a stoolpigeon—one of the workers who joined the same night as Hudson—leading to Hudson's dismissal in January, 1932 along with the other workers who had joined at that meeting. Members of the other Stockham CP units were not fired but were intimidated into inaction (Hudson 1972).

Out of the shop, Hudson and John Beidel, also fired from Stockham, began to build the party in their neighborhood and on their relief jobs. They put out leaflets, initiated conversations, talked up the party's program with people who showed interest, and recruited. They moved people to action.

A group of relief workers were building a highway—as a condition of receiving relief but for no additional pay. In the spring of 1933 Doc Carter was late getting his tools on a relief job. The white straw boss cussed him. When Carter cussed him back, the boss pulled a gun and shot at him. Carter ran away uninjured. After the cops left, the other workers shoved the boss into a ditch, someone grabbing his pistol and running off, making sure he didn't know who pushed him. The boss called the cops and relief officials, and everyone was sent home. Carter was worried; so workers stayed with him that night. Carter visited Reverend Sears—an important minister. (Carter was unaware that a black minister became "important" only by cooperating with the authorities.) Sears reassured him that since he hadn't taken the boss's pistol, he wasn't in danger from the cops. Disarmed by Sears's reassurances, Carter was unprepared when, the following day, four cops arrested him, carried him to jail, and beat him badly. When Carter's wife visited him, he told her to tell everyone to join the reds because cops will beat you anyway, whether you are a communist or not (Carter had opposed the party).

Hudson was summoned and called for a meeting. They wrote and mimeographed leaflets about what had happened, then held an open-air meeting at a local ball diamond. Hundreds showed up, and it was decided to form a committee to question

---

[4] Painter uses this quote as her epigram for the book.

Sears about his role in Carter's arrest. The committee consisted of committed communists (not Hudson) who were not known in that neighborhood. When they got to Sears's church, many people were there from an earlier meeting. First one, then another, from the committee questioned Sears about Carter's arrest. Sears pulled a shotgun from behind the pulpit and dared those who were questioning him to come closer. Panic ensued, with everyone in the church trying to flee, even jumping out of windows. The incident devastated Sears's reputation and size of his congregation. Although Carter spent six months in jail, the CP-organized workers deterred black ministers from cooperating in the arrest and beatings of black workers.

The party's actions—often initiated by non-party workers (such as Doc Carter) who turned to the CP for help—addressed evictions, problems on relief jobs, or inadequate relief benefits. In 1932 the party set up block committees for unemployed workers. Hudson says,

> We was always busy-bodies. We didn't wait for people to come to get us when they didn't get they grocery order or they coal order from the welfare. We would go around to see what the condition was.... We make it our business to go see this person, find out what the conditions was. And if the person was willing for the unemployed block committee person or the Party person to work with them and help them get something, we'd work with them.
>
> Painter 1979: 138

If the person was unwilling to work with the reds, the comrades would leave it alone. If the person wanted help, the block club leader or party member would organize a meeting, usually less than ten neighbors of the affected person. The committee would visit that person, let the person tell what happened, encourage everyone to give an opinion, then typically form a small committee—three or four—to accompany that person to the welfare office, asking for volunteers so that the group had both party and non-party people. At the welfare office, they would be insistent but not militant, arguing points but not making demands. After that visit to the welfare office, they would organize a larger—perhaps 25–30 people—but secret meeting at someone's house, because people in the neighborhood would want to know how it came out. Parallel methods might be used to address evictions, but when meeting with landlords and real estate companies, they might remind them that empty houses were often burned or disassembled for firewood. Block committees that organized among the unemployed met every week, read the *Daily Worker* or the *Southern Worker*, and discussed Scottsboro or other party campaigns. These methods built the party: by 1934 the Birmingham party had one thousand members, overwhelmingly black. The powerless were empowered.

Reliance on and empowerment of ordinary workers is also shown in the way the party organized the writing and distribution of literature under conditions of illegality. When industrial workers were dissatisfied with issues on the job, a party member would

> pick out one or two of the issues, and try to sample this one person, these two, few people, you draft a leaflet on just that one grievance.

> The leaflet don't have to talk about everything, just talk about one thing. You tell what's going on, tell how it's happening, but let the workers help to write it. Don't you write it. Involve them all the way through. Make them believe that they somebody. In other words, make them feel that they doing it, and not you doing it for them.
>
> 191

The party member would then show how to fold and distribute the leaflets in the shop without being seen, in this way empowering that industrial worker to agitate among other workers.

That same empowerment of others applied to Hudson's work as a section leader of the unemployed work: "In the section, I got two or three people. I got just two or three people, I sit down with and we talk, we plan. Each one go back to they group and on down. That's the way we did it." Hudson led others, who led yet others (just as the industrial worker involved in the leaflet was learning to lead co-workers).

Hudson describes how the party organized a city-wide leaflet distribution. Suppose, for example, Hudson was responsible for distributing leaflets in the Collegeville area; they would be left at certain places in this area.

> So now I got to see to each one of these people getting they share and going back to they group. They go, get every member there involved, get ready to put the leaflets out Wednesday night. It was just like a network.
>
> I didn't have to worry about what was going on outside Collegeville. They going to see to they task. I'm going to see to my tasks. All I got to do is see my two-three people and they get they people. They put the leaflets out, come on back to the house. That's just how easy it was. In thirty minutes, we'd cover the whole city of Birmingham with leaflets. It was easy because it was well organized, very well organized.
>
> 192

This was under conditions of illegality! The leaflets would be distributed in the dark, put out in communities or in a shop or mine. And there was check-up. If a party member was responsible for an area, but no one saw any leaflets in that area, there would be an investigation, leading in one case to the exposure of a "comrade" as a police informant. This tight organization and discipline, assignment of responsibility and check-up empowered workers and made them responsible to a collective, the collective enabling them to influence how people were thinking, what they were discussing, and what was happening in the city of Birmingham.

What did such actions have to do with the party's goal of proletarian revolution? It might seem that such reform struggles and organization of political propaganda are irrelevant. However, we should understand these struggles as a revolutionary might. Here I present some analysis that may be unfamiliar to the reader in the hope that the reader can better understand Marxist thought and practice. Marx advocated what he called "the dictatorship of the proletariat," where workers ran society democratically, making and implementing laws. His model was the Paris Commune of 1871. But in capitalist society the capitalist class through political parties it controls makes the rules. In our daily lives we often live in fear of losing our jobs, being disciplined at work, not having enough money, and so forth—various consequences of not conforming to rules that we had no part in making. We may adapt by becoming not only fearful but passive, waiting for orders or instructions, afraid to stand up to authority. We live under the dictatorship of the bourgeoisie

If the dictatorship of the working class is to be possible, we must train ourselves in a different approach where we learn to take initiative and organize, as Hudson exemplifies not only in his own conduct but in the ways the party's activities empowered *other* workers to do the same. The party's recruitment in Birmingham and in the party-led Share Croppers Union (SCU), which had 12,000 members at its peak, shows that they had some success. The same point, if with a bit of hyperbolic flourish, was made by Marx in a dispute within the Communist League in 1850, when he said, "We say to the workers: 'You will have to go through 15, 20, 50 years of civil wars and national struggles not only to bring about a change in society but also to change yourselves, and prepare yourselves for the exercise of political power'" (Marx 2010 [1851]: 403). Of course, the struggles communists led in Birmingham hardly qualify as "civil wars" or "national struggles," but the point remains: workers must change in order to take power. In practical struggles such as Hudson describes and led, they learn how to take initiative, work collectively, act in a disciplined way, make rules, and understand society. These activities helped not only Murphy, Beidel, and Hudson to grow and change but many others as well.

What is communist leadership? The central task is to develop the leadership of others. A leader empowers others, making herself replaceable, preparing them to lead society, preparing for proletarian revolution. Hudson's early organizing exemplifies communist leadership.

The work of the CP changed after the Seventh Comintern Congress in 1935 with its line of a united front against fascism.[5] The CP sought to enter more mainstream organizations such as the National Association for the Advancement of Colored People (NAACP), the Committee for Industrial Organization (after 1938 the Congress of Industrial Organizations [CIO]), and churches not primarily with a goal of building the party and preparing for revolution but rather with the aim of building these organizations in a united front with non-communists and turning the political tide in an anti-fascist direction.

In Hudson's case (but not universally) this led to a retreat from the empowering of workers just described in favor of what was often a more top-down approach to organization. While Hudson did involve rank-and-file workers in the *founding* of a United Steel Workers of America (USWA) local, of which he was president from 1943 until the anti-communist purge of red union officials at the end of 1947, he took pride in his honest and principled advocacy for the interests of workers, white as well as black. What seemed to take second place was *empowerment* of the rank and file on the

---

[5] See Dimitroff 1975 [1935] for the new line and Dutt 1974 [1934] for the more revolutionary earlier line that it supplanted.

shop floor; he did *for* workers rather than helping them to fight for themselves, as he had in the earlier unemployment work.

The Communist Party becomes anti-racist

The CP (Workers Party until 1930) was originally a largely immigrant party; many members brought anti-black ideas and behavior into the party. The party also attracted black radicals and revolutionaries, particularly from Harlem, who were inspired by the Russian Revolution and believed, with Lenin, that socialist revolution could be an alliance of the working class with oppressed nationalities. They (Claude McKay, Cyril Briggs, Oscar Huiswoud, and others) repeatedly raised the issue of the CP's racism at meetings of the Communist International (Comintern) in the 1920s. The Sixth Comintern Congress in 1928 stated the "Third Period" line: after a revolutionary period (at the end of World War I) and a period of capitalist stabilization, the world was entering a Third Period of crisis and revolutionary opportunities. Communists were instructed to bolshevize their parties (become professional revolutionaries), to prepare the working class for seizure of power, winning masses to socialist revolution. This congress also set the CP on the path of becoming an interracial anti-racist party.

Black communists from the US had come to Moscow to study at the University of the Toilers of the East (KUTV). KUTV student Harry Haywood, working with Charles Nasanov, developed the line about black self-determination. Black people in the Black Belt[6] were a separate oppressed nation within the US. Communists must seek an alliance with this oppressed nationality around allied goals of proletarian revolution and self-determination for black people in the Black Belt. This line was adopted by the Sixth Congress, which instructed the CP to advocate the right of self-determination for southern black people, to combat Jim Crow and any other racist treatment, to advocate and practice full social equality for black people, and especially to intensify its work among black people and combat "white chauvinism" inside the party and the working class as precondition for class unity (Naison 1983, Solomon 1998). This line made a remarkable difference in the CP's work, but not immediately.

The turning point occurred in 1931, after nearly ten years of struggle to rid the CP of racism. Harry Haywood's *Black Bolshevik* (1978) gives the fullest account. In late 1929 and 1930 the CP intensified efforts to organize among the growing unemployed group of workers, leading to recruitment of black members in numbers much greater than before. Growing black participation in the party and party-led groups occasioned conflicts and slights. In national clubs and cooperatives where the party had a presence, black workers were mistreated: refused service at a Lithuanian cooperative restaurant in Chicago and denied jobs at a Russian cooperative restaurant in Gary. The pivotal case occurred at the Finnish Workers Club in Harlem: black people arriving to attend a dance were treated quite rudely. CP member August Yokinen, a janitor at the club, failed to come to their defense. Worse yet, when the issue was raised at a meeting, he

---

[6] Majority-black counties stretching from the Atlantic Ocean through Louisiana.

said he agreed with the mistreatment: if black people started coming to the club, they would want to use all of the facilities including the Finnish baths, and "he for one did not want to bathe with Blacks" (354).

Haywood writes, "the list of racist manifestations was long and growing; clearly a crisis in the Party's mass work was building up. Further advance required a renewed drive, a counter-offensive on the question" (352). Black comrades Briggs, Maude White, and Haywood wrote up the various incidents and presented them to the party leadership at a meeting in January 1931. Briggs, speaking first, "was sore as hell." Then Haywood spoke. Finally White—returned from three years study at the KUTV and assigned to lead work in the needle trades—described the repeated failure of white leaders of the party-led Needle Trade Workers Industrial Union (NTWIU) to deal with anti-black injustices. Afraid of driving away white workers, they tolerated white members hiring black workers to do their work at much lower pay: "she burst into tears and asked to be relieved of her leadership responsibilities in the needle trades unless she were given more support" (353).

Haywood continues, "An awkward silence settled over the room." After some other responses Clarence Hathaway called "for some dramatic action to resolve the crisis" and "proposed a public trial of those involved in the incident at the Finnish Hall." This was a turning point for the CP—and for anti-racism in the US. An anti-racist campaign began within the party. The CP expelled members who would not oppose racism.

The Yokinen trial was held in the largest hall the party could rent in Harlem on March 1, 1931. Fifteen hundred attended, black and white, most standing. The prosecutor Hathaway stressed two points. First, given the history of betrayals by others who promised fairness and equality, black people would never believe the Communist Party meant it unless the party proved its sincerity by its actions. Second, the capitalist enemy promotes racism to exploit all workers and especially exploit and oppress black workers, a special oppression that undermines the entire class, including white workers. Yokinen's actions and his defense of them were a crime against his class. It is impossible for the Communist Party, which seeks to lead the working class, to tolerate that crime: "They, the white workers, must boldly jump at the throat of the 100 percent bandits who strike a Negro in the face." Hathaway stressed that this is what Yokinen and the other communists in the Finnish Workers Club failed to do. In his defense of Yokinen Richard Moore argued for clemency on the ground that Yokinen's crime was shared by many others in the party who fail to attack racism. The arguments made by both Hathaway and Moore helped to transform the CP. The "jury" (of seven black and seven white comrades) rendered the verdict that Yokinen was expelled from the CP but could apply for readmission after a period during which he led anti-racist struggle in Harlem (Communist Party USA 1931).

Why was this trial so important? Mark Naison writes, "Never before had a political movement, socialist or otherwise, tried to create an interracial community that extended into the personal sphere, and defined participation in this community as a political duty" (1983: 47). Harry Haywood believed that this trial was "a historic event in the battle for Black rights" whose impact "was tremendous throughout the country.... It was the first time the revolutionary movement clearly and openly declared war on this pillar of American imperialism [that is, racism]" (1978: 357). I agree with these assessments. It clearly influenced many people. Lowell Washington, a black worker in Chicago, states how it affected him to meet white workers thoroughly committed to fighting racism:

> Those guys really threw me. I mean here were these white fellas who were helping us out, really meaning it. I'd never seen anything like it. They took up things that really mattered—jobs, food, places to live. You might not agree with them all the time, but you had to stand with 'em when they was fightin' for you. You'd be a fool not to.
>
> Halpern and Horowitz 1996: 45

Something new in the history of Marxism had happened in the Comintern resolutions, applied and popularized in this trial and the booklet the CP issued with its speeches. Racial injustice had been defined as a central issue of class oppression and exploitation, a "pillar of imperialism," in Haywood's phrase. A decisive struggle had been made within the CP that racial injustice was a concern not only of its most direct black victims. It was an attack on the entire working class, benefitting only capitalists. Combatting it was the political duty of every communist. White communists must actively oppose anti-black injustice.

More was to come: promoting this line in party-led unions. (Party-led "dual unions" were to be revolutionary unions separate from the mainstream AFL unions which discriminated against black workers.) As mentioned, Maude White was frustrated by the absence of support for her work in the NTWIU, a supposedly revolutionary union. White had a strong anti-racist class line. The union *officially* opposed subcontracting, which led to black workers' wages being one-third to one-half those for white doing the same work, but did not fight the practice. The union ignored special oppression and exploitation of black workers. So it had few black members. In his speech at Yokinen's trial Hathaway alluded to a NTWIU strike which black workers did not honor because of the NTWIU's racism. Less than a year after the Yokinen trial, the party held a trial of "Joe Birns, a white furrier, charged with using abusive language to Maude White and stating publicly that 'it would be better if we had no Negroes in the trade at all.'" The trial itself followed a script that paralleled the one of Yokinen's trial—guilty but contrite, sentenced to suspension from the union, and required to engage in anti-racist activity—but it also included a judgment that the union must "move against members who exploited blacks under the subcontracting system" (Solomon 1998: 143). While Solomon does not say whether there was progress on this issue in the short term, we will see that this demand that all communists fight racism influenced CP union work in the remainder of the 1930s and beyond.

The Unemployed Councils (UCs)

Two important campaigns beginning in 1930 and 1931 had inspired many black people to join the CP or party-led groups: the campaign around unemployment, relief, and evictions and the campaign to free the Scottsboro Nine, accused of rape and quickly sentenced to death.

William Z. Foster estimated that the 1.25 million people participated in demonstrations in various cities March 6, 1930 demanding unemployment insurance (Foster 1952). How could this small party organize so many? California communist Dorothy Healey described how she learned (as a fifteen-year-old) to organize:

> Everybody was working very hard on small practical tasks.... We took the question of organization very seriously.... You started with small demonstrations in relief offices, or in various neighborhoods around the city, and then built up to a big central demonstration.... We brought new people to demonstrations as a way of increasing their knowledge of the power of collective endeavor. We learned that the consciousness of human beings is not a static thing. We learned to watch and measure the process of growth of the people participating. And we could see that organization gave them a power that they hadn't ever had before, that perfecting that organization was our greatest, indeed our only hope for success.
>
> Healey and Isserman 1990: 32–3

Healey's words not only explain how a party of less than ten thousand could organize more than a million but also give lessons for anti-racists today: like Hudson's words, they show how organization and discipline can empower people who otherwise lack power.

By the middle of 1930 the party decided that the unemployment struggle needed a new organization, soon forming Unemployed Councils (UCs). The direct actions of UCs were brilliant; most spectacular were anti-eviction struggles, replacing furniture removed by deputies, backed often by large crowds gathering in support. (My detailed account is from New York and Chicago, but UCs were doing similar work across the US.) Harlem had a campaign against high rents and slum conditions, targeting black slumlords as well as white. In Chicago UCs' anti-eviction struggles were so popular that "When eviction notices arrived, it was not unusual for a mother to shout to the children, 'Run quick and find the Reds!'" (Drake and Cayton 1945: 87). By early August 1931 Chicago UCs were stopping between three and five evictions each day.

On August 3 a large crowd (up to 4,000) marched from a UC rally in Washington Park to restore the furniture of 72-year-old Diana Gross. A fight broke out with the cops, and three UC members were killed on the scene. That evening the body of another UC member was found badly mutilated. In the week that followed five to ten thousand rallied every evening in Washington Park denouncing capitalism and police violence. A funeral march for the victims, all black men, was planned. Over 165,000 leaflets for the funeral were distributed by the CP and allied organizations. Sixty thousand marched in the funeral procession, one-third white. Another forty thousand watched. This was the largest and sharpest struggle, but similar UC activity occurred throughout the US. (Naison 1983, Solomon 1998, Storch 2007).

The UCs would turn on gas, electricity, and water, leaving a sign "Restored by the Unemployed Councils" (Storch 2007: 113). Chicago mayor Cermak declared a moratorium on evictions, but it must have been short-lived because by the spring of 1933 UCs were still restoring the furniture of evicted people (Solomon 1998, Storch 2007).

UCs fought at government relief offices and private charities responsible for providing some minimal assistance to the poor. In 1932, the effects of the depression being more severe, people became more desperate. Harlem UCs adopted a "strategy of stimulating disorder": If UC members and other demonstrators met resistance from relief officials, they "camped in the bureau offices and remained there until they received aid" (Naison 1983: 76). They resisted police actions by overturning furniture or fighting police. When arrested, they carried the fight into the courts—loudly and in numbers.

Chicago UCs helped people to get benefits from relief offices, "demanding money for rent, food, clothing, and utilities" (Storch 2007: 116). "[C]ouncil members became effective in shepherding clients through red tape and getting results" (117). The UCs' work put "the needs of blacks ... on the table as the most compelling aspect of the needs of all working people" (Solomon 1998: 152). Demonstrations empowered workers to fight for their own interests, training them as fighters. Many joined a UC.

Out of struggles such as these membership in UCs on the South Side of Chicago grew to over one thousand and by 1931 over eleven thousand members citywide (even more by 1933); over four hundred communists provided much of the leadership (Storch 2007). Lowell Washington explains that for the first time in his life he could speak his mind to white people "and not having to worry about saying something that might rile 'em up" (Halpern 1997: 110). Claude Lightfoot "became a communist when he joined an 'eviction riot' and witnessed how whites 'shed real blood in defense of Negro workers'" (Solomon 1998: 156).

The Scottsboro Campaign and the International Labor Defense

The Scottsboro struggle, spearheaded by the CP-led ILD, led many black people to join and some to lead the CP. On April 9, 1931 eight of the nine Scottsboro defendants were sentenced to death.[7] The sentences were in response to incidents fifteen days earlier. When black youth fought with white youth, all hoboing, the white youth tried to get the black youth in trouble. The black youth were charged with rape when two young women chose to avoid trouble for themselves by claiming they were raped (Horne 1997). Legal lynchings were a common response to black people who challenged norms of submissiveness—as the Scottsboro youth did—and an important part of racist terror, which was integral to the discipline and exploitation of black labor. The CP's national and international struggle to free the Scottsboro youth resisted this terror, the first such massive resistance since the Civil War.

The CP and ILD responded to Scottsboro early and forcefully. Before the trials were concluded, ILD members had won the trust of the parents of three of the Scottsboro youth who were from Chattanooga. The communist attorneys treated the parents respectfully as fellow-workers in a common struggle. (NAACP

---

[7] The exception was thirteen-year-old Roy Wright.

representatives in contrast called the parents dense and dumb.) By December all of the rest of the youth and their parents had decided to go with the ILD, and in January the NAACP withdrew.

The CP and ILD thought that only mass action could save the youth; mass action also empowers workers, challenging the culture of racist legal lynchings with leaflets to and rallies before millions of white and black workers. It built a communist movement and prepared workers to seize power. May Day demonstrations in 1931 included speeches about Scottsboro; in Harlem white communists held street corner rallies, drawing thousands into Harlem demonstrations in April, May, and June, uniting black and white. Reaching out to workers, asking them to participate in the struggle to free the defendants gives each a role to play and a little bit of power, as we could see from efforts in Birmingham.

As reds persisted, black workers in Harlem were drawn closer and into the CP. What was happening in Harlem was also happening on the South Side of Chicago; Drake and Cayton write, "The Communists' defense of the nine Scottsboro boys stirred the imagination of the Negro people, and thousands of them joined committees and participated in demonstrations" (1945: 86). Later they report on a 1938 Bud Billiken back-to-school parade (an important, longstanding tradition on Chicago's South Side) where an observer in their research group was walking alongside the march just behind the Young Communist League's float with the slogans "Black and White Unite" and "Free the Scottsboro Boys." He reported that a wave of applause greeted the float over the entire five-mile route of the parade with shouts of "Yes, free the boys!" and "Them's the Communists. They don't believe in no differences. All's alike to them" (737). In Chicago hundreds of black people joined the CP.

Mass actions spread globally. Mark Solomon writes, "Demonstrations spanned the globe from Havana to Europe, to Moscow, to Australia and New Zealand, to Japan, South Africa, and Latin America" (1998: 197).[8]

The party combined practical struggles with political education: the UCs had party fractions that focused on red politics and recruitment. There were schools on communist theory in many cities. At the KUTV in Moscow communists often studied for several years, as did Maude White, Harry Haywood, Al Murphy and many others. There were also national or regional schools such as the one Hosea Hudson attended.

Black communists were three percent of the CP in 1930; by 1938 they were nine percent of a party with 50,000 members, thoroughly incorporated into party leadership (Green 1980: 163, Howard 2008: 9). The CP had transformed itself through political and practical struggle into an anti-racist party. It created a mass movement against racism that permanently affected the US, making the extreme racist terror that continued in the South an object of hatred among many workers and others in the North and West.

---

[8] None of the defendants was executed. Four spent six years in prison before charges were dropped. Four were paroled after serving longer sentences. One escaped prison and died in a Michigan prison, having been convicted of manslaughter there (Horne 1997: 84).

More communist anti-racist practice

The anti-racism of the Yokinen trial, the UC work, and the Scottsboro campaign was part of a much broader fight against racism. Here I list and summarize the main political lessons of a *few* of the many struggles of the early and mid-1930s.

- In 1932 World War I veterans marched on Washington demanding a bonus they were due. Communists successfully fought racial segregation of many units, and the color line was smashed in the veterans' encampment (Solomon 1998: 74).
- San Francisco longshoremen in the International Longshoremen's Association (ILA) struck the docks in May 1934. The union local had always barred black workers. CP members and others—with Harry Bridges (a close ally of the party) in the lead—fought to end that ban and to make central to the strike the demand for a union hiring hall where all—including black dockers—would have an equal chance to get work. They won, and black dockers became leading fighters for the union, rather than strikebreakers (Foner 1981, Nelson 1988). (See Quin 1979, Chapter XVIII for a full account of how the hiring hall worked.)
- In California's San Joaquin Valley in 1933, 15,000 cotton pickers struck. Workers had often been divided by race and nationality: white, black, filipino, and mexican. The strike was met with violence—arrests, beatings, shootings—by "law enforcement" and the guns of growers, who at least twice shot at and killed and wounded strikers. Law enforcement did nothing (Daniel 1981). The strike held firm. Racial barriers broke down in strike camps: black and white workers (many from the South) "ate from the same dishes, drank from the same jug, and stood shoulder to shoulder on the picket lines" as "whites elected Negroes as heads of the camps, captains of picket lines and other offices," learning that "the Negro was ... a comrade, fighting by their side" while also coming to respect mexican strikers as class warriors (Evans 1933: 8–9).
- In Birmingham area coal mines in 1930 black workers were subject to racist conditions: the wider screens we saw earlier in Ohio, no pay for "dead work" (time spent preparing for and cleaning up after mining), assignment to lower-paid and less-skilled jobs, and greater disadvantage from seasonal layoffs. UMWA leaders were useless. Communist miners fought racism. Black communists gave leadership to two wildcat strikes in the first half of 1934, leading white as well as black workers in struggle. Communist fliers distributed in mining camps demanded equal pay, more pay, access to more skilled jobs for black workers, an eight-hour day, free transportation to and from the mines, and price cuts at the company store. UMWA leaders sold out for minor changes. In another red-led wildcat strike against conditions that particularly harmed black miners UMWA officials helped mine bosses to break the strike, then helped them to fire communists and bar them from the mines (Kelley 1990, Solomon 1998, Woodrum 2007). White workers were coming to see the need for unity and to recognize how terror against black people undermined all workers.
- At Funsten Nut in St. Louis black women nutpickers—working in horrible dusty conditions without adequate restrooms and taking home between three and four

dollars a week—led a strike including white workers slightly less oppressed and exploited. In May 1933 they walked out, eventually involving 1,400 workers, nearly half of the nut processing workers in the area. Strike committees in each shop met daily to plan activities. CP and UC members helped feed 1,200 each day. After eight days Funsten granted equal wages, union recognition, and a wage increase (Feurer 1996, Fichtenbaum 1991). This strike shows a lot: powerless black women were empowered to lead; following the discipline of a collective, they asserted themselves; they "helped generate a wave of worker unrest" especially among other oppressed workers to form unions and strike at other nut processing plants, in laundries, in electric plants, rag and bag workers, and in the Chicago garment industry (Ervin 2017: 51). Many so inspired were white, the most oppressed and exploited black women giving leadership. Introduced to the struggle of the Scottsboro youth and understanding the youth's oppression was linked to their own, Funsten workers became aware of systematic oppression that targeted black workers for special oppression and terror; they became aware of a revolutionary alternative, discussing conditions in the Soviet Union. Several workers joined the CP (Gebert 1933: 804). Black women became leaders of their class.

Some lessons of the CP's practice in the early 1930s

The short review here of some important strikes give an inadequate sense of the *many* strikes and other struggles the CP led during this period and the ways it transformed people's lives. Yet many victories were short-lived. As soon as the nutpickers strike was over, Funsten, needing to make more profit, planned layoffs and a move to San Antonio. In September huge reductions of its St. Louis operation began, then later closure of three factories in East St. Louis; by 1934 most of Funsten's St. Louis production had moved—despite union resistance to closings. Five years later in San Antonio, the other center of pecan processing, mexican women led a strike of ten thousand against a different processor. A strike victory was followed by a layoff of ten thousand and mechanization of processing.

When workers earned wages that allowed them a minimally decent life, their labor was not profitable enough. Alabama coal bosses, with inferior coal seams, needed cheap labor. They used terror, beatings, killings, and surveillance of miners' lives. In the end they mechanized. Black miners, once the majority of miners, were 11 percent of miners in 1980. The machines were run by a small labor force of mostly white miners (Woodrum 2007).

In California's Central Valley, the cotton strike was followed by other labor actions as cotton strike organizers Pat Chambers and Caroline Decker moved to orchards around the Bay Area. A growers' association decided to get rid of them: they arranged and financed a trial of seventeen communists, Chambers and Decker included, under California's "criminal syndicalism" law, and both spent time in the penitentiary (Daniel 1981, Olmsted 2011). The killings, beatings, and incarceration devastated labor organizing in the Valley.

These events repeat the lesson of earlier strikes: under capitalism workers' gains against racial injustice and exploitation generally are temporary, to be followed by a counter-attack. With the backing of the state and capitalist organizations generally, capitalists win. The main gains of these strikes are the ways *people* are transformed, becoming lifelong fighters for revolution. The CP so emphasized the reform and failed to stress the *limits* to reform (as just reviewed) that they failed to train people as *revolutionaries*. While they stressed the *preferability* of the Soviet Union to US capitalism, they did not stress how capitalists *must* oppress and brutalize workers to make profits, that reforms are limited, revolution necessary.

The CP's anti-racist understanding

When workers at Funsten Nut and striking cotton pickers in the San Joaquin Valley became fighters, they did so to achieve material gains in capitalist society, not to end capitalism and make proletarian revolution. For a communist these struggles help us to develop the understanding, organization, and skills to make revolution and run society. Most workers had other goals, and these other goals, when communists work collectively with non-communists, can pull communists to downplay the need for revolution. This seems to be what happened even in Third Period work. Probably the hardest thing for communists to learn—in our time and that earlier one—is to do revolutionary communist political work among those who do not have revolutionary goals in mind.

From the CP's Marxist perspective, anti-racist class unity was foundational, a "sacred" duty, and a revolutionary necessity. In the Harlan County coal miners' strike of 1931 some miners argued for racially segregated kitchens to avoid giving owners a pretext (violating Jim Crow laws) for attacking. CP members "argued back for six or seven hours; they finally convinced the workers to eat in the same kitchen" (Solomon 1998: 105). As a result of their practical organizing, communists "had come to believe that racial segregation and the savaging of black identity represented both an institutional foundation for American capitalism and its weak point. To compromise with racism in any way strengthened capitalism and wounded its most potent foes" (128). Communists must understand and teach that racism harms not only black people but the entire working class, including those identified as white. Spreading this understanding was particularly difficult for Birmingham communists, but in the strike wave in 1934 party union activists "were able to show that ... wage discrimination against blacks was also passed on to white workers" (293).

A new Marxist understanding of race and class is emerging: racism is inseparable from class oppression and fighting racism is a Marxist duty. On this view the fight against racism must *lead* all working-class struggle: without fighting racism we are ignoring the unequal oppression of workers, the particular harms done to black workers on account of race. Hence any "unity" based on ignoring racism makes the working class vulnerable. Capitalists will exploit the underlying disagreement about the reality of racial oppression to divide workers. As the CP repeated constantly (during this period) white workers have a special duty to "jump at the throat" of any racists. Such actions created a ground for unity.

These practices—class unity based on complete racial equality, anti-racism as integral to class struggle, and black working-class leadership—form the kernel of a race-centered Marxism that can guide anti-racist activists today and an important advance made by the Comintern and the CP in the US.

Reform and revolution

The revolutionary aspirations of communists were expressed in Langston Hughes' 1932 poem "Good Morning, Revolution," which opens with the lines "Good morning, Revolution:/You're the very best friend/I ever had." Imagining the use of radios by revolutionary workers, it closes with these lines:

> Broadcasting that very first morning to USSR:
> Another member the International Soviet's done come
> Greetings to the Soviet Socialist Republics
> Hey you rising workers everywhere greetings
> And we'll sign it: Germany
>> Sign it: China
>> Sign it: Africa
>> Sign it: Poland
>> Sign it: Italy
>> Sign it: America
>> Sign it with my one name: Worker
>
> On that day when no one will be hungry, cold, oppressed,
> Anywhere in the world again.
>
> That's our job!
> I been starvin' too long,
>> Ain't you?
>
> Let's go, Revolution!

Hughes expresses the revolutionary aspirations of many party members in this early period (Hughes 1992).

As the CP engaged in anti-racist practical struggles, party members focused on reforms, building unions and wining strikes. They failed to explain the *necessity* of a revolutionary struggle to end capitalism. In fact, as we will see, some very committed members of the CP may never have believed in revolution or came not to believe in it. The CP became a great party of anti-racist struggle, but not a revolutionary party.

Communist work in the CIO

Now we come to the greatest anti-racist working-class movement in US history and its defeat. That movement was grounded in workers' militancy on the job and the dignity and mutual respect achieved by it; their sense of self-worth and their dependence on and respect for co-workers lay the basis for anti-racism. Because of space limits I can review only some highlights.

The unions making up the Congress of Industrial Organizations (CIO)—initially in 1935 a committee within the American Federation of Labor, but by 1938 its own federation of unions—organized entire industries (auto, steel, electronics, etc.) rather than trades (carpenters, electricians, etc.). Communists acted as leading organizers of the new federation and soon won leadership of local and national unions. Whether nationally or in union locals, workers often respected communist leadership, but few agreed with socialism. Communists won respect by providing leadership on issues such as pay and conditions of work, especially conditions that enabled workers to control their own jobs. Most important, the CP encouraged anti-racist struggle, as we will see. Because workers usually did not agree with socialism and because communist unionists often concealed CP membership, they were vulnerable when attacked for their politics. These attacks ultimately drove them from the unions. CP members seemed to think (somewhat magically), "If I win the workers' respect as a good unionist, then as they come to realize that I am for socialism, they will be persuaded of the need for socialism." According to Harvey Levenstein (1981: 338) even CP leader William Z. Foster believed this.

The anti-racism of red-led CIO unions

I cannot do justice to CP achievements. My purpose is to give the reader a taste of what workers can do. I do not give a "balanced" account of CP activity. Since my purposes are practical, my concern is the CP's *best* work and the weaknesses *it* contained. These lessons, both positive and negative, can help us learn how to fight as they did—but better.

CIO organizing was facilitated by the passage in 1935 of the National Labor Relations Act, which established the National Labor Relations Board (NLRB) to supervise elections to determine union representation. The victor in a representation election was legally entitled to collect union dues used to represent workers' interests.

In 1949 and 1950 eleven unions were expelled from the CIO for being led by communists. (Rosswurm 1992: 1–2 names these unions.) I will not discuss the anti-racism of all of them. There is much missing here.

UCAPAWA-FTA

The United Cannery, Agricultural, Packing and Allied Workers of America (UCAPAWA) became the Food, Tobacco, and Agricultural, and Allied Workers Union (FTA) in 1944. It developed black leadership at the local and regional levels. Moranda Smith worked at the Reynolds tobacco plant in Winston-Salem, North Carolina. For a year Karl Korstad trained her to become FTA director for the Southeast Region, from Virginia to Florida (Korstad 1992). At Reynolds in Winston-Salem Local 22 developed *many* black workers as leaders (Korstad 2003). Reds taught workers to read and write, lead meetings, give speeches, and organize other workers. Party literature revealed a wider world of national and global exploitation and presented a socialist alternative. Black workers Henderson Davis and John Mack Dyson became, respectively, Memphis leader of the CP and a union local president. (Memphis was at least as repressive as Birmingham.) Yet black workers, backed by their union, dropped deferential postures expected of them and asserted themselves forcefully against the bosses, negotiating contracts (Honey 1993).

The union participated in civil rights struggles in Winston-Salem and Memphis, where voting rights were denied. It combined the fight against material racial oppression on the job with broader political struggle. It empowered those most beaten down by capitalism to fight for themselves and to lead other workers. It developed black women as leaders (Korstad 2003).

How were black workers being trained to lead? Karl Korstad describes how Donald Henderson, the communist union president, led meetings:

> He knew how to listen. He made everyone feel free to participate in the discussion. No one was "put down." When he did speak at length, he drew from the consensus that was developing in the meeting as well as from the depth of understanding he had acquired through the years.
>
> Korstad 1992: 78

If Korstad trained Moranda Smith to follow that same approach, then, even though Korstad was not a communist, he was modeling a communist understanding of leadership: to draw out and summarize the experience and understanding of the collective.

The union strove for and, to an extent, achieved interracial solidarity. The workers at one major cottonseed oil plant in Memphis were mostly white while at another mostly black, all strongly union. Workers decided that, to discourage strikebreaking, pickets at both plants should include both black and white workers. When workers went on strike, Korstad observed:

> For the first time in Memphis, as far as we could learn, black and white workers picketed together. At first, the black workers stayed together, as did the whites. Within a few hours they were completely integrated. They had things they wanted to say to each other.
>
> 82

Lawrence McGurty was a Memphis packinghouse worker who joined FTA; attending a picnic of FTA workers, he was thrilled by something he had never seen before: "to my utter amazement [I] found the entire union membership, Negro and white, drinking beer, shooting craps, and having a great time together" (Honey 1993: 232–3).

International Longshore and Warehouse Union (ILWU)

ILWU's (formerly Pacific Coast ILA) anti-racism was remarkably uneven. White workers were sometimes consistently and explicitly anti-black. ILWU dockworkers in

Portland barred black workers until the 1960s. Earlier in this chapter we saw how the ILA's 1934 strike ended the color bar in San Francisco's ILA local. Left leadership was able to abolish discrimination in the hiring hall and on the docks, prohibiting segregated work gangs. The ILA became bargaining agent for longshoremen in Pacific Coast ports (Nelson 1988).

When in 1937 West Coast dockers moved from AFL to CIO, forming the ILWU, the constitution barred racial discrimination.

ILWU's leadership often fought courageously for anti-racist principle. As World War II came to an end and shipping slowed, longshoremen feared for their jobs. Cleophas Williams, hired during the war, had been exposed to the CP's philosophy of class unity and collective struggle in required union classes. At a 1945 meeting a white worker challenged Harry Bridges about "how he intended to deal with the 'excessive number' of blacks" once work slacked off. At first Bridges just attacked the capitalist system for forcing workers to compete for jobs but then addressed the more immediate issue. Howard Kimeldorf paraphrases Williams's account: "if work ever slowed to the point where there were only two workers left on the docks, he [Bridges] personally believed that one should be black." Williams was "taken aback." What Bridges said was

> very shocking to me because there was no political gain for him by making this statement. There was no gain even among blacks at that particular time because many of the blacks were still on probation, so they couldn't vote. I considered it a statement of conviction. I was shocked. I had read and been exposed to some of the left-wing forces, but I had never heard anyone put his neck on the line by making a public statement of this kind.
>
> Kimeldorf 1988: 148

United Farm Equipment and Metal Workers of America (FE)

Organizing began at two large neighboring plants of International Harvester (Harvester) in Chicago, the Tractor Works and the McCormick Works. Workers at the Tractor Works had formed an underground union; two Tractor Works activists joined the CP, one of them black. In 1937 the union at the Tractor Works—no longer underground, having won a raise in wages in 1936—affiliated with the CIO. In 1938 FE was launched as a CIO organizing committee and won a representation election at Tractor Works. Grant Oakes, an early organizer at Tractor Works, and Gerald Fielde, a machinist from McCormick Works, became chairman and secretary-treasurer of FE; by 1941 they were joined on FE's staff by two labor writers, DeWitt Gilpin and Milt Burns. All four were in or close to the CP—for at least some of this time. After years of effort, several votes, and much stalling by Harvester, FE won its first contract granting recognition in 1942, the year the FE became a separate union within the CIO.

Communist thought greatly influenced FE's actions, even during World War II when Fielde, Gilpin, and Burns were in the military. As Burns put it, "The philosophy of our union was that management had no right to exist" (Gilpin 1992: 125, 2020: 6). The union's philosophy was to empower workers on the shop floor, oppose management abuse, make decisions democratically, and fight racism. These are connected: when workers fight management to advance their common interests, they are readier to recognize and oppose injustices to other workers. We will explore *why* this connection holds.

FE leaders fought for racial equality on the shop floor, to promote black workers into more skilled positions, to secure black leadership within the union, and to mobilize white workers in those struggles. At Tractor Works FE secured an agreement to "promot[e] Negro workers in the machine shop" (2020: 101). FE fought for plant-wide seniority, which gave seniority rights to black workers hired in unskilled positions to bid into skilled jobs. They forced a Peoria hotel to abandon Jim Crow policies and allow black delegates to stay at the hotel. Black workers were leaders of FE locals in percentages much greater than their percentage among the workforce. Toni Gilpin[9] writes that FE "challenged ... the racism prevalent among the majority-white membership," which "deepened African American support for the union, but it also transformed many whites as well." Workers, fighting in unity on the job "developed personal affinities that carried past the plant gates and into their homes" (315–16), transforming its members and winning their love and loyalty.

FE relied on the militancy of black and white shop stewards leading shop floor battles. (A shop steward is the lowest level of leadership in most unions.) Workers at Harvester were on piece rate (pay determined by quantity produced). Management was continuously re-timing jobs in order to lower piece rates, hence either lowering the worker's pay or forcing him to produce more for the same pay. FE stewards helped workers to fight the adjustments. "FE officials, both local and national, wielded the contract in the workers' defense, employing it when it was useful, abandoning it when it was not" (Gilpin 1992: 194) because the leaders believed that management had no right to exist. Stewards on the shop floor had real power; "a strong and relatively independent battalion of stewards functioned at the heart of the union" (196). FE utilized lots of stewards (one for every 35–40 workers) who, by contract, were paid by management when doing union work. They often roamed the shop floor encouraging workers to grieve anything they thought unjust. At the same time management was sending around time-study men to examine piece rates and adjust them if they were "too high." Workers were trying to produce efficiently to increase their pay but not overstress themselves. They resisted efforts to lower pay or increase work pace to a point they found stressful. Workers—backed and led by FE stewards—fought management to control the shop floor.

It worked something like this: when management says, "We have the prerogative to determine the piece rate," the steward says, "The hell you do" and goes around to all the workers in the area, saying "we're going out." They walk out. They are on strike, not officially, but they are not working, holding a continuous meeting, as they sometimes called it, outside the plant. The walkout or "wildcat strike" is a violation of the contract, but to FE leaders that made no difference because management had no right to exist. When management would respond by suspending workers or suspending or firing the shop steward, a wider walkout, sometimes the whole plant, might result. When piece

---

[9] Toni Gilpin, whose work informs this subsection, is DeWitt Gilpin's daughter.

rates were lowered at East Moline's Harvester plant, workers had a plant-wide slowdown, working only for their base pay, not producing beyond the absolute minimum. Management suspended 2,000 workers. FE national leadership raised money for East Moline workers and threatened to shut down all FE-controlled Harvester plants. Harvester gave in, restoring the previous pay rate.

When the steward says, "we're going out," workers walk out. They assume that their steward would not call them out without good cause. This is generalized. So each worker knows that if something he finds unjust happens to him, other workers will unquestioningly back him up. These practices built solidarity among the workers and a strong sense that *they had power*, not stable, taken-for-granted power, but power requiring constant vigilance and willingness to walk out. It worked, and management hated it.

Contempt for bosses, shop floor militancy and power, and solidarity among workers lay the basis for anti-racism. Judith Stepan-Norris and Maurice Zeitlin (2003) found that red-led unions were not only more militant and democratic than the others but also more consistently anti-racist. It makes sense that militancy on their own behalf and anti-racism are linked. If workers are not fighting, it can seem that nothing will change. If nothing will change, then what benefits one worker, harms another (workers competing for promotions to higher pay grades). Applied to racial groups, capitalism can make it seem that what benefits black workers harms white. But in struggle for their common good workers can advance together. Collective struggle requires willingness to stand up for co-workers against injustices to them. Black workers see they can fight racial injustice. White workers can recognize *racial* injustices as *injustices*.

How was anti-racism manifested in the two FE locals Toni Gilpin (1992) reviewed in detail, Local 108 at McCormick Works and Local 236 at Harvester's Louisville plant?

McCormick Works, with older, ethnic workers was considered the "weak link," the target of repeated UAW raids to defeat FE in NLRB elections. Yet it was anti-racist from the beginning. In 1942 FE workers forced Harvester to admit black workers to the cafeteria, from which they had been barred. Bruno Bartnick describes what they did:

> So, we says, all right, let's fight Jim Crow here. So we got four blacks and four whites, and we let the blacks go first. Then when they stopped them, we surrounded them, and we said, we're not going to let anybody near this place unless you let these people eat. And they haggled and haggled, and finally one of the guys from industrial relations comes over, and said, alright, let them go. That was a great thing.
>
> Gilpin 1992: 256[10]

A 1951 Local 108 flyer gave a rationale for such actions: "The prime reason for the persecution of the Negro is to divide them from their white brothers in the struggle for decent wages" and "the unity of Negro and White workers means higher wages" (245). This and another flyer asked union members to support a southern black man charged with raping a white woman.

---

[10] A similar struggle occurred in Louisville, unsuccessful in 1948, later successful.

The Harvester plant in Louisville, Kentucky, opened in 1946. Local 236 was brilliantly anti-racist. Harvester had gone to Louisville, a southern city of non-union, low wage work, purchased a war production plant cheaply and added buildings to make the largest industrial complex in the state with 6,000 workers producing the Farmall Cub tractor. Many workers were World War II veterans, young and unmarried. FE sent organizers. Black CP member Frederick Marrero got a job in the plant. By February 1947 Marrero had recruited 100 percent of the 53 black workers at the plant into FE. James Wright, later a national leader of FE, was one of them. A custodian, Wright "appropriated" useful documents from the trash and passed them on to other FE members. The union then knew management's next move. Wright reported that all workers, black and white, were told "the FE's program was integration" (297). An FE pamphlet about its Louisville local wrote that organizers explained that "the policy of the union was economic equality for all" that "the only way to beat Harvester's low wages was to unite the Negro and white workers," that "southern bosses for generations had played Negro workers against white, and white against Negro," and that "there was a direct connection between this and the fact that southern workers are the lowest paid in the country" (1992: 297–8, 2020: 165). FE won an NLRB election in July 1947; in September Local 236 struck against the southern wage differential. With the help of FE national leadership, in defiance of injunctions limiting pickets, and despite many arrests, workers held strong—no black Local 236 members crossed the lines—shut production, and won a wage increase that, while not ending the southern differential, cut it roughly in half. James Wright thought the strike "unified the people" (1992: 306, 2020: 169). It laid the basis for the militancy, democracy, and anti-racism that characterized Local 236.

Earlier I described FE's constant contest with Harvester over piece rate cuts; workers were ready to walk out to assert their will. Local 236 was the most extreme example of that, with the highest rate—of all FE plants—of work stoppages (as many as two per week on average) not authorized by the contract (wildcats). Often the threat of a walkout would get the matter settled to the workers' satisfaction. Most walkouts were small—not always. In summer 1950 Harvester announced that any work stoppage to argue a grievance would lead to suspension of the steward. In the next few days the company suspended seven workers; all but one were stewards. Local 236 replied that the workers' actions were a contractually authorized response to Harvester contract violations. Four thousand workers walked out; after three days, Harvester agreed to negotiate and then soon rescinded the suspensions and gave the workers back pay. In 1952 workers responded to a piece rate cut with a slowdown, working only for minimum pay. Harvester fired six stewards and committeemen. Two hundred workers walked out immediately, leading to their suspension. When a union meeting decided that Harvester had voided the contract, the whole plant walked out. After five days, Harvester agreed to negotiate, leading to the reinstatement of the stewards (but still allowing their suspension) and of the two hundred who had initially walked out.

Other conflicts led to dismissals. In 1948 and 1949 three stewards were fired after walkouts. There were other firings for harassing management outside the plant. In 1949 the company fired two black leaders—the only two black workers in an otherwise all-white department—including union pioneer Frederick Marrero. This led to a walkout by all the workers in the plant. A workforce over 85 percent white walked out to defend two black leaders! The firings were sustained. Still, the wildcat displayed the anti-racism that made Local 236 "the closest to the most perfect union" in James Wright's words (1992: 292, 2020: 154).

Local 236's civil rights efforts were extensive, fighting to integrate segregated parks, taverns, and hotels. Efforts to integrate white parks were not fully successful. In a white park, a cop ejected a racially mixed group; later a large squad of cops beat a larger group (Wright says someone informed cops of their plan); a later group of picnicking husbands and wives was allowed to stay for an hour. They brought white workers to integrate a black park, where police did not object; some white workers frequented the park after the first effort. They successfully integrated one hotel but failed at another. While many union members socialized across racial barriers in the union hall and one another's homes, they got a reaction when a mixed group went to the black club Top Hat. When they went in, a crowd of about 125 black patrons gathered around them. Wright defended his white co-workers to the crowd and pointed out that if the group had gone to a white bar, he would be beaten. "That's what we ought to do to them," someone said. James Wright: "'No, you ain't going to do that,' I said. So they quieted down, and it got so where [the white workers] would go to the Top Hat, and after about 12 trips, they'd just go, there by themselves, just go to the Top Hat" (Gilpin 1992: 367–8).

Local 236 members were involved in more conventional activities, political campaigns, struggle for "job creation through public works; an expanded relief system; higher pay for city workers; a tax increase for high-priced property; and an unemployment insurance program which paid benefits to striking workers" (360). In addition Local 236 fought to integrate hospitals. All of these activities involved white as well as black workers.

Earlier I wrote that when black and white workers oppose injustices to themselves and co-workers, they are more likely to oppose racial injustices. I am not the only person to address this connection. Anne Braden, a Louisville journalist (probably a CP member), was involved in FE. Were FE workers different from other Louisville workers? Braden told Toni Gilpin that white workers at Harvester "were no different from the white people working in the Ford plant here or the distilleries or the tobacco companies," that their experience and expectation had been only racism against black people. But "they had a different experience when they got [into the plant] ... It was something totally different from what workers in the Ford plant and elsewhere were hearing and therefore they acted in a different way. ... To me it was amazing, the kind of turnaround that people's minds had simply because they were in a different setting and what was acceptable in the old world was not acceptable when you walked into that union hall. (1992: 370, 2020: 218). On the same question Wright said

> They'd go along with [blacks], eat with them, go places with them, go hunting with them, walk out with them, work on a machine with them, have fun in the shop with them. That was a new thing for [the white workers]. That union had put what people call today in people some kind of religious—I don't mean a biblical religion—I mean a religious feeling of them sticking together.
>
> 1992: 370, 2020: 217

Some (for example, Robinson 2000 [1983]) have written that white racial attitudes are cultural: European culture has always had a negative attitude toward things dark and Africa-descended people. Braden and Wright have a contextual view: attitudes respond to the environment and the activities in which people engage.

Are these changed attitudes connected to their militancy as workers, as I had suggested? Braden says that white workers would respond to injustices to black workers that "this just isn't fair. You're not treating that guy right and I'm not going to put up with it" (Gilpin 1992: 346, 2020: 215). One white worker told Braden that, as he was brought up, black people "were something to look down on. But when I went to work at Harvester I saw something different." Black workers "were some of the best leaders the union had; they were the ones you could depend on to stick up for you when you got into a fight with the company; they knew what to do and they weren't afraid. You can't help but respect them," and soon "you think of them as just people like yourself" (Braden 1999: 47). Braden continues that standing up to the bosses gave the workers "a sense of strength and dignity that the workers in most Louisville plants did not have." That dignity meant that "they no longer needed the Negro . . . as an outlet for their own frustration and worries; for the Negro workers it meant they could look at the white workers without bitterness" (48; also Gilpin 1992: 346; 2020: 216). While this is a different account of the connection from the one I suggested earlier, they are not inconsistent, and they may capture different aspects of how white workers can change and make possible a *broader* fight against racial injustice.

Conversely, when Harvester crushed Local 236 and reasserted their dictatorship over the shop floor, when workers once again accustomed themselves to submitting their will to the bosses' orders, racism re-emerged among some white workers (2020: 290–1). This makes sense. When we accept abuse at work, we can come to think of it as normal, acceptable behavior and begin to abuse our co-workers and others. Struggle against the ways we are brutalized opens the door to broader struggle against racism and sexism. Acceptance of the bosses' mistreatment can normalize such behavior and lead us to mistreat others.

United Auto Workers Local 600

Local 600 was the UAW local at the huge Ford Rouge complex in Dearborn, Michigan. The three-thousand-man Service Department gunned down a score of workers at the 1932 Ford Hunger March—five died—and beat or arrested (or both) workers caught with union materials before firing them. Ford controlled Dearborn and its police. Paid snitches posed as workers. Paternalism complemented terror: Ford donated to churches and hired through these connections, creating loyalty, real or feigned. Others bought their jobs or bought a Ford car to get (and later keep) a job. Ford hired black workers—as much as fifteen percent. Anti-union terror and paternalism were meant to prevent formation of a union.

In 1927 Bill McKie, a fifty-year-old immigrant from the United Kingdom, started at Ford as a sheet metal worker. He was struck by the "Ford face" of workers, a blank expression that made no eye contact; workers did not speak to one another. When McKie asked his foreman about the union, he was told never to utter that word again if he wanted to work at Ford. Workers were in constant fear, concentrating only on their work, and fled the plant running at the end of a shift (Bonosky 2000). This is alienation from oneself, from one's humanity.

The CP in Detroit had helped organize the Hunger March in 1932 where three thousand workers and unemployed marched on the Ford plant. In the funeral procession for those killed between fifty and a hundred thousand marched or watched. The local was forged from this early work. Underground union activity grew. In 1937 the CIO launched UAW organizing at Ford. Beatings by Ford service men prevented leafletting at the plant. So organizers canvased for Ford workers in neighborhoods of Detroit and Dearborn. The CP-led International Workers Order (IWO), an alliance of immigrant groups influential among Polish and other Slavic workers, gave organizers access to Ford workers. A cadre of black workers—recruited from earlier UC work—argued with other black workers for the union and against loyalty to Ford. In 1940 the NLRB ordered Ford to stop interfering with union organizing. In February 1941 open organizing began, union posters and buttons appearing everywhere, union stewards taking up workers' grievances with foremen. By March 1941 some buildings or departments were sitting down to win grievances. On April 1 eight grievance officers were fired in the rolling mill; fifteen hundred workers sat down. The next day—at the agreed time—committed unionists developed by the CP pulled the switches in buildings throughout the complex, shut production, and led 50,000 out of the complex. On April 3 the entire complex was ringed with workers' automobiles blocking entrances. Ten days later Ford capitulated, agreeing to an NLRB election, held in May; the UAW won with 70 percent of the vote (Stepan-Norris and Zeitlin 1996).

At its peak membership Local 600 was larger than most CIO international unions, over 60,000 workers in the late 1940s and almost certainly many more during World War II (Stepan-Norris and Zeitlin 2003). It was run democratically: officers were elected for one-year terms. As black worker, union leader, and communist Dave Moore explained it, officers who did not serve the workers who elected them "didn't last but one term, and they were gone and forgotten" (Stepan-Norris and Zeitlin 1996: 8).

The "Ford face" frozen with fear was replaced by the faces of human beings fighting for themselves. Archie Acciacca said, "[W]e started getting security, and we started living like human beings. . . . If we thought something was wrong, we'd have something to say about it—before you could never say it" (120). Walter Dorosh said, "Right after we got organized, the supervisors were afraid. They were hiding. We had real power. . . . The guys were just—they felt free. Boy what a wonderful feeling" (120). Dave Moore observed, "[I]t was a big change in attitude. . . . They were more defiant to the supervisors. They had their say so. [If a guy] was involved in an argument [with] the foreman . . . everybody in that department could stop work and come to [his] defense" (121). Paul Boatin emphasized that while other union officials would file paper grievances and settle them in private, the red-led Progressive Caucus, handled grievances "where the workers could see the committeemen arguing with the supervisor in front of the workers, so they'd get a feeling that their own sentiments would be strengthened, their own education would be enhanced," (121) developing workers into fighters and leaders. This is a complete turnaround from the "Ford face."

With FE we saw that when workers fight for themselves, they are more open to fighting racism, white as well as black workers. The same was true in Local 600. Moore emphasized that leadership was crucial: he mentioned the names of three communists who were early organizers and leaders of Local 600 and says they

> demonstrated by action "... All of us got to be together. We should not be divided on race. What happens ... to Dave Moore as a black man [happens to] Sally Jones as a white woman." And this was instilled in the Ford workers. They had a close-knit brotherhood there ... because of the leadership.
>
> 135

Moore mentions some hotels would not house black delegates. Then, he says,

> That hotel was almost tore apart and would have been torn apart if they didn't give them a room. White guys was doing it for us. And we even had run-ins with other locals of UAW.... Some of the white guys from other locals around the country [would say], "Just what the hell are you doing, ... he's a Negro, he can't do it, he can't eat in this room with the rest of us." [But] these [Local 600] white guys, "God damn it, if he don't eat in here, nobody is going to eat..." And we put up a picket line, sometimes we did. The white guys themselves would organize.
>
> 135–6

These principles carried into the local's social life: interracial dances, choral groups, and picnics where black and white children played together; a majority-white local would select a black woman as beauty queen; black and white workers were in and out of one another's homes.

Shelton Tappes tells the story of two workers, friends, a black man and a white woman, who regularly ate lunch and left work together. She was disciplined, accused of clocking him out. A grievance was denied at the first step of the grievance procedure; the grievance man did not appeal. Tappes told him to appeal it. The man and woman were childhood friends; he walked her to the car where her husband was waiting; the families were close, taking vacations and socializing together. Tappes showed that the foreman was too far away to have seen what she did at the time clock. She was reinstated with full back pay. In another case Tappes tells of the trial of two union committeemen who objected to a white woman who had lunch with black women every day, her friends. The committeemen worked with management to get her fired. Tappes recalls a big union meeting at a high school on a Sunday, where Paul Boatin, a communist leader, "was at his best that day. He made a speech I'll never forget. Oh, he roasted those two guys, so he recommended that they set up a trial committee and these fellows be kicked out of the union pending trial and everything he proposed went over" (142). At the trial they were found guilty and suspended from the union.

Dave Moore remembered struggles for integrated housing. Moore emphasized acceptance of black residents throughout Detroit. He recalled

> Housing became an issue. Certain places in the city didn't want blacks. Projects were being built. We in Local 600 were insisting that these projects being built by the federal government, using [our] money, is open to everybody.... And they

tried to pit some of our own white guys against the blacks, moving in different projects. But we—the whites and the blacks—would picket and demonstrate together.

We fought for integrated housing... [He imagines speaking to a white person objecting to a black family in his neighborhood.] "We got a damn war going, our future is at stake, and you say Hitler is the enemy. Damn it to hell.... The guy's on the verge of going to the army to give up his life of [sic] defense of you, and you're telling us that he can't live here. Here, he got his draft papers in his pocket, and looking for a place for his family to live to go to defend this place, and you tell me that he can't live here. Well, to hell with that crap." And ... these were things that were did by guys from Local 600.

Asked whether efforts to integrate housing were successful, he responds

Oh yes, oh yes. I'll give an example. You take the Sojourner Project out here in northeast Detroit. You take the Herman Gardens over here on the west side, that was one. And you take the neighborhoods themselves, where individual housing, where blacks had never lived before in some neighborhoods here in the city of Detroit.... we had what you call a flying squad at Local 600. Wherever there was a trouble spot you had this flying squad. These were the guys we called the head crackers, black and white. (I got my uniform home yet.) And wherever there would be a trouble spot ... the flying squad from Local 600 is going over to give this guy some help.

Stepan-Norris and Zeitlin 1996: 136–7

A Local 600 flying squad showed up on March 17, 1942 to defend Rouge worker Frederick Hagan and his family after rocks had been thrown at his house by organized racists. Dominic Capeci (1984: 131) reports that "members of UAW Ford Local 600 stood vigil," but since these were "head crackers," they assuredly were prepared to do a lot more than watch if there was trouble. Racist intimidation failed. "Head crackers" can intimidate too.

I would infer that the defense of the Hagans was not an isolated incident but representative of the anti-racism of auto workers under the leadership of black and white communists during the war.

At this point Moore assures us that "the *true* history ... [of] the labor movement ... has never been written ... from the standpoint of the rank and file ... especially the participation and contribution that the blacks made" (137). Walter Reuther made it a point to drive communists from the union and conceal their accomplishments, at the same time concealing many contributions of black workers. Moore complains of the concealment and the emerging racism of the UAW under Reuther's leadership. Reuther's five-year contracts had a no-strike provision: employers could fire workers who wildcatted, and Reuther would not object. Workers still would walk out or turn to sabotage to exercise their power. Reuther's effort to defeat Local 600's red leadership failed. Ford had another solution: they slowly killed Rouge; today 6,000 workers produce trucks. With the international against them, Local 600 eventually began to look like other locals, but that took decades. Assessing the state of unions in the 1980s,

Dave Moore says, "[T]oday there are concessions. The order of the day is pitting one plant against another plant ... one department against another department ... one worker against the other worker—which we fought so damn hard to eliminate" (129).

United Packinghouse Workers of America (UPWA)

Figure 5.1 UPWA logo.

By the mid-1950s UPWA was the largest working-class civil rights and anti-racist organization in the United States, with more than 100,000 members. That was a remarkable accomplishment. Earlier in the twentieth century the packing plants had been centers of racial strife. This sub-section tells the story of that development.

Much of this story focuses on Chicago, the largest meatpacking center in the US during the first half of the twentieth century. Black workers had entered the industry there to break strikes in 1896 and 1904 and to supply labor during World War I.

Brooklyn native Herb March was assigned in 1930 at age seventeen to go to Kansas City as Young Communist League (YCL) organizer for that region of several states. His work included Scottsboro-type struggles and hunger marches as well as organizing UCs and among meatpacking workers in Kansas City. In 1932 he met and married another young communist Jane (Jacinta) Grbac, she moving to Kansas City. They moved to her family home in Chicago in 1933 after she had become pregnant. Herb found work at Armour, the largest and most viciously anti-labor plant in the stockyards (March 2017).

In this Third Period the CP was organizing Trade Union Unity League (TUUL) industrial red-led unions. March and other CPers were building the Packing House Workers Industrial Union (PHWIU), emphasizing racial unity and equality, appeals that resonated with black workers on the hog kill and beef kill, departments that could shut down an entire plant. Many joined. March was fired as a suspected organizer but managed to get rehired using a different name—until he got fired again (Halpern 1997, March 2017).

Organizing took off when the CIO formed the Packinghouse Workers Organizing Committee (PWOC) in 1937, using communists such as March and socialists such as Charles Fischer in Kansas City but retaining top down control (March 2017: 220, Horowitz 1997). PWOC in Chicago adopted clasped black and white hands as its symbol (later becoming symbol of the union). As March put it, "From the inception our union kept fighting against the discrimination and was able to win the confidence of the black workers. This whole concept of black-white unity was at the heart of the organization" (Halpern and Horowitz 1996: 42). Here we can see the CP's idea from the early '30s that anti-racism must spearhead class struggle.

PWOC work wove together fighting company racism, empowering workers on the shop floor, encouraging and developing black leadership, and addressing the bigotry of some white workers. All were essential to unity.

Struggles at Armour mobilized shop floor power and fought racism. When two workers were fired at the Armour Soap Works, PWOC organized a "grievance committee" to meet with management; the committee consisted of three or four essential workers from each department. During the meeting the bosses started getting calls from several departments: "we can't get any work done because these workers aren't there." The fired workers were reinstated. In another incident butcher Wally Strabawa, who had joined PHWIU in the early '30s, was fired for cooking meat (obtained from the plant) on steam pipes for his work crew. Again a committee met with management, again with key personnel. Each time the bosses tried to explain the firing, the workers replied, "Are you going to reinstate Wally?", nothing else, no discussion. As it became clear to management that they were not going to get production, they reinstated Strabawa (March 2017: 169–72). Horowitz (1997: 76) reports, "Black butchers openly backed Strabawa in the confrontation with management" and that "[w]hites reciprocated by supporting efforts to end management's practice of placing a black star on the time cards of black workers." Leon Beverly makes the stars' purpose clear: "When they get ready to lay off, all they do is say, 'Well, here's a black star, we'll lay this one off'" (76). In 1938, when Armour laid off high-seniority butcher Charles Perry out of turn, "white and black killing-floor workers sat down to protest management's action and secured a commitment from the company to remove the star and rehire Perry" (76), another exercise of shop floor power (Halpern 1997: 146 also connects these struggles).

Strabawa, who was white, got along well with his black co-workers. When he got married, some of his black co-workers showed up for the ceremony; they were turned away by the church ushers, with the pastor's approval. March says, "A committee went to the pastor and raised hell. 'You embarrassed Wally and excluded his friends! That is not acceptable'" (March 2017: 174). The union's pressure forced the church to open its doors to its Mexican neighbors, and it joined the red-led Back of the Yards Council.

Anti-racists integrated bacon departments at Armour and Wilson, often shown to visitors: they featured white women packaging sliced bacon in a clean environment. Black workers in hog kill and beef kill (who could shut down the whole plant) demanded and won integration of bacon. (Halpern and Horowitz 1996: 52) (Similar struggles occurred in Ft. Worth, Kansas City, and Waterloo, Iowa.)

After the war the Wilson UPWA local "succeeded in placing black apprentices in the skilled white mechanical gangs" and "utilized the contract's anti-discrimination clause to force the reinstatement of ... a black worker who was fired after punching a foreman who called him 'Sunshine'" (Halpern 1997: 180). Earlier at Wilson when a racist foreman "refused to allow a black to fill a vacant scaler's position, claiming that 'coloreds can't count too well,' workers purposely miscalculated their cuts and then punched out early feigning an inability to read the clock." The black worker got the scaler job. Halpern writes, "Building on the growing feeling of interracial solidarity forged by these kinds of spontaneous displays, the local scored another victory when it extracted an official apology from the company for ordering three long-service black employees out of sight when a visitors' tour approached their work area" (153).

Addie Wyatt in Chicago, seeing how the union was fighting for women's rights and for black women particularly, attended a union meeting during the war. She "saw a picture I have never been able to forget.... Here were workers who were learning ... how to band together to improve their lives through collective bargaining, political and social action. And I wanted to be part of it" (Horowitz 1997: 165). She became an important leader at Armour.

Workers forced the companies to hire black workers. At Swift in Chicago in 1938 work stoppages forced the company to agree to hire black workers in their proportion to the Chicago population (Halpern 1997). During the war the union in Chicago, Kansas City, and Omaha won the inclusion of more black women in the plants and in a wider range of jobs (Horowitz 1997). In 1948 UPWA won a non-discrimination contract provision at Swift, then enforced it by sending matched pairs of black and white applicants for jobs. When Swift hired the white applicants but rejected the black, the union had proof of discrimination. This forced Swift to change its practices and hire those applicants with back pay. This precedent led to defeating racial discrimination in hiring at other plants (Halpern 1997, Robinson 2011).

It was important in these (and the many other) struggles to address the racist attitudes of some white workers. L. C. Williams, a Fort Worth Armour worker, did this with great skill, telling white workers

> ...just because you was getting twenty cents more than I was getting for the same work, really ... this was just another one of the things that the company was using to make money off both of us.... I would say to them, "You know, as long as this company can keep this kind of thing between us and keep it going, and you support it, then we're never going to get this company on a solid front." ... Not only were you suffering, but I was suffering. Now I was probably suffering more but ... you're suffering too, because we both could get more if we eliminated this thing.
>
> Halpern and Horowitz 1996: 116

Williams understood that anti-black injustice (lower pay) was used by the company to undermine *white* as well as (more obviously) black workers. Saying this to white workers, he built class unity based on a shared recognition of how racism directed against one group of workers undermines all workers, a point made in UPWA literature. *That* understanding laid the basis for united anti-racist class struggle, the only way forward for the working class.

In 1943 UPWA became a separate union and chose Ralph Helstein, PWOC's lawyer, as president. Though a liberal, Helstein was March's buddy and a deeply committed anti-racist. He led the union in securing non-discrimination clauses in contracts settling the 1948 strike (which was otherwise a failure). Helstein commissioned a study to determine workers' racial attitudes. Discovering considerable racial prejudice among white workers, Helstein—with strong support of black and white communists and other black union officials—undertook to transform UPWA into a thoroughly anti-racist union.

Working together with black workers can change white workers' attitudes. Kansas City Cudahy steward Marian Simmons "found that integration of the women's departments and dressing rooms reduced racial tensions. 'We became friends,' she recalled. 'We had a sort of a family going among the women, the blacks and the whites.'" Anna Mae Weems, who was elected steward in sliced bacon at Rath in Waterloo by whites who had opposed her hiring, noted, "They looked to me as someone to protect their rights" (Horowitz 1997: 226). Still, there were limits. Weems notes, "They never really wholeheartedly accepted me" (Halpern and Horowitz 1996: 136). Limits are to be expected: hundreds of years of racist conditioning are not going to disappear in a day or year or even a decade.

This fight is not for the impatient. Robert Burt, a hog-kill worker at Rath, endorsed this protracted approach to dealing with white workers who were "buddy-buddy" about unity in the union, but when black workers entered previously all-white departments, "the hatred arise" (Halpern and Horowitz 1996: 131). While not minimizing the bigotry of his white co-workers, Burt stressed the *company's* responsibility to open up jobs to black workers. Union leaders would hold a department meeting to make it clear to reluctant white workers "well the time's gone, you know, so we had to put that across . . . the company didn't do their job. We take the attitude, that's up to the company to carry out. But as far as union [member] against union [member], we didn't take that type of attitude" (132). Emphasizing the *company's* racism, Burt strove to make anti-racist struggle a united working class struggle. He patiently combatted the bigotry of white co-workers.

As early as 1937 union activity had begun to break down segregation in taverns near Chicago's stockyards as workers gathered in racially mixed groups to organize (Horowitz 1997). By 1939 the unity built in Chicago packinghouses by PWOC had broken an earlier racial boundary, and black people could walk safely west of Ashland Avenue (March 2017: 175). Civil rights activism mushroomed after the transition to the UPWA. With an anti-racist president and many equally anti-racist communists in positions of responsibility, black workers led the fight often with participation of white co-workers.

In Kansas City "interracial delegations of packinghouse workers organized by [Cudahy worker] Marian Simmons, a UPWA official, pressured stores along . . . the main shopping street in Kansas City, Kansas . . . to serve and employ blacks" (Horowitz 1997: 224).

In Chicago white people rioted against black people moving into a previously white area. In 1946 there was a housing shortage for returning veterans; the Chicago Housing Authority built Airport Homes, a project near Midway Airport. When two black families—one a packinghouse worker and his family—moved in, two thousand racist white people protested; Chicago cops sided with the racist mob. Eighteen UPWA locals "sent teams of packinghouse workers to the Airport project each night to guard the homes of the black families." During the day they "called upon white residents and attempted to win their support." Black families stayed. Lowell Washington believed that once the union "got involved, it don't matter how, it made us stronger all across the board." These actions strengthened white activists and "affected other white workers as well." Halpern writes, "most white packinghouse workers in this period accepted the union's anti-discrimination activities" (Halpern 1997: 216–17).

Essential to these struggles were initiative and leadership of black UPWA members and active participation of white members, mostly committee activists, stewards and other union officers, "who rendered critical institutional support inside the union, participated in integrated public protests, and provided the bodies for carefully crafted tests of discriminatory practices" (225). It is a protracted struggle to win *most* white workers to understand that racial oppression of black workers is *their own* oppression; participation of white people conveys the message that anti-racist struggles are *class* struggles, not "black struggles."

In Waterloo, Iowa, white workers going into bars with co-workers experienced the mistreatment of their black co-workers—as Charles Pearson puts it, "They were witnessing that this did happen"—and became committed, along with black workers, to the project of integrating. They integrated bars and taverns around the Rath plant.

Anna Mae Weems, whom we met earlier, became active in the union's Civil Rights Committee and then was able to lead a take-over of the Waterloo NAACP from the "respectable" black leaders and link it with the union. She took a lead in national union anti-racist actions and resolutions (139–40). Workers challenged the schools, Jimmy Porter says,

> because they did not have black teachers. People would advertise for housing to be sold, when black folks would show up all of a sudden the place was rented. We start setting people up to have a white member to go in there and check, and have a black person to go in and take them to court.

They did the same thing in a tavern "and have those white people testify that this did happen to them. Even some paying a hell of a price to their neighbors as being traitors to their own race. The union had people who would do that" (142).

These achievements of the 1940s and 1950s deserve to be known by today's anti-racists, particularly the class-based anti-racism as exemplified by L. C. Williams' and Robert Burt's ways of combatting prejudice among white co-workers and organizing a broad anti-racist movement on and off the job. This can be a model for us: don't give up; dig in for the long haul; never accept racial injustice, but recognize that workers—black and white alike—can change, grow, develop, and become anti-racists.

Repression and reversal

Communists forged working-class anti-racism. After World War II red-led unions were either demolished or diminished as centers of working-class anti-racism. I will not go into detail—only summarize and cite sources where details can be found. I focus on why capitalists had to defeat them. The last section of the chapter elicits lessons.

At the end of 1945 things looked rosy. The Soviet Union and the US had been allies during the war. Communists believed that US patriotism and support for the Soviet Union were compatible. However, having been invaded and having suffered catastrophic loss of life (twenty to forty million), the Soviets sought to protect themselves with allied states in Poland, Germany, Czechoslovakia, Hungary, and the Balkans, frustrating US and European imperial ambitions. A Cold War between the US and the Soviets dominated the second half of the twentieth century.

For communists the Soviet example sustained hope of socialism. Although the Comintern was abolished in 1943, CP members were accused of being unpatriotic agents of a hostile government. The CP did not "openly declare that their aims can be attained only by the forcible overthrow of all existing conditions," including the overthrow of the US government. It insisted that it was patriotic, that it believed in peaceful and lawful transition to socialism based on majority will. Violence would occur only if there was violent resistance to that will. Socialism was the fulfillment of the "American democratic promise."[11] Abandonment of revolution was no protection. The Smith Act of 1940 made it illegal to advocate the forcible overthrow of the US government. Trials led to prison terms.

Historians (for example, Ellen Schrecker 1992, 1998) believe the CP's identification with the Soviet Union led to its repression, a view supported by anti-communist rhetoric. However, another reason would have led to the attacks in any event: the bosses' loss of control of the shop floor, which the CP helped to create. *Whenever* workers have control over their work lives, the capitalists, having lost control, attack and defeat shop floor power: in the mines of Alabama, among nutpickers, among California farmworkers, and in red-led CIO unions. Workers' power on the job created conditions where workers, white as well as black, opposed racial injustice. Capitalists cannot tolerate that.

At the war's end huge strikes hit auto, steel, electrical, meatpacking, railroads, and coal mines, neither initiated nor led by communists. They represented massive frustration experienced by millions of workers. Yet communists became the target.

At a November 1945 conference with union leaders capitalists expressed anxiety about "the right to manage," but union representatives would not concede that anything was exclusively management's responsibility (Brody 1993: 159). Recall from Chapter 4 TCI chairman Don Bacon's words to stockholders in 1904: the company must "fully control its own operations, untrammeled by union restrictions." Neil Chamberlain (1948: 40) wrote that any effort to undermine full managerial authority "would raise dangers to the whole business structure." Testifying before Congress Charles Wilson, General Motors chairman and soon to be Secretary of Defense, agreed. David Brody (1993: 165) writes, quoting Wilson, "Only by legally confining collective bargaining to 'its proper sphere' ... could 'what we have come to know as our American system' be

---

[11] Elizabeth Gurley Flynn's speech at her trial defending a peaceful and lawful transition to socialism is available at https://awpc.cattcenter.iastate.edu/2017/03/21/statement-at-the-smith-act-trial-april-24-1952/. See also William Z. Foster, History of the Communist Party of the United States, especially Chapter 35 (available at https://williamzfoster.blogspot.com/).

saved from a social revolution 'imported from east of the Rhine'" (referring to Soviet socialism); unions have tried to push "farther and farther into the area of managerial functions." Managers told Chamberlain (1948: 41, 79, 286) that union officials often had more shop floor authority than foremen. Another automobile boss told Chamberlain (41), "If any manager in this industry tells you he has control of his plant he is a damn liar." Through their union, workers exercised a veto over the orders of a foreman.

This was unacceptable: to maintain or expand market share and make profits, a firm must produce as efficiently as possible. To produce efficiently management must control the shop floor. If it does not, the company will go under to competitors that do. Some of the managers E. Wight Bakke interviewed in 1945–46 said exactly that (Bakke 1966: 29–30).

When workers (at Ford, for example) had no control over their work lives, going to work was horrible. The unions gave workers dignity and humanity, a voice in their work lives, an effective will in control of their own bodies. That voice made work tolerable for workers but was unacceptable to management.

Capitalists need productive efficiency. Workers need to feel like human beings at work. These needs are contradictory.

The bosses had to regain shop floor power. Unions had to let bosses control the shop floor. Those CIO unions that would cede power to bosses had to prevail. Anti-communism was central to this process. Working-class anti-racism based on shop floor power had to be stopped.

The Taft-Hartley law of 1947 made unions with communist officers ineligible for NLRB representation election; union officers had to sign an affidavit that they were not CP members. By 1948 CIO union bosses were signing the affidavits and preparing to attack CIO communists. Red-led unions were expelled or left the CIO in 1949 and 1950. The CIO lost well over one million members (Levenstein 1981, Rosswurm 1992).

Walter Reuther, as head of UAW's General Motors (GM) division, led a long 1945–46 strike. Gains were modest, but Reuther had posed as a fighter. At the March 1946 UAW convention he assumed presidency. In March 1946 Reuther said "he intended to unite 90 percent of the union against the 10 percent with 'outside loyalties,' by which, he said, he meant the Communists" (Keeran 1980: 256). In early 1947 Reuther helped defeat an eleven month left-led strike by UAW at Allis-Chalmers. Then Taft-Hartley was passed. Communists were under constant attacks. At the November 1947 convention Reuther removed communists from influence in the UAW central office.

Reuther advocated wage hikes to stimulate the economy, hikes that would expand production and—Toni Gilpin's paraphrase—lead to "efficient production, high output, low prices—and both wages and profits augmented in the process," insisting that "his demands would benefit GM, the auto industry, and American business as a whole" (Gilpin 1992: 178). If the company could not afford a wage increase, the union should scale back its demands. Reuther endorsed a "business code" maintaining that a "union leader should promote the welfare of business as well as that of employees" and encourage practices that will "improve the competitive position of the company" (181). Reuther signed five-year contracts that tied wage gains to productivity, not a bigger piece of the pie, but a bigger pie. UAW *endorsed management discipline of workers* who violated the contract. Workers gained economic benefits and security but lost shop floor power. Work became well-paid wage slavery. Other anti-communist CIO leaders also preached cooperation with capitalists, suppressing workers' self-activity that would interfere with profitability.

Red-led (or influenced) unions had a different approach. FE leaders and Helstein of UPWA refused to attack strikes initiated by workers in violation of the contract (on Helstein see Robinson 2011). These unions encouraged shop stewards and committeemen to take up grievances and defend workers. Power was with the rank-and-file, often by different means: FE workers stopped work, as did meatpackers. In Local 600, union representatives defended workers or were voted out. Dave Moore describes how he handled workers' grievances:

> if [the foreman] started to explain to you . . ., you could just stand there and look at him, and say, 'Well, look I want this did, understand, Fred? I don't want any more of this you harassing her or him. Now, if I have to come back in this department, goddamit, your production stops.'
> Stepan-Norris and Zeitlin 1996: 177

Stepan-Norris and Zeitlin (2003) agree: "by denying management the 'right' to exercise unilateral authority over production," the shop floor in red-led unions "embodied an altered balance of class power in the workers' favor" (188). As long as the capitalists controlled the state, the power of workers was limited. Capitalists had ultimate power. They bided their time, then counter-attacked.

Workers' self-assertion created self-confidence and mutual respect. With red leadership, this led to anti-racist action. But it was intolerable to capitalists who had to produce efficiently. The communist-led unions had to go. The Cold War made anti-communist witch hunts more popular, but—earlier examples show this—even without the cold war, capitalists, the media, and the state would have combined to smash CP power in the unions and support a Reutherite labor movement that would allow them to produce efficiently.

Anti-communism won out. UE was decimated by raids; FE, after defeating many UAW raids, gave up and was absorbed by UAW, unable to afford the many election contests that the wealthy UAW could launch. UPWA merged with AMC, which was absorbed into UFCW. Ford largely shuttered Ford Rouge.

UPWA (and other red-led unions) fostered social unionism. Workers assert themselves on the shop floor *and* in the larger society. They fight for themselves at work and for racial justice on and off the job (Horowitz 1997). That tradition is lost to the working class today. Capitalists could not tolerate these unions. Moreover, their history has been erased. Anti-racists need to know that history.

Lessons of communist anti-racism

In the early 1930s, prodded by the Comintern and black communists, the CP developed a line that the fight against racism leads the struggle of the entire working class. The work of the CP inside CIO unions brought that line to its fullest development. The fight against racism must lead because material inequalities among workers—in pay, in the skill or cleanliness of their work, in unemployment—divide our class. When inequalities seems stable and unchangeable, we tend to rationalize or resent them: the less oppressed look down on those more oppressed, and more oppressed workers resent the less oppressed. The working class can unite only by fighting racial (and gender) injustice.

Anti-racist battles were grounded in shop floor militancy that required workers to rely on one another. Militancy built workers' respect for themselves and for one another. They fight injustice to another as injustice to themselves. In so many industries workers described the coming of militant unionism as making them feel alive, like a person with rights, as conveying dignity and respect, as having power. Meatpacker Gertie Kamarczyk said that, after the union came in, she "felt like a human being with real rights, a real whole person for the first time in my life" (Halpern 1997: 166). UAW 600 workers said similar things as did many meatpackers. One black meatpacker said that the pre-union days were "like a bad dream gone" (153). William Raspberry said "It gave me dignity. I felt like a human being. I felt like a person" (Halpern and Horowitz 1996: 83). With shop floor power setting limits to what the bosses could do, workers can express their own will.

This sometimes spawned broad anti-racism. Workers in Detroit, Louisville, Chicago, Waterloo and many other places took flying squads from the workplace to battle racism outside. A small but significant group of white workers joined black workers in these battles. When examining the work of FE, we saw how this is connected to shop floor power. Workers can change when they see the opportunity to fight together. Black workers overcome passivity and fight their own mistreatment. Seeing black workers as fighters for their class, white workers can reject racial bigotry.

But both rights gained and anti-racist class unity are unstable. They require vigilance and struggle, cannot be taken for granted. The capitalists and their representatives must control production. Competition requires capitalists to be flexible and agile, to produce efficiently, to be able to change production accordingly. Shop floor power has to go. Anti-racism has to go. Communists have to go.

The suppression of workers' self-activity required more than the removal of communists, as David Brody (1993) makes clear. In steel, rubber, and elsewhere, militancy persisted. The final suppression occurs in the late 1970s and 1980s as we see in Chapter 6. They have to do it, and they do.

Many CIO organizers were radicalized in the CP work of the early 1930s. As John W. Anderson puts it, "The people who organized the CIO and UAW ... were ... people ... looking forward to a new society." Their sacrifices "were not those for a nickel an hour, but for something far greater" (Levenstein 1981: 54). However, they took their eyes off the prize. The vision expressed in Hughes' "Good Morning, Revolution!" inspired communists: a non-capitalist society based on collectivity, mutual respect, and finding meaning through developing and contributing our abilities in labor that serves others (Gomberg 2007). In The Third Period revolutionaries believed that revolution outside the Soviet Union served Soviet needs. With the Nazi ascent to power in Germany, the Soviets felt an immediate threat. They believed that Soviet interests—and the interests of Communist Parties elsewhere—were better served by making alliances with liberals than by organizing for revolution. This was the line of 1935's Seventh Comintern Congress of a united front against fascism.

Based on this new line, communists in the US buried their revolutionary politics. They didn't cease to believe in socialism or publish socialist literature, but in their activism, socialism took a back seat. In their union work they depended on the NLRB and the War Labor Board to win rights for their unions. Unions built on capitalist law can be destroyed when the law changes. Taft-Hartley was the beginning of the end for red-led unions.

Activists such as Herb March and many others came to *believe in* the reforms they were winning. Dorothy Healey says:

> For the first time we had close ties with top national labor people like John L. Lewis.... By 1938 the Party was abandoning its "fraction" meetings and shutting down its shop newspapers. That made it easier for us to get along with non-Communists, both locally and nationally.
>
> Healey and Isserman 1990: 74

She adds that the issue of how to fight both for workers' immediate needs and for socialism needed to be answered. It wasn't. If the goal is to "get along" with people who abhor revolution and communism, then they did what was necessary. If the goal is to persuade workers of the *necessity* of revolution, burying red politics is a disaster. CPers ceased to think as communists who understand that capitalism cannot allow workers to have rights. (March himself even voiced contempt for the study of theory.) They were caught off guard by the counter-attack. They shouldn't have been.

Communist achievements were less than meets the eye. Two characteristics of 1935–1945 were unusual. First, the unrest of the early 1930s—the veterans' Bonus March, the Hunger Marches, and eviction struggles of the UCs are examples—persuaded liberals that workers had legitimate grievances and should be empowered to express these (Barenberg 1993). The National Labor Relations Act of 1935 created a framework for workers' empowerment within the confines of capitalist society: protection for workers' right to form unions and laws to decide which union would represent workers. The red-led unions relied on this framework created by bourgeois law. It enabled them to oppose racism through union propaganda, training schools, and discipline of workers' racial bigotry. They were legally entitled to control the union treasury. But what capitalist law creates, it can take away. Capitalists concluded that workers had intolerable power.

Second, the period of World War II was unusual. The US government was purchasing much that workers produced. More production and more workers were needed. The War Labor Board sought to ensure that production was uninterrupted. Where this required concessions to workers, these were made. Capitalists could tolerate concessions: competition between firms was muted during the war. Capitalists could make huge profits even if they were not producing with maximum efficiency. This is not a characteristic of ordinary capitalism. Under ordinary circumstances capitalists must be able to control the shop floor and organize it efficiently to compete with other capitalists.

When the war was over, competition resumed. Profitability—success in competition—required regaining control of the work floor to maximize productive efficiency. Capitalists realized this. The communists didn't. They had reformist illusions that the gains they had made 1935–1945 could be sustained. This error was fatal to building a communist movement.

I don't mean to suggest that if the CP had had a more revolutionary line, they would not have been crushed as leaders of unions. The best that could have happened is that communists emerged from this defeat with a revolutionary party, with their eyes still on the prize of communism, understanding the fight against racial injustice as key to that development. The struggle to end racism in the US (and elsewhere) may take fifty years, a hundred years, a thousand years, or ten thousand years. The job of communists is to understand what must be done, to struggle here and now as best we can, to understand the line of march (as best as our limited knowledge allows), and to dispel illusions about capitalism in ourselves and others.

These criticisms of the limitations of the CP's work in the CIO are not offered with any sense of superiority. The courage and commitment of these red fighters is awe-inspiring. Still we must learn from them and try to do better.

This story should, however, stress the anti-racist achievements of the red-led unions. The CP enabled workers to win dignity for themselves and co-workers. This dignity and mutual respect lay the basis for a broad anti-racism on the job (winning hiring or promotion of black workers into previously all-white departments) and in the larger society (fighting for integrated neighborhoods, bars, restaurants, and hospitals).

Why is white supremacy so common today in the thought of white workers? The answer lies in the story of this chapter. Anti-communism among white workers, triumphant after World War II, reinforced racism.

Themselves deprived of dignity on the job, workers reverted to that losing approach of shoring up their self-esteem by demeaning others. Jim Wright noted this in Louisville after FE's defeat in the 1952 strike (Gilpin 1992, 2020). Powerless people abused at work tend to take it out on their co-workers or their families. This is the logic of our accepting capitalist indifference to our humanity: treating others inhumanely becomes normative, the expected and acceptable behavior; racism becomes acceptable and expected.

Many unions (the remnants that survive) have become centers of and enforcers of racism. With the CP's defeat, the tradition of working-class anti-racism was lost to us. Without communist theory and practice as an alternative, white workers gravitated toward white supremacy; black workers, seeing the indifference of white workers toward racial injustice, lose confidence in their co-workers and gravitate toward politics of black identity.

6

The Creation of Today's Racism

Overview

This chapter surveys three things: origins of huge wealth disparities between black and white families, disparities which are the material basis of black-white racial division; the Civil Rights Movement of the 1950s and 1960s, its achievements and limitations; and federal policies which created hyper-vulnerable workers—workers without rights—in the aftermath of civil rights and urban rebellions of the 1960s. The first two, I cover briefly, the third in greater detail.

The New Deal: deepening racial inequality

Racial injustice is *transformed* and *recreated* in response to struggle: sharecroppers replace work gangs of enslaved people; Jim Crow is enforced in response to the Farmers Alliances; when workers unite and win wage gains, machines replace workers; anti-racist communist working-class leaders are jailed and expelled from unions; factories move from the urban north to rural areas, particularly in the South; unionized urban meatpackers are replaced by undocumented immigrants and others in right-to-work states; sharecropping disappears when it becomes more efficient to produce crops with chemicals and machines. No longer a rural agricultural population, black workers labor in urban centers and suffer high unemployment. Segregated nearly all-black schools in nearly all-black neighborhoods create poor prospects for many in the next generation. The prospects for most white children are not as bad, and white families have, on average, much greater accumulated assets. There is deep racial inequality within the working class. This disparity is largely the result of policies of the middle and late twentieth century, the story this chapter tells.

The New Deal was a constellation of laws and directives of the Roosevelt administration, starting in 1933. For the first seven decades of the twentieth century the Democratic Party was a coalition of northern urban politicians—thought to be defenders of workers and small businessmen—and southern segregationists, "Dixiecrats." New Deal legislation created relief for the unemployed, public works jobs, labor protection (minimum wage, right to organize unions, forty-hour week, unemployment insurance, prohibition of child labor), old age insurance (Social

Security), and, after 1944, extensive benefits for returning veterans; the legislation has a reputation of improving things for the "little guy."

Black workers did not get the full benefits of New Deal legislation. Either the law prescribed universal benefits administered locally (relief and public works jobs), or most black workers were excluded from the benefit (Social Security and labor legislation), or discrimination made benefits unavailable to black people (housing, education) (Katznelson 2005).

Relief and public works jobs in the South were administered by local racists who made sure that black people got less.

Legislation excluded categories of labor that black people did. Agricultural labor and domestic service—sources of black employment—were not covered by old age assistance, unemployment insurance, rights to organize unions, forty hour work week, and prohibition of child labor. The 1947 Taft-Hartley law *extended* to food processing workers exclusion from organizing protection; many more black workers labored there.

The racism of these laws is *intertwined* with harm to many white workers. While in 1940 55 percent of southern sharecroppers were black, the other 45 percent were not. While the exclusions of domestic and agricultural labor from old age insurance and unemployment insurance made two-thirds of black workers ineligible, they also made 40 percent of white workers ineligible (Katznelson 2005). The majority of domestic servants were not black (Evans 2009). The southern "racial order" was at the same time an order that guaranteed low wage *white* labor. It was *racist* (a disproportionate harm to black people). At the same time the *majority* of its victims were white (because white people were a larger percentage of the population).

There are, then, these two dimensions to racism: it particularly disadvantages black people and hence is *racism*; the effects of racism are rarely or never experienced by black people alone. US-born white people, asian, mexican, indigenous and immigrant workers of all "races" are caught up in similar oppression. Yet the *rationale* for the laws was often to preserve the "southern racial order."

With the onset of World War II many black people moved north or west to work in industry. (Mechanization of southern agriculture accelerated in the later 1930s; black labor became increasingly superfluous.) Black workers' increasing presence in industry combined with the CIO's militant multi-racialism (when under left influence as in Memphis and Birmingham), led Dixiecrats to oppose unions. When they thought of unions as bastions of white advantage, Dixiecrats supported labor legislation in 1935 and 1938. As left-led multiracialism emerged in the late '30s and intensified during the war, Dixiecrats sought to limit black rights to organize.

The war created more racial injustice. Initially black people were not called up (segregated facilities had to be prepared). By the end of 1942 10 percent of soldiers were black, a year later 11 percent. Military Jim Crow caused their education and skills to fall further behind those of white soldiers, who had greater opportunities for training.

In 1944 the GI Bill of Rights became law: soldiers returning from the war received aid in buying homes and in college or other post-secondary training. Eventually veterans became, on average, more affluent than non-veterans. Most black veterans couldn't take advantage of these benefits. In the South most schools were closed to black veterans; enrollment at historically black colleges was kept low; banks would not lend black veterans money for homes. In the North colleges and universities would not admit black applicants. Black homebuyers were excluded from white neighborhoods, and banks would not lend in black neighborhoods.

Ira Katznelson (2005) emphasizes the *Dixiecrat* influence on national policy, slighting racial injustice inherent in *northern* practice: New Deal housing policies insured that urban areas would be segregated by race and that many black neighborhoods would become slums.

A 1933 law created the Home Owners Loan Corporation (HOLC) to refinance mortgages and prevent foreclosures. HOLC's Residential Security Maps determined likely future value of a home based on its neighborhood. Working with realtors and banks, HOLC color-coded neighborhoods green, blue, yellow, and red, in declining order of likely future home value. "Red-lining" marked neighborhoods where mortgage-lending was thought to be a poor risk. Residential Security Maps were part of a *uniform, national method of appraising* home value. Black neighborhoods were red-lined, mortgages virtually unattainable, the HOLC writing in one case that relatively new houses had "little or no value today, having suffered a tremendous decline in values due to the colored element now controlling the district" (Jackson 1985: 200). Even a small number of black residents caused the neighborhood to be red-lined.

The Federal Housing Administration (FHA) was established by the National Housing Act in 1934. Together with the Veterans Administration (VA), established by the GI Bill in 1944, it transformed housing for millions of—mostly white—working-class families through mortgage insurance—government payout to the lender in the event of foreclosure. Insurance made loans a safer bet for banks, which gave lower interest rates, longer mortgage terms, and lower payments. Purchasing a house became cheaper than renting.

For the FHA and VA, as for HOLC, black people in a neighborhood meant declining values and no insurance. The FHA would not insure a housing project whose residents were black nor homes in black neighborhoods. In 1948 FHA Commissioner W. J. Lockwood wrote that "the FHA 'has never insured a housing project of mixed occupancy' because of the expectation that 'such projects would probably in a short period of time become all-Negro or all-white.'" (209) The problem was not projects would be all-white; the FHA was encouraging that (including restrictive covenants barring black residents). By FHA standards, only all-white is acceptable.

Cheap mortgages and all-white suburbs encouraged white families with the means (often nothing more than a steady job in the 50s) to abandon the city for the suburbs. Cities became increasingly places for disadvantaged minorities. Newark, Gary, and Detroit are extreme cases, but the same phenomenon is common throughout the North. Chicago's population dropped from 3.6 million in 1950 to 2.9 million in 2000.

Federal policy intensified racial segregation of urban areas. The policy *lowered* home values where black people lived by denying mortgage insurance and home improvement loans. It created all-black slums. It *reinforced prejudice*, giving white people an economic incentive to prefer all-white areas. These policies continued through the early 1960s.

Imagine instead that federal policy had offered *financial incentives* (in the form of a large tax credit or mortgage interest subsidy) to families who moved into census tracts where their "race" was in the minority, the greatest incentive to those who were in the smallest minority. Under such a policy home valuations would have developed differently.

Where black homeowners could not get mortgages, entrepreneurs stepped in. "Contract sellers" panicked white residents into selling cheap, jacked up the price (by an average of 70 percent in Chicago's Lawndale neighborhood), and sold the property to a black person "on contract," with a large down payment, high interest, hence high payments (due to the high initial price and the high interest), and a provision that, should the buyer miss *a single payment*, the property reverts to the contract seller and all monies paid to the seller are forfeit. Contract sellers made a killing (selling the same property several times) despite the decline in property values resulting from this practice. Black buyers had high payments. They often subdivided properties into many units, trying to cover payments by renting to others. The neighborhood became a slum. White observers clucked their tongues about black "culture of poverty" and neglect of their property (Satter 2009).

In 1966 the FHA ended its red-lining practices. The 1968 Housing and Urban Development Act established FHA home mortgage insurance targeted for urban neighborhoods. However, racism in housing did not end. The pattern will be familiar from the discussion of contract selling: speculators bought property cheap from whites often panicked into selling. Property was resold at a much higher price to a black family. The FHA insured the mortgage, and people moved in with as little as $200 down payment. An appraiser was paid to give a high appraisal, making FHA insurance possible. The speculator filled out forms indicating that the buyer's income was adequate to pay the mortgage, which it often wasn't, making up numbers. The mortgage company collects from the FHA in the event of default; so it had no incentive to ask questions. Appraisers and particularly speculators and mortgage companies made out like bandits. Overcommitted homebuyers abandoned the buildings, which became empty, boarded up, or burned or torn down. The victims were black homebuyers, who could not afford the high payments, and neighborhood residents, whose homes lost value as abandoned buildings multiplied. The FHA was being defrauded. Hundreds of thousands of homes (25,000 in Detroit alone) became abandoned as a result of this program (Boyer 1973, Satter 2009).

These unscrupulous lending practices led to reforms. But in the words of Patricia J. Williams (2008) "the 'ghetto lending' practices of the 1960s [and earlier—PG] have metastasized, spreading across class, race and regional boundaries.... If such practices began in neighborhoods where there was disrespect for the property rights of certain Americans, it's come round to bite us in the tail." Practices that victimize black people first and hardest harm others as well. Sub-prime mortgages enticed buyers into loans with high interest but low payments (balloon and ARM mortgages, with negative amortization—debt grows because payments are less than interest charges). Practices of the 1970s were repeated on a larger scale, affecting many more people. Underwriting mortgages without checking people's income or debt, altering figures to make sure the mortgage met underwriting standards, getting false appraisals, putting people in the most expensive possible mortgage with the highest fees to the mortgage company were common practices at the biggest mortgage underwriters of the 2000s: Countrywide, Fremont, NovaStar, and others. The debt was then sold to major financial institutions. This mortgage debt was at the center of the economic collapse of 2008: Fannie Mae, Freddie Mac, AIG, Citicorp, Goldman Sachs, and other big wall street banks and brokerages were selling (and holding) financial instruments backed by high-interest mortgages, but the mortgages were often junk. Much of this was justified politically on grounds of access to housing for urban minorities (Morgenson and Rosner 2011).

Black people were more likely to be victimized. Fifty-five percent of loans to black people were subprime compared with 17 percent of those to white. (Sixty percent of black people receiving subprime loans were eligible for prime loans.) Despite racial disparity more white people than black were victimized by subprime mortgages (United for a Fair Economy 2008).

Devastated all-black areas of Detroit, St. Louis, or Chicago—abandoned buildings, empty lots—are the result of gouging of black homebuyers—ready victims because racism made it hard for many black people to find housing.

New Deal policies and their successors widened racial inequality within the working class. They tended to make many white (and some black) people more conservative. Most workers had once lived in rental housing. In the twentieth century this began to change in the boom of the 1920s, then went into decline in the 1930s, only to grow rapidly after the end of World War II. Owner-occupied housing increased from 43.6 percent in 1940 to 66.2 percent in 2000. There is large racial disparity in home ownership. According to a 2017 Stanford report (Grusky and others 2017: 4) "In 2014, a full 71 percent of white families lived in owner-occupied housing, as compared with 41 percent of black families and 45 percent of Hispanic families." White homeowners accumulated significant equity, black homeowners comparatively little. In 2019 median household assets for non-hispanic white were 13.3 times median black.[1]

People's identities can shift from "working class" to "middle class" and "homeowner." In *American Babylon* Robert O. Self (2003) traces how white residents of the East Bay of the San Francisco area changed. In 1946 there was a general strike in Oakland in support of efforts to organize downtown retail clerks. In 1964 voters passed Proposition 14 *repealing* legislation prohibiting discrimination against black people in housing. In 1978 voters passed Proposition 13 limiting property taxes (funding schools and other programs). New Deal programs widened the economic divide among workers, marked by race. Many homeowners developed a conservative consciousness that undermined social justice. Workers will not launch a general strike for their common interests when racism divides them.

I have argued that the fates of black and white workers—particularly the most oppressed white workers—are deeply intertwined, that anti-black injustice harms oppressed white people. The logic of housing is different. Because of government and mortgage lender policies, white homeowners *gain* property value by excluding black people from their neighborhoods. Because of injustices to black families, children suffer. Suffering can affect their school performance. Hence white families prefer not to

---

[1] See the table for Wealth and Asset Ownership at https://www.census.gov/data/tables/2019/demo/wealth/wealth-asset-ownership.html.

send their children to schools attended by large percentages of children from poor black families; they believe, not unreasonably, that the prospects for *their own* children would be worse in those schools, and they feel it is a parental duty not to disadvantage their own children in this way. (Likewise, black parents with resources and options try to find schools for their children where the students are not overwhelmingly from poor families, particularly black families.) These considerations seem to weigh in favor of the rhetoric of "white privilege" or white advantage.

But, as Sheryll Cashin (2004) argues, white people pay a price for segregation of schools and neighborhoods. Along with better services come high home prices that often require overcommitting time. Cashin writes that in a society of winner and loser neighborhoods and schools, "those in the middle of the income spectrum, of whatever race, have to work harder and harder to stay in or get to the 'winner' column" (199–200), thus paying a price in more stress and less leisure and family time.

Moreover, there is evidence that growing racism is undermining white opportunity when we measure these by homeownership rates. Millennials have the lowest homeownership rate for white people *and* the greatest racial disparity in homeownership rate (that is, white vs. black)—compared with the previous three generations, Gen X, Boomers, and Silent (Choi and others 2018). A larger percentage of white people (than previously) are being locked out of the housing market. The same thing is happening to black people but to an even greater degree.

The strongest case for white benefit is based on housing equity, where racial exclusion seems to advantage white homeowners. Yet even here there is evidence that the main trend is for there to be *greater inequality within the working class*. This inequality harms white people who lack computer engineering degrees from Stanford.

The rise and fall of civil rights

After World War I, black soldiers returned to the world of segregation they had left, leaving many bitter. White racists insisting that black people stick to their place in the racial order instigated pogroms in East St. Louis, Chicago, Tulsa, and elsewhere. Antiracists responded. The NAACP and others in Harlem organized a march of 100,000 protesting the East St. Louis pogrom of 1917 in which at least one hundred black people were killed.

World War II mobilized so many for the war effort that black soldiers were unlikely to accept the old racial order. William Ashby, a Newark Urban League member, summarized the feelings of veterans:

> I'm tired of all this goddam crap. Tired of hearing the white man say, "I can serve no niggers in my restaurant," tired of being told "I ain't got no place for colored in my hotel." Why, hell, I've been to Europe. Hitler leveled his bullets at me. Missed. I went to the Pacific. Mr. Hirohito sent his madmen to blow me to hell in their planes. I'm still here. Why don't I tell the white man, "Take your goddam boots off my neck!"
>
> Sugrue 2008: 132

The Cold War was developing between the US and the USSR and China. The post-war period included proxy wars in Korea, Vietnam, and Afghanistan (1980s anti-Soviet war leading eventually to the rise of the Taliban, an unintended consequence). There was struggle for influence throughout Asia, Africa, Europe, and the Americas. As former colonies became independent countries, the Soviet Union highlighted racial injustice in the US in propaganda to persuade people that the US was no model of social justice. These efforts put pressure on ruling elements in the US to jettison southern Jim Crow.

Some action against Jim Crow was from the top: President Truman's 1948 order abolished racial separation in the military; in 1954 the Supreme Court ruled in *Brown v. Board of Education* (of Topeka) that racially segregated schools were inherently unequal.

However, grassroots activism ended Jim Crow. The Montgomery Bus Boycott of 1955–1956 lasted 381 days, ending with a Supreme Court endorsement of a district court ruling that racial segregation in transportation was unconstitutional. The solidarity of the boycotters encouraged other challenges to Jim Crow throughout the South, including the 1960 Greensboro sit-ins at Woolworth's lunch counter against their policy of not serving black people. After six months of protest, Woolworth ended this policy. The late 1950s and early 1960s saw protests against Jim Crow throughout the South, including the Freedom Rides of 1961 that challenged segregation on buses and were met by vicious beatings organized by the KKK in Birmingham. Freedom Summer of 1964 in Mississippi brought many from the North to organize for voting rights and led to the murder of three activists, two of whom were white, sparking much national sympathy for the civil rights struggle and forcing the hand of the US government. This led to civil rights legislation in 1964 and 1965 which abolished much of Jim Crow and secured voting rights (Payne 1995, Woodward 1974). This summary of the southern struggle omits many hundreds of other struggles, giving only a hint of what actually happened.

People in the North fought its own Jim Crow. The North did not insist on separate bathrooms, drinking fountains, and segregation in transportation, but "There were colored hotels and white hotels, Negro bars and white bars ..., black restaurants and white restaurants.... [A]musement parks, bowling alleys, and roller rinks" either did not allow black people to enter or allowed it only on certain days. Black people could not usually use public swimming pools (Sugrue 2008: 131). Black travelers might use *The Negro Motorist Green-Book* to guide where they could sleep and eat. Throughout the North in the 1940s, 1950s, and into the 1960s downtown movie theaters commonly either did not admit black patrons or segregated them inside the theater. Many towns and cities had schools which were reserved for black students, even (usually) in violation of state law.

Thousands of battles were fought throughout the North to end these practices of segregation, often led by the Congress of Racial Equality (CORE), by local civil rights groups, by the NAACP, sometimes led by ministers, or by members of the CP or other left organizations (including the CP-led Civil Rights Congress). These struggles continued from the 40s through the 50s into the early 60s. By that time most northern

Jim Crow had ended in these public spaces. Here the Civil Rights Movement was victorious.[2]

Besides the struggles to desegregate public venues, the central civil rights struggles were for jobs, schools, and housing. The build-up to war in the late thirties and early forties eased unemployment for white people, less so for black. In response A. Phillip Randolph launched a March on Washington Movement (MOWM) to culminate in a mass march on July 1, 1941 for black inclusion in defense-industry employment. The Roosevelt Administration disliked the movement, tried to stop it, but finally issued a directive forbidding racial discrimination by defense contractors and establishing a Fair Employment Practices Commission (FEPC) with no enforcement power. Randolph called off the march. The FEPC publicized a few cases of employment discrimination, but black workers remained a tiny fraction in defense industries.

There was a second upsurge of attention to black unemployment in the early to mid-1960s (peaking in 1963). Activists, having largely achieved non-discrimination in restaurants, hotels, and theaters, turned attention to jobs, often led by CORE. The Department of Justice counted 1,412 civil rights demonstrations during the summer of 1963, a level of activism that continued into 1964. And black people were hired for many jobs where they had been excluded or under-represented (Meier and Rudwick 1973, Sugrue 2008).

Besides having an unemployment rate double that of white folk, black people often worked the dirtiest, most dangerous, most noxious, and lowest-paid jobs, deprived of opportunity to use seniority to improve their position (Nelson 2001). Despite the formation of black caucuses in many industries in the '60s (and white workers joining those causes to resist do-nothing union leadership), black workers continued to be confined to the worst jobs.

What were the gains in the struggle for racial equality on the job? From the 1930s through the 1960s black people gained access to many government jobs. The Roosevelt administration tripled the number of black federal workers in its first two terms. In the 1960s black workers gained employment as bus, streetcar, and subway operators, jobs largely closed to them earlier. Frustration with high unemployment, low-wage jobs, confinement to ghetto slums, and especially police brutality led to urban uprisings from 1964 (Harlem) through the early 1970s. Many black workers were hired into the auto industry after the Detroit uprising of 1967. Gains in industry were offset by the decline of urban industry in the US, so-called "deindustrialization," which really consists of three processes: increasing use of technology to decrease need for labor; export of jobs to countries with lower wages; movement of jobs within the US from northern cities with many black workers to the South and to small towns—low-wage, non-union areas. This occurred in meatpacking, auto and many other industries.

White people sympathetic to the struggle against southern Jim Crow felt threatened by black demands for jobs and advancement in a labor market where opportunity was limited. White public opinion about racial injustice shifted. While the struggle for

---

[2] A qualification: the desegregation of downtown public venues coincided with the suburbanization of white people and the rise of malls and cineplexes.

public accommodations was clearly winnable, the struggle for equality in the labor market threatened the entire American social order, where black labor had, for three hundred years, been more oppressed. Civil rights activists became aware that the task of achieving racial equality in labor was monumental and became discouraged (even as they were winning victories) by the difficulty of the task (Gomberg 1994).

Black workers experience hiring and job discrimination. There is evidence from interviews that people responsible for hiring (even black personnel people) negatively stereotype black workers, particularly black males. Once hired, black people experience job discrimination, treatment to which many white colleagues are simply blind (Kirschenman and Neckerman 1999). Experiments done by black and white testers in low-wage job markets in Milwaukee and New York City show that white applicants are called back or offered a job *twice as often* as black people; this is an effect of racial identity alone (Pager 2007).

Black jobseekers are closed off from opportunity by segregation. Employers commonly recruit for unskilled jobs by asking current employees, "Do you know someone good? We need a new person." Hiring is through social networks. Neighborhoods, schools, churches, and social associations are segregated, creating large black disadvantage. For sixty years the unemployment rate for black workers has been double the rate for white.

Highly educated black people have made remarkable strides. The Obama presidency was a symbol of this. But schools segregated by race and class ill-serve black children also handicapped by poverty. Civil rights activists opposed separate and inferior education for black students, North as well as South. In the North school segregation was largely due to neighborhood segregation; northern cities contained large black ghettos. Many neighborhoods became slums. The Civil Rights Movement of the 1960s and thereafter made some effort to overcome residential segregation, but little changed. Residential segregation of black people is far greater than that of any other group (Massey and Denton 1993).

When students' school assignments are by residence, residential segregation ensures school segregation. 1960s court cases challenged school segregation in some northern cities by arguing that school segregation had been maintained beyond what color-blind considerations of residence would warrant. These cases often led to court rulings requiring busing to integrate schools. But white families were abandoning the cities for the suburbs. Court orders did not lead to school integration. Detroit was paradigmatic of this trend, and was the focus of a court case, *Bradley v. Milliken*. In 1972 Judge Stephen J. Roth ruled that Detroit had segregated its schools but that the remedy required fifty-three surrounding districts as well to participate in an area-wide desegregation plan. Under this plan white families in the Detroit metropolitan area who wished to avoid integrated schools had no place to flee (except private or parochial schools). How did white people respond? Alabama segregationist George Wallace won the 1972 Michigan Democratic Party primary on an anti-busing platform. The strength and openness of white opposition to busing for integration must have been very demoralizing to millions of black and white people who hoped to live in a society without racism. In 1974 the US Supreme Court struck down Roth's decision, ruling that multiple districts could be required to participate in desegregation efforts only if it was shown that they had all cooperated in creating segregation; the court rejected Roth's broader view that the districts themselves were arbitrary and constituted segregation in practice (Cashin 2004, Sugrue 2008).

The ruling effectively ended efforts to desegregate schools in the North. The culture emerging from the decision created "color blind" racism: publicly people don't say that race is the reason for their decision about housing and schools; such decisions were treated as private matters of individual right to choose. People can be called racist for pointing out that the consequence of housing and school choices is to segregate schools by race. Because many white (and some black) families avoid schools where the student population is significantly black, large numbers of black children, particularly the most disadvantaged, are in schools with other children from similar families. To the extent that educational advantages confer employment advantages, the overturning of Roth's *Bradley v. Milliken* ruling secured racial injustice in both areas.

Residential segregation leads to segregation of social networks, churches, clubs, fraternities and sororities, and other groups. Segregation exacerbates inequality in educational opportunities, adding to difficulties that segregated networks make for finding jobs.

The Civil Rights Movement defeated segregation in restaurants, movie theaters, and other public places. But three central social practices that create inequality and division within the working class—job disadvantage, segregated education, and segregated neighborhoods—were not ended by the civil rights struggles.

Left forces were largely absent from the Civil Rights Movement, particularly after the mid-1950s. The US government launched an attack on the CP and on the party-led Civil Rights Congress in the late 1940s and early 50s (Horne 1988). This government attack marginalized anti-racism grounded in a left analysis. The Civil Rights Movement that emerged in the 1950s did not place racism in the context of exploitation of workers and benefits to capital of a divided working class. The absence of left analysis weakened the Civil Rights Movement (Gomberg 1994). It reinforced white supremacist thought and white identity among white workers, who are not hearing that they too are victims of anti-black racism.

Workers without rights: recreating racial injustice

We have seen the origin of huge racial wealth inequalities and the disadvantages for black people arising from segregation of neighborhoods, schools, and voluntary associations such as churches. More was needed to reconstruct racial injustice. Racial slavery and Jim Crow had provided the US with abundant cheap and flexible labor, people who (because of force or terror) worked under conditions others would not accept. The US government created new systems of fear to replace Jim Crow racism, creating again workers without rights.

By "workers without rights" I do not mean workers lacking *legal* rights. I mean workers so vulnerable that their bosses know they are unlikely to assert any legal rights they may have. Consider these three (hypothetical but realistic) examples: (1) A twenty-two year old black single mother of two young children, their sole support, works in a chicken processing plant in central Mississippi; her paycheck pays rent that keeps her family from homelessness. From repetitive motions at work she has developed carpal tunnel inflammation so painful that she cannot sleep at night without soaking her arms in cold water to numb the pain; when the pain awakens her she soaks them again. The company doctor tells her to go back to work. So she endures pain. Eventually she expects to become disabled and to try to get disability relief, as her mother did. (2) An undocumented Mexican immigrant works at a club stocking the bar with beer, wine and liquor. During a snowstorm the managers, concerned about snow on the roof, ask him to shovel the roof. He complies. That evening someone gets sick in the men's restroom; the managers tell him to clean up the vomit and feces. He complies. Undocumented do what others will not do. They believe they cannot refuse. (3) A black ex-felon, convicted of selling small amounts of marijuana at work on an earlier job (supplementing his low pay), works at a fast food restaurant. At the end of his shift, clean-up of the restaurant is not complete. The manager tells him to clock out and continue working. When he complains, the manager replies, "I did you a favor giving you a job; now I need a favor." The worker complies.[3]

In the first case changes in welfare law, absence of her children's father (who is in prison), and complicity between her employer and state officials leave the worker little choice but to endure pain until she is disabled. In the third case the bosses' demand is illegal, but the worker, being vulnerable, went along. In the second case the worker, subject to deportation, will not refuse a task. In all three cases their bosses know that the workers are unlikely or unable to assert rights. Effectively they are workers without rights. The rest of this chapter tells how racism was *recreated* to replace Jim Crow.

Function and social change

Vulnerable workers and high unemployment are *functional* in capitalist society, where firms must make profits in competition with other firms. Doing business cheaply gives a competitive advantage. It's cheaper to do business with labor that will work hard, flexibly, and efficiently for wages lower than competitors pay. A vulnerable worker is more likely to work hard for low wages and comply with employers' requests. So the presence of low-wage pliable labor enhances profits. A *society* where workers are vulnerable creates—for firms operating there—a profit advantage over firms located in societies where workers are less vulnerable. In that sense vulnerability has a function in a capitalist society.

Saying that something is functional does not substitute for a historical narrative of its origins. I have given such narratives. Those most deeply and directly affected were identified as "black," but, given labor competition, others whose labor competed with black labor were also held down. Historical narrative is compatible with functional analysis.

---

[3] The first example is based loosely on Stuesse 2008, the second on Gomberg-Muñoz 2011, and the third on conversations with Chicago State students.

Capitalist society creates limits to what is likely to exist within it. Imagine a country whose working class had engaging labor, security, cultural and educational opportunities, and housing and a physical environment that are healthy, comfortable, and lift our spirits. In competitive capitalism firms operating in that country would have higher labor costs and be at a competitive disadvantage. Vulnerable labor is functional. It will continue to exist in some form.

We who seek social change need to be aware of function. We may protest treatment of vulnerable workers or policies which create vulnerability. But capitalists benefit from vulnerable workers. So when one form of racism is protested and ended, another form of racism replaces it. We have seen this repeatedly. Racism is functional. Vulnerability is functional. Poverty is functional. Creating a society where all workers can flourish requires us to abolish capitalism.

In the pages that follow we see how, after the Civil Rights Movement, the role that black labor had historically played was *recreated* for black workers and others. What role had black labor played? Enslaved black labor producing cotton created US wealth and made the US a capitalist power. After the Civil War black sharecroppers—and white and mexican—continued to produce immense wealth. Migrant black and other farmworkers moved from Florida to New England seasonally harvesting fruit and vegetable crops and processing these crops for freezing and canning (Thomas-Lycklama a Nijeholt 1980). In cities black workers assumed increasing prominence in basic industry, including meatpacking and, by the 1960s and 70s, automobile and steel. However, they often had dangerous and low-paying jobs. Black workers, especially women, cleaned up and cared for children and the elderly. Black workers were central to the US labor force. The work that black workers have done historically has to be done by someone, and much of the US economy has depended on black labor. Others besides black workers also toiled under inferior conditions and were exploited and oppressed more severely than white male workers: Mexican *braceros* (migrant farm workers deported when their labor was not needed), chinese and filipino labor in the West and indigenous in the Great Plains, many immigrants, women, and children. The Civil Rights Movement and urban uprisings of the 1960s demanded that black workers have the same rights as others. To whatever degree this demand was met, racism was transformed.

The relative decline of the United States

At the end of World War II, the US had been dominant. To give a measure of US dominance: in 1953 the United States produced *more than double* the amount of steel, cement, electric power, and motor vehicles produced by any other industrial power (in motor vehicles the next highest production was by the United Kingdom, whose production was only 15 percent of US production). By the late '60s that dominance was quickly fading. Other powers challenged US hegemony—the Soviet Union challenged the US militarily, supplied more energy to Europe, and sponsored movements to remove former colonies from the Euro-American sphere. Japan and Germany were making inroads on world markets including the US auto market. New smaller producers—Korea, Taiwan, Brazil, Philippines—were beginning to build their own steel (and, in the case of Korea, auto) industries. More recently China has emerged as the US's main competitor. The US had some peculiar disadvantages: while at the end of World War II its capital stock was far more productive than others', by the end of the 1960s other capitalist countries were beginning to surpass US productivity. The US was in relative decline. Worker safety and environmental protection legislation also increased manufacturing costs. Increased competition and higher capital costs led to declines in profit rates (Anonymous 1971, Armstrong and others 1991; compare to Arrighi 2003, Bowles and others 1990, Brenner 2006, Glyn 2006, Parenti 1999, Perelman 2002 for similar arguments).

By the mid-1970s international competition, a sharp hike in oil prices in 1974, the decline in profit rate, and high wage settlements combined to create "stagflation," a high inflation rate combined with a stagnating economy and growing unemployment (US withdrawal from Vietnam ended labor shortages). Capitalists needed to make it cheaper to operate a business in the US.

US capitalists renewed their capital, replacing older technology with new, increasing efficiency, decreasing the need for labor. Capital renewal further weakened labor's position by creating surplus labor. In 1981 Reagan broke the air traffic controllers' strike. It was now open season to attack workers and unions. Paul Volcker, appointed by Jimmy Carter to chair the Federal Reserve Board in 1979, raised interest rates to several points higher than the inflation rate to induce a recession (which occurred) and increase unemployment. The ensuing recession had a highly unequal racial impact: while the unemployment rate for white workers rose in 1983 to 9.3 percent, for black workers it rose to a staggering 21.1 percent (Pew 2016: 26)! The suffering dampened workers' militancy: between 1965 and 1979 in the US on average 1,520,000 workers each year were involved in work stoppages of more than 1,000 workers; between 2000 and 2014 the average was 111,870 per year, a drop of over 90 percent (calculated from United States Department of Labor 2016: Table 1). As unemployment rose and strikes fell, bosses threatened to move jobs overseas or out-of-state. They cut wages and benefits. Some moved to rural areas in the North or to the South, others to Mexico or to Asia (virtually all electronics production). Rural areas, the South and non-US destinations had no labor unions, lower wages, few or no benefits, lower taxes, and few or no environmental or safety protections. Actual or threatened moves intensified workers' fears. Bosses demanded and workers made concessions to try to keep their jobs (often eliminated anyway). As a result of all of these attacks, unionization of workers in the private sector dropped from a high of over 30 percent in the 1950s to 6.4 percent in 2016 (Mayer 2004, US Department of Labor Bureau of Labor Statistics 2017b).

All of this worked—up to a point. Depressing wages and intimidating workers helped capitalists to survive and broke the remaining shop floor militancy. But the fundamental problems were not solved: the international economy is competitive; wage concessions in one company, industry, or country lead to wage concessions in others as workers compete for jobs in a "race to the bottom." The US is still in decline relative to other powers, particularly China.

The recreation of state-centered racial injustice

The policy changes described in what follows should be understood in the context of this continuing attack on workers. The historical role played by black labor and labor of children, women, and immigrants has come to be filled by workers without rights: women who work in exchange for an assistance check from the state (workfare and similar programs) or under the threat or reality of being cut off from assistance, undocumented immigrants, and people under the control of the penal system or with a felony conviction.

These groups act as an anchor limiting what other workers will achieve. For example, a woman whose husband (or father of her children) is in jail or prison has limited options; she is desperate for work under any conditions that may be offered. Others must compete for jobs with the most desperate and disadvantaged workers. Competition drives down all workers.

The crucial changes occurred primarily at the federal level. First, the welfare program Aid to Families with Dependent Children (AFDC, earlier ADC) was replaced by Temporary Assistance for Needy Families (TANF) in legislation passed in 1996: aid was limited to five years, and after two years of aid further aid was contingent on adult participation in labor. Second, immigrant workers became undocumented. New numerical quotas on immigration, particularly from Mexico, were imposed just as a massive US-Mexico guest worker program ended. Economic changes in Mexico cut wages and forced people off the land, leading to more immigration. So immigration was increasing from areas where workers had diminished access to visas. Third, by the mid-2000s the *rate* of incarceration in the US was *five times* the rate of the early 1970s. Nearly 40 percent of those incarcerated are black, and 60 percent are either black or latin. Black people are incarcerated at a rate *five times* the rate of non-hispanic white people. Federal and state governments passed laws creating mass incarceration.

What unites these programs is their effect on workers seeking jobs or currently employed. None was *advertised* as a program to create cheap, malleable, and vulnerable workers. Welfare reform was supposedly intended to reduce welfare-dependency and give mothers pride as workers. Immigration reform was said to take control of the border with Mexico and penalize employers for hiring undocumented workers. The changes in policy that led to mass incarceration were alleged to stop drugs, battle gangs, and limit street crime. All of these together have created thirty million workers without rights.

Welfare reform

TANF replaced AFDC in 1996 federal legislation. TANF limits lifetime assistance to sixty months and to twenty-four months unless adults work (these are the federal guidelines; states develop particular programs within the guidelines). The justification of the change had been prepared by theories—propounded by famous professors—that poor people in general and black people in particular were genetically inferior or culturally deficient. Newspapers and television news carried stories about the dysfunctional "underclass" harmed by crack addiction and government dependency, a theme championed by Charles Murray (1984). Politicians embraced some of these ideas, and their campaigns popularized them, Reagan, for example, promoting the myth of the welfare queen living lavishly on welfare fraud. The ideas gained hold, in one form or another, among racially victimized people as well as white.

What was the legislation's effect? When public assistance exists, workers have alternatives to work under the most exploitive and degrading conditions, a "back-up" in the form of public aid. Removing that back-up forces people into the labor market in desperation. They accept whatever is offered. Since there were no or inadequate provisions for child care under the new law, the law created additional strain on relatives who watch the children of working parents (students at Chicago State University will miss class looking after the children of a parent, sister, cousin or aunt). Under the reform more workers had little ability to say "no."

In *Making Ends Meet* (1997) Kathryn Edin and Laura Lein studied 379 low income single mothers, 214 receiving some assistance from the old welfare system (the study was done before the reform) and an additional 165 receiving no such aid but relying primarily on low-wage work. Of these women all but one relied on *other* sources of income besides either welfare or low-wage job. So before welfare reform, neither low-wage work nor state assistance was enough to enable mothers to support their families. The changes made under TANF made mothers *even more* reliant on low-wage work. In 1996 there were over 4.43 million families receiving welfare assistance. By 2009 the number had dropped to 1.77 million (United States Census Bureau 2012: 364). It is hard to know how much of this drop is a *result of* the change in the law (most people on welfare had always preferred to work and rarely stayed continuously on welfare more than two to four years). Still, the decline gives a rough measure of how many have been forced to labor under whatever conditions they can get. More recent studies of the law's effects confirm the hardship. Women must care for children but lack adequate income to do so. The law forces them to work (Collins and Mayer 2010, Henrici 2006).

Competition for jobs makes it harder to improve wages and working conditions. People who *must* work to survive can be used as strikebreakers. Employed workers are aware that many are desperate for work. So they are deterred from striking. Employers can use those desperate for work to replace any workers inclined to organize or rebel. In poultry processing and in border *maquiladoras* employers encourage or enforce short-term employment to prevent organizing (Stuesse 2016). A large number desperate for work has an "anchor" effect on other workers. It depresses struggle to improve wages and working conditions.

These changes recreate *racial* injustice. While in 2010 the ratio of non-Hispanic white people to black people in the US population was 5.3 to 1 (there were 5.3 times as many non-Hispanic white people as black in the US), the ratio of white to black dependence on TANF was 1.7 to one (United States Census Bureau 2012: 10, 353). Black families were 3.1 times more likely to be under the discipline of TANF than white families, a disparate racial impact, but the majority of whose harmed were white. (I couldn't find more recent comparable data.)

Undocumented migration[4]

After the Mexican-American War of 1846–48, current borders were established, mostly unguarded. People crossed it as they had for millennia. As California agriculture developed in the second half of the nineteenth century, big growers needed seasonal labor. They tried others but eventually settled on Mexican (and, to a lesser extent, Filipino) labor, recruited when needed, deported when not. In 1942 the official *bracero* program began. From 1942 to 1964 there were 4.6 million *bracero* entries from Mexico (since many workers came repeatedly, the number of workers was between one and two million). In some years the number who entered outside the program or any official channel of immigration ("illegally") probably far exceeded the number of *braceros*. After the end of the *bracero* program in 1964 Mexican workers continued to cross in order to work (mostly in California but also in Texas), often without documents. These undocumented workers worked alongside others in the fields. Efforts to *limit* immigration were opposed by businesses dependent on immigrant labor and by politicians representing those interests.

In 1965 national quotas were abolished that had been imposed by the Immigration Act of 1924. In 1968 a cap of 120,000 on immigration from the Western Hemisphere was enforced for the first time (there had earlier been no numerical limit). In 1976 the 1965 law was amended to impose a limit of 20,000 from any single country from the Western Hemisphere (Massey and others 2002: 43). So in eleven years legal immigration from Mexico went from being unlimited to being limited to 20,000. Later legislation further limited the number of visas.

Mexican immigration was caused not only by job-pull but also by deprivation-push. In the 1970s economic stagnation, which hit many countries, including the US, hit Mexico. A series of devaluations of the Mexican peso, starting with a floating of the peso in 1976, then further devaluations in the 1980s and 1990s cut real wages for Mexican workers. A structural adjustment initiated by US banks, the International Monetary Fund, and the World Bank, led to privatization of industries, elimination of trade barriers, and removal of supports for Mexican agriculture. Mexican grain markets were flooded with cheap US-produced grain (cheap because US production is capital-intensive), including dumping of surplus grain. By 1995 one-third of Mexico's grain consumption was of grain imported from the US. Life in the countryside became untenable for millions of Mexican workers, who either moved to Mexico City (metro area population over 21,000,000 in 2019) or other Mexican cities or left for work in the United States. US-based businesses took advantage, moving production to Mexico. Migration of rural workers to Mexican cities depressed wages there. Urban workers seeking to maintain or improve their living standard moved to the US for jobs: 1.8 million during the 1980s, 4.9 million during the 1990s, and 4.4 million between 2000 and 2005. As the border became more heavily patrolled, workers stayed rather than return to Mexico.

---

[4] This section is indebted for much of its information and analysis to Ruth Gomberg-Muñoz (2011), especially Chapter 2.

US businesses depend on undocumented labor. Workers in the following categories were estimated to be more than 10 percent undocumented in 2008: landscaping (28 percent), household servants (23 percent), garment labor (23 percent), agricultural labor (20 percent), animal processing, various manufacturing labor, building maintenance (all 19 percent), bakery workers (not retail) (17 percent), car washes (17 percent), construction (14 percent), taxi and limousine drivers (14 percent), fruit and vegetable processing (13 percent), restaurants and other food services (12 percent) (Passel and Cohn 2009: 32).

This labor force works under the conditions offered, in fear of state action. Businessmen dependent on undocumented labor and politicians who represent them ensure that no law *effectively* deprives them of this labor. Increased border enforcement and raids *never* rid the US economy of this labor but ensure that workers are terrorized and pliable. In the words of Ruth Gomberg-Muñoz: "[T]he opening of borders to trade and finance, accompanied by the 'closing' of borders to workers, has had the effect of illegalizing—but not stopping— transmigrant labor.... [B]order policies do not stop labor migration; rather they generate inequality by assigning illegal status to a segment of the global labor force" (Gomberg-Muñoz 2011: 34).

Jeffrey Passel and D'Vera Cohn (2009) estimate that 5.4 percent of the US labor force is undocumented, more than 8.25 million workers. These workers are constantly threatened by state action. Nearly 360,000 were deported annually 2008-2015 (United States Immigration and Customs Enforcement 2016). The undocumented are workers without rights and a boon to bosses, large and small, who employ them.

How mass incarceration creates workers without rights

Group stereotypes change. Well into the twentieth century, black workers (and people enslaved before 1860) were stereotyped as pliable and willing workers for simple labor, much as Mexican immigrants are now. Racist terror—black workers were lynched, beaten, or maimed if they rebelled—created the behavior behind the stereotype. Black workers worked long and hard under conditions usually worse than those for white workers. Black workers brought North to break strikes fostered the stereotype of black people as a "scab race."

During the 1930s, as union organizers (under communist influence) aimed to include black workers, stereotype and reality changed. Black workers joined and led the new industrial labor movement. To this day, black workers are union members at a higher rate than white. Militant black caucuses in the 1960s and 1970s destroyed the stereotype of the submissive and compliant black worker. But then who would work long and hard for low pay under whatever conditions were offered? Part of the answer, as we have seen, is undocumented immigrants and poor women (disproportionately black) who must support their children— vulnerable workers without assertable rights.

There is another part of the answer. Mass incarceration has transformed a large segment of the black male working class into workers without rights—at the same time it has done the same to a larger number who are not black males.

In 1925 the incarceration rate in state and federal prisons was 79 per 100,000 US residents or .079 percent; that represented a low point. Between that time and 1973 it fluctuated around a rate of 100, usually a little but not much more. In the late sixties the rate fell into the 90s where it remained until 1973, when it was 96 (United States Bureau of Justice Statistics 1982). Then it began a rise. In 2009 it was 502. To return to the 1973 rate of incarceration, four out of every five prisoners would have to be released from prison. (Michelle Alexander [2010] puts the point in this way.) If we add the people held in local jails, the total incarceration rate was 752 in 2009 (United States Census Bureau 2012: 218).[5] How did this happen?

While, as I will argue, mass incarceration is functional, we need to understand how it developed. With mechanization of southern agriculture and use of chemical herbicides eliminating much labor, many black people migrated north and lived in segregated neighborhoods. Early in the Kennedy administration black youth without jobs were called "social dynamite" and "potentially the most dangerous social condition in America today" (Hinton 2016: 29). Kennedy's assault on juvenile delinquency focused on education and job training. Lyndon Johnson's War on Poverty created Head Start and Job Corps. These programs saw urban black people as suffering from "social pathology." Black individuals needed to change, both in their skills and in their mindset, to take advantage of opportunities.

In 1964 first Harlem and then Rochester rose up in rebellion against the police. A year later Watts in Los Angeles witnessed the largest urban uprising in US history (up to that point). Echoing the calls of conservatives for "law and order," Johnson launched the War on Crime with the Law Enforcement Assistance Act of 1965. Police might provide a recreation center with a pool table and library. Cops would act as counselors to youth (114). Elizabeth Hinton writes, "White House officials and Congress championed a law enforcement strategy that merged the War on Crime with the War on Poverty, forging a network of social service and surveillance programs.... These urban interventions provided a foundation for the rise of the carceral state" (61). With each rebellion, policies became more about punishment, less about "helping" youth.

While Hinton traces the influence of northern liberals on the rise of mass incarceration, Michelle Alexander (2010) emphasizes the influence of southern racists. In the 1950s and 1960s southern segregationists shifted from defending "states' rights" and "tradition" to calling for "law and order." The targets were black protestors and insurrectionists and student radicals. This strategic retreat happened as most southern white voters shifted from the Democratic to the Republican Party. Richard Nixon emphasized "law and order" in 1968, opposing urban uprisings and student radicalism. Parenti explains, quoting Nixon advisor H. R. Haldeman: "'[President Nixon] emphasized that you have to face the fact that the whole problem is really the blacks. The key is to devise a system that recognizes this while not appearing to.' That 'system' was the war on crime and the criminal justice buildup" (Parenti 1999: 12). Calls for law and order were later embraced by Clinton, who put 100,000 more cops on the streets. Mass incarceration grew more rapidly in Clinton's terms than before or since.

Bruce Western (2006) emphasizes that *northern* white Democratic voters also shifted to the Republicans, based on opposition to northern civil rights struggles and

---

[5] No statistics going back to 1973 are kept for jails, but we can assume a similar rate of increase for jail populations. Rates have dropped slightly since 2009.

urban uprisings. Western's model suggests that working-class voters are driving policy; he omits capitalist interests. More plausibly, elites, through financial and institutional control of political parties, persuade voters to support policy initiatives created by capitalists and their intellectual and political allies. We will return to the issue of capitalist gains from mass incarceration.

Alexander shows how mass incarceration works, but many of us who live in or near all-black or mostly black neighborhoods see it often: young men assuming the position against a car or the side of a building. "Driving while black" (DWB) entered English as a name for a "crime." The Fourth Amendment was to protect citizens from unreasonable searches and seizure. The War on Drugs has ended that protection, particularly for poor black people: cars are stopped on the pretext of a minor traffic violation, for example, a broken or missing taillight. The officer requests permission to search the vehicle. Most folks say "yes," fearing consequences if they say "no." The same sort of "consent search" can occur—without the vehicle stop—on the sidewalk or on a bus: "May I speak with you?" says the officer. "Will you please put your hands up and lean against the wall?" he continues. Most do not realize that they are legally entitled to say "no."[6] The Supreme Court interpreted compliance with these "requests" (which sound like commands) as consent.[7] 95 percent, sometimes 98 percent or more, of these searches find nothing. But if they conduct enough searches, they arrest many.

These and related practices account for much growth in incarceration. Other factors—more common use of prison as a sentence and longer sentences—amplify the number swept into the system (Western 2006: 50).

The racism comes partly in whom they search. A 2007 Illinois study shows that black drivers are three times as likely as whites to be searched by state police (Northwestern University Center for Public Safety 2007: 10). City cops concentrate their searches in black neighborhoods, particularly targeting young males. The cause needn't be racial animosity; more probably it is lack of social power. Cops don't look for illegal drugs at a fraternity party at an elite university: sweeping up well-connected students would be bad for police. So poor people, particularly poor black people, are the main victims. Parenti summarizes: "[W]hile African Americans constitute only 13 percent of all monthly drug users, they represent 35 percent of all drug arrests, 55 percent of all drug convictions, and a staggering 74 percent of all drug prisoners" (1999: 239). Most growth in prison population is related to drug offenses.

Mass incarceration creates five groups of workers without rights: inmates who labor, people with jobs on work-release or in halfway houses, people on probation or parole, ex-felons (people with a felony conviction on their record), and the female partners or others who depend on men in the first four groups. Mass incarceration links millions of families, especially black families, to the "criminal justice" system.

Here are the 2009 numbers before a recent decline: 7.3 million directly in the system, 760,400 in jail, 1,524,513 in state or federal prisons, 4,203,967 on probation,

---

[6] Empirical evidence indicates that very few people, particularly women and young people, feel free to decline to speak with police who ask to speak with them (Kessler 2009).
[7] These ways of phrasing the police questions are borrowed from Alexander (2010: 65-6), as is the point about consent not being real.

and 819,308 on parole (United States Census Bureau 2012: 217).[8] Christopher Uggen, Jeff Manza, and Melissa Thompson (2006), using conservative demographic assumptions, estimated the 2004 ex-felon population at 11.7 million. Of adult males 12.8 percent are either current or ex-felons; 33.4 percent of black adult males are either current or former felons. Ex-felons are no longer under the direct control of the system but encounter a number of barriers—legal restrictions on employment, access to public housing, education, and other benefits. Many current or former felons enter the labor market as workers with diminished rights. Forty jurisdictions (out of the fifty states plus the District of Columbia) require parolees to seek employment, and similar requirements are made of probationers (Alexander 2010: 145). So if we add the five million on probation or parole to roughly twelve million ex-felons, at least seventeen million, mostly males, enter the labor market without rights.

The stereotype is that black males, particularly young ones, do not work, but while unemployment is high, most work. As recently as 1997 56 percent of prisoners had a full-time job at the time they were arrested (Uggen and others 2006: 295).[9] Others must have worked part-time. People who supplement legal income with extralegal income are in the labor force. So are many of the seventeen million who are either on probation or parole (likely high labor force participation) or are ex-felons (lower participation). These are particularly vulnerable workers, with very diminished rights, who often work the lowest wage jobs, some off the books.

The stigma of race amplifies that of felon or ex-felon: in a low-wage labor market, black job applicants with a clean record were no more likely to be called back or offered a job than white applicants who were just released from prison (Pager and others 2009). So while, for a white candidate, a prison term cut their chances in half, so did being black rather than white. In Pager's Milwaukee study a prison record cut a black applicant's chances of getting a further interview or offer by another two-thirds; this is the equivalent to one-sixth the chance of a white worker with a clean record (Pager 2007: 70).

Mass incarceration—especially its anti-black element—controls the most oppressed of our class, what Karl Marx called capitalism's "relative surplus population" (1976 [1867]: 781 ff.). After a brief post World War II period of expansion (and diminished international competition), US industry began a rapid decline in the 1970s. Capitalists abandoned much urban industrial production in favor of small towns and the South— where unions were weak and workers desperate—or they moved out of the US. Black urban workers were now relative surplus population. Mass incarceration was the method of control.

This control also disciplined the remaining workers. In *Capital* Marx wrote, "The overwork of the employed part of the working class swells the ranks of its reserve, while, conversely, the greater pressure that the reserve by its competition exerts on the

---

[8] In 2018 a bit more than 6.4 million were in jail or prison or on probation or parole (United States Bureau of Justice Statistics 2020). The number of parolees grew, but the number in each other sub-category declined.
[9] I have been unable to find data about labor market participation of ex-felons, http://www.noi.org/about-million-man-march/

employed workers forces them to submit to over-work and subjects them to the dictates of capital" (789). Mass incarceration increases terror in black neighborhoods. It reminds employed black workers of the consequences of deviation from capitalist order.

Despite high unemployment and high incarceration, black workers are central to the workings of the US economy, to our health care system, the industrial economy of the South, Amazon warehouse work, letter and package sorting and delivery, and urban transit, among other essential tasks. We should reject that unwarranted stereotype of black people as not working. Disproportionately black schools usually do not prepare black children for challenging and interesting work but for *essential low-status jobs*. Visits to or letters to or from carceral institutions, letters from parole or probation officers—these remind black workers of the dangers of non-conformity, the need to go to work and do their jobs.

Alexander denies that mass incarceration helps to control labor. She cites Loïc Wacquant:

> He emphasizes that the one thing that makes the current penal apparatus strikingly different from the previous racial caste systems is that 'it does not carry out the positive economic mission of recruitment and discipline of the workforce.' ... [Mass incarceration] views African Americans as largely irrelevant and unnecessary to the newly structured economy—an economy that is no longer driven by unskilled labor.
>
> 207

This common view is exactly wrong. Mass incarceration makes workers vulnerable and disciplines even more of us through fear.

Cheap food, cheap chicken

We need to draw together several threads. Black labor was central to the development of the US as a world power in the nineteenth century, providing the largest export crop, cotton. In the late nineteenth century and the first half of the twentieth black (as well as white and mexican) labor continued to create wealth in plantation crops of cotton, rice, and sugar as well as in mining, meatpacking, food crop harvesting and processing, and basic industry. Black workers were demeaned and vulnerable; they worked for lower wages and in worse conditions than others. Their vulnerability limited what white workers working alongside them could gain.

From the 1940s through the 1970s two things happened: first, black people, unwilling to be demeaned and vulnerable, demanded the same rights as others. Second, as the stagflation of the '70s developed, it became clear that the US was declining economically relative to Japan and Europe, as well as new rising economies in Asia and Latin America. The capitalists' response to the crisis was to weaken the position of workers, lowering wages, and attacking unions. But now it was harder to use black workers—disproportionately unionized—to undermine the position of other workers (although black youth were used as strikebreakers in that period). New sources of vulnerable labor were needed.

The three changes reviewed in the last section were the main sources of new workers without rights: curtailment of welfare, a huge increase in workers classified as "illegal," and a rise of carceral discipline. The transition from AFDC to TANF forced at least 2.5 million additional parents into the labor force; 8.25 million undocumented workers are in the labor force; in 2018 roughly 6.4 million people were in jail or prison or on probation or parole, plus roughly twelve million ex-felons, totaling over eighteen million under the discipline of the penal system (United States Bureau of Justice Statistics 2020). In total, more than twenty-nine million people labor or seek jobs without rights.

This section is about cheap food, particularly cheap chicken. Cheap food is central to social control. Many of us do not like our jobs but console ourselves at the mall or on the internet, buying smart phones, flat panel television sets, computer games, iPads, and other electronic wizardry. These keep us under control. But many of us are far from affluent: how can we afford it? Workers in Asia who make these things work long hours for low pay. And we don't pay much for food. Cheap food facilitates social control.

In the US people spend less of their income on food than in other countries. Comparing budgets for eating at home in 2015, in the US the figure is 6.4 percent for food and non-alcoholic beverages, the lowest percentage in the world (United States Department of Agriculture 2016b). When people spend less on food, this leaves more money for other stuff.

Cheap chicken is a central cheap food. In the US per capita consumption of chicken is roughly 80 pounds per year, turkey roughly 20 pounds per year. The four largest chicken processors control nearly 60 percent of the market. Roughly a half million workers are employed in meat slaughtering and processing (including poultry), but less than 3 percent are covered by a union contract. Real wages of workers have declined since 1976. Turnover rates are high, in some plants as high as 400 percent per year; the lowest estimate of turnover is 40 percent annually (Kandel 2009).

Employers encourage high turnover to prevent unionization. In her study of central Mississippi poultry workers, Angela Stuesse (2016) was told by union members that the new hires from the area replacing undocumented workers were unlikely to stay. "When I asked [union steward Patrick] Herring if this would be a problem for Tyson, he shrugged, 'No. They'll just replace 'em. That's what they want!' ... high rates of attrition do much more damage to organizing efforts than to company profits" (183).

Mississippi has 25,000 workers in the poultry industry, concentrated in central Mississippi, where three of the top five chicken producers (Tyson [1], Sanderson Farms [4], and Koch Foods [5]) all have plants. There are a few white workers left in the industry. It relies primarily on black and undocumented labor. Black labor is likely to be particularly vulnerable in this area, partly because of the tradition of intense segregation and subordination of black people in Mississippi and partly for reasons I have suggested here: Mississippi has the second highest (to Louisiana) rate of incarceration in the US leaving many black women without male family members to help support themselves and their children, and many men doubly stigmatized as black and ex-felon.

Poultry producers particularly like undocumented labor. In fact, as black workers organized unions in both poultry processing and catfish farming and processing, capitalists turned to undocumented workers to lower wages and reduce worker prerogatives.

Not only do many white workers harbor anti-black stereotypes which serve to divide poultry workers, but black and undocumented workers are also divided. Stuesse found that undocumented workers quickly accepted the racist stereotype that black people did not want to work, and black workers see undocumented workers as eroding rights they had gained. Undocumented workers, cultivating the self-stereotype as willing workers, may see black anti-management militancy as confirming anti-black stereotypes.

The growing presence of undocumented workers in the industry is used by management to depress wages and undermine working conditions, which can be brutal. Line speeds require workers in deboning to perform 20,000 motions per shift. Repetitive stress injuries are common, turnover high. Company doctors routinely misdiagnose or minimize injuries. Management tells injured workers to stay in the plant, even doing nothing; they don't send them home, which would require an injury report. Injuries are greatly underreported (250–61). Injuries to workers have a "crippling effects on entire communities," one town of black families having "'three generations of cripples' all of whom had worked in poultry" (265).

Since workers—particularly the undocumented—are often fired for getting injured, Bureau of Labor Statistics reports of declining injuries should be regarded instead as reflecting the growth of undocumented labor (263). Management's approach is to ensure an oversupply of workers, treat them as disposable, and replace injured workers with new ones. A high enough percentage of the most vulnerable workers helps bosses avoid workers' compensation claims.

Divisions between vulnerable workers—black and undocumented—undercut union organizing, lower wages, and speed up the pace of work. Central Mississippi is representative of wages and working conditions throughout the southern-based poultry processing industry. Workers in Arkansas frequently pee in Pampers they wear to work because management will not allow them to take a break to use the restroom; in Mississippi workers may pay a supervisor to use the bathroom (Oxfam America 2018). This is why chicken is cheap.

Chicken is not atypical in food processing. In a 2006 *Chicago Tribune* article Dawn Turner Trice described the vicious conditions endured by Mississippi Delta catfish workers, mostly black women. They were sexually harassed, and their bathroom breaks were timed; the bathroom stalls lacked doors. Workers had formed a union twenty-five years ago that won some rights, but subsequent importation of undocumented workers undermined gains workers had achieved (Trice 2006).

Beef and pork processing traced an arc from the brutal conditions at the beginning of the twentieth century (portrayed in Upton Sinclair's *The Jungle*) through the CIO period of the 1930s–60s that transformed meatpacking into a relatively decent working class job at union wages (Halpern 1997; Horowitz 1997), then to its current descent into conditions which are, arguably, as bad as ever. Under the innovation of Iowa Beef Packers and then later Cargill and ConAgra, beef and pork processing moved from the unionized urban centers of Chicago, Kansas City, and St. Paul to small towns in right-to-work states where unions were weak—in areas closer to cattle feed lots. Huge packing plants opened; workers are being drawn from the world's displaced peasants (including failed US farmers) into work at a blistering pace that reduced living mammals into the small pieces we see in the supermarket. Bodies wear out from the frenetic pace, long hours, forced overtime, six and even seven day weeks (Horowitz 1997, Human Rights Watch 2004). Workers are easily replaced.

Stoop labor harvesting crops is notoriously difficult. When Georgia enacted legislation prescribing harsh penalties for using fake identification documents to get jobs and empowering police to interrogate criminal suspects about their immigration status, growers could not find workers to pick their crops. The state government tried to use unemployed people on criminal probation as farm workers, but the probationers did not relish stooping to pick cucumbers for long hours in the hot sun (Brumbach and Henry 2011). Fruit and vegetable processing is not much easier. While it lacks the horror of slaughtering animals who resist dying, it can be fast-paced and repetitive, leading to repetitive stress injuries. If changes in meat and poultry processing are indicative, conditions in other food processing have also deteriorated.

Who are the workers in these industries? Certainly undocumented, likely many who are ineligible for government support under TANF, people who are either on probation or parole or are stigmatized by a felony conviction (no one seems to collect this information), and partners of the incarcerated. Management uses vulnerable labor to depress wages and working conditions in agricultural labor and meat, poultry, and other food processing. Depressed wages and brutal working conditions make food cheap. Because food is cheap, the rest of us can buy toys to give our lives an empty meaning.

What goes around comes around

The extra oppression experienced by workers without rights is a two-edged sword. One edge—the one just explained—is that cheap food means that urban workers with modest jobs can buy smart phones and other gadgetry. For those inclined to the language of "privilege" for intra-class inequalities (I am not) these could be regarded as privileges of urban workers. The other edge of the sword is that the extra oppression and exploitation of some workers lays the basis, politically, for attacks on the *less* oppressed workers.

In 1975 19.5 percent of US workers were in unions (Mayer 2004); in 2016 10.7 percent are in unions (US Department of Labor, Bureau of Labor Statistics 2017a), in private industry 6.4 percent; government workers are a labor stronghold with 34.4 percent in unions (US Department of Labor, Bureau of Labor Statistics 2017b). Unions can bargain for better pay. They can resist oppressive working conditions. They have often won important benefits such as paid sick days and personal days, paid vacation (sometimes as much as three or four weeks), and pensions which enable workers to retire comfortably. Unionized workers, primarily public employees, are the last workers with rights.

Unions in the United States are primarily "business unions," not "social justice unions" (as the old UPWA was). This narrowness lays them open to attack. Former Governor Scott Walker of Wisconsin can say, "We can no longer live in a society where the public employees are the haves and the taxpayers who foot the bill are the have-nots." In this way Walker appealed to the resentment of voters toward workers who may be (and may not be) better off than they are (Johnson 2015). In Illinois politicians invoke the stereotype of the incompetent teacher just collecting a paycheck while students fail to learn. The result is to eliminate teachers (disproportionately black) who have devoted much of their adult lives to working with disadvantaged children. So the years of disparaging people on welfare, attacking poor black women with the stereotype of having children to boost a welfare check, the years of talking about a "crack epidemic" scourging black communities and the need for a "war on drugs," leading to mass incarceration of young black men, the years of attacking immigrants as "taking our jobs" are followed by a period where the resentment of people about the deterioration of their living standards is mobilized to attack public sector workers who have (sometimes) slightly better pay, more employment stability, sick and vacation days, and pensions. What goes around comes around. The divisions in the working class, failure to mobilize against attacks on welfare mothers, immigrants, and black youth, lead to attacks on workers with more rights.

These attacks, however, have a racist edge. As I pointed out urban unionized teachers who are said to be incompetent are often black. And transit workers, health care workers, and teachers are often providing services to black and latin workers or their children. When these workers are laid off, services deteriorate for those most in need and with the fewest alternatives. What goes around comes around—and then back again in a race to the bottom.

The year 2020 and thereafter

The spring and summer of 2020 brought massive demonstrations against police killings. The torture-murder of George Floyd was recorded on a cell phone. Breonna Taylor was killed in her own apartment in a "no-knock" drug raid. Racist vigilantes chased and shot black jogger Ahmaud Arbery. Many more have been killed. Millions in the US and worldwide marched in anti-racist protests. These large crowds of black, latin, asian, and white people—particularly the young—should hearten anti-racists.

Police killings of our youth are a consequence of the carceral state, ever-present policing of working-class black and latin neighborhoods, and police attitudes regarding youth as a danger to be controlled—at all costs. While incarceration declined roughly twelve percent between 2009 and 2018 and may not rise again, it won't fall much either. As I write in 2022, Joe Biden, speaking in support of his "Safer America Plan" said, "When it comes to public safety in this nation, the answer is not 'defund the police,' it's 'fund the police'" (Biden 2022). Threats of jail, prison, beating or death have disciplined US workers and youth since the middle of the nineteenth century. Don't expect that to change.

It is hard to anticipate the future of immigration and illegalization or state control of immigrants. One possibility is that something like the old *bracero* program will be resurrected, where workers can enter on a temporary work permit. Registration with the government as a non-citizen (the government knows where you are and how to find you), like illegalization, disciplines workers. Further affecting immigration is dislocation in the world economy and surplus population, mostly displaced peasants or people in areas run by drug bosses, who flee to the US. Now most seeking to enter at the southern border are not Mexican and are seeking asylum. Misery creates instability. I don't know how this will develop further.

Part Two

Fighting and Ending Racism

7

Is Racism Interracial?

In order effectively to oppose and eventually to end racist social organization it helps to understand what it is. It is often called "white supremacy" or "white privilege," phrases which suggest that white people corporately (as a group) have power or that white people benefit from racism. Our historical chapters argued otherwise, on both points. Here we consider whether anti-black racism is something done by white people to black people.

Two models of racism

One model is that racism is interracial, acts by a member or members of one racial group against a member or members of another racial group; it is an *intergroup* phenomenon, where people act as members of *their* group in a way that excludes or harms members of another group. A second model is the racial harm model; racism is harm to people because of their racial identity, regardless of who or what inflicted harm, provided that their racial identity generally leads to greater harms (racial harm to a white person is not racism).

The racial harm model acknowledges racism that is obscured or precluded by the interracial model. First, agents of racism may not be white people generally. They could be a ruling class with power, as was obvious in the case of colonial Virginia; laws such as those forbidding a "negroe" from striking a "christian" were made by a small group of the biggest planters. Chapter 6 reviewed legislation that recreated vulnerability among workers, disproportionately black or latin. The second model acknowledges that a capitalist ruling class (not necessarily white) can be the main source of racism. When that class creates racial harms, it does not act as white but as capitalists seeking profit and stability.

Second, racial oppression occurs in segregated environments where black people are locally in charge. Those in charge may be the *immediate* agent of oppression and mistreatment. My years teaching at Chicago State University—top administration and campus security overwhelmingly staffed by black people—taught me this lesson. Assuming an interracial model of racism, many did not acknowledge that black people can be immediate agents of anti-black racism. Their not acknowledging as *racist* anti-black harms done by black people, it was harder to oppose them. We can acknowledge this without suggesting incorrectly that black people are racism's *main* source.

This chapter argues that the second model is more helpful to practical struggles against racial harms to black people. If we don't oppose *all* racial harms to black people, regardless of who inflicts them, then we give black people a license to harm other black people. Calling them racist and recognizing that anti-black racism can take this form strengthens anti-racist struggle.

The interracial model of racism

Imagine the following dialogue:

> **Latrice** I just saw the video of the black teenager shot by a cop last night. That was so wrong and so racist: he was walking away when the cop shot him in the back.
> **Kevin** How can that be racist? The cop was black.

Kevin is probably working with an interracial interpretation of racism. Granted, we could interpret Kevin to be saying that because black people do not share anti-black bias, the cop's actions were not affected by the perceived race of the teenager. If Kevin was right in that conclusion, it *might* not be an instance of racism, even on the racial harm model, provided that the race of the victim was not relevant to his likelihood of being shot in some *other* way besides the racial perception of the cop. However, when people say things like what Kevin said, they commonly mean that, whatever the cop's thought, it could not be racism because racism is interracial. It is (put simply) something white people do to black people.

Racism is commonly thought to be interracial

Most philosophers do not address carefully how racism is to be defined. Lawrence Blum (2002) gives definitions of racism and related failures, but these concern moral wrongs done by individuals. My concern is with racist *society* and individual acts as constituting it. Elizabeth Anderson (2010) gives a systematic account of racial injustice. Charles Mills (1997) uses the term "white supremacy" for what I have called racist society. That term avoids the suggestion of the term "racism" that our concern is the psychology and moral character of individuals (a suggestion Blum accepts). However, it suggests that white people as a group have power.

Anderson gives a careful account of racial injustice. (My discussion of Anderson assumes that what she means by "racial injustice" corresponds to what I mean by "racism.") She starts with group (or categorical) inequality. She writes that in order to understand racial injustice we need to begin "from a structural account of the systematic disadvantages imposed on people because of their race" (2010: 6). She continues that group inequalities are tied "to paired social categories, such as black/white" (7). She argues that there are social processes by which a social group secures an advantage "by closing its ranks to outsiders," a process which she calls (borrowing from Charles Tilly 1988) "opportunity hoarding" (7–8). Opportunity hoarding is practiced especially by *non-elites*, while elites reap advantages through what Tilly calls "exploitation." She modifies Tilly's account of group inequality but concludes, agreeing with Tilly, that "the central cause of categorical inequality is the exclusion of one group from equal access to critical resources controlled by another" (16). Call the excluded group A and the group that controls the resources B. If B *controls* the resources, then presumably B *causes* A to be excluded from the resources. She explicates the phrase "systematic disadvantages imposed on people because of their race" (essentially the racial harm model) by offering an interracial model, essentially that all systematic racial harms are interracial.

Relations between groups are modes of conduct by which one group acts in ways that affect the other group's interests (17). Group inequality is unjust "if it *embodies* unjust social relations, is *caused* by unjust relations (interactions, processes) ..., or *causes* such unjust relations" (18). But "relations" here must mean relations between *groups*, and the *injustice* must be *intergroup*, specifically interracial, injustice. Therefore unjust racial inequality implies unjust group *relations*, which in turn imply (in the case of anti-black injustice) the *agency* of someone white (at least not black) which unjustly *causes harm* to someone black. This is the interracial model of racism.

An interracial model such as Anderson's *can* be developed to accommodate the racism of the cop's actions in our imagined dialogue: the cop's killing of the youth is caused by unjust group relations; white people have shown unjust contempt for black life; this is an unjust group relation, and it causes the cop's action; because this white attitude is influential, especially among police, the cop's actions are caused by unjust group relations between white and black people. This narrative assimilates the racism of a black cop to an interracial model. He is, in effect, acting white, perhaps fearful of white supervisors or internalizing white racism.

There is no simple argument for rejecting the interracial model. Still, assimilating black people's anti-black racist psychology to the interracial model of injustice assumes that black people who harbor anti-black racial stereotypes and endorse anti-black social philosophies are thinking white. Are they?

Joe Feagin, a leading anti-racist sociologist, accepts the interracial model of racism. In his book *Systemic Racism* (2006: 217) Feagin writes

> Periodically, there is discussion in the white-controlled mass media about African Americans taking more responsibility for their own communities. This discussion is usually led by white Americans or their conservative black acolytes.

Feagin adds that black people have always acknowledged the need for individual responsibility. Why does Feagin characterize black conservatives who believe that black people take insufficient responsibility for their communities as "acolytes" of white people? An acolyte is literally a minor altar attendant or altar boy in a religious service, a very demeaning term. White conservatives are not called acolytes. Black conservatives are the "altar boys" of white people, according to Feagin. When someone as profoundly anti-racist as Feagin slips into demeaning black people, this is likely the result of framing racism as interracial: a black person who embraces a racist account of black inequality is thinking white and serving white people.

This is wrong. Over the years, in opinion surveys, black and white respondents have been asked whether lack of motivation is an important cause of disproportionate black poverty and unemployment. Years ago there was a large racial difference of opinion on this question, with white people much more than black believing lack of motivation is an important cause of black poverty. Recently the difference is not so much—between forty and fifty percent of both black and white people tend to think lack of motivation is a major cause. Yet black people, much more than white, believe that discrimination is an important cause of black poverty (Krysan and Moberg 2016). So many black people believe that *both* discrimination and lack of motivation cause black poverty. How are we to make sense of this?

Now (in contrast to the 1960s) many are pessimistic about an end to racism. Suppose you believe black people face discrimination but that this won't change. The remedy has to come from black people themselves. They have to "run faster." (This is the advice the professor/role-model in John Singleton's film *Higher Learning* gives a young track athlete complaining of racism.) A double standard—extraordinary efforts by black people—is the only "answer" people have. (People who deny the reality of discrimination—more white than black—don't think this represents a double standard, just holding black people to the same standards as white.) Because many black people are pessimistic about a non-racist future, they can only blame black people for any failure to succeed in racist society: black effort can change, not social racism. Black conservatism can have origins besides "thinking white."

In addition, black people sometimes *accept* racist views of (poor) black people. When Louis Farrakhan and the Nation of Islam organized a Million Man March[1] in 1995 around the theme of black men atoning for failure to take responsibility for their families and children, when Barack Obama gave a Father's Day speech to an approving black audience around the same theme of black male irresponsibility (Alexander 2010), and when Bill Cosby (2004) told a cheering NAACP audience that poor black people don't hold up their end of things, defended police shooting black people for theft, and ridiculed, among other things, naming practices of some black parents, black people were agreeing with a very racist anti-black view of poor black people: they create their circumstances through irresponsibility or stupidity. Racist culture, rationalization of one's own advantages, and pessimism about social change can similarly influence black and white people. Black people who adopt anti-black thought and actions needn't be acting white or fearful of white people.

The race relations model

The term "race relations" implies the interracial model of racism by reducing racism to a matter of relations between races. Stephen Steinberg's *Race Relations: A Critique* (2007) lays waste to the mysticism (a term borrowed from Oliver Cox) and deception implied in the term "race relations."

---

[1] http://www.noi.org/about-million-man-march/

Steinberg writes

> "[R]ace relations" is the language of the oppressor, whereas "oppression" is the construct—the rhetorical weapon—of the oppressed.... Whereas the race relations model assumes that racial prejudice arises out of a natural antipathy between groups on the basis of difference, "racial oppression" locates the source of the problem within the structure of society. Whereas "race relations" elides the issue of power, reducing racism down to the level of attitudes, "racial oppression" makes clear from the outset that we are dealing here with a system of domination, one that implicates major political and economic institutions, including the state itself. Whereas "race relations" implies mutuality, "racial oppression" clearly distinguishes between the oppressor and the oppressed.
>
> 16–17

As to solutions, while one model suggests radical social change, the other suggests something like marriage counseling, a "solution" that helps to perpetuate racial oppression. The use of the term by politicians and others involves the same evasions and deceptions. It suggests that two groups of roughly equal social power are having trouble getting along.

While Steinberg is good on issues of power, oppression, and the state, he drops the ball when it comes to identifying the oppressor, which he implies is white people, lumping together capitalist oppressors with people who are also oppressed. Steinberg breaks with the race relations model of racism but not with the interracial model.

White corporate agency

Consider the idea that white people corporately (as a group) are the *agents* of racial oppression. Charles Mills writes, "on matters related to race, the Racial Contract prescribes for its signatories... an epistemology of ignorance... producing the ironic outcome that whites will in general be unable to understand the world they themselves have made" (1997: 18, original is all italics). I shall focus on the idea that whites corporately *made* the world of racism. Recall from Chapter 1 the 1680 law that prescribes "thirty lashes on his bare back well laid on" for any "negroe or other slave" who may raise his hand to strike any "christian." The law was made by the Virginia legislature, composed of the wealthiest landowners. Whom would a "negroe or other slave" raise his hand to strike? The master? Not likely. More likely, a "negroe or other slave" would get in a quarrel with another servant with whom he was working or perhaps an overseer, and that quarrel could easily lead to blows. That small-time "christian" did not *make* this world of proto-racism; he is shaped by it. The intended effect of the law is to give the common "christian" a sense of entitlement and superiority against "a negroe or other slave." Accepted as applying to daily life, the law eventually secured this effect. (But you can imagine people refusing to report a co-worker.) What was true in 1680 Virginia was true in the post-Reconstruction South: the legislature was controlled by the planter class, in collusion with northern finance and merchant capitalists. *They* are the authors of racism. They passed and enforced the vagrancy laws that created a slave workforce for the mines. Today the mass incarceration which has replaced Jim Crow is a consequence of punitive legislation passed by capitalist-financed politicians and of racially targeted police stops (many by black cops). Mills is wrong about who made the world of the "Racial Contract." Thinking of "white people" as the oppressor distorts the historical evidence.

Steinberg writes, "[W]e have a subjugated people rising up through a grassroots movement to challenge a system of state-sponsored racism that amounted to what Howard Winant has aptly called 'a racial dictatorship,' enforced by legislatures, courts, police, and in the final resort, by the lynch mob" (2007: 16). It seems that lynch mobs—and, we could add, anti-busing mobs, mobs attacking black families that move into a neighborhood, and so forth—make non-elite white people authors of racism and hence could make it interracial.

In one case I know first-hand about racist mobs. I was part of an anti-racist summer project in Boston in 1975 that fought against anti-busing mobs there. The base of the mobs was South Boston, the neighborhood of the very poorest, most oppressed white people. However, this racism was organized by city hall politicians (Louise Day Hicks and others) who displayed the acronym ROAR in huge letters in the windows of City Hall. ROAR stood for Restore Our Alienated Rights and was the main anti-busing group in Boston.

The police were involved too. The first night I arrived in Boston the car I was driving was pursued by a racist mob. Here is what happened. Soon after we arrived, our hosts received a call that comrades had experienced trouble at a radio station in downtown Boston. Four of us volunteered to investigate, and I drove. We saw nothing unusual when we drove past the radio station. I drove around the corner and parked down the block. Two people got out to investigate. When they got to the corner, some racists recognized them from previous encounters. The couple ran back to my car, the mob pursuing them, got in, and I pulled away. At the end of the block the street was blocked by cars waiting at a red light. We were still being pursued. I escaped by driving over a curb, across some sidewalk, onto an intersecting street, and through a green light. As soon as I had escaped the mob, I was pulled over by the police. I showed the cop my driver's license, as requested. It was a Missouri license. "Why don't you go back there?" he said. Cops pulled me over and tried to intimidate me. They did nothing against the racist mob chasing my car. Race mobs in Boston did not represent white Bostonians generally: they also terrorized anti-racist white people

The Chicago race riot of 1919 did not come out of the actions of white workers from the meatpacking plants; it was organized in part by Ragen's Colts, an irish youth gang in service to the Democratic party—as well as other irish youth gangs. The Democratic Party establishment felt threatened by the growth of a black neighborhood on the border of the irish Canaryville neighborhood. (Barrett 1987: Chapter 6, Haywood 1978: 81–2)

Building a white front in the South required lynch-mob terror directed against any white people who might ally with black people. Moreover, lynchings were sometimes advertised in newspapers in advance and even organized as regional events. This organization would be beyond the abilities of people without elite connections and organizational experience and skills, not in the domain of white sharecroppers and poor dirt farmers. Poor white people who participated in these racist lynching festivals did a horrible thing. I make no excuses for them. However, it is a distortion to regard white people corporately as the authors of racism; as in Boston, racist mobs often terrorized white people.

Racism was created and is sustained by capitalists and their political servants through laws, courts, and police. Non-elite white people themselves struggle for survival, work, dignity, and a future for their families. They sometimes committed terrible crimes, as did the mobs of Irish immigrants who attacked and murdered black people in New York City in the 1863 draft riot. They too were victimized (though not as viciously) by the same capitalist system that attacks black people. They are potential and sometimes actual allies in anti-racist class struggle. They didn't create and don't control capitalism and its racism. White people are not, corporately, the agents of racism.

White benefit? Or unequal oppression and exploitation?

The interracial model of racism can be differently defended: even if it is agreed that white people are not corporately the *authors* of racism, it can be argued—Charles Mills has done this—that white people corporately are *beneficiaries* of racism.

Arguing against the idea that white people benefit from racism, I said I thought the phrase "unequal oppression and exploitation" better caught the duality of *inequality* (even extreme inequality) between the average conditions of black and white workers and *common exploitation and oppression*. Both black and white workers are often deprived of dignity and control of their own labor. Both often suffer from economic insecurity. White people do not benefit from systematic anti-black injustice.

"Paul, you are wrong: a white and a black applicant go for the same job. The white person gets it because of racism. The white person has benefited from racism."

A white person can benefit from a *particular racist act*. At the same time that act is part of a *system of racism*. That system drives down workers, white as well as black. So when we talk about benefit we must be clear about benefitting from a particular act or benefitting from a system. I am denying that white workers benefit from the *system* of anti-black racism.

Earlier we saw many cases where non-black people were harmed by anti-black racism. Maryland and Virginia non-slaveholders suffered economically as early racial slavery expanded. With the expansion of cotton plantations in the antebellum South, white people who did not own other people became trash, expendable, useless. After the Civil War the extension of cotton into Texas and elsewhere set black, mexican and white labor in competition; racist oppression of black and mexican labor drove down white labor. When racist terror intensified at the end of the nineteenth century, black labor became preferable to white tenants and croppers, who might resist oppression. When black workers entered coal mines, many white miners united with black seeing how "an injury to one is an injury to all." The southern wage meant lower wages for white workers; even white tire-builders in Memphis who "benefited" from job reservations had wages lower than their northern counterparts. Red-led unions defeated racist job reservations by showing how anti-racist unity benefited all workers.

Like me, Du Bois and many other authors I cited believe the conditions of black and white labor are linked. Jacqueline Jones's *The Dispossessed* reviews how black and white people became sharecroppers, sawmill workers, coal miners, cannery workers, and oyster shuckers. The lives of rural black and white labor were intertwined. She explains (1992: 77–8)

> The life experiences of poor white rural households overlapped in significant ways with those of their black counterparts during this period [1870–1930] and constitute a vital, if relatively neglected part of the history of the Jim Crow South.... The lien law that reduced sharecroppers to wage laborers applied equally to workers of both races, as did fence laws, vagrancy and contract enforcement legislation, and high personal property taxes.

Jim Crow voting restrictions "reduced white voting strength by an average of 25 percent (and black strength by 62 percent) throughout the South." Racism brutalized rural black people and held down rural whites. The oppression was *un*equal; that is what made it *racism*. Policies that oppressed black people *more* than white people, oppressed the poorest whites, and there were many of them.

The word "benefit" is relative and comparative, but not obviously. The hidden issue is "benefit compared to what?" In the case of benefitting from a particular racist act, the comparison may be obvious: A is hired rather than B because of racism toward B. A has benefited compared with the result of fair treatment where B would have been hired.

When we speak of benefitting from a *system* of racism, the comparison is not obvious. To what are we to compare a particular system of racism to discover whether someone or a class of people have benefited from that system? We have seen two kinds of comparisons: *temporal* comparisons, where the introduction or intensification of racism may harm or benefit particular groups; and *regional* comparisons, where the greater intensity of southern racism and greater divisions among southern workers harmed those workers compared with northern workers. In both cases anti-black racism harmed many workers who were not black. To these we can add the regional comparisons of Michael Reich in *Racial Inequality* (1981). Reich compared forty-eight metropolitan areas in the US to see how the degree of racial income inequality affected the income levels of non-black people. Greater *racial* inequality tended to be associated with greater inequality *among* white people and *lower* income for most white people. Reich's statistical argument supplements the historical studies in this book.

However, all these reasons concern how workers fare in *capitalist* society. For a communist the main reason is this: in a communist society workers can fully experience their humanity, working in order to benefit others in a system that can make sense to all of us, as we meet one another's needs (Gomberg 2007: Chapter 13, Kandiyali and Gomberg forthcoming).

While workers may respond to their own economic insecurity in racist ways (for example, supporting Trump), they don't benefit from a capitalist system that drives them down, although less so for white than for black workers. What should we call what we observe? Is it white benefit? "Unequal exploitation and oppression" better describes it.

Summary: racism is not interracial

The interracial model of racial injustice defended by Elizabeth Anderson is implied in the language of white supremacy, white domination, white privilege, and white racism. While it may be natural to understand racism as interracial, provided we accept racial identities (I argue for this conclusion in the next chapter), it is hard to justify doing so. The race relations model of injustice prevalent in sociology and in much common rhetoric is wrong. Neither white corporate agency nor white corporate benefit seems accurate; they cannot support the interracial model.

A racial harms model of racism

What is racism? I defend a model which is not interracial: in racist society we are called "black" or "white" (and by other names, but this book focuses on this central case). People assigned to different racial categories have different experiences. Still, we live in the same racist world and can be similarly (not identically) affected by it: people thought of as white can be victimized by anti-black injustice, and people thought of as black can adopt anti-[poor] black attitudes and philosophies and may exploit and oppress other black people. Here I develop and defend this model.

The definition of race and the meaning of race

A society is racist if and only if social inequality is organized by how people are racially identified and some racially identified groups are especially harmed thereby. By this definition the US is a racist society. Black people are incarcerated at a rate five times that of non-hispanic white people. There is overwhelming evidence that police are about eight to ten times more likely to stop a car if it is driven by a black person. Pretext stops and "consent" searches are concentrated in black neighborhoods. Black people suffer disproportionately in the legal system in part because they, on average, are less able to afford the best legal assistance, but poverty too is disproportionate because, for example, employers, including black employers, are reluctant to hire black workers, especially male workers. Black people experience double the infant mortality, higher morbidity, and shorter life expectancy. The evidence is sufficient to conclude that the US is a racist society by the definition given.

But a definition of racism does not tell us why it arose in the first place or why it persists despite three hundred years of struggle against it—in particular why, when it is defeated in one form (racial slavery, Jim Crow) it arises in a new form (mass incarceration). Those are issues of what I have called the *meaning* of racism. Race was created by a ruling capitalist class to supply a labor force that it could control. Capitalists have learned that it is easier to defeat labor insurgency if workers are divided. Nothing seems so effective at dividing workers as oppressing and exploiting them unequally and then marking the inequality in some way that is fairly obvious, by appearance (racial or gender), by dress (as with some Muslim workers), or by the language they speak. These ways of dividing, controlling, and unequally oppressing workers are virtually universal now in the capitalist world. They work: they not only divide workers against one another; they also create a hyper-vulnerable class of workers whose desperateness can be used to undermine conditions for other workers. This form of social control was invented in what became the US; its original form is anti-black racism.

The Rationalization Principle explains part of its effectiveness. (The Rationalization Principle states that whenever a society appears stable to the people who live in it, they tend to rationalize it, to think it is just or fair or at least better than any alternative.) Workers compare themselves with other workers who may not be as well off as they are. To the extent that the society seems stable and change does not seem to be on the horizon, workers may rationalize to themselves why they are better off by supposing that there is something lacking in that other worker (Lamont 2000). Thus, rather than uniting and opposing the capitalist boss, workers compare themselves to other workers and direct their emotional energy to blaming them, not just those worse off than they are but even those better off. This only works, however, if workers are oppressed unequally; unequal oppression is the material basis of racist social thought and of black resentment of white workers.

Racist social thought

Racist society was created and then re-created: the Virginia laws creating the status of "slave" and assigning it exclusively to black people and the laws designed to create contempt and separation from poor white people; the protection of slavery in the Constitution and its expansion in the first half of the nineteenth century; the creation of the sharecropping system for agricultural labor in the South and then of Jim Crow in response to the unity of the Farmers Alliances and the Populists; mass incarceration and undocumented immigration in the most recent period. With every struggle against racism, it has been recreated by those in power, not by white people generally. Racism creates huge racial wealth gaps and differences in the life prospects of the young. These material inequalities are the foundation of racist social thought.

How do we understand a world where race is such a significant marker of social inequality, particularly a world where, among residents of black urban neighborhoods, many are unemployed, few have well-paying jobs, and public schools offer little opportunity of a better life for the young? Are these conditions caused by ruling class oppression and racism, supplemented by indifference or hostility from many white people? Or is it the result of moral and other failings of the residents of those neighborhoods? The last idea I call "racist social thought." In this subsection I examine why racist social thought is so easily accepted. Capitalist-controlled media and their think-tanks often promote racist social thought. Still it would not have much hold on the rest of us if it did not coincide with psychological needs. These psychological tendencies may affect those identified as white and as black in similar ways. But not in every case. The principles I discuss are social identity, ego-defense, and rationalization.

Social Identity

Individuals typically identify themselves by social categories, as a male or female, as a Christian, Jew, Muslim, or nonbeliever, as an American, Finn, or Nigerian, as a spouse, parent, sister, or son, as an electrician, philosopher, teacher, or architect, as a conservative, moderate, liberal, anti-racist, or communist, and as black, white, latin, or asian. These categories are typically normative in the following sense: when someone identifies as a Christian, American, or parent, as examples, she develops a conception of what behavior is required to be a good Christian, a good American, or a good parent. If the identity is central to our conception of who we are, the norms are central to our personal morality, the behavior we expect of ourselves. Salient identities ground strong norms of conduct.

White identity developed in contrast to black identity. For people for whom a white identity is salient (it may be underground, coming to the fore when people choose mates, neighborhoods, and schools for their children) negative stereotypes of black people may be a reason for embracing their whiteness. White identity can also imply extreme individualism and self-reliance, grounding racist thought toward people who depend on government aid. Similarly, while black identity can be interpreted in accordance with various norms of what is implied by being black, it is often associated with a strong sense of loyalty to black people and a need to defend the group's reputation (Lamont 2000). So black identity can lead to hostility to ideas that would damage the group's reputation and hence to a rejection of racist social thought. However, other principles can operate similarly for black and white people.

Ego-defense

For successful people, whether categorized as white or black, ego-defense can lead to negative racial stereotypes. It gratifies one's ego to attribute one's success to one's own virtue and to attribute the failures of others to their failings. The tendency to think this way can translate easily into racist social thought when people are confronted with the disproportionate poverty and unemployment among black people: if my success is due to my own virtue, what explains their absence of economic success? This tendency may be as strong among successful black people as among successful white people; if so, it would explain the widespread conservatism and stigmatization we saw earlier from Farrakhan, Cosby, Obama and especially their audiences. On the other hand, those who are among the have-nots can defend their egos by supposing that the system is unfair or racist (if they are part of a disadvantaged minority), that they are the victims of affirmative action (if they are white and a have-not), that the successful are money-grubbers or unscrupulous or were born with a silver spoon in their mouths. I am not saying that all of these ideas are wrong, only that part of their appeal—for the relatively dispossessed—is that they can help to salvage self-esteem.

Ego-defense may also explain why even *disadvantaged but ambitious* black students I have taught thought negatively about high school classmates who dropped out or are not in college. Aware of racism but determined to succeed, it would enhance my students' optimism about their own prospects for success to think that those who fail failed because of not being sufficiently determined to succeed: "All I need to do is keep trying and not give up." This can easily translate into blaming less successful black people for their lack of success.[2]

Rationalization

Rationalization operates most similarly for black and white people, for advantaged and disadvantaged. The Rationalization Principle holds that when a society seems stable and change unlikely, people rationalize the social *status quo* by thinking it just. Rationalization may occur because it is disconcerting to suppose the system is unjust but won't change. As I argued earlier, much conservatism among black people seems a response to not seeing possibilities for change; the "solution" to racism lies within them: to advance within the system, despite the increased obstacles. Black people who think this way are in greater unity with white people who think the same way (but who are less likely to acknowledge widespread discrimination against black people).

Do we live in the same world?

Do people called "black" and people called "white" live in the same world? It might seem the answer is "no." How could someone white know the daily assaults black people experience because of how they are perceived? When I go to the mall or walk down the street, people think I am white and treat me accordingly. When my young black male friends go to the same mall, they experience something else. How can someone who is not black know what it is like? Yet we do live in the same world. We do experience different things, although our experiences track gender, age, language style, attire, and bodily adornments as well as race. In fact *individuals* have different experiences, but people of the same gender or the same racial appearance will have a lot of experiences in common. One way of coming to understand the world in which we live despite the biases of how we may be treated as individuals is to ask and *listen*. The world in which we live is a racist world, where our experiences differ because of how we are perceived racially.

Earlier I reviewed development of racist society and changes in the forms racism takes. Actions of the state were and are central to the creation and re-creation of racism. Current formally color-blind laws are enforced by agents of the state in such a way that black people, particularly black working class youth, are targeted. Supreme Court rulings that statistical evidence—even if the police stop only black people and never white—is never evidence of racial bias; the rulings protect police stops from legal challenge, cementing the racism of mass incarceration. So the abuse continues.

---

[2] Social Identity Theory may explain this as an effect of adopting an identity corresponding to one's *aspirations* rather than one's current status. See Reynolds and others 2013: 237.

It's about power, and in racist society black racial identity (often amplified by youth and other factors) signifies lack of social power: you can do whatever you want to that person and get away with it. This is the effect of the racial inequality that Elizabeth Anderson documents and analyzes. At Chicago State University, where I taught for most of my adult life and where the student population is overwhelmingly working class black people, two students—Willie Preston and Brittany Bailey—ran for student body president and student representative on the Board of Trustees on a platform of opposing the administration of the university president, Wayne Watson. They won the election by overwhelming margins. So Watson voided the election and tried to suppress the results of the election. (They were obtained over a year later under the Freedom of Information Act.) Later, on a complaint from the provost, Angela Henderson, allied with Watson, Preston was expelled from the university, and Henderson obtained an order of protection that he be barred from campus because, she testified, she felt threatened by him, implicitly invoking the stereotype of the violent black male.

All of this could be done to Bailey and Preston because they were racialized as black. Because they were "black," Watson and Henderson knew they could get away with it. Preston's and Bailey's being racialized based on their physical appearance made them liable to abuse. Watson and Henderson are also black. This is racism according to the second model of racism. I don't see how it could be racism by the first model unless you say that in some way Watson and Henderson are thinking white. They, like the rest of us, live in a racist world that makes black people subject to this sort of treatment from people with greater power, which Watson and Henderson had locally. Similarly the Watson administration targeted a black professor who opposed his administration (invoking the stereotype of the sexually predatory black male) in a way that they did not do with non-black faculty.

Racism is not interracial

In this chapter I have argued for the racial harms model of racism, according to which racism is harm that black people experience on account of their racial identity. It better fits the origins and recreation of racism than the interracial model. It explains why black people are still subject to so much abuse even in relatively segregated environments where black people (such as Watson and Henderson) are given authority. The racial abuse model, if accepted, would enhance the struggle against racial abuses of black people in these segregated environments—but not just in those. Yet most of us seem intuitively to understand racism as interracial. Hence the protest against the abuses of Bailey and Preston was much less than it would have been had Watson and Henderson been white. I speculate that Watson, sensing that this would be the case, was further emboldened to abuse Preston. Why do people so readily believe that racism must be interracial? The next chapter answers that question.

8

Alienating Race and Fighting Racism

"As long as you think you're white, there is no hope for you. As long as you think you're white, I'm going to be forced to think I'm black."
        James Baldwin speaking in the film *James Baldwin: The Price of the Ticket*

Several years ago at a conference on the legacy of slavery I had several friendly conversations with another philosopher. Shortly after the conference ended he e-mailed me: "I wish you all success, including in your efforts teaching philosophy to my people." I wrote him back: "Is it OK if I think of them as my people?" (I am socially perceived to be white; the philosopher and roughly ninety percent of the students I taught are thought to be black.) He replied with some of his thoughts on identity. I replied to him and he to me several times. Finally I wrote that not to think of my students as my people would be a disaster for me as a teacher. I had to think of them as my people.

We should alienate racial identities, which tend to create a racial distinction between "my people" and "not my people." Alienating racial identities makes it easier to accept people of another "race" as our own and build larger anti-racist struggle. Moreover, alienating race is helpful to identifying and effectively opposing racism, especially as it affects the most disadvantaged black people in the most overwhelmingly black environments. We should replace racial identities with class identities that can ground anti-racist class unity and struggle for a non-racist, non-capitalist society.

This chapter is about recognizing and fighting racism. Recognizing an act as racist can lead to more fierce opposition. Whether we recognize an act as racist is affected by how we think of our own identity. When we apply to ourselves the racial identities of racist society—black, latin, asian, white, indigenous—we tend to think racism is interracial. While accepting racial identities makes *interracial* injustices salient, it obscures racism which is *not* interracial. Moreover, acceptance of racial identities can undermine the broadest and fiercest opposition to racism.

The social psychology of group identity

Try an experiment in your imagination. A black customer approaches a sales counter at a major department store. A clerk is standing several feet away behind the counter facing at an angle where she could probably see the customer out of the corner of her eye. As the customer approaches, the clerk turns and walks away. Was the customer ignored because she was black? You may think, "Yes, probably." Does it make a difference to your answer whether you imagine the clerk as racially categorized as white or black (I did not specify the clerk's racial identity)?

When we apply a racial identity to ourselves, we are less likely to view the (possible) slight of a black customer as racist when the clerk is racially identified as black. If we accept those identities, we tend to think of (anti-black) racial slights as something a white person does to a black person, not as slights black people experience on account of their racial identity. But if a white clerk can slight a black customer because she is black, can't a black clerk do the same—even if it is less likely? (I am *not* suggesting that black people are the *main* source of anti-black racism.) Thinking of racism as interracial obscures some racism and make it harder for us to oppose it. Here I explain why our own acceptance of a racial identity influences us to think of racism as *interracial*.

In the 1950s the dominant psychological theory of group conflict was realistic group conflict theory (based on work by Muzafer Sherif and others 1988), that in-group favoritism, intergroup conflict, and out-group stereotyping arose from conflict of interest over scarce resources. Henri Tajfel's work tried to determine how much real conflict of interest had to exist to elicit in-group favoritism. The surprising discovery from his experiments and experiments by colleagues was "none." These experiments were called "minimal group" experiments because there was no basis for group assignments. Subjects still showed in-group favoritism.

This favoritism was elicited by experiments that asked, for example, a subject—assigned to group A—to allocate points among two other subjects, one identified as also an A, the other as a B. At the end of the experiment the points would be translated into monetary reward. There was a *tendency* (qualified by fairness) for As to award more points to As than to Bs, and for Bs to award more to Bs than to As. Among the choices allowed in some experiments was to choose between point allocations that maximally favored the in-group and point allocations that gave more points to members of both groups (an A could allocate 7 points to an A and 1 to a B or 19 points to an A and 25 to a B). Subjects have no direct interest in their allocations of points because they are allocating points to others. But if they assume that others will act as they do, they should maximize in-group points and hence their own likely payout at the end of the experiment. But they did not do that. To the extent that they deviated from equality (fairness), they did so in the direction of in-group favoritism (the 7 versus 1 distribution) rather than in-group point maximization (the 19 versus 25 distribution) (Tajfel 1981).

Why did they favor their group? In identifying with a group we establish a connection between esteem for ourselves and the status or rank of the group. Hence in favoring group members we elevate esteem for a group with which we identify and, indirectly, ourselves. Elevating esteem for self is in our interest (Tajfel and Turner 1979).

This is called social identity theory: for any group identity we accept, we tend to favor that group. If the theory is correct (and I will assume that it is, at least approximately), it has consequences for how anti-racists should fight racism.

If we accept racial identities, we tend to understand racism as intergroup, something white people do to black people (oversimplifying). The connection is this: A consequence of accepting a social identity is we easily think in terms of "my people, my group" and "not my people, the others." Thinking this way, we tend to favor our own group. Now suppose that—I believe this is true—we intuitively understand that people tend to favor their own group. Then most will think that black people will tend to favor black people and white people favor white people (even if we all try not to be prejudiced). Then we easily infer that anti-black racism is an in-group out-group phenomenon, the way that white people behave toward the out-group. This is how racism is commonly understood: people believe that black people can be racist toward white people—because they think racism is intergroup prejudice and discrimination.

"Paul, now you have confused me. You started with an example where you suggested that a black sales clerk could slight a black customer. Then you explain that social identity theory implies that when people accept a racial identity they tend to favor their own "race." Isn't there a contradiction between the implications of social identity theory and what you ask us to imagine, that a black sales clerk might slight a black customer and favor a white one?" It is confusing, and the reality is complex. Social identity theory implies that people who accept racial identities tend to favor the group with which they identify. But we are subject to *other* influences besides the influences of our social identities.

Specifically in the US black people are disproportionately poor, have less formal schooling, and, on average, work lower wage jobs or have higher unemployment. For reasons I have explained (the Rationalization Principle) if we do not rebel against our society, we have a tendency to rationalize why people are in a worse off position by saying, "It's their own fault; they deserve it." For people who identify as white, rationalization tends to *reinforce* effects of racial identity. For the white-identifying person a black person is "the other" (an effect of racial identification), and a black person is a member of a group that is at fault for being poor, is inferior (an effect of rationalization). For black people the effect of rationalization can *contradict* the effect of racial identity. Racial identity can cause them to identify with and favor black people. Rationalization can cause them to look down on and slight black people. (Think of Cosby and his NAACP audience from the last chapter.) Black people too tend to identify the black body with low social status. We are contradictory beings. Sometimes the Rationalization Principle, which influences the psychology of black as well as white people, will cause black people to act in a racist way toward other black people.

When we accept racial identities we tend to view racism as an intergroup phenomenon. So anti-black racist acts committed by black people can be more difficult to recognize. Acceptance of racial identities and the consequent view of racism as interracial can be harmful to identifying and opposing it.

What does it mean to accept an identity? Suppose we are a group of ten anthropologists—in physical appearance a representative sample of people from Los Angeles or Chicago. We come from another planet where race is unknown (go with me on this) to visit a typical large city in the US with the purpose of understanding the society we are visiting. We are looking around at the society, how and where people live, who does what work, who socializes with whom, and then we notice that, as we interact with others, the people we are visiting start calling some of us "black," yet others "latin," some "white," and some "asian." We don't understand at first, as these distinctions based on appearance are unknown to us, but eventually we realize that these people use these categories in the way they organize *their* society. *They* pay attention to these things and treat people (including us) differently based on how they perceive us. *We* find this way of doing things puzzling. What we don't do is accept these categories as applying to us. To us they are alien categories.

While the people we are studying may believe racism is interracial, we don't. We see it as a way of treating people based on their (racialized) appearance. We realize that people act differently toward others based on how their racialized appearance signals social power or the lack of it or invokes a racial stereotype. We recognize the effects of group identities in how people think of themselves and others. But we also recognize the effects of power inequalities and rationalization. In fact, as we carry our studies further, we discover that anti-black prejudice and discrimination are felt and practiced as much by black people in power as by white (Kirschenman and Neckerman 1999, Wilson 1996: 130–2). While this is racism—a response to the racialized appearance of another person's body—it is not an intergroup phenomenon. Rather it seems to involve racial stereotyping, something that does not have to be a reaction to a member of a racial out-group (the Cosby speech again). We see racism differently because we don't accept the categories our study subjects are using to discriminate. They are alien to us.

Now consider the consequences of accepting racial categories and applying them to ourselves. When we do this, we tend to view the world from *inside* the category, to think *as black* or *as white* (and so forth). When we do that, we tend to think of racism as interracial. In perceiving our social world, our assumption that racism is interracial can block awareness of *other* reasons people think and act in racist ways.

Here are two examples of how thinking of racism as interracial may block understanding of it: (1) Black people can accept racial stereotypes of black men as irresponsible fathers or black youth as criminal. The racial appearance of the body of a black person who is also poor may trigger a negative stereotype based on belief that poverty results from moral failings—a consequence of *rationalizing* the present social order. Black people can do this, not just white. (2) Those with greater relative power may tend to take advantage of those whom they perceive being vulnerable—here the racialized body acts as a symbol of social vulnerability (more on this soon). In both examples black as well as white people may engage in racial stereotyping and racist anti-black behavior.

These and other psychological tendencies can lead to abuses which are not interracial. When we accept racial categories, these other sources of racism tend to be obscured. Recognizing that people favor their own groups, we infer that racism is intergroup.

Anthropologists from another planet will understand racism more accurately than people who think from within racial categories. But what about anti-racist activists? I argue in this chapter that thinking like our anthropologists, striving to make racial categories alien, is helpful to seeing and opposing racism. Let us turn to that argument.

"Othering" people and racist social thought

In a speech before the convention of the NAACP in 1992 presidential candidate Ross Perot twice used the phrase "your people" to his audience: once in talking about black people suffering most when there are economic problems, again in the context of black people suffering from crime. People in the audience were offended, but why? Surely he was right on both points. But the language he used reaffirmed his white identity; to affirm an identity which does not belong to others offends them; for Perot, white people are "my people" while black people are "your people." It reminded his audience of centuries of white people affirming their whiteness to marginalize and discriminate against black people. It was insulting even though the *content* of what he said was not racist. What Perot did was to "other" black people. Consider two other examples.

The Racist Rally. You are shopping downtown, when, coming around a corner, you encounter a street-corner rally by a white supremacist group. Surrounding the rally is a crowd of black hecklers. Directing his words to the hecklers, the speaker says:

> You hecklers should give it a rest. You black people are your own worst enemy. You want to sit around all day and live off welfare at the taxpayers' expense. You have babies rather than getting out and getting an education. You expect the government to take care of you rather than getting off your ass and getting a job. You go around killing each other and doing drugs rather than contributing to society in a constructive way. When you have a little money you blow it on fancy rims or expensive purses or clothes rather than healthy food or paying the rent. Before you people complain about racism, you need to look at yourselves and stop causing yourselves problems.

First the speaker "others" his black audience, asserting his whiteness in contrast to the audience's blackness. This othering is carried by the word "you." But he also articulates a view of black people which attributes their social position to moral failings. These ideas would rationalize the current society, implying that it is not racially unjust, but that the bad social outcomes black people experience are their own fault. This is racist social thought combined with white identity. Now let's try another story.

The Barbershop. You wander into the barbershop on a Friday evening to get a haircut. One man is complaining that white people just will not give a black man a chance. Another customer replies:

> C'mon, man, we black people are our own worst enemy. We want to sit around all day and live off welfare at the taxpayers' expense. We have babies rather than getting out and getting an education. We expect the government to take care of us rather than getting off our ass and getting a job. We go around killing each other and doing drugs rather than contributing to society in a constructive way. When we have a little money we blow it on fancy rims or expensive purses or clothes rather than healthy food or paying the rent. Before we complain about racism, we need to look at ourselves and stop causing ourselves problems.

For those who may not be in the know, this sort of talk in all-black environments (a barbershop, a college lunchroom) is not uncommon, and while some may disagree, few call it racist. The speaker's words combine racist social thought with black identity—carried by the word "we." My point is this: the very same ideas *appear* different depending on the identity (especially the affirmed identity) of the speaker. But the racism is the same.

People who vigorously affirm their black identity may feel more at liberty to disparage black people, that is, to endorse racist social thought or to commit racist acts. Alienating race helps us to identify and oppose racist social thought and material injustices. If we fail to alienate race, we may, thinking racism is interracial, think that thought or actions must be held or done by a white person to be racist. Someone's perceived identity may obscure the content of the thought or action.

"But, Paul, the speaker in The Barbershop intends his remarks constructively while the speaker in The Racist Rally is vicious and hostile to black people." There is certainly a difference in emotional tone, but the conclusion that the speaker in The Barbershop intends his remarks constructively is unwarranted. People who say these things may be asserting their superiority and putting on a show. (Constructive remarks might take an *individual* aside and try to help that person to break a drug addiction or find work.) Our speakers assume that people have enough income, but lack of income and wealth is a much larger problem. Racist social thought locates black disadvantage in moral failings, as the speakers in The Barbershop and The Racist Rally both do. Acceptance of racial identities *obscures* the racism in The Barbershop while it *highlights* it in the Racist Rally.

Seeing and fighting racism when black people are in charge

In predominately black segregated environments racism can occur at the hands of black agents. I will describe instances of such racism. These environments are crucial in the fight against racism. The greatest racist oppression is experienced by black people most deeply cut off from elite (mostly white) environments—being cut off itself makes life harder. Those most cut off and most oppressed must *lead* the fight against racism.

I concentrate on an incident in the early 1990s at Chicago State University. I have changed the names because so many years have passed. I joined protests of this incident. Because of that I knew some participants well, and they explained in detail what happened. In the last chapter I mentioned some recent egregious similar incidents. The incident that follows illustrates further how racism may occur in majority-black environments.

Calvin Miller was sitting with four other Chicago State University students around a study table in the university library. Calvin, a 40-year-old student with epilepsy, had sat down to help Reginald Jackson with an English paper. Samuel Howard, a campus police officer, and James Phillips, a student, started "playing the dozens" (an exchange of insults often focused on people's mothers). The exchanges between them became loud and vulgar, and Phillips seemed to be getting the better of the exchanges. Samuel Howard left.

Howard soon returned with Pamela Bonner, another police officer. She said there had been a report of a disturbance in the library. (I later was told that someone had called campus police, complaining of the disturbance Phillips and Howard were making. If so, Howard "played dumb.") Howard asked everyone around the table to show their university IDs. All complied. Phillips continued to curse Howard even more vigorously. Except for Calvin Miller the students were young, healthy, relatively big, and athletic. Miller was older, smaller, and slighter. Holding the student IDs, Howard asked Miller, "Do you go to this school?" Miller was angry and challenged Howard: "Yes. What's it all about?"

Howard started to beat him. I speculate that Howard was humiliated and angry at Phillips's verbal assault and picked the person who had challenged what he was doing and an easier target. The beating lasted several minutes, slamming Miller's head into the wall, making a large hole. Miller started having seizures. The students who had been there and others who heard the commotion protested.

Miller was taken to jail where he was strip-searched and charged. (The charges later were dropped, a common sequel to police beatings.) When Terence Turner (one of the students at the table) and Miller protested the beating to the office of the university president, they were told by Carmelita Smith—executive assistant to the president—that they should drop the issue: "Chicago State is a black university, and a lot of people would like to see us fail. If this was a white university like UIC [University of Illinois at Chicago] it would be swept under the rug." Samuel Howard was never disciplined.

All the people I have mentioned are socially identified as black. Calvin Miller was beaten because he was black. It was a racist beating. A white man of similar age and attire (neat and conservative) probably would not have been beaten under the same circumstances.

What would likely have stayed Howard's hand had Calvin been perceived as white? The median white family has many times the financial assets of the median black family. White people are more likely to be connected by family and friendship to people with money and some political influence. Then if you add the university setting, Howard might intuitively fear that Calvin is related to a professor. Fear of social power can make cops and others more respectful of people perceived as white. Seen as lacking social power—connections and financial resources—black people may be subject to abuse. They "ain't shit," beaten because they are beatable: a person can beat them and get away with it.

I am not saying that there were no other reasons why Calvin was beaten. He was smaller and hence less a physical threat. He challenged Howard, which provoked the beating. Black people are rarely beaten *solely* because they are black (it does happen). Other factors may be at work. But race is a factor too. Identified as black, Calvin was more likely to be mistreated.

Contempt for black people is pervasive in racist society. Black people are not immune from this attitude. Contempt (or lack of respect) grows from the correct perception that, generally, black people have less social power, have less economic resources and political connections to protect themselves. Many immigrants and poor white people do as well. This element of racism—contempt based on perceptions of powerlessness derived from appearance of one's body—illustrates the close alliance between the social psychology of racism and the social psychology of contempt for the working class. A person perceived as white but whose dress identified him as homeless might be beaten in the same situation. In Calvin's case it was the racial appearance of his *body* that did the work. Perception of powerlessness based on racial identity subjects black people to abuse. This is racism.

That does not mean that the police officer, who may well be black, harbors hatred of black people (even if he has contempt for black people). He may be angry at his spouse or at his supervisor or (as I speculated in the case of Samuel Howard) at another person. But he will beat or abuse the one whom it is easiest and safest to attack. Calvin's blackness signaled his (likely) inability to retaliate to the beating or abuse. So poor black people or working class black people, particularly youth, are often subject to beatings or other abuse on account of their racial identity. More advantaged black people (Henry Louis Gates, Jr.[1]) who are not recognized as being more advantaged may be similarly attacked; their racial identity, which is associated with a group that in general lacks social power, causes them to be treated on that basis rather than on the basis of their actual social power.

Nor should we think that in beating Calvin Miller Samuel Howard was "acting white." To think this is to import the interracial model of racism into a situation where the injustice was not intergroup injustice.

Racism here is based on the racialized body as signaling lack of social power. This racism is different from the racist social theory that arises from the rationalization principle. The workings of the rationalization principle may cause some people, reflecting on disproportionate black poverty, to assume that lack of ambition or moral failings explain why many black people live in poor neighborhoods, attend poor schools, work low wage jobs, or are unemployed. The racism represented by the actions of Samuel Howard does not arise from intellectual reflection. Surrounded by racist practices, people unthinkingly adopt these as norms.

While there was protest against the beating of Calvin Miller, protest was limited because Samuel Howard, Carmelita Smith, and the president of CSU, Deborah Cramer, were black. Accepting racial categories and thinking from *inside* them, many thought racism must be interracial, making it harder to perceive the racism of the beating.

Racial solidarity with black administrators further blunted protest. Race-consciousness among direct victims of racism can entrench racism. The South African apartheid government used African police in the townships. In the US, after the rebellions of the 1960s, black police, police chiefs and mayors held local power in cities with large black populations. This practice helped to blunt protest against the continuing abuses experienced by black residents of many segregated ghetto neighborhoods. At one time it had been easy to identify racism as the attitudes and practices of white people that showed contempt for black people. Now, when many black workers and youth deal with black officials in positions of power, race-consciousness makes it difficult to see and oppose racism.

---

[1] Harvard professor Gates was arrested when trying to force open the front door of his Cambridge home (it was jammed).

Accepting racial categories as applying to ourselves and others, we see racism as being "white racism," something unjust done to black people by white people, as an *interracial* phenomenon. In "black" environments r*ace*-consciousness defeats ra*cism*-consciousness. If we think "race" is what is important, that it represents some real ground of commonality and loyalty, anti-black injustice at the hands of black people will be less visible to us. When a black cop beats a black man, we may not recognize it as racism; we may tend to think that the race of the victim was not a cause of the beating. Protest is more muted, and racism thrives.

Disadvantaged black workers and youth have the most intense experience of racism. Their racial identity is amplified by dress, speech, and manners that reinforce the racial message about their class status. They often inhabit intensely segregated environments where enforcement of injustice is typically at the hands of black people. A student at Chicago State once said to me in class that, growing up, he had never experienced any racism. When I asked him to say more, he said he had never been around any white people. Although the conditions of his life were intensely racist, he did not recognize them as such.

This last story raises a further issue: so far we have discussed seeing and fighting particular racist *acts* where agents are racially identified as black; we have not discussed the *institutional* racism of black-led institutions. Students at Chicago State cannot go into the bookstore to select their books for the coming semester. They hand a copy of their schedule to the clerk who then goes and selects the textbooks for them. Students have a long wait because only a few clerks are hired. This wait could be avoided if students were allowed to get their own books. But bookstore management complains of theft. The bookstore can save itself time, effort, and cost of finding an alternative method of dealing with theft by simply not letting students come into textbook aisles. Given this racist policy in place, it can save money by not hiring enough clerks to make the student wait times shorter.

"Well, doesn't the bookstore have a right to make a profit?" Providing services to low-income people in a respectful way may not be profitable. Part of the experience of racism is that low income black people experience poorer services and pay more for them. Racism is deeply woven into the economics of capitalism—it is institutional.

At Chicago State the classrooms were often not clean, nor were the chalkboards or whiteboards. That seems a trivial example compared with the beating of Calvin Miller. True, but we may fail to appreciate institutional racism in segregated black environments. Everything tends to be a little worse, a little neglected. There are many small slights: long lines for financial aid, long lines at the bookstore, no student access to textbook aisles, light fixtures missing, broken plumbing and missing toilet paper holders in the bathrooms, broken doors, locked classrooms, stained ceilings, filthy air ducts, non-functioning elevators, dirty whiteboards and erasers, and no chalk at the chalkboards. About each one you can say, "What's the big deal?" Any one or two of them could be on any campus. But they add up. They demoralize teachers and students, conveying a constant message that we "ain't shit." If you pick on one instance, people can say that it is not very important. But the negative message these conditions convey is important. It is important to struggle against these racist conditions, not accept them. Given segregation, some students may not recognize them as racism, having no experience with conditions at more elite institutions.

In segregated black-led institutions someone's racial identity is not going to tell you where they stand on issues of racism. Black people who administer racist institutions have to be opposed, and the injustices have to be identified as what they are, racial. The alternative would be to curtail the struggle against racism at segregated, largely black institutions. Perhaps most important, black workers will lead class struggle in the US and revolutionary struggle as well. The most oppressed black workers will be disproportionately in the lead. So what happens at schools like Chicago State and other segregated black institutions is critically important to class and revolutionary struggle.

In the effort to oppose racism—the ways in which people identified as black are harmed thereby—it helps to alienate race. Racial categories are necessary for practical struggles only in an alienated way: to identify how imposed racial categories are part of a system of oppression.

Suppose anti-racists in segregated black environments call the racism of black people with local power "racist." Suppose they organize against them on the basis that they target black people for mistreatment. These are more likely to happen when activists strive to alienate race. Then they can more readily perceive the racism of black people in charge. Moreover, another consequence of alienating race, they will not exclude or marginalize non-black people in anti-racist struggle. They will not think of anti-racist struggle as a "black struggle." The result would be inclusive, powerful anti-racist struggle. It is possible—I believe likely—that movements against racial injustice where black people are in charge will open the door for wider struggles against racism.

Movements at black-led institutions are likely to be disproportionately black-led (it would be odd if they are not). They can be inclusive and nevertheless deeply anti-racist, struggling against the subtle slights and unconscious racial framing that can poison relations in multi-racial movements. (In Chapter 5 we saw how the CP sought to deal with these slights.) At the same time they don't have to emphasize racial identities of people in the movement in a way that makes a broad movement impossible.

Seeing and fighting racism when non-black people are in charge

Racism looks different where few or no black people are in charge. Here racism tends to come from white people who ignore a black person's professional qualifications, educational background, middle class attire and manners, or other marks of social status. Laurence Thomas (1990) brilliantly describes being surrounded by security police at a "midwestern university," picked out as suspicious purely because of his racial identity, despite the markers of being a professional.

Injustices discussed in this section come from people perceived racially as not black; the interracial model of racism makes the injustice *more* salient. In a predominately black institution such as Chicago State there is a tendency for racism to pervade everything, a thousand slights or inconveniences. In a "white" environment anti-black racism takes a different form—being *picked out* for treatment *different* from others. This stings!

That doesn't mean fighting it is easier. The interracial model can imply that this is a black concern, that it is not the special concern of white people or, at my present institutional home, white, mexican, and asian (black students being roughly two percent of students). When people think they are white (or latin or asian), they are less likely to feel black oppression as their own oppression and oppose it actively. They are more likely to buy into anti-black racial stereotypes. Black students at my current campus have been subject to racist attack. Protest came mostly from black students.

I do not oppose all identities. Working class identity builds class solidarity. Particular identities such as parent or sister can be integral to our sense of self. Racial identities are harmful to fighting against racism, undermining anti-racist solidarity. Alienating race makes it easier to include *all* who would oppose racism in the anti-racist movement.

White identity is the most vicious. Many who identify as black interpret black identity as resistant of racial oppression and as expressing racial solidarity against it and for mutual aid. White identity does not have a parallel anti-racist meaning. While white identity is "normative" in many situations—not mentioned, but taken for granted—it can be affirmed in an underground fashion, as when someone might say, "I am an American!" meaning "a white man." If the distinctive affirmation of blackness can often mean "do not oppress me," affirmation of whiteness is affirmation of superiority. Whiteness was created to make a distinction between and to rank (originally) black and white workers (enslaved or free). Whiteness persists for the same reason. Thus Baldwin's epigram that opened this chapter.

Response to the 2020 murder of George Floyd showed the potential of working-class unity. In Houston alone 60,000 marched in a funeral march for him—in the middle of a pandemic! This march brought together young people of our class—black, white, asian, and latin.

The arguments of these last two sections are connected. The most forceful and massive movement against racism will develop as black people in segregated mostly black environments call the actions of black people in power racist and invite white people to join the struggle and as white people alienate white identity and regard the struggles against anti-black injustice as struggles for "their" people. While I have not emphasized this point, it is also true that other victims of US racism—people identified as latin, asian, arab, and indigenous—also must recognize that these categories, to the extent that they were created by and sustained by capitalist society, are ways of dividing workers and oppressing and exploiting them unequally. *All* racism, no matter which group is the target, must be opposed in a united struggle. The fight against racism is the key to forging unbreakable working class unity. Alienating racial identities—all of them—strengthens anti-racist struggle.

Alienating race

I have sketched what I mean by finding an identity alien to us—the anthropologists from another planet. Unlike the anthropologists, we have learned racial identities. For us, this means we must alienate race. Understanding racial categories as instruments of oppression can lead us to alienate race, widening and strengthening anti-racist struggle. Alienating race does *not* mean denying the reality of race in organizing inequality. It is meant to have the *opposite* effect, to sharpen perceptions of and opposition to the ways that racial categories are used to create inequality. Racial inequality is central to inequality within the working class. To alienate race is to alienate capitalism: racist society is not *my* society. It is the society in which I find myself and to which I set myself in opposition (the anthropologists from another planet become activists). Opposition to capitalism is defended in the last three chapters.

Alienating race is a *process*. It may help to understand this process if I review other identities I have alienated, to see similarities and differences involved in alienating race.

I am not sure when in my childhood that I "discovered that I was a jew."[2] At a Cub Scout dinner about the age of seven or eight someone called me a "damn jew." It hurt my feelings. My father was born into a Jewish family but never identified himself as a Jew in religious practice. My mother was raised vaguely Protestant and liked Judaism. I was sent to a Reform Jewish Sunday School for two years, but when I was eleven my father pulled me out and sent me to an Ethical Culture Sunday School. That only lasted a year. I eventually "realized" that I had a "Jewish name." That was enough to make me a jew.

But am I a jew? In high school and college I thought it acceptable to tell jokes invoking anti-jewish stereotypes because I was a jew. (I stopped telling such jokes and took antisemitism more seriously when I became active against racism in the 1960s.) In Jewish tradition whether one is a Jew depends on whether one's mother is Jewish. My mother liked Judaism and was certainly welcomed at (liberal Reform) Temple Emmanuel in San Francisco, but she never converted as far as I know. So, to most Jews, I was not a Jew. But to an antisemite, I was a jew.

I decided to handle the question in this way: if you are an antisemite, then I am a jew; otherwise not. As to the "otherwise not," it seemed to me that since I was not Jewish in belief or religious observance or in my culture (in college I met students who really were Jewish in culture, coming from homes where Yiddish was spoken and whose family members had died in the Holocaust), there was no reason to call myself a Jew. Had I been in Europe during World War II I would have been considered a jew, and that was enough to cause me to identify strongly with European jews in the Holocaust. But it was not enough to make me call myself a jew, since I also identified increasingly with black people who had fought racism or been its victims. As to my decision that if you are an antisemite, then I am a jew—that seems obvious: I am what the antisemite means by "jew," and he does not care about my convictions or culture or my maternal ancestry. He cares about my "race."

This, then, is what I mean by alienating an identity: I came to realize that I was jewish only in the sense that an anti-jewish racist would call me a jew. I was not a jew. What I was *called* could not determine what I *am*. But that does not mean that I lessened my opposition to antisemitism, and I would *never* deny to an antisemite that I am a jew. But my opposition to antisemitism is grounded in my being an anti-racist.

---

[2] The word "jew" here was intended racially, hence lower case. By Haslanger's (2000) criterion this is a racial category, referring to suppositions about the *religious traditions* of one's supposed ancestors.

For me alienating a jewish identity was easy because the criterion used by Jewish tradition was in conflict with the judgment of my identity based on my paternal ancestry. I had to decide. In most cases we don't realize that we *can* decide on our own identities, at least when it comes to racial identities.

There is a qualification here. I said I have alienated a jewish identity, but whether I am a jew is contextual. In a context where antisemitism is in play, then I am a jew because I am what the antisemite means by a jew. That is true generally of identities, even alienated ones: what you are does depend on context. But, when it is up to me to decide what I am, I am not a jew. Because of pervasive racism, black identities are much harder to alienate; black people are constantly reminded that they are "black."

I came to alienate American identity even though every social voice said I was an American.[3] Alienating American identity, for me, was grounded in my political thinking. In the summer of 1967 I first actively opposed the Vietnam War. We went door-to-door asking people to sign a petition against the war. Some of the people I talked with agreed that the war was wrong but insisted that we had to "support our boys." At first I questioned what it meant to "support our boys": did we support them by supporting the war or by opposing it? I put out a leaflet (the first I had ever written) attacking the use of that phrase to justify supporting the war. The point of the leaflet was that "supporting our boys" meant opposing the war. I was very proud of the leaflet. But another anti-war activist criticized it: he told me that I had pandered to patriotism and racism against the Vietnamese. The phrase "our boys" carried the implication that we should care more about "our people" than about "those people." I had accepted the idea that a Vietnamese life was worth less than the life of a US soldier. He said I should challenge that idea, not go along with it. I couldn't disagree.

My active opposition to the war forced me to confront the question of who were "my people." Were Americans my people in a way that the Vietnamese were not? I did not believe that. I did not identify with US actions in Vietnam. Was *my* country doing these things? I cannot say when I stopped using "we" for the US and its actions, when I stopped identifying myself as an American. The word "we" is the most profoundly political word in the English language. Much of how we think politically depends on who we think the "we" is. As I re-read US history, the European invasion and continuing genocide of indigenous peoples, the history of US interventions around the globe and of the origin of slavery, and as I came to understand the continuing racism against people of African descent, indigenous peoples, and others, I came to believe that racism and imperialism were central to the US national project. I did not identify with that project. I stopped thinking of myself as an American.

I have a US passport, which I need if I am to travel outside the US. When a form requires it, I will check the box "native born US citizen" because legally I am a citizen. So in some contexts I am an American. But I have alienated an American identity. I don't use the word "we" for the US. When others use it, I notice their use. There is a gulf between us. We understand differently who we are and perhaps what it means

---

[3] I here use the word "American" even though it is inaccurate and offensive. The proper term might be "United Statesian," but there is no such word. So I use the incorrect word "American."

to be an American. I do not identify with racism and imperialism. I have *chosen* not to identify with that nation as my nation. (That does not mean I identify with another nation. I don't identify with any nation.)

I do not offer these words to persuade *you* that you should not identify as an American (although earlier chapters were intended to undermine identification with the US). I am trying to illustrate the process of and some motivations for alienating an identity.

Racial categories such as black and white involve different issues. European science developed racial categories, and the ruling group in Virginia and eventually the US embraced them. Thomas Jefferson called white people "homo sapiens Europaeus." An owner of enslaved people called some of us "white" and others "black." The rulers of Virginia—slave owners all—wrote those categories into law. The categories were invented and are imposed as categories of oppression and exploitation. Their imposition is hostile to us.

As I mentioned in the Introduction, I first became politically active against racism in 1970 on my campus as a graduate student, coming to the defense of Charlie McNeil, a black campus worker. Other activists encouraged me to combat racial segregation on our overwhelmingly white campus by getting to know and befriend black students as well as workers whom I met distributing literature at the unemployment office. After visiting a black couple who lived in a black Boston neighborhood (I had met the husband at the unemployment office), as I returned to my car, cops pulled me aside and asked, "What are you doing here?" My wife and I were invited to dinner by the family of another young black worker I had met at the unemployment office; it was the first time I had eaten dinner in a black family's home.

I had grown up in a San Francisco neighborhood usually attending all-white elementary schools. I learned anti-black racism on the playground, at the same time learning I was white. I even repeated anti-black words. So I tell the stories of my social contacts as a young adult with black people as social equals to try to show how difficult it is to overcome the racial segregation our society creates. As a young adult I began that process.

On my first teaching job I continued to be active against racism on campus, protesting an admissions policy that used "aptitude" tests that disadvantaged black applicants on our predominately white campus. We held rallies in support of the 1971 rebellion at Attica State Prison in New York, protesting apartheid in South Africa, and attacks on black students in the busing struggle in Boston in 1974 and 1975. I was befriended by some black students who taught me to dance The Bump and helped organize a baby shower for me and my wife. In the middle of the night a year or so after my daughter was born, I received a call from one of the students; he needed my help to get his girlfriend out of jail. Later my wife and I attended their wedding and met his maternal grandmother, who was white.

Later, when this friend and I were both postal workers (after I had been denied tenure on that first academic appointment), he told me what happened when his grandmother died. She had grown up in a small all-white town in Southern Illinois but moved to St. Louis in the 1920s where she met, fell in love with, and married a black man. They started a family and lived as husband and wife in St. Louis's black ghetto, raising their children. Periodically she would visit her family in southern Illinois, but she never told them of her marriage and family. Then as an old woman with grandchildren and great-grandchildren she died (her husband had died earlier). Her St. Louis family brought her body to the town where she had grown up to be buried. Needless to say, her birth family then discovered who she was.

Through all of this I was seeing and getting to know things that most people identified as white never learn. But I still thought I was white, just a white anti-racist. When I was teaching at Chicago State, I realized the barriers that racial identities were creating. Many semesters my students enjoyed my teaching until we came to the topic of race. Then I became white, almost as if a wall suddenly appeared separating us. The first time I taught the class Philosophical Issues of Race and Society one student came to the first class but never came back. I was told that he did not want to take a class on racism from someone white. Once a student said to me "Well, you're not really white." Another time I was called a reverse Oreo (white on the outside, black on the inside). I took these as compliments, but also as ways that students could accept and befriend me without letting go of their idea of what it means to be "really white."

My students' belief that I was white was making it harder for me to say things that I wanted my students to think about. For example, I argued that it was necessary to engage in social action against racial disadvantage. I would explain how in our society many black people are socialized for failure. In that context I pointed out to my students, as an example, that the seven-year graduation rate for incoming freshmen from Chicago State was less than 20 percent. My purpose in giving this example was to argue that, despite the rhetoric that Chicago State University was "Opportunity U," the predominate social reality was that incoming freshmen students were not graduating. Most freshmen were being socialized to lower expectations. Instead we needed to fight the barriers that were making it so hard for people to graduate.

Some students reacted, "There it is again, a white man telling black people that they can't 'make it.'" Had I not been perceived as white, my statement could have been accepted for its content and intent. Being perceived as white, I learned to couch my points in caveats and warnings to make it crystal clear what I am and am not saying. All of that forced me to think about and explain these issues clearly and carefully. But that is beside the point. The point is that my students' perception of me as white was a barrier to teaching them, particularly about racism. It was harder for me to teach and be heard by my students because of our perceived racial identities. If they should not accept those identities, then I shouldn't either.

My understanding developed most in thinking about the beating of Calvin Miller. We organized to support Calvin and go to court hearings on his being charged with attacking Samuel Howard. A number of the students in my classes and some others went in support of Calvin. But I realized that the protest was limited because Howard was black, and he was being defended by the black university administration. Few of us saw the beating as racist. That led me to ponder why. People seemed to think racism was interracial. They did this because they *accepted* racial identities. To see much of the racism at Chicago State, it is helpful to alienate racial identities. You can see that people are mistreated because of how they are identified racially. You realize that it makes little difference who does it. I concluded that alienating race strengthens opposition to racism.

To summarize: there are two reasons to alienate race. First, seeing one another through racial categories can distort relationships and separate people who are not identified as black from the struggle against anti-black racism. Second, accepting racial categories can obscure racism because accepting them leads us to look at racism as an interracial phenomenon; the direct agents of injustice against black people can be black.

"But, Paul, your story of how you alienated race is of no use to a Black person. For you alienating race was no big deal. You were not constantly being dissed on account of your race. People accept you and treat you with respect. So what have you given up? For us the problem is totally different. We are constantly reminded that we are Black. Identity is contextual. We are always in a racist environment; so we are always Black. Taking pride in and affirming our blackness helps us to survive constant racist assaults. Moreover, while the normative content of whiteness is racism, Black identity implies *resistance* to racism. Many anti-racist struggles arise from black people acting on Black anti-racist identity and on racial solidarity. So there is no comparison between *your* story of alienating race and what that would mean for *us*."

I agree that alienating white identity is different from alienating black identity. I cannot, from my life experience, tell a story of what it is like to alienate a black identity. But the force of my arguments remains: alienating racial identities helps us to see and oppose racism and to unite the working class to fight injustice against our people. We are all part of the working class.

Also, there may be more similarity between alienating white and alienating black identities than might appear at first. We seek to alienate racial categories as the *enemy's* categories: the capitalist class created and sustains race through law. Racist culture arises as people reconcile themselves to racist law and practice. This is the *enemy's* capitalist system to which we seek an alternative. In *The Souls of Black Folks* (2007 [1903]: 8) W.E.B. Du Bois recollects a childhood experience, the "peremptory refusal" of a greeting card by a classmate. From experiences of being seen by others *as a Negro* emerged "double-consciousness." He explains that racist culture only lets a black person "see himself through the revelation of the other world." Double-consciousness is "this sense of always looking at one's self through the eyes of others."

The idea that our world "only lets [us] see [ourselves] through the revelation of the other world" applies to revolutionaries of all "races": we are seen and see ourselves through the racial lenses of a society we reject. We (black and white revolutionaries) go back and forth between two consciousnesses: one adapted to a racially unjust world where we act and think according to its categories—no one can completely avoid this—and, for the revolutionary, one that rejects that world, its categories, and the ways we are seen racially—rejects them as belonging only to the enemy. So while I acknowledge that black and white people have different experiences, there is also a similarity in the double consciousness I propose (different from Du Bois's) toward which both black and white people *can strive*, of thinking *outside* the world of race, as well as—inevitably—inside.

An example: twenty-five years ago I participated in a study/action group for young comrades or potential comrades in downtown Chicago. We rallied and distributed literature, had some free time, then came back together for study, discussion, and evaluation of the rally. During the free time one of the young black people was accused of purse-snatching by a shopper downtown. She called the cops, and a cop was detaining and questioning the young man. My comrades approached me. In racist society I represented a stereotypical power figure "middle-age, educated white male." I was best suited to talk with the cop. I assured the cop that we were a church group teaching moral values, and that the young man was surely misidentified. It worked. Then we met afterwards for study and discussion.

In talking with the cop, I played the white role and recognized the social power the cop was likely to give to me based on appearance and personal style. In our discussion afterwards we *strive* to think of one another as comrades and as individuals with our particular strengths and weaknesses but not to think of one another or ourselves through racial lenses. We cannot fully succeed at that, but we can see that those categories have their importance only because *they* represent the way the capitalist enemy has organized society.

The paradox of this chapter

I have argued that we should alienate racial identities, regard them as names for us imposed by people and social institutions hostile to our interests. There is a paradox here. People do not accept or alienate identities because of argument, philosophical or otherwise. It is a process, as my description of my own alienation of racial and American identities shows. The process does not consist of reading an argument, as my readers are doing. It consists of working through one's own beliefs, commitments, and goals. It is a process of deciding who one is. As a teacher and anti-racist I found it helpful to alienate white identity in order to teach better and to identify and oppose racism.

Not everyone will be a teacher, but all of us can be anti-racists. As I became active in opposing racism, two things changed. As I have explained, I became aware that in a struggle for change people do not line up based on their racial identity but based on their opposition to the particular way that racism is manifesting itself and their perception of whether it is racism (which can be affected by whether *they* have alienated race). As I also explained, as far back as 1970 when I was first involved in anti-racist struggles, I strove to overcome segregation in my friendships. It is hard to convey to someone how important it is to break that wall of segregation, how important it is to who we think we are to become in-and-out-of-one-another's-house friends across the divide of segregation. It brings home to our consciousness in a way that nothing else can how meaningless and vicious it is to categorize one another by race.

You, my reader, must work through who you are and your own commitments and goals. Still, the arguments made and processes described here can be useful to another person. Some of you may feel that you have already gone down part of the same path. Others may not have, but what I have written may place before you a possibility you may not have considered. So what I have written here can be useful to others in sharpening their own struggles against racism and in working through their own process of alienating race.

9

Race-Centered Marxism

Introduction

The last two chapters were about what racism is and about alienating racial identities. Both chapters addressed expanding and sharpening the fight against racism.

Communist anti-racism aims to *abolish* racist society; only communism can do that. Communism in the future requires anti-racist struggle today. In discussing the work of Hosea Hudson and the Birmingham CP in Chapter 5, I explained the connection: for a Marxist, today's practical struggles *change us* so that we learn to work together and run a new communist society in what Marx called "the dictatorship of the proletariat." These last three chapters explain communist anti-racism. This present chapter is about how race-centered Marxism guides practical struggle. The last two are about the necessity and possibility of communism.

Du Bois and Cox: pioneers of race-centered Marxism

W.E.B. Du Bois in *Black Reconstruction in America 1860–1880* and Oliver Cromwell Cox in *Caste, Class, & Race: A Study in Social Dynamics* have shown a path to race-centered Marxism—even if I am not in complete agreement with either and even though neither book is fully Marxist.[1] Still, both wrote masterfully about the entanglement of race and class. Today's anti-racists need their understanding.

Du Bois' *Black Reconstruction* argues that the creation of racial oppression and exploitation and division between black and white workers are central to the history of the South. His careful recounting of the achievements of Reconstruction conventions and governments demolished the vicious racist stereotypes that dominated textbooks and were popularized in D. W. Griffith's *Birth of a Nation*, a Ku Klux Klan propaganda film promoted by President Woodrow Wilson. In South Carolina but also in other states these conventions and governments expanded suffrage and instituted free and compulsory public education for black and white children. They banned discrimination. They sought land for freedmen and poor white people. They engaged in serious reasoned debates over policy and law.

---

[1] For relevant criticism of *Black Reconstruction* see Bunche 1935, Harris 1989 [1935], Miller 1935; and of Cox see Watson 2014.

His history of the achievements of Reconstruction is set in the context of the struggle between southern workers and their capitalist bosses. His first two chapters are entitled "The Black Worker" and "The White Worker"; the third is entitled "The Planter." Du Bois calls the Reconstruction governments "proletarian" (although he backed away from the idea that they were dictatorships of the proletariat on the ground that workers did not "rid themselves of the dominion of private capital" [1962 (1935): 381, note]). With the end of Reconstruction, the northern capitalists in alliance with southern planters re-established capitalist rule. He calls this rule "oligarchic," acknowledging the acquiescence and participation of non-elite white people. However, he insists that the preponderant power and influence was that of "property," the northern capitalist class and its southern allies. Together they re-established the plantation economy with the use of black and, increasingly, white agricultural labor. In his chapter on the end of Reconstruction he argues that northern capitalists and their southern allies "delivered the land into the hands of an organized monarchy of finance" and "overthrew the attempt at a dictatorship of labor in the South" (580). This dictatorship of capital manipulated "the white labor vote" (as in the North) and deprived "the black voter by violence ... of any vote at all." Racial division neutralized "the labor vote in the South." All of this reinforced "the capitalistic dictatorship of the US, which became the most powerful in the world, and which backed the new industrial imperialism and degraded colored labor the world over" (630).

The clearest expressions of Du Bois' Marxism in *Black Reconstruction* are his assertion that slavery and racism are harmful to white workers and his insistence on a fundamental unity of interest between black and white labor. Describing the participation of non-elite white people in the Confederate military, Du Bois writes that the slave system degraded white soldiers "equally with the black slave" (29). In the aftermath of the Civil War "poor whites joined the sons of the planters and disfranchised the black laborer, thus nullifying the labor movement in the South of a half century or more" (131). He quotes approvingly Senator Henry Wilson of Massachusetts saying, "the man who is the enemy of the black laboring man is the enemy of the white laboring man the world over" (217). In his account of the overthrow of Reconstruction he writes that there is "an absolute difference between those who were trying to conduct the new Southern state governments in the interest of the mass of laborers, black and white, and those North and South who were determined to exploit labor, both in agriculture and industry, for the benefit of an oligarchy" (240). In defeat the late nineteenth century Populists "realized that it was not simply the Negro who had been disfranchised in 1876, it was the white laborer as well. The South had since become one of the greatest centers for exploitation of labor in the world, and labor suffered not only in the South but throughout the country and the world over" (353). After the Civil War white labor organization in the North did not reach out to or include the freed people and other black workers. "Thus," he writes, "labor went into the great war of 1877 against Northern capitalists unsupported by the black man, and the black man went his way in the South to strengthen and consolidate his power, unsupported by Northern labor" (367). The result was a disaster for both groups.

In recounting the defeat of Reconstruction and the development of Jim Crow, Du Bois stresses that southern white workers joined their class enemies to create a racist society that robbed these very workers of power and of a decent wage. Du Bois thought that something else was possible: a united struggle by black freed people and poor white people for decent land, breaking up plantation estates (673). Reconstruction governments began to empower freed people and white workers who joined them. "There was but one way to break up this threatened coalition, and that was to unite poor and rich whites by the shibboleth of race, and despite divergent economic interest" (680). By 1873 "The Northern reform movement had begun to unite itself with Big Business and Super-Finance, and to sympathize with the Southern planters" and "time was now ripe for open war on the labor of the Black Belt" (684). Secret terror organizations, especially the Ku Klux Klan but others as well, unleashed a "campaign of racist terror." Grant did not suppress the racist terror, and the Supreme Court moved to suppress Reconstruction and undercut the Fourteenth and Fifteenth amendments. Du Bois comments, "It is significant that the very center of Northern capitalistic power, which protected and buttressed the new monopoly of Big Business, turned, and with the same gesture freed land and capital in the South from any fear of control by black and white labor" (690). Black people were disfranchised, and "widespread and determined exploitation of black labor" grew (696). There was crushing taxation of the poor. Black people had no redress in the courts. Convict labor expanded, enslaving new generations of black workers. North and South, opportunity was curtailed. Life was cheap, particularly for black people but for white as well.

Du Bois observes that in theory the oppression of workers "would throw white and black labor into one class, and precipitate a united fight for higher wage and better working conditions." However, the ruling class developed "a carefully planned ... method, which drove ... a wedge between the white and black workers." Although they have "practically identical interests," they "hate and fear each other so deeply ... that neither sees anything of common interest." White workers are low-paid but are "compensated in part by a sort of public and psychological wage," the so-called "wages of whiteness" (700). Yet after explaining the various advantages to whites in public respect, political positions, and schools, and the corresponding public humiliations heaped upon black people, Du Bois summarizes, "The result of this is that the wages of both classes could be kept low.... Thus every problem of labor advance in the South was skillfully turned by demagogues into a matter of inter-racial jealousy" (701). Du Bois believed that the "public respect" accorded to white workers was "chump change": the children starved in rags while their father was called "Mr."

Du Bois is not without hope, but it is hope tempered by an understanding of the obstacle that racism creates. He writes that only the determination of white capitalists "to keep the black world poor and themselves rich" blocks the road to a "kingdom of economic equality." He envisions "a world without inordinate individual wealth, of capital without profit and of income based on work alone" as "the path out, not only for America but for all men. Across this path stands the South with flaming sword" (706–7). In a more optimistic mood he wrote that despite the defeat of Reconstruction "the rebuilding, whether it comes now or a century later, ... must go back to the basic principles of Reconstruction ... Land, Light, and Leading for slaves black, brown, yellow and white, under a dictatorship of the proletariat" (635).

Du Bois often expresses a superficial anti-racism, to unite "two groups of workers with practically identical interests." This goal represents a superficial anti-racism because it does not address the *unequal* oppression and exploitation of workers, the essence of racist social organization. But Du Bois is a deep anti-racist. Early in *Black Reconstruction* Du Bois reviews how the world economy is built off of the exploitation of workers of color, the "dark and vast sea of human labor in China and India, the South Seas and all Africa; in the West Indies and Central America and in the United States" that is "driven, beaten, prisoned and enslaved in all but name" and produces "the world's raw material and luxury—cotton, wool, coffee, tea, cocoa, palm oil, fibers, spices, rubber, silks, lumber, copper, gold, diamonds, leather" and more (15). The low prices of these materials produced by the brutal exploitation of workers of color creates the wealth of European and American capitalists. For Du Bois "the real modern labor problem" is that out "of the exploitation of the dark proletariat comes the Surplus Value filched from human beasts.... The emancipation of man is the emancipation of labor and the emancipation of labor is the freeing of that basic majority of workers who are yellow, brown and black" (16). The task of ending the super-exploitation and super-oppression of the "dark proletariat" is identical with the task of ending the exploitation and oppression of all workers—this task and this understanding express deep anti-racism. Anti-racism leads class struggle.

Du Bois shows how to write a Marxist history of racism, understanding the role that race plays in the class struggle, that working class unity requires workers to address racist oppression and exploitation. While his Marxism is not identical with the Marxism defended in this book (he embraces black identity, while I seek to alienate racial categories), it points the way to race-centered Marxism.

Oliver Cromwell Cox's masterwork is *Caste, Class, and Race* (1970 [1948]); the last section, on race, was published separately in 2000. Writers on race often ignore Cox; Charles Mills dismisses his account as "class reductionistic" (2003: 181). This is wrong. Cox is a brilliant interpreter of racist culture, showing how racial demeaning is connected to demeaning people on account of their class. Racist culture arises from material oppression. He identifies both what is common to other class oppression and what is distinctive and vicious about racial oppression.

Racial oppression is a form of capitalist oppression of the worker. Caste relations arise in a particular pre-capitalist society, while race is modern and an invention of capitalist society. Race relations are, he writes, "labor-capital-profits relationships; therefore, race relations are proletarian bourgeois relations and hence political-class relations" (Cox 2000: 21). If one reads this out of context, it is easy to dismiss Cox as "class reductionistic," adding nothing to the understanding of race and racism beyond the observation that it originates in capitalist society. But Cox says much more, both about class oppression and about what makes race unique.

The brutality of racist oppression can make us lose sight of the brutality of class oppression, apart from its racial dimension. Cox's account of class oppression—and racial oppression as a special case—starts with the capitalists' need for labor. "[T]he slave trade was simply a way of recruiting labor for the purpose of exploiting the great natural resources of America." Black and indigenous workers "were the best workers to be found for the heavy labor in the mines and plantations across the Atlantic." White workers were used and kidnapped for that purpose, but ultimately black workers were selected and reduced to slavery. Race "was not an abstract, natural, immemorial feeling of mutual antipathy between groups, but rather a practical exploitative relationship with its socio-attitudinal facilitation—at that time only nascent race prejudice" (17). "The capitalist exploiter" is "opportunistic and practical." So he "will devise and employ race prejudice when that becomes convenient." White workers early on "had to endure burdens of exploitation quite similar to those which colored peoples must bear today" (18).

For the capitalist, the worker is, like a machine, "an item of cost—that is to say, ... both a necessary and important factor of production." The worker "should be paid only so much as would be sufficient to keep him alive and able to labor" (24). Low wages kept production costs low and kept the worker eager to work. Poverty is useful. Cox quotes Mandeville, "in a free nation where slaves are not allowed of, the surest wealth consists in a multitude of laborious poor." If people are reluctant to work, George Berkeley asked whether "sturdy beggars may not be seized and made slaves to the public for a certain term of years?" Cox also quotes William Temple in 1770 saying that the "laboring people should never think of themselves independent of their superiors for, if a proper subordination is not kept up, riot and confusion will take the place of sobriety and good order" (25). For capitalist ideologists, the worker is a thing that must be controlled—by requirement to work for a welfare check, by poverty, workhouses, slavery or other legal enforcement—in the interest of profitable production.

Thus the capitalist treats the worker as a thing. The worker is not just a thing but a living human being. How is this contradiction to be resolved? Cox writes, "To 'commoditize' the capacity of persons to work is to conceptualize ... as inanimate or subhuman, these vehicles of labor power." It is "the immediate pecuniary interest of the capitalists ... to develop an ideology and world view which facilitate proletarianization." The capitalists "show by any irrational or logical means available that the working class of their own race or whole peoples of other races, whose labor they are bent upon exploiting, are something apart: (a) not human at all, (b) only part human, (c) inferior humans and so on" (181).[2]

English rulers of the seventeenth and eighteenth centuries needed to turn the idle poor into productive workers. Nineteenth-century theorists distinguished among white people fit to rule and small and swarthy south Italians, Jews, and Slavs who must be ruled (Painter 2010). Twentieth century eugenics and IQ testing incorporated the same view, including Richard Herrnstein's "IQ" (1971), which argues that equal opportunity has resulted in a (largely black) lower class which is a "genetically inferior residue" of the rest. Thinking of the poor as subhuman continues to this day; Kevin Williamson trashes Trump voters: "take an honest look at the welfare dependency, the drug and alcohol addiction, the family anarchy—which is to say, the whelping of human children with all the respect and wisdom of a stray dog" (Williamson 2016). So in this view humans "whelp" children. The poor are subhuman. Race and class cannot be separated, although race must be distinguished as a *species* of class oppression.

---

[2] Fifty years before Charles Mills wrote in *The Racial Contract* that in the system of White Supremacy, people of color are subhuman, Cox showed that capitalists and their spokesmen adopted this view of workers.

Racism goes further. Here the human body itself is the locus of social contempt. The horror and viciousness of racism is that it stigmatizes the human body. Capitalism demeans proletarian identity as subhuman. Racism attaches subhumanity to a person's *racialized physical appearance*. Cox writes that race prejudice is "prejudice marked by visibility, physical distinguishability" (2000: 36; cf. 117). Race, unlike other representations of class inferiority, attaches to a whole people: "In the case of race relations the tendency of the bourgeoisie is to proletarianize a whole people—that is to say, the whole people is looked upon as a class—whereas white proletarianization involves only a section of the white people" (30).

The fact that even black capitalists and professionals who dress and act in non-proletarian ways are subject to racist treatment does not show that race is independent of class oppression. Rather racial oppression of black *professionals*, based on the racialized body, is rooted in the class status of black people generally. Vicious anti-black stereotypes (stupid, lazy, oversexed, dirty, smelly, criminal, etc.) are stereotypes of workers generally, as the history of class stereotypes readily shows (for example, Gould 1981, Morgan 1975).

"But, Paul, racist culture likens black people to monkeys and apes. Surely this is not a general anti-working class stereotype but uniquely part of anti-black racism." I agree. However, this is not an objection to Cox's point (with which I agree) that anti-blackness is identification of a human body with demeaned proletarian status. Race is a *species* of anti-working class oppression.[3] Part of that particularity of anti-blackness is to identify the black *body* as ape-like. Generally—there are exceptions (Irish had been stereotyped as ape-like)—this particularity is not shared with other anti-working class oppression. But that fact no more shows that anti-black racism is not part of anti-working class oppression than does the fact that humans are the only fully bipedal primate show that humans are not primates.

So Cox's theory that race is proletarian class status is not "class reductionist" in any negative sense. It understands the psycho-social harms of racial oppression as a species of the same psycho-social harms experienced by proletarians generally. (Workers who rebel against their oppression do not experience the same harms.) But these harms are intensified by being attached to the human body itself, to *who I am*.

One function of race is to divide the working class: "both the Negroes and the poor whites are exploited by the white ruling class" but this requires "the maintenance of antagonistic attitudes between the white and the colored masses." The bosses most fear "a *rapprochement* between the white and the colored masses" (168). The violence of race prejudice and stereotyping is explained by the natural resistance to oppression by the oppressed and the capitalists' need to maintain racial oppression: "it is the human tendency, under capitalism, to break out of" extreme oppression, but "the determined counterpressure of exploiters ... produces ... race prejudice," which arises as one of the "legal contrivances of the white ruling class for securing mass support of its interest." Race prejudice "is an attitude of distance and estrangement mingled with repugnance,

---

[3] As the quote from Williamson above shows, poor white workers are also likened to animals ("stray dog"), however based on their behavior not their bodies alone. However, see also Gould 1981 for earlier attempts to identify a working-class body type.

which seeks to conceptualize as brutes the human objects of exploitation." Prejudice is "strained even at the very few points where sympathetic contact is permitted between the people" (170).

Cox is like Du Bois but adds that the effort "to conceptualize [black people] as brutes" grows out of the need to deter white working class sympathy for black workers. While Cox is right to emphasize that the capitalists have power and control the laws, workers are not totally passive. Caught up in a society we did not create, workers may rationalize racial identities and act on those rationalizations, taking up racist culture, accepting the stereotypes of our fellow workers (and even sometimes of ourselves) and developing and acting on these. Workers can become active agents of racism.

What I have just written about workers' agency merely supplements Cox's account of the demeaning of workers generally and the special demeaning of black workers. His explanation of these is a brilliant contribution. Du Bois emphasizes a point that Charles Mills also stresses: the centrality of the labor of people of color worldwide to capitalist production. From these contributions, then, we can build race-centered Marxism.

Race-centered aracial Marxism

The racial organization of labor is central to capitalist social organization. The fight against the racial organization of labor and racist oppression leads class struggle. In Chapter 5 we saw how the CP put that idea into practice. However, only classless communism can *end* racism. *Aracial* race-centered Marxism adds something more: race-centered practical work should be combined with striving to *alienate* racial identities. A united anti-racist working class movement can overthrow capitalism and create classless communism, a society without race.

"But, Paul, to identify racism we must employ racial identities. A black person fighting racism is recognizing that her own identity grounds racist treatment. So the contradiction is still there." In reply: the identities used to recognize racism are alienated identities: people are harmed because racist society identifies that person, even oneself, as black.

Here I present the view. In the next chapter I show only communism provides the solution to racism. In the last chapter I argue that we may reasonably strive for classless communism.

Marx recognized the importance of race to working class organization and unity (Marx and Engels 1975: 222), but it is not central to his *economic* theory. European proto-capitalists used indigenous and African slave labor to mine the gold and silver of the Americas, enabling coinage that lubricated trade. Lumber was taken and sugar was grown, harvested, and processed by brown and black workers in the Americas. Slave-produced cotton, indigo, and other plantation crops of the Americas produced the raw materials of European mill production. When the US Civil War curtailed cotton exports from the South, European capitalists used Egyptian and Indian land and brown or black people to grow the cotton for European mills. Marx was aware of all of this; it appears in *Capital I* in a discussion of "primitive accumulation" and briefly elsewhere (end of Chapter XXXI). But it needs to be centered in an account of capitalist economy.

Worldwide dark-complexioned labor, intensely oppressed and exploited, *continues* to mine minerals; grow, harvest, and process crops; husband, transport, slaughter, and process beef, pork, poultry, and fish; scour the world's oceans for tuna, salmon, and other fish; produce commodities in factories, and provide labor for services. Oppression and exploitation are *unequal*. That inequality is a material reality. Racist culture rationalizes the racial organization of labor. The world capitalist economy, society, and culture are all racist. The development of racist social organization and the rise of capitalism and modernity are the same process.

The contribution of US capitalism to this global process was the racial organization of labor *within* the borders of a single nation. Racial categories were written into law. Race structured domestic social organization beyond the labor process—for example, Jim Crow laws mandating segregation. Racist culture rationalized racist social organization, including the racial organization of labor. As Cox noted, capitalism dehumanizes the worker; race transfers that dehumanization to the human body. Racist culture intensifies racial divisions within the working class, extends and intensifies racial oppression, sometimes setting racist mobs—including many workers—to attack black, mexican, indigenous, and filipino or other asian people.

These are not just facts about the past. Black (and other hyper-vulnerable) workers continue to work the dirtiest, most dangerous jobs at the lowest wages with the greatest job insecurity and highest unemployment. Low-paid black women work in nursing homes and provide home health services. Racial material oppression beyond the workplace leads to segregated neighborhoods, churches, shopping centers, health services, and schools. Generally, these are worse for black people. Black people pay more for insurance, mortgages (if available), and other services, while often getting inferior service.

Any Marxist theory—if it is to describe adequately capitalist economy and social organization, if it is to describe how workers are both exploited and oppressed—must put the racial organization of labor, both internationally and domestically, at the center of its account.

Race-centered Marxist thought is not original here, but we combine race-centrism with aracialism. Practical Marxists have believed that fighting national oppression meant defending rights of oppressed nations to self-determination (Lenin 1964a [1914], Stalin 1975 [1913]).[4] Communist parties of the twentieth century transferred this line to "racial" groups, defending the right to organize based on race or nationality. That line made it easier for Du Bois, who embraced a black identity and Pan-Africanist politics, to join the US Communist Party in 1961. The race-centered Marxism defended here is aracial: we should strive to alienate the enemy's identities and abolish the racial categories used to organize unequal exploitation and oppression, but we cannot succeed in either striving without overthrowing racist society.

When workers accept the racial categories of capitalism as applying to themselves, that acceptance divides the working class and encourages in-group/out-group behavior among workers, at worst leading to pogroms and lynchings, but surely separating

---

[4] See Gomberg 2018 for criticism of Lenin's defense the right of nations to self-determination.

non-black people from the fight against anti-black racism. In addition, aracialism can strengthen the fight against racism in segregated predominately black environments.

Even more important, to create a fully communist society we need to alienate race. Du Bois' phrase "the dictatorship of the proletariat" is derived from Marxist thought. This refers to workers' control of state power and use of that power in a class dictatorship to suppress remnants of capitalism, sexism, and racism. But, as Marx emphasized when he summarized what was original in his thought, the dictatorship of the proletariat is a historical stage leading "to the abolition of all classes and to a classless society" (Marx 1975 [1852]: 64). The core of Marxist thought is a conception of history as leading to communism (a classless society) with the working class (proletariat) as agent of that transition from capitalism to communism. Marx's "Critique of the Gotha Program" (1974b [1875]) again states the communist goal. However, only a united working class can create communist society. So the practical imperative of Marxism is to unite the working class as a class. But how?

Concerning race, there are two barriers to class unity. One is the failure of most white and some black and other workers of color to acknowledge that capitalist social organization is deeply racist: when a person is identified with a race which is especially exploited, oppressed, and demeaned in capitalist society, the identification leads—*on average*—to a shorter life, more illness, lower wages, and less security. All workers, particularly white workers, must recognize this if unity is to be possible; workers should understand the world in the same way, and it is possible to do that if that is how the world actually is and we can all come to know this.

The second barrier to unity is our acceptance of racial identities. When we accept those identities we accept the power of the capitalist enemy to name us, names invented to rationalize his treating us differently according to these names. If we reject that we should be treated differently on account of these racial categories (as is implied in the fight against racism), we should reject the categories themselves as the invention of the same capitalist forces that made racist laws and control the capitalist economy and state. When "white" workers accept that they are white, they can begin to think in terms of "white interests" and accept stereotypes of those who are not identified as white. The same is true of "black" workers; accepting that they are black, they can think in terms of the interests of "the race" and stereotype "white" people as inherently racist or as all well-off. All of these divide our class. Struggling to alienate these categories (we cannot fully succeed) and to acknowledge their role in racial oppression can help unite the working class as a class. For these reasons the Marxism defended here is not only race-centered but aracial. We should strive for the understanding that just as we have no country, we have no race. This understanding helps us to put the fight against racist super-exploitation and oppression at the *center* of the fight for communism.

Who are my people? Whose oppression is my oppression?

"An injury to one is an injury to all."

IWW slogan

Much thought among activists (on college campuses and elsewhere) is dominated by the idea of multiple and overlapping systems of oppression (White Supremacy, Patriarchy, Heteronormativity, Capitalism) or dimensions (matrices, axes, vectors) of oppression (class, race, gender, nationality, immigration status, sexuality, ability, age and others).

According to this analysis different people are oppressed by different systems of oppression, women by Patriarchy, black (and other racially oppressed peoples) by White Supremacy, gay people by Heteronormativity, workers by Capitalism. What oppresses one person may not oppress another, who may even benefit. When black people resist anti-black oppression, non-black people who join them in the struggle are their allies. And similarly for the other systems and dimensions of oppression: the categories are (1) those directly oppressed by those systems or on those dimensions, (2) those who benefit from the oppression, and (3) allies in struggle who are not oppressed on that dimension.

This way of thinking about oppression arose primarily from work by black feminists familiar with different forms of oppression. In 1977 literary critic Barbara Smith (1979 [1977]) argued that—besides the invisibility of black writers to many white critics—black women writers were even more invisible and black lesbian writers suffered yet another form of cultural suppression and oppression. Twelve years later UCLA law professor Kimberlé Crenshaw (1989) pointed out how—one of her examples—black women auto workers were denied status in a lawsuit seeking restitution for discrimination against black women (General Motors would not hire black women when they would hire black men and white women) because, while both black people and women were protected classes, black women were not. This led her to use the term "intersection" in her title for the particularities of oppression experienced by people who were simultaneously members of two or more oppressed groups. Smith's and Crenshaw's essays are grounded in real experiences and real problems for which they sought solutions.

In 1977 the Combahee River Collective (CRC), a group of black feminists including Smith, laid out a systematic account. The ideas in the influential CRC statement were taken up by others, particularly black feminist academics and activists in struggles on campuses and elsewhere. I choose to explain and criticize the CRC statement because it was early, arose from activism, and summarizes a view common among activists (although activists may not appreciate the subtlety of the CRC analysis). The CRC opposes "racial, sexual, heterosexual, and class oppression" and seeks to develop "analysis and practice based upon the fact that the major systems of oppression are interlocking" (Combahee River Collective 2000 [1977]: 264). While "intersection" refers to overlapping of different oppressions, "interlocking" implies that different oppressions cannot be completely separated. The CRC statement focuses on harms from interlocking oppressions, from "racial-sexual oppression which is neither solely racial nor solely sexual, e.g., the history of rape of Black women by white men as a weapon of political repression" (267). For the CRC oppression includes class oppression: it is "difficult to separate race from class from sex oppression because in our lives they are most often experienced simultaneously."

> Liberation necessitates the destruction of the political-economic systems of capitalism and imperialism as well as patriarchy. We are socialists.... [W]ork must be organized for the collective benefit of those who do the work ... and not for the profit of the bosses. Material resources must be equally distributed among those who create these resources.
>
> Combahee River Collective 2000 [1977]: 267–8

The CRC prioritizes fighting oppression grounded in their own identity: "We believe that the most profound and potentially most radical politics come directly out of our own identity, as opposed to working to end somebody else's oppression" (267). What is meant by our own as opposed to "somebody else's" oppression? It cannot mean our *individual* experiences of oppression, which are unique to each. If we fight only what oppresses each as an individual, we cannot act together and are powerless. Rather what is meant is fighting around oppression that comes "directly out of our own identity," an identity shared with others. What is our identity? Whose oppression is "somebody else's"?

While the CRC recognized that some struggles opposed someone else's oppression, they did not, for that reason, hold back from such struggles. In 2017 Keeanga-Yamahtta Taylor published interviews she had done with CRC members including Smith. In those interviews Smith reiterates the CRC's commitment to coalition with others; prioritizing "our own" oppression does not meaning ignoring harms to people who don't share one's identity. Her examples seem to show that it is the *conjunction* of black, woman, feminist, working class, and socialist identities that is "their own" identity: examples of *coalitions* (presumably fighting oppression which is "somebody else's") include working with socialist feminists, union organizing, and supporting men of color. Sharing one or two identities with others is not sufficient to make their oppression "our own" (Taylor 2017: 62).

Systems-of-oppression analysis is different from a Marxist understanding. The disagreements are primarily strategic and factual but can be expressed abstractly. For a Marxist, while there are many forms and grounds of oppression, there is only one *system* of exploitation and oppression—racist and sexist capitalism. There is only one solution—communism. (I argue for that conclusion in the next chapter.) Only the working class can create communist society, but it can do so only if it is united. The working class can unite only if *all* workers recognize and oppose the *extra* burden of exploitation and oppression borne by black (and other) and women workers. Hence anti-racism and anti-sexism must lead working-class struggle.[5] Claudia Jones (1949) defends this view, emphasizing the vicious oppression of black women.

---

[5] It should be possible to develop a parallel analysis of sexism: that the fight against gender oppression and super-exploitation must lead working-class struggles.

Figure 9.1 January 27, 2007 anti-war demonstration Washington, DC.
Credit: Nicholas Kamm AFP via Getty Images

Figure 9.2 May 1, 2007 demonstration Los Angeles, California.
Credit: David McNew Getty Images News

Because it emphasizes differences in our identities and differences between systems of oppression, systems-of-oppression analysis tends to fragment the working class. In 2007 there were three important demonstrations: a January 27 demonstration of 500,000 in Washington against the US occupation of Iraq, huge May Day marches in several cities on May 1 (roughly 100,000 in Chicago alone), and a September 20 demonstration in Jena, Louisiana against the judicial attacks on black high school

Figure 9.3 September 15, 2007 in Jena, Louisiana protesting prosecutorial racism against black youth.
Photo by Robert Sabo/NY Daily News Archive via Getty Images.

students. The first was overwhelmingly white immigrants, the second overwhelmingly latin, and the third nearly all-black. Why the separation? *All* forms of oppression identified on a systems-of-oppression analysis *harm the working class*.

Who are my people? Whose oppression is my oppression? On the CRC analysis not all of us are oppressed by the same thing. This is true because we do not share identities. The CRC then strove to qualify this: different oppressions interlock; they cannot be fully separated (at least in experience); we need to form coalitions with others who do not share our identity. The consequence of their analysis, however, was to fragment movements of resistance. Distinguishing between systems of oppression, distinguishing "our own" oppression and "somebody else's" divides our class. CRC could not put the toothpaste back into the tube.

On a Marxist view an injury to one worker is an injury to all workers. When black people accept the identity ascribed to them in racist society, they naturally tend to view police killing of a black working class youth as happening to their people; that oppression is their oppression. For those who identify as workers that killing is an attack on our people; that oppression is our oppression. When, as in Ferguson or Baltimore, people rebel against police killings, this is not a rebellion of oppressed and allies but of members of the same class, of comrades (Dean 2019).

The struggle against racial oppression is central to uniting the working class as a class. That unity makes it possible for workers to win power and end capitalism with all its forms of oppression. Racial divisions drive down the working class. They are sustained by unequal oppression and exploitation. Emphasizing racial oppression is *not* divisive! Ignoring *unequal* oppression is the path to working-class *disunity*.

Marxism also differs from many if not most systems-of-oppression partisans about the facts. Specifically, for a worker racially identified as white, the oppression of a worker racially identified as black is her own. Earlier chapters contained many examples illustrating how white workers were driven down by anti-black oppression. Here I add another.

Consider black and white infant mortality. In the US black infant mortality is 2.4 times white infant mortality, an increase from a ratio of 1.6 to 1 in the 1950s (Collins and David 2009). In 2010 the US ranked 30th among nations in infant mortality, worse than any other affluent nation. It might seem that the poor infant mortality of the US compared with other nations is due to the poor infant mortality for black children. But if we consider only white people in the US as if they were a nation, then the infant mortality would be 28th in the world, an improvement of only two places; a white baby in the US is 2.4 times more likely to die than a baby in Japan or Finland (David and Collins 2014). Why?

Let's consider a systems-of-oppression (White Supremacy) or axes-of-oppression analysis. It might go something like this:

Black people are *explicitly targeted* by racial oppression, which makes black infant mortality 2.4 times white. White people are targeted by capitalist exploitation and oppression, which makes their infant mortality less; capitalism treats health care as a privilege rather than a right. As a result all workers suffer worse outcomes, including white workers. Black workers are doubly targeted, by the capitalist oppression they share with white people and by White Supremacy. White people experience the harms of capitalism but benefit from White Supremacy.

(This analysis employs an additive model of multiple oppressions that many reject but is common among activists.)

Why is infant mortality for white people in the US so much worse than in capitalist Finland and Japan? Anti-black racism causes the death of *white* babies in the US (compared with Finland and Japan). Anti-black racism seems to cause something parallel to the "southern wage" we saw in Chapters 4 and 5: conditions for white people in the US will be worse than those for people elsewhere where racism is less severe. Racism targeting black workers *harms white workers* in an anti-black capitalist society.

A major cause of the black/white disparity in infant mortality in the US is the higher incidence of low birth weight among black infants as well as very low birth weight (less than 1500 grams., roughly 3.3 pounds). Collins and David (2009; also Collins and others 2004) show how chronic stresses—called allostatic load—causing low birth weight are more prevalent in black mothers (determined by blood markers of stress). In addition black mothers often lack access to the best pre-natal and infant care—because of racism.

How does anti-black racism cause greater mortality among white babies in the US? My answer is a speculation, subject to further inquiry. My speculation is that, just as black mothers in the US experience greater stress as a result of racism, so white mothers in the US also experience greater stress because of anti-black racism. This speculation draws together five things: anti-black material racism (worse conditions generally for black people), racist explanations of black inequality, individualist social thought, severe US economic inequality, and worse conditions for US workers, including white workers.

First, as we have reviewed at many points, black people suffer lower wages, vastly inferior accumulation of assets, fivefold greater rate of incarceration than non-hispanic white people, poorer health, lower life expectancy, and greater poverty. Moreover, this is widely known to be true.

Second, why are black people generally worse off? In the most recent surveys over half of black and white people in the US think that lack of motivation explained black poverty (an even higher percentage of black people thought it was discrimination, some giving both explanations) (Krysan and Moberg 2016). This is racist social thought. Explaining poverty as due to lack of motivation is a fallacy: it transfers a factor relevant from an *individual* point of view (what to do if you are out of work) to a *social* problem (unemployed should look harder for jobs). It makes no sense: if everyone unemployed tried harder to find a job, the unemployment rate would not change nor would the number of available jobs (Gomberg 2007: Chapter 2). The key point is that black and white people *believe* that lack of motivation causes higher poverty among black people. They blame people who suffer unemployment. This blame causes people additional stress. The *individual* is responsible for her own condition.

Racism and individualism are conjoined twins of oppression. Individualism is much stronger among white people (Lamont 2000). Jonathan Metzl interviewed many white people oppressed by lack of access to adequate health care. The white people stereotyped themselves as independent, not relying on government programs. Such programs were identified with black and immigrant dependency. Contempt is heaped upon those who accept government aid. Consequently, many white people will not accept government aid, even when they need it (Metzl 2019). Residents of the town Jennifer Sherman studied would drive long distances to use their food stamps in order to avoid shame in their own community (Sherman 2009). The notions of white independence and black dependency are conjoined twins.

Third, individualism (you are responsible for your own life) puts greater stress on people, including mothers, than does a more communal culture. Robert Bellah and others write that individualism "provides little encouragement for nurturance," but nurturance is precisely what expectant mothers need. The US is unique among nations in its individualist culture (2008: xiv), and this fact might help explain why white infant mortality is so much higher than in other countries. Moreover, racism and individualism are cultural factors partly responsible for lack of access to health care, not only for black mothers but for white mothers too.

Fourth, the US has greater economic inequality and poverty generally (than in Japan or Finland). The Gini score (measuring economic inequality) for Japan was .55, for the US .81, showing much greater inequality (Brandmeir and others 2016). This means more poverty and economic stress generally are experienced by people in US society.

Fifth, now tie all of this together. Racism has divided the working class, weakened unions, encouraged a culture of individualism, and driven down conditions for black people and, though to a lesser extent generally, white people along with them. The capitalists increase their share of wealth. There is greater economic insecurity especially for the lowest paid workers and unemployed. Poverty creates stress, and this can affect maternal and child health, especially for black mothers and babies, but for white mothers and children as well. Not only is there more poverty and insecurity. There is also a culture of individual responsibility. Ideas of universal opportunity and individual responsibility are pervasive in racist culture. The culture puts pressure on people.

Instead of a society where health care, housing, and nutrition are secure, where the culture is collectivist, nurturing, and supportive, we have a society where our basic needs are insecure (not just for black people but for many white people as well), where the culture is competitive, individualist, and judgmental. For these reasons people in the most racist capitalist societies, particularly the US, experience greater stress, and white mothers are affected by this stress as well as black mothers, although not to the same degree. Now add to all of this the mother's need for nurturing and support during pregnancy, the physical stress of childbirth, the hormonal stress of the postpartum period, and a society where a mother, including a white mother, may be "on her own" with little social support and help during the time of pregnancy and after birth. This is a recipe for poor infant health and higher mortality. Greater material insecurity and more intense individualism are effects of racism, the resulting deep divisions among workers, and the unchallenged sway of the capitalist class.

All of this needs more research. Three issues particularly need to be investigated: the connection between individualism and racism; the connection between individualism and maternal stress; evidence that expectant mothers in the US experience greater stress. Further evidence could either confirm or undermine my speculation about the connection between racism and higher white infant mortality in the US.

I introduced the discussion of infant mortality by asking whether, for workers racially identified as white, the oppression of workers racially identified as black is their own oppression. I have argued that it is.

This example—of racial and international differences in infant mortality—illustrates and defends Marxist anti-racism: racism harms our entire class, but unequally. Where, among nations, racism is more severe, the less oppressed workers are worse off than workers are where racism is less severe. Workers in the US are worse off than workers in other industrialized countries by many measures, not just infant mortality. Racism is a major culprit.

The primary reason racism harms the whole working class is that it inhibits the movement toward communism. Workers need unity to overthrow the capitalist state and build a communist society. In capitalism we are deprived of our humanity by working for a wage rather than working collectively for each other. As we will see in the last chapter, we thrive when doing what is useful to ourselves and to one another. We are fully human. We experience joy and humanity in serving others (Solnit 2009). When doing wage labor, we may feel occupied and engaged (as in a game); mostly we wait for the end of a work shift. Classless communism enables us to live as human beings; racist capitalism never can. But communism is possible only when workers unite as a class, and such unity is impossible without recognizing and fighting racism. All workers have an interest in fighting and ending racism.

It makes a difference whether we embrace a systems-of-oppression analysis—where your oppression is not my oppression—or see ourselves as oppressed, though unequally, by the same system. On that second view, we all have a direct interest in fighting racist capitalism. We are not divided into the oppressed and their allies. We are all oppressed by the same system. This understanding grounds working class identity and unity, making it possible to unite our class into a revolutionary army that can defeat the power of capitalists and create a communist world. Racism will be wiped out.

Working class unity needs more than race-centered Marxism. Many great thinkers and activists (W.E.B. Du Bois, Eric Williams, Walter Rodney, C. L. R. James) developed race-centered Marxist politics. However, they tended to combine it with a strong and positive identification with blackness. Our hatred of capitalism and our determination to replace it with classless communism are strengthened if we combine race-centrism with aracialism: the capitalists create not only racism but even the *categories* through which racism is organized. We should struggle against racism and at the same time the racial categories that capitalism creates to sustain that injustice. Those categories were created by the capitalists and belong to them. We should alienate them and at the same time intensify awareness of and determination to end racism. Aracialism helps to build class unity, making communist society possible.

Some objections and replies

"Paul, you write that anti-black racism makes all workers' lives worse. You call for sharper anti-racist struggle. You also call for communist revolution. But if struggle can defeat racism and lead to improvements in our lives, why do we need revolution? And if struggle can't lead to improvement, how is it possible to unite workers against racism? I don't get it."

Workers' gains through struggle are turned around. In Chapter 3 we saw that the southern planters allied with northern capitalists undermined the heroic struggle against slavery in the Civil War by instituting convict leasing. They rebuilt southern agriculture based on black sharecroppers, now joined by many white and mexican workers. The gains of the Farmers Alliances and the threat of the Populists led to Jim Crow. In Chapter 4 we saw that when Alabama coal miners defeated racial divisions, the capitalist state used the national guard to defeat miners militarily; only the armed seizure of state power could stop this. In Chapter 5 we saw anti-racist working class movements that explicitly addressed anti-black practices were defeated by the anti-communist onslaught 1945–1955, which outlawed communist leadership of unions and jailed communists. When Jim Crow was defeated, mass incarceration took its place in disciplining black labor. Whenever racism is defeated in one form, it is rebuilt in another. Capitalists need compliant labor subject to racist terror, which indirectly disciplines other workers. Only communist revolution can end this.

"Paul, many of us experience capitalism as queer and working class or black and working class or immigrant and working class, and these experiences are very different from others."

If we see the particularities of our experiences as part of an overall picture of how our class is exploited and oppressed, the fact that my *experience* is different from others' is not divisive. We identify with all oppressed workers. *They are all us.* Differences in our experiences are real, but if we take them to ground different identities, those identities divide us politically and practically. Is the oppression of a black lesbian worker my oppression? The answer has to be "yes." My *experiences* are not the same, but the *oppression* of another worker is my oppression. That's what it means to identify as a worker. Our experiences are different and often not chosen, but our identities are chosen and political.

"Paul, you seem to be implying that the oppression of a black lesbian *capitalist* is not your oppression and that you are not opposed to it. I disagree. If we are to oppose racial and other injustice we must oppose these as they affect *everyone*."

Racism arose and is sustained as an attack on the working class, the class with which I identify. Racism includes "collateral damage" to some black capitalists. Do I oppose it? I am indifferent. *Revolutionary* Marxism (communism) has implications that differ from common anti-racist views. The working class and the capitalist class are the only two classes that are sufficiently large and actually or potentially organized that they can rule society. There is, over the long term, a struggle to determine which class rules. If the working class seizes power, defeats the capitalists as a class, and reorganizes society in an egalitarian collectivist way, workers can eliminate exploitation and oppression of one human being by another. This contest is a violent struggle for state power. In this sense the capitalists are the enemies of workers. Winning the class struggle requires indifference to harms to our enemies (Gomberg 1990, on partisanship and the partisan's attitude toward enemies).

"But when the CEO of Sony's emails were leaked, a supposedly feminist site published details of her Amazon purchases. The site mocked her in a really invasive and sexist way. It was an expression of contempt for women. It played on vulnerabilities of women in a pervasive culture of sexual objectification. That was hitting her as a person, not as a capitalist, and in a way that was harmful to other women too."

I agree. A sexist attack on a capitalist can promote sexist culture and indirectly attack workers. We should object to it on *those* grounds, not as a harm to a capitalist.

"You write, 'we must all understand the world in the same way.' Must we all think alike?"

We don't all think alike because we have experienced and know different things. But we listen to one another and, through listening and sharing, strive for an objective grasp of the world, using all of our experiences. In that objective grasp we come to understand the world in the same way. The collective is smarter than the individual.

Collective knowledge is not individual knowledge. In the research at CERN that led to the confirmation of the Higgs Boson one paper had 2,800 authors, and no one of them understood everything that, collectively, they had discovered (Merali 2010).

Summary of race-centered Marxism

To summarize, race-centered aracial Marxism builds on the contributions of Du Bois and Cox but differs from much writing about racism and from other Marxist accounts in seven ways:

1. The struggle against racism is the struggle to end all capitalist oppression and exploitation, not just in the US but everywhere. Because capitalist norms are enforced by the power of states—their militaries and police—racism and all similar injustice to workers cannot be ended except by destroying that power. This means revolution. The society that emerges as an alternative to capitalism must abolish all structures that maintain social inequality, struggle for social relations that enable us to flourish by advancing the flourishing of others, establishing communist social relations. The next chapter defends the conclusion that only communist social relations can end racism.
2. Racism is not interracial. Racist social organization grows out of laws and policies developed by capitalist ruling classes, originally in colonies such as Virginia but more recently in the laws and programs such as those developed by the US government since the 1960s (as detailed in Chapter 6). Racist culture rationalizes racist social organization.
3. Opposition to racism is not determined by racial identities. Both those who protested the killing of Michael Brown in Ferguson, Missouri and the police, national guardsmen, and government officials dispatched to control the situation included people identified as black and people identified as white. Which side someone is on is not determined by their "race."
4. We must be conscious of underlying racist inclinations and attitudes within the anti-racist movement and within ourselves. Racism and racist culture have influenced all of us. The battle against anti-black racism must be largely (but not exclusively) led by black people. People categorized by racist society as black or white are likely to be affected by those categorizations: people categorized as white may find it easier to step forward as leaders in racially inclusive situations. Part of the struggle against racism is to battle these effects of racism.
5. We should strive to alienate racial identities, eventually to destroy racism and racial categories which organize it. We struggle to think of "black" and "white" as "the enemy's name for us," not who we really are. We should strive for working class identities, communist identities.
6. We engage in a *worldwide* battle against racism and particularly the worldwide organization of unequal oppression of workers, largely based on whether those workers are or are not of European ancestry. Our struggle must be international, internationa*list*, and anti-racist, fighting the special oppression and deeper exploitation of workers of color worldwide.

7. All racism is linked and anti-racists must fight all its forms. Waves of anti-muslim, anti-immigrant, anti-mexican, and anti-asian racism have recently swept through the US. They are all part of a system of racism based originally and currently on the forceful appropriation of indigenous lands and degradation and terror directed against black people.

10

A Society Without Race

What vision of a society without race can inspire anti-racists?

The only alternative to racism is a communist society where we flourish together by contributing to one another's flourishing. In this chapter I explain and defend this vision of communism. I show why other anti-racist proposals will not destroy racism.

Capitalist societies inevitably harbor racism or something similar. In a communist society there is no money. We don't work for wages. People work in order to serve the needs of all. This is possible and can be made plausible to others. It can inspire day-to-day anti-racist activism with reasonable hope of such a communist future.

To sustain anti-racist activism, we must believe that the task of ending racism is not hopeless. We need reasonable hope of a society without race. What makes hope reasonable? The historical chapters argued that racism was created by and benefits capitalists. They will oppose its elimination. That's a very small class. However, that class controls state power, is relatively well organized, and has allies. We can expect the military and courts to try to sustain racism (at least in some form). Moreover, there are many who have spent their lives in service to the capitalists' task of controlling the working class: police, many in the system of "justice" and "corrections," workplace supervisors, professional ideologists, and others; we can expect most of these to ally themselves with the capitalists in the struggle to eliminate racism. So a force sufficient to end racism must be able to overcome its likely supporters, people who endorse the capitalist system.

That force must be large but not necessarily the majority. If we are to have a reasonable hope of ending racism, we need a vision of a society without race that can inspire a *very* large group of people and win less visible support from many who, while not activists, could see that a society without race would be better.

Therefore, to be *inspired* to end racism we must be able to see that we and our children or grandchildren would be better off in a society without race. The struggle for a society without race cannot ask people to violate moral commitments to their children to do what they can to secure their future. If a society without race would make their children worse off, then fighting for such a society would violate a moral obligation. If their children would be better off, anti-racists can see activism as fulfilling a duty. Moreover, if we can see that most of us would be better off, people who just want to be left alone will be sympathetic with the cause of activists and may defend and protect them.[1]

People *as they are now* must be able to recognize that we would be better off in a society without race, making our task more difficult. Many of our values are shaped by racist capitalism, for example extreme individualism, competitive success, and prestige in a racist social hierarchy. So the "better off" I defend is not according to these values.

We have other values, not tied to racist capitalism, by which we would be better off in a society without race. We value friends and family; we enjoy using our minds, developing our abilities (physical as well as others), solving problems and being engaged by the work we do. We value cooperative and comradely relations with others, not just with intimates but others as well. We value a positive physical environment. We would like to believe that a good life for ourselves is not achieved at the expense of others. We value good health and confidence in the abilities of our bodies. We value security in our possession of all of these goods. A society where these goods could be available to all of us simultaneously would be better.

However, goods can be available to all of us simultaneously only if they are of unlimited supply. A good is of unlimited supply if and only if there is as much of it available to us as we may want. Air, for example, is ordinarily of unlimited supply. Your having enough air to breathe does not affect my having enough air to breathe. We don't compete for goods in unlimited supply. They are available to all of us simultaneously. If one of us has that good, it does not diminish the opportunity for everyone else to have that good. In a society where our relations with others are comradely and cooperative, each person's having a good *enhances* opportunity for others to have it. Consider friendship: suppose a society fosters development of moral qualities that make us admirable and likeable; development of friendships would encourage the development of other friendships, as people see that we get along, like, and even cherish one another. The tendency of goods to multiply can be true of complex abilities when those *who have* an ability *help others* to master the same ability.

This requirement that the most important goods be in unlimited supply is important for how we think of a society without race. Race is used to organize inequality among workers, some significantly more oppressed than others. Racial inequality divides the working class, directing resentment toward those closer to one's social position. It concerns goods in *limited* supply. If they were in unlimited supply, one person's having them would not negatively affect their availability to anyone else. Some goods—for example, security—might easily exist in unlimited supply. But security is not likely to be in unlimited supply unless other goods are: if some are living much better than others, those with less will seek the goods possessed by those with more. If the disparity is severe in goods needed to survive, deprivation leads to desperation. Even relative deprivation of goods primarily of prestige value or deprivations that represent symbolic humiliation can harm a person's dignity, inspiring rebellions such as the urban uprisings of the US in the late 1960s. Absent collective struggle, people express alienation

---

[1] In Mississippi in 1964 people who would not register to vote supported the movement in less obvious ways (Payne 1995). In Vietnam in the 1960s Vietnamese who did not actively resist the US invasion did not tell US soldiers where booby traps were, but they didn't step in them.

by victimizing others, particularly those nearest, creating insecure households and neighborhoods. The most important goods must be available in unlimited supply.

As I will argue in the section that follows the requirement that a society without race make the most important goods in unlimited supply requires both that we not separate racial from other inequality and injustice and that we change how we live together.

Why proposed remedies to racism would not correct it

Any proposed remedy to racism must meet this standard: enough people must be capable of seeing it to be preferable to current racism that they would organize themselves and others to realize it. I know of no vision of a society without racism which meets this standard except for the communism defended here. I will not attempt an exhaustive survey of alternative views; I will confine myself to Elizabeth Anderson's *The Imperative of Integration,* Charles Mills' defense of reparations grounded in racial exploitation, and David Lyons' radical proposals for equal opportunity.

Elizabeth Anderson's integrationism

We discussed Anderson earlier, in Chapter 7. Her view assumes an interracial model of racial injustice, that white people corporately are agents of injustice; she lets capitalists off the hook and assimilates poor and powerless white people to capitalists. We saw that her interracial model doesn't fit the facts. Here I focus on the *practicality* of her proposals.

Anderson writes as a moral philosopher arguing for a moral imperative to integrate US society, ending the marginalization and exclusion of black people from the most desirable social positions. I write as an anti-racist activist and social philosopher seeking a movement which could end racism. There are other important differences. Her argument addresses racial injustice, considering it apart from broader social issues, particularly class exploitation and oppression. I have argued that racism is integral to the class structure of US society and cannot be remedied without ending capitalist exploitation and oppression of the working class. Related to the last point, she seems to envision that inclusion of more black people among elites will improve the situation of more disadvantaged black people (Anderson 2010: 110). My experience as a teacher in an environment where black elites held local power (at the university)—and white politicians toadied to them in order to get the "black vote"—has given me innumerable lessons that race and class cannot be separated, that black elites freely practice anti-black racism against less advantaged black people, and that the interracial model of racism is wrong and harmful to anti-racist activism.

Leave these disagreements aside. Do her proposals to integrate dominant institutions without more radical social change offer hope of racial justice? In the final section of her last chapter, "The Hope for an Integrated Future," she explicitly addresses the question how *likely* it is that integration will be realized. She reviews state-centered policies to bring about integration: offering housing vouchers and ending class-restrictive zoning in order to integrate neighborhoods; implementing aggressive state policies to advance integration, particularly of schools; and aggressive affirmative action programs in employment. Yet, she believes, there is a problem with all of this: "While implementation of these mostly state-centered policies would have important effects, at foreseeable scales their impact would be modest compared to the vast scale of de facto segregation" (189). She mentions some resistance to racial integration, including white flight from some cities when courts ordered busing to integrate schools. She writes, "the project of integration cannot be left to state initiative alone," and mentions voluntary efforts. She cites legal changes reinforcing segregation and comments, "this state of affairs is just how whites want it" (189). She asks whether her integrationist theory is unrealistic but says it is not. She writes that it is "based on an empirically grounded diagnosis of the causes of unjust race-based" inequality and that integration can "undo those causes and thereby reverse their effects." What it asks of is us not "impossible or unreasonably difficult for people" to do (190). Instead, she believes, people are simply *unwilling* to do what is neither "impossible" nor "unreasonably difficult" for them to do. She thinks opposition to integration "is based more on anticipatory fear than on evidence" (191).

It is not clear from what she writes whose opposition to integration or which people she means. Given her interracial model of injustice, the answer may just be "white people." If so, it unfairly lumps together non-elite white people who have normative responsibility for their children's education with capitalists who benefit.

This is a true story: a friend who is sincerely and resolutely anti-racist decided to put her two sons in private schools; she felt the risk to them, particularly the one who was struggling in school, was just too great in the neighborhood, largely working-class racially mexican, school. She did this with regretful awareness that such decisions, repeated by others, contributed to the isolation of working-class minority children in their own schools. But she did it. She had a duty to her son, who was struggling. Even an anti-racist parent can contribute in a small way to the isolation of poor children in their own schools.

Anderson says integration "does not prescribe normative standards that are impossible or unreasonably difficult for people to meet," but she does not engage these problems: (1) there is limited opportunity for places in society that provide economic security and engaging work; (2) many people work low wage, often part-time or seasonal, insecure jobs with few benefits—or are unemployed or incarcerated; (3) children in some schools end up with these poorer situations at a much higher rate than children in other schools; (4) schools influence to some degree the prospects for their students (even if families play a bigger role); (5) parents should secure—as best they can—their children's futures; (6) parents, in light of the above, are normatively influenced to select good schools for their children; and (7) a high percentage of black (or latin) students from low-income families in a school make it more likely that the students in that school will not do well. Therefore, like my anti-racist parent whose integrity as both an anti-racist and as a parent I admire, good—even anti-racist— people make choices that often further isolate poor minority children in their own schools, and these decisions have a normative basis in parental duties.

When I asked Anderson about this (electronically), she replied, "I don't think of integration as primarily a demand addressed to individual parents or children, to make huge sacrifices for some collective ideal." But that makes her presentation in the last pages of *The Imperative of Integration* confusing, for she says that state-centered policies are not enough and then cites "white flight" in response to busing for integration. While we can acknowledge that many who left central cities in response to court orders of busing to integrate schools had unjustified fears, we cannot say they were not motivated to do the best by their children. Moreover, these decisions to move were made by individual families, not corporately by "white people." Some had ignorant stereotypes of black people; not all did. The result can be "white flight" as well as the abandonment of the cities by many black people who can afford to move.

Raising the point that schools prepare us for a life of work and that so much work is unchallenging (at best) and insecure, with many working for low wages or part-time (and many others suffering unemployment), I asked Anderson what sort of future opportunities she imagined for people living in an integrated society. She replied, "There are lots of economic and social policies that would be needed ..., which I don't discuss in my book. It's only chipping off one problem of a much larger system that also sustains other kinds of injustice." I agree with that. But does a project of identifying a non-racist society for which we are supposed to be *hopeful* makes sense without addressing much broader injustice beyond that experienced specifically by black people? I think not; the whole issue of sustaining hope of a non-racist future cannot sensibly be raised without specifying in more detail the sort of society which one is proposing. *The Imperative of Integration* doesn't do that. It doesn't show that people don't have good reasons to make choices—as parents, for example—which would defeat integration.

Charles Mills on reparations

Perhaps a more plausible account of racial justice might directly create racial equality overall. Charles Mills argues that racial wealth and other economic inequality is due to unjust racial exploitation of black people by white people. He suggests a solution: "The ideal for racial justice would ... be the end to current racial exploitation and the equitable redistribution of the benefits of past racial exploitation" (Mills 2004: 48). I interpret Millsian redistribution to imply wealth transfers from white to black until the two groups are equal in wealth (thus repairing racially exploitive transfers from black to white). The proposal for wealth transfers derives from Mills' interracial model of racism.

Such wealth transfers might not end racism—for three reasons. First, if redistribution did not attack economic inequality generally, many black people would suffer racism. Suppose racial inequality is eliminated but total inequality is the same. Black and white people will be proportionately represented among those who live in neighborhoods with the most limited educational opportunities, the highest unemployment, and the greatest concentration of low-wage and part-time jobs. Consider a black family nearly as disadvantaged in the racially egalitarian society as any black family is now. It is likely suffering racism. Racism does not impact all black people to the same extent. For example, lighter complexioned black folk have, on average, experienced less severe injustice than darker folks. Not to be misunderstood: this is but one obvious way that racism impacts black people very differently. If we imagine a "racially egalitarian" society which retains much inequality within each race, black people who are worse off would be those most victimized by racism. The society would be racially unjust.

Second, many white people have been victimized by anti-black racism (and a few black people have benefited). Someone must pay for racial redistribution. Should victims of racism be made to pay again because they are white? These issues go to the heart of the interracial model of racism: who benefits from it? To simplify, let us focus for now on wealth disparities. Mills proposes that white people corporately have benefited from racial exploitation; so even if they, or their ancestors, did not all commit the injustices, they might have to pay for them. Wealth transfers must come from the beneficiaries of injustice. Here is a simple plan for creating wealth equality: divide black people into a hundred equal groups from the wealthiest to the poorest and do the same for the white people; then transfer wealth from the wealthiest one percent of white people to the wealthiest one percent of black people until the two groups are equal in wealth per capita; then repeat the process for each percentile. You can imagine this more fine-grained, and perhaps you can even imagine it being accomplished through taxation; that does not change the essence of the proposal. The analysis of "who benefits?" implicit in the plan is that white people benefit and the wealthier a white person is, the more that person benefited; so reparations cost all white people and cost rich white people more. This corrective is consistent with Mills' account of who benefits. But his belief about who benefits is incorrect.

We saw in earlier chapters many cases where non-black people have been harmed by anti-black racism. Anti-black racism in the South explains much of the extreme poverty among southern white people. The history of anti-black racism is locked into a complex story of unequal exploitation among people called black or white. While we find huge racial inequalities, we also find, intertwined with these, inequalities among black people and extreme inequalities among white people. White planters got rich from the labor of white and black sharecroppers; racist exploitation of black and mexican sharecroppers facilitated exploitation of white sharecroppers. Wealth transfers from beneficiaries to victims of anti-black racism requires a non-racial identification of beneficiaries and victims. Mills' "racial exploitation" analysis and the corrective proposal it suggests do not do that.

Third, racism cannot be disentangled from other non-racial injustices. If we could separate racial from other injustices and victims from beneficiaries, then perhaps we could simply transfer wealth from beneficiaries to victims, leaving social structure intact. If, however, it is impossible to separate racial economic injustice from exploitation generally, the demand for racial justice has radical implications.

Consider the system of sharecropping: how do we separate "racially unjust" exploitation of black sharecroppers from the "ordinary" exploitation of white sharecroppers? In the sharecropping system there was a "reckoning time" at the end of the year: after calculating the resources the sharecropper had received from "the man" and the crop returned, the owner told the sharecropper the debt or credit for the year. But was the system of sharecropping itself a form of illicit wealth transfer or only that portion we can ascribe to falsely claimed debt? How can we identify which debts are falsely claimed and what was a just price to charge the sharecropper for the supplies used? (Many economists reject the notion of a "just price," arguing that any price is just as long as people will pay it.) Now consider the white sharecropper working for the same planter as a black sharecropper. Is the wealth extracted from him just while that from the black sharecropper is unjust? The planter can get more from the white sharecropper by threatening to replace him with a black person. This example is not insignificant. A huge amount of wealth was accumulated through sharecropping and tenancy, which formed the basis of cotton production for longer than slavery did. Sharecropping was founded in mainstream capitalist norms of property ownership. We cannot separate wealth due to racism from the rest.

Banks and other financial institutions have redlined neighborhoods in a way that has limited opportunities for black people to accumulate real estate wealth. Most likely, like much racist discrimination, redlining was profitable. Were poor white people also harmed? In Chapter 6 I described the sub-prime mortgage scam that specially victimized black homebuyers. What are we to say about similarly victimized white homebuyers?

Much racism in education is the effect of housing segregation and the funding of schools from local property taxes. I doubt that housing segregation is unprofitable to real estate interests. Generally rich and poor people do not share neighborhoods, and people often pay huge premiums to live in exclusive neighborhoods. Using local property taxes to fund schools is not explicitly racist and is inseparable from opportunity hoarding that harms many white people too. Affluent suburban communities resist regional or state-wide funding that would equalize educational opportunities; while the urban communities are disproportionately black, the commonly accepted norm is that people advance their children's' opportunity by hoarding opportunity, thus limiting opportunity available to others who are more disadvantaged. This form of racism is not condemned by current norms and is not separate from the attempts of well-off white people to distance themselves—particularly their children—from poor people generally. This nearly universal practice most deeply harms the poorest children, in the US disproportionately black and latin.

Practically, we cannot bring about racial equality without addressing non-racial inequality. This becomes clear when we specify exactly what racial equality would look like. Consider two extremes. If we specify racial equality as redistributing the current poverty, crappy jobs, unemployment, and miseducation to different people, then the objections made thus far apply: (1) for many of the most disadvantaged, we retain the effects of our current racism; (2) for the rest, we are inflicting the same or similar harms on different people. If we specify racial equality as leading to a society where the potential of all children is developed and each is encouraged and allowed to contribute whatever abilities she develops to society, we are imagining a radically different social order that challenges capitalist norms of justice.

The first way of imagining racial equality presents insuperable practical difficulties: it would not improve the overall situation of those who are most disadvantaged but change their skin tone. It would fail to inspire black people and provoke fierce resistance from white folk who would be harmed. This is a sure recipe for maintaining the status quo. The second scenario has the potential to inspire a united working class but would meet fierce resistance from the capitalists. Its practical difficulties are enormous but, in the right situation, could be overcome.

We cannot separate racism from other injustices. Many if not most white people are harmed economically by anti-black racism. Moreover, many of these injustices—racial and otherwise—seem to arise from the ordinary workings of capitalist markets as businessmen seek to make maximum profit at minimum risk. Therefore, if we understand reparations as a reform that would transfer wealth from white to black people without undermining or questioning fundamental capitalist norms, it makes no sense.

David Lyons' radical anti-racist egalitarianism

Anderson and Mills address racism without addressing other harms. This approach can't give us a workable solution to racism. People seem to have normative reasons for acting in ways that lead to segregation (my criticism of Anderson). Racial equality may not eliminate racism (one criticism of Mills). Limiting themselves to *racism*, their proposals are unrealizable. In imagining a society without race we have to imagine social changes that go beyond race narrowly understood. The prospect of such changes must be capable of inspiring enough people that they could form a force sufficient to overcome powerful resistance to racial justice.

Anti-racist reforms combined with radically egalitarian ones would seem likely to meet that standard. Such reforms are articulated by David Lyons in his "Corrective Justice, Equal Opportunity, and the Legacy of Slavery and Jim Crow" (Lyons 2013: Chapter 5). There Lyons argues, in the context of a discussion of reparations for racial injustice, that we can identify a continuous agent responsible for racial injustice throughout US history, an agent that can be held accountable for insuring reparations: the US government. He writes that the US government needs "to ensure that social arrangements provide a fair share of favorable life prospects for each child" (106), particularly because so much disadvantage is the result of past and current injustices that affect children. He insists that the US government owes *corrective* justice, "to eliminate unfair inequalities that it has wrongfully promoted" (106, Lyons' italics omitted). He calls his proposal a National Rectification Project. Citing massive injustices to indigenous peoples, Mexican Americans, Asian, Latino, and other immigrants in addition to the horrors done to black people, he proposes to "focus on the most basic needs of children, in order to ensure equal opportunity on the least controversial basis possible" (107).

More specifically he proposes that the government must insure "prenatal care for mothers, postnatal care for mothers and children, and adequate nutrition, which school breakfasts and lunches can help provide" including "substantial outreach programs to overcome language barriers" and other obstacles to participation (107). He calls for "affordable, well-maintained family housing" which is safe and pleasant. Children must have "adequate individual attention" in school with small classes. All children must be provided "with adequate exposure to cultural and technical developments" so that none are disadvantaged in work or schooling. "Children must have adequate time with their parents," implying that pay must be sufficient to allow parents to support families with reasonable work hours. There must be "adequately staffed day care" and transportation to jobs and other places. His point is that "poor children's life prospects cannot be improved significantly without aiding their parents" (107–8). All of this implies radical changes in work (higher pay for fewer hours) and working conditions, and in expenditures for housing, transportation, and support services for children (with much higher pay for those who provide these services).

Lyons goes on to call for programs to address the wealth gap between black and white families (he doesn't say "eliminate"). He writes that many of these goods and services should be provided free, including transportation and health care. He notes that these programs would benefit not only people identified as disadvantaged minorities but also impoverished white people. He adds that we need to address what he calls "the moral component" of injustice, not just the meeting of material needs but the combatting of the vicious ideas, attitudes, emotions, and practices that have stigmatized and degraded particularly black people, but others as well.

I think it is plausible to suppose that such a program, well laid out and explained, would attract support from many people, perhaps eventually from enough to overcome opposition to it. It projects a vision of a society where every child is cared for and nurtured and those responsible for their care and development, both parents and other workers, would receive the support to make this possible. It is hard not to be inspired by such a vision. So Lyons' proposal meets the standard proposed earlier of being able to inspire sufficient support.

However, his proposals harbor fatal problems. First, Lyons is proposing radical reforms that would provide every child with resources and education to eliminate disadvantage. Lyons writes, "Fair competition in what is sometimes called 'the race of life' requires a substantially equal set of opportunities and resources" (105). He accepts the idea of a "race of life." So he is talking about fair *competitive* opportunity. We are to imagine that some of our children will be architects, engineers, physicists, or philosophers while others will work picking or processing crops, raising chickens or catfish or slaughtering them, working in fast-food or other restaurants or doing factory work. That's the race, who gets the good jobs, who gets the crappy ones. Lyons never questions this organization of labor but imagines a fair competition to determine where children end up: the children of poultry processing workers and the children of electrical engineers have a fair chance at the more interesting, challenging, safer labor.

This will never happen. As I have argued elsewhere (Gomberg 2007, especially Chapter 3), children will tend to be socialized for opportunities in numbers that at least approximate the opportunities that will be available to them—call this The Socialization Principle. To do otherwise is to socialize many for what only a few end up doing, a recipe for social instability and discontent as well as a waste of resources. So all societies socialize their young for opportunities that will actually exist for them. But in societies that divide labor in the ways with which we are familiar, *opportunity* (for the most interesting jobs requiring the most intensive and extensive training) *will inevitably be radically unequal*, in ways with which we are familiar. This is a necessary result of socialization. Without imagining the reorganization of labor, an issue Lyons does not address, his proposal for fair opportunity does not make sense.

The communism I propose would reorganize labor to share both simple and more complex, skilled labor among all. It is compatible with The Socialization Principle to develop the talents of each child with the prospect that developed abilities could be contributed to society—provided that labor is shared in these ways (Gomberg 2007, Chapters 7 and 8).

Second, Lyons' proposal runs afoul of the political-economic arguments in Chapter 6. He is proposing that the needs of all families with children for adequate housing, nutrition, health care, child care, safe neighborhoods, security, education, and other social services be met. Jobs would be safe and well paid; parents would have sufficient time with their children. Any capitalist society which adopted such a program of benefits for workers would have a wage bill that would make goods produced and services provided under these conditions much more expensive than comparable goods and services produced and provided by workers who are more exploited and oppressed. The pressure of competition between capitalists creates a race to the bottom for workers.[2]

The US is a declining power, particularly relative to China. US capitalists face competition from all over the world. Hence there is pressure to decrease costs. This explains the terrible conditions under which food is harvested, processed, and slaughtered and the shipping of garment production elsewhere (except in a few sweatshops). Much manufacturing also goes to lower wage areas, and wages tend to stagnate or decline for all but the most highly skilled workers.

Despite its obvious appeal to those who oppose racial injustice, Lyons' proposal fails in two ways. First, it imagines the restructuring of *opportunity* to make it equal and universal without imagining the restructuring of the *positions* for which we seek opportunity to make them available to all. It would thus have us imagine equal opportunity for a *limited number* of lives of engaging labor. This won't happen. Second, in imagining conditions of work that provide security, sufficiency, and leisure for all, it pushes beyond the limits of what capitalist economies make possible for workers. We need to consider a solution yet more radical than Lyons'.

Only communism can end racism

In order to end racism we must be able to organize sufficient force to overcome those who benefit from racism. "Benefit" is a relative term: benefit compared to what? If the only alternative to racist social organization is a society where white people are at greater risk of the very harms of which black people are now at greater risk, then white people benefit compared with *this* alternative. If that is the only alternative to racism, then, it seems to me, there is no hope of a society without race. To sustain hope of a society without racism I must try to show how the *vast majority* would be—and could see themselves to be—better off in a society without racism. Only communism offers reasonable hope of this.

Racism is a way of organizing inequality within the working class. When not all workers can live well (by capitalist standards), it enhances social control and becomes

---

[2] Funny story: at a conference on "The Moral Legacy of Slavery" Lyons presented this proposal. In the discussion Charles Mills pointed out that realizing Lyons' proposal was incompatible with capitalist economic organization. In the break between sessions, I congratulated Charles on his comment. "Paul," he replied, "you misunderstood. I meant that as an *objection*."

an increasingly common feature of capitalist social organization to create *significant inequalities* among workers. Then workers focus their attention on the relative advantages and disadvantages of those closer to their social positions who naturally attract their attention. Anger at the relative advantages of others and contempt for others based on relative disadvantages—rationalized by racist social thought and allied ways of thinking about inequality—replace class struggle. Capitalists get off the hook.

Once racism—inequality among workers marked by the "racial" appearance of a person's body—develops in capitalist society it tends to spread. Racism depends on and promotes the moneyist conception of the good, that what makes life good are the goods and services money can buy. Inevitably these are in limited supply. If we think that these are what makes life good, then a person's having more money will be rationalized as signifying that the *person* has greater relative worth (Gomberg 2016). To say that they are in limited supply is to say that not everyone can have as much as they want; some get them only if others don't. These inequalities are very important to people. As Du Bois argued, they can even get people (poor southern white people, in his example) who are—at a national level—exceptionally poor to be "content" with their poverty as long as they have *more than others* (black people) to whom they compare themselves locally. They may have inferior schools (as southern white people did), but they compared their schools to those of the black people around them, which had even fewer resources. In this way capitalists could pay a low wage (including social wage) to all, as long as there was sufficient inequality to induce racial distrust and racist social thought among white workers. Similarly in the current period the extreme oppression of workers in agriculture and food processing (hugely disproportionately latin and black) keeps workers divided and creates relative advantages for urban workers. The capitalists must make profits under conditions of intense national and international competition. As a result not all workers can be well off. So racism is functional, creating relative stability and control of workers while depressing hourly and social wages for all workers.

No responsible parent will endorse a social change that would expose their children to greater risk of a bad life. Many white parents think racism insulates their children, at least to a degree, from the prospects that befall black people. Opportunity for good lives is limited; many end up unemployed or in low wage mind-numbing jobs with few or no benefits and little security. So whatever a society without race would be, it will not be one that would replace the oppression experienced disproportionately by black people with "fairly distributed" oppression. We can't build a winning movement for *that* "solution." Race organizes relative winners and losers among workers (where the "winners" are often not very well off) in the struggle over goods in limited supply.

The communist alternative is *to make the most important goods of unlimited supply*. Social values and social structures must change. We cease to value ever more consumer goods, desire for which can be multiplied indefinitely, always in limited supply. Instead, we come to value a life of intelligent, creative, constructive activity, a life useful to others.

We must change social structures so that everyone can have *these* goods without diminishing their availability to anyone else. If we share labor, each doing a share of whatever labor cannot be made interesting and challenging—perhaps harvesting and processing food, packing and shipping necessities, some factory labor, much cleaning up—then no one's life is consumed by such labor. Each has opportunity and *social encouragement* to develop more complex abilities. We each have reason to encourage others to develop and contribute their abilities, for we will have inspiring architecture, welcoming and nurturing public spaces and urban landscapes, public health, medical services, particle physics, philosophy, sculpture, music, opera and drama only if people develop these abilities and contribute them to the rest of us. This more challenging and, for those who develop their abilities in these areas, more engaging labor is available to all in unlimited supply provided that this labor too is shared among all with the relevant competence. When everyone contributes simple labor—giving all of us time to develop more complex abilities—and contributes mastered complex skills, each can earn esteem for these contributions. These important goods can be available to everyone in a non-competitive social environment. Everyone's contributions make possible the contributions of others. Each flourishes by enabling others to flourish.

In *How to Make Opportunity Equal* (Gomberg 2007) I explained how labor sharing might work and dealt with several objections, including how to deal with people who do not willingly accept the principle of labor sharing (Chapter 7). I showed how it promised to transform relationships from competition for limited opportunity to nurturing for unlimited opportunities, where each person's accomplishments enrich the lives of others (Chapter 8). In another essay (Gomberg 2016) I have discussed further problems: how contributing labor can be both a duty and a good (47–8); why jealousies of others' accomplishments and status rivalries would diminish or disappear as all are able to make useful contributions for which they are rightly esteemed (49–50); why norms of labor contribution would enhance the natural connection between esteem and contributions to a common project by making the connection normative as well (47; also 2007, Chapter 13).

At the center of racism is the racist organization of labor, where the dirtier, more back-breaking, more dangerous, simpler and more tedious labor has been done disproportionately by black people or by immigrant or women workers. When labor is divided in this way a negative stigma attaches to the simpler labor and to the workers who do it. By sharing both simple and more complex labor, we erase that stigma. We abolish this racial (and gendered) division of labor. We can unite all workers around a vision of a communist society where we flourish together. It is no simple task to persuade a critical mass of workers that we will flourish together in this way, but, it seems to me, it is *possible*.

In the last chapter I investigate the processes by which enough people might come to see that communist society is worth working to bring about. There is a reasonable hope of persuading enough of us that we would be better off in this alternative communist social organization. There is reasonable hope of such a future.

11

Reasonable Hope?

People must be able to hope before they can act; they must possess not only ideals and a sense of mission, but hope and confidence that they will be able to realize their ideals through their own actions.

Maurice Meisner[1]

An objection

"Paul, you haven't shown that there is reasonable hope of a society without race. To sustain reasonable hope you must show what might lead to the communism you described and that there is reasonable hope that these things will occur.

"How can you possibly imagine a revolution occurring? How many must suffer and die in futile struggle? And how could you be optimistic about the *results* of any revolution? The Soviet Union has given way to capitalist Russia, and China is communist in name only. How much cruelty and suffering are you willing to advocate in pursuit of your communist dream?

"You say that capitalism and modernity are based on racist social and economic organization. Then you say the only solution is communism. But communism is vanishingly unlikely. Your argument will more likely *discourage* anti-racists than inspire activism.

"Because of the immense suffering that any struggle for communism is likely to cause, because of the unlikely prospect of communism and because the likely effect of your argument is to *discourage* anti-racist activism, not inspire it, your advocacy of communism is wrong, both morally and practically."

Is there reasonable hope of communism?

Urban uprisings and revolutionary situations

Revolutions in the twentieth century arose from urban insurrections in Russia and in response to oppression of rural people in China. However, the percentage of the

---

[1] Meisner 1999: 35.

world's population doing agricultural work is in steep decline caused by mechanization, high-production seeds, chemical fertilizers, and herbicides. So I focus on urban uprisings.

Mass contentions such as general strikes and uprisings are not sufficient for communist revolution but seem necessary for urban-based revolution. Such events can occur, as they did in Tunisia in December 2010 and January 2011 and in Egypt in January 2011, when people feel they no longer want to live as they have and develop "contempt for death" (Lenin 1962 [1906]: 178). Both uprisings were preceded by many years of working class contention including strikes (Beinin 2016). In the US, urban uprisings occurred in 1964 in Harlem in response to the killing of a resident by police, on a much larger scale in Watts the following year, and then emerged in many cities— in 1967 Detroit and Newark witnessed large scale rebellions against police and national guard—in the rest of the 1960s into the early 1970s. These uprisings were limited by the low participation of non-black people. Politicians called for "law-and-order," and legislation led eventually to mass incarceration.

With rare exceptions general strikes and urban uprisings do not lead to profound political change. When the Egyptian army was welcomed by rebels in Tahrir Square, it meant that nothing positive was likely to come from the uprising. Mubarak was gone, but what followed continued the essence of Mubarak's policies. The army and police are linked socially and organizationally to local and international capitalists, implementing policies favorable to capitalists and repressing working-class or radical dissent that threatens their interests. With few influenced by communist thought, most occupiers of Tahrir Square did not understand that (I suppose some did). So they welcomed the army.

Some situations offer revolutionary possibilities. Lenin discussed several times what constitutes a revolutionary situation. He wrote, "It is only when the *'lower classes' do not want* to live in the old way and the *'upper classes' cannot carry on in the old way* that the revolution can triumph" (Lenin 1966 [1920]: 84–5 emphasis in original). Workers, or at least the leading segment of workers, must realize the need for revolution and "be prepared to die for it." The rulers must be divided among themselves, causing various factions to draw the masses into contests between rulers: "the masses ... uncomplainingly allow themselves to be robbed in 'peace time', but, in turbulent times, are drawn both by all the circumstances of the crisis and *by the 'upper classes' themselves* into independent historical action" (Lenin 1964b [1915]: 214, emphasis in original). Most of us most of the time want to be left alone. We feel we cannot affect the direction of society; we don't think much about how it should be organized. But for the reasons Lenin gives, crises and contests between ruling class factions can change that. Only when the ruling class itself is weak and divided, only when factions of it mobilize the masses for their own reasons, is there revolutionary opportunity for the exploited and oppressed to change the course of history.

None of the mass uprisings or other instances of contention in Arab nations in 2010 and 2011 or in the US in the 1960s occurred in revolutionary situations, which often arise in wartime particularly where a ruling class is suffering military defeat or a country is invaded and occupied by outside forces. These situations occurred in the First World War in Russia and in the Second in China. They require not just suffering and anger on the part of the exploited and oppressed, but division and vacillation on the part of the ruling class.

"But, Paul, it has been over seventy-five years since the end of the last world war. Surely you don't think revolutionary situations of the sort you imagine are likely to arise soon." The revolutionary thought of Marx and of Lenin arose from an estimate that capitalism was inherently unstable and prone to crisis, even, as Lenin argued in *Imperialism* (1964c [1916]), world war. A society can be extremely oppressive of masses of workers and peasants but, if stable, can last for thousands of years. Can capitalism be made tolerably stable? Can wars be limited and confined, avoiding global conflict? If the answer to these questions is "yes," then there is no reasonable hope of profound change. If both can reasonably be answered "no," then hope for communism may be reasonable.

In the current period the main threat to global stability is long-term strategic conflict between the US, a declining power, and China, a rising power. Can global conflict between these two powers be prevented? I estimate that it cannot. Hope that revolutionary situations will arise in the future is reasonable.

"Paul, that's just a philosophy of 'worse is better,' which is morally repulsive." To seek to make things worse is morally repulsive. Those who have power will risk revolution to try to maintain (in the case of US rulers) or gain (in the case of China's rulers) global ascendancy. Communists fight against inter-imperialist war but cannot prevent it. To believe we cannot prevent it is not morally repulsive. To believe that war will likely provide revolutionaries with opportunities to create a communist society is not repulsive. So reasonable hope for these reasons is not morally repulsive.

The revolutionary situation Lenin described is not enough. There also must be many communists who have strong personal relationships with many non-communists; as a result of these, enough people will follow communist leadership to make communist revolution and communist society possible. This is the task of the rest of this chapter.

How people are transformed through struggle

For communist society to be possible people must change. People change in the course of class struggle. This section shows how and why.

In April of 2010 I interviewed six former workers at Stella D'Oro bakery in Bronx, New York. In August 2008, 138 workers struck against Brynwood Partners; the strike lasted eleven months. Brynwood had bought Stella D'Oro from Kraft Foods. Brynwood's plan was to break the unions, making the company more profitable, and then re-sell it. After an eleven-month strike the National Labor Relations Board ruled that Brynwood had bargained in bad faith and ordered that Brynwood resume collective bargaining with the union, reinstate the workers on the terms of the expired contract, and give them back pay. After the workers returned, Brynwood announced that it had sold Stella D'Oro to Lance, Inc., a non-union company, which shut the Bronx bakery in October 2009 and moved production to Ohio (*New York Times*, Oct. 6, 2009). The striking workers lost their jobs.

The workers had been asked to make concessions that would cut their effective hourly pay by $3. They might have accepted these, but Brynwood also demanded that the cookie-stackers, women workers in a lower pay category, take an additional $1 per hour cut the first year of the contract and then a *further* $1 per hour cut *each of the other four* years of the contract for a total of a $5 per hour cut in addition to the $3 per hour cut (at the end of five years their pay would be $13/hour). This was too much. The proposal enraged the workers.

Before the strike workers had cooperated well and, when conflicts arose, settled these through intervention of union leaders rather than through management. They sang songs during the winter holidays, brought food for single men, and celebrated one another's birthdays. They cooperated with lower-level management in making production. Management left them alone if they took extra break time to celebrate a special occasion for a worker.

Two themes emerged during the interviews. First, during the strike the sources of self-pride were very different from what they had been. Before the strike workers typically took pride in providing for their families and doing well with their children. During the strike workers valued their contributions to the common effort, anticipating norms and values of a communist society (Gomberg 2007: Chapter 13). Strikers also identified strongly with and developed pride in the working class as a fighting class which doesn't knuckle under to the capitalists. Second, while all workers felt that *relationships* to one another had changed during the strike (becoming like family, much closer to one another), four workers felt that *they* had changed as a result of the strike, becoming more communist in their ways of thinking and acting.

Before the strike Maria (all names pseudonyms) had taken pride in putting her children through college despite her surgeries to repair damage caused by her job. This source of self-pride does not challenge capitalist norms. She felt she had to strike to preserve her dignity: "I take 32 years in this place and I feel like somebody throw something in the garbage and doesn't appreciate nothing... .If we had taken those kind of contract..., I don't respect myself." Bill told me, "We felt the women were being abused ... and they were the hardest workers there." Francisco told me, "The job these ladies doing over there was so hard ... have problems, ... have surgery, ... and then say after twenty years, ... now you gonna make less money. That's not fair! ... These people don't ... know what is humanity."

What Maria, Bill, and Francisco say seems to accept the capitalist idea that our value is represented by what people will pay for our labor. But that assessment is one-sided. The *resistance* to the insult, which disrespected their work, insists on the human worth of the worker and her labor and was anti-sexist. Francisco told me the women's job required a quickness and dexterity that few could attain. Before the strike the workers had accepted the sexist norm of paying women cookie stackers less than male bakers. Brynwood pushed the sexism so far that the workers, women and men, rose up against it.

In fighting Brynwood workers began to embrace communist values and norms: that workers and what they contribute have value, that women deserve respect equal to that for men. These norms resist capitalist norms that diminish or dehumanize workers.

In the strike communist values emerged. Mutual respect and bonds of friendship grew. Strikers shared child care so that parents could participate in strike activities. When a striker died during the strike, a collection was taken for the family. When a union supporter died, strikers helped to move his things. A collection was taken for a striker who needed surgery. Strikers discussed together financial and other personal and family problems. Maria told me, "The strike becomes day by day more strong because one supports another.... we feel like a family because some bring food ... for everybody." Chuy said, "If there was a loaf of bread, if there was twenty people, we supported twenty people. That way was guaranteed." Bill said, "We made sure everyone was taken care of, if there was anything missing at home or whatever, any problems, we shared this all together." Later he explained, "Now we're discussing issues at home—we're not just talking about work—something ... about the family, if we are able to help each other out in any way.... During the strike everything became pretty much personal." Sharing food, sharing problems, solving problems collectively—strikers valued one another in a struggle to which each contributes. This expresses a communist value. Each is valued and esteemed for their contributions, reinforcing in each a sense of self-worth. Workers valued promoting the good of all, the beginning of a communist community.

Workers developed *class* consciousness. Outside support for the strike helped strikers feel more positive about the struggle and themselves. A newspaper deliveryman dropped a bundle of papers every day for the strikers; the strikers might give him water. Every week a fire truck driver stopped with water, fruit, and salad for the picketers. Sanitation and telephone workers stopped to show support. A woman stopped to pray with them. A car wash customer gave twenty dollars every week. One supporter would bring pizza, another donuts and coffee. Workers would stop by after their work shift on another job and donate money for lunch or pizza. In a Latin American country, a banner was made supporting the strike and carried in the May Day parade there. Then the banner was shipped to the US, where it was used in demonstrations here. Several people stressed that the strike was known all over NYC, all over the world. Support from communists was helpful. Bill said that the communists "was like a wall we were able to lean on. They would be out here practically every day, pick up the spirit, we'll set rallies and they'll be part of it big time, they spread the word all over ..., let the whole country know about the strike." The outside support helped strikers see that they were part of a *class*, the working class.

Class consciousness arose also from the struggle as a fight against management, which had contempt for the workers, thinking they would be easily defeated. Workers took pride that they had hurt management. Alex said, "We show to the bosses, we not stupid, we have a power to do things, ... we not chicken.... And we show to the labor movement like if you get together and be united you can accomplish a lot." Francisco told me,

> The guy said, "Listen, Reagan defeat the controllers.... Reagan disappeared them and we're going to disappear you," just like that. ... They say "the time of the ignorants is finished," they called us "ignorants," and I said, "we going on strike for eleven months, in eleven months you people ... against the 'ignorant' you cannot produce in this plant. Who the ignorants?" ... And I said "The people who produce

are the workers. We can defeat the capitalists because the people who produce, who can build things, are the workers."

Maria said, "We demonstrate we have the power.... We bring a lot of ... political people [communists and others], and then we demonstrate those people to have the power.... we have a victory." Later she observed, "[The working class] is the majority, we build this company, and we make it, I feel so proud to be in the class obrero."

The sources of workers' self-pride changed during the strike. They had taken pride as good workers and providers. In the strike they took pride from the recognition they received from others outside the plant and from one another as sisters and brothers in struggle and for making a good fight and hurting management. The breadth of support for the strike led some to take pride in themselves as members of the working class. Everyone thought the strike resisted the capitalist norm, emphasized by Cox, that workers are less than fully human.

Did this struggle change them? Four, all immigrants, felt it had. For Victor, Francisco, and Alex, it reminded them of the radicalism of their youth in their countries of origin. They felt that the strike reminded them of things they had known but had "forgotten" with their concern to keep a job and care for their families. Maria had no radical background but liked the communist literature she received and was inviting people to communist events, as were Francisco and Alex. Those two joined a communist party and committed themselves to communist activism. All four said, that having been in struggle and aided by others, they no longer could look the other way when workers in struggle needed help.

Bakery union leaders thought the Stella D'Oro strike too small to be of concern. So rank-and-file workers exerted their own leadership. Workers' initiative and self-activity introduced them to elements of communism. Participation of communists in strike support, bringing students and workers from other jobsites to the picket line, organization of rallies, preparation of fliers, and distribution of communist newspapers together led some workers to think about and embrace communism as an alternative to the capitalist society they experienced.

How might a large group of communists develop?

The Stella D'Oro interviews, by themselves, prove nothing about reasonable hope of communism. They illustrate how a very few workers can change in struggle. Daily life in capitalism can lead those workers to "forget" again.

Reasonable hope of communism requires not just a revolutionary situation but also a *large* group of communists with sufficiently strong relationships with many other workers that they could lead a critical mass to overthrow the capitalist state and establish a proletarian dictatorship committed to communism. In this section we inquire what might lead to the development of a large group committed to communism.

The current situation in the US seems bleak: as we saw in Chapter 6, strikes have declined 90 percent from the period 1965–1979. Open white supremacists have taken to the streets and even stormed the Capitol building. Nearly half of voters in the 2020 presidential election in the US voted for a candidate who encouraged racism toward immigrants. On the other hand, there was an uprising in Ferguson, Missouri in 2014 and 2015 against the police killing of Mike Brown and the decades-long practice of using black motorists as a piggy-bank to support local government. Responses to the torture/murder of George Floyd and other racist police killings in 2020 mobilized many mostly young working class people (in Houston 60,000 marched to honor Floyd's life). Still, they fall far short of the urban uprisings, mass demonstrations, large strikes, and campus uprisings of the 1960s. These in turn were small compared with the red-led movements of the 1930s and 1940s and other militant working class struggle of the nineteenth and first half of the twentieth century (Brecher 2014). What could possibly justify any inference from the small struggle at Stella D'Oro that a large group of communists might develop?

As I noted earlier, Marx argued that capitalism tends to be unstable and crisis-ridden and Lenin that interimperialist rivalries lead to global war (the ultimate instability); these arguments are plausible. Accelerating climate change further undermines stability and amplifies instability caused by economic crisis and war. Climate change, smaller proxy wars between imperialists (as in Syria), intense poverty, drug gangs, and oppression by local gangs and militias all cause mass migration. As I write in 2023, the Russian invasion of Ukraine and the defense of Ukraine by the European Union and the US have sharpened global divisions with China, India, Brazil, and many other countries allied to varying degrees with Russia. This is not the place to explore these complicated issues in detail. Still, I think it reasonable to anticipate greater instability.

As instability grows, so will strikes and other working-class contention, such as the protests of police killings. In these struggles a segment of workers may develop a communist understanding of their situation, as happened at Stella D'Oro but on a larger scale. Mass uprisings, such as those of the Arab spring are likely to occur. In a climate of heightened class struggle, of frequent strikes, of demonstrations on campuses and in the streets against racism and in support of striking workers, many could embrace communism as an alternative and become communist revolutionaries. It won't happen unless mass working-class struggle becomes common, but in mass struggle the communist segment can become large.

In the interviews of Stella D'Oro workers I showed how communist consciousness and commitment can grow in struggle (even this very small one). Since future instability offers greater opportunity to recruit communists, it is reasonable to hope that our efforts will make the communist segment of our class grow.

Communists, non-communists, and communist revolution

Something is missing in my argument that a large group of communists may develop: this development requires not just instability but communists with sufficiently strong ties with other workers that they can recruit them to the communist movement. What *relationships* must exist between communists and others for non-communists to become communists and for communists to lead non-communists in proletarian revolution?

Whatever influence communists had on Stella D'Oro strikers was due to their consistency in showing up at picket lines, their bringing others (family, friends, students, co-workers) to the picket lines, the support for the strike in their unions, churches, and other organizations, their organizational support in the form of rallies, leaflets, and other literature, their distribution of communist literature to the workers, and their presence in the lives of these workers away from the strike (such as helping a worker with his job search). Moreover, communists were more likely to influence the family, friends, students and co-workers whom they brought to the strike—people with whom they spent time in daily life—than to influence strikers. As the strikers became closer to each other by visiting one another's homes and getting to know their families, so communists—if they are to influence others—must make their lives open to non-communists and intertwine their lives with non-communists. Only through such personal intimacy can non-communists develop confidence in communists. Others evaluate our ideas as we exhibit their meaning in our lives, not just as words out of our mouths (or off our keyboards).

Both in words and, to the extent possible in capitalist society, in their lives communists must express communism. The CP of the 1930s through the 1950s engaged in massive organizing efforts that led to the formation of unions and other organizations that had millions of members. However, those communists hid revolutionary goals from most whom they knew. Many viewed their participation in unions as their party work. In the end many denied that revolution was needed.

If the activity of communists is to lead to communism, some arguments of this book should guide their work. Opposition to racism disadvantaging black, latin, indigenous, asian and other workers (especially black workers) must lead united working class struggle. The struggle must be based on a common understanding of *unequal exploitation and oppression*. Workers *share* a common exploitation and oppression by the capitalists as workers. But they share these harms *unequally*: generally black and other racially oppressed workers are *more* oppressed, experience more diminished opportunities, have the prospect of shorter lives, poorer health, less economic security, and greater likelihood of incarceration. This is a generality that workers must recognize as a basis of their unity.

They should also recognize that it is only a generalization: white children growing up poor in Appalachia, the Ozarks, or in small towns everywhere experience constricted prospects, as do children in the poorest sections of cities and suburbs. Recognizing racial oppression does not mean thinking that it exhausts the ways our class is brutalized and oppressed. When workers recognize unequal racial oppression but at the same time are attentive to *all* the ways in which workers can be exploited and oppressed, workers can unite as a class. Fighting racism and sexism must unite our class.

Most important, communists should proclaim their vision of a communist world, where work is not for a paycheck but to do something useful for others, where labor—both simple and more complex—is shared, where the abilities of all children are developed so that they can contribute them to others, where we flourish by enabling others to flourish.

The vision of a world without racism and the reasonable hope of creating such a world is necessary to sustain anti-racist working-class struggle. More or less spontaneous instances of working-class rebellion, while often exhibiting courage and solidarity, are frequently undertaken without an overall outlook about what is to be achieved and how the particular tactics used are to achieve it. Where there is a goal, it is some reform of the present order. People have illusions about how readily capitalism can be reformed. The strategy of the bourgeoisie is twofold: (1) wait, for time is on their side, and desperation can give way to despair; (2) exact a price, particularly from the leaders. Eventually the rebellion subsides, or a settlement is reached. Reforms may or may not be won, but even if they are, the condition of the working class generally has less to do with the amount of working class rebellion and more to do with the general state of capitalism, whether there is expansion or contraction, and how that general state affects a particular country, region, or industry. In circumstances where a conscious communist movement has developed, individual workers and groups of workers may come out of these struggles looking to communism for answers to questions about why the reform struggle did not achieve its goals and seeking to understand the general historical development of capitalism. Depending on the bonds of friendship between communists and non-communists, the conscious communist segment among the workers may become large.

What relationships would enable communists to give revolutionary leadership in a revolutionary situation? Mass uprisings sometimes occur in revolutionary situations; when there is a sufficiently large conscious communist segment of the working class (not necessarily the majority) with deep and broad ties with others, that segment can lead others in revolution, as happened in Russia's October Revolution (Rabinovitch 2007, 2017).

As in Russia communists must be *inside* the capitalist military during a war, winning soldiers not to fight working-class soldiers of another land, but to overthrow their own rulers, a strategy of "revolutionary defeatism," as the Bolsheviks called it. Bolshevik influence inside the Russian military made revolution possible, as Bolshevik soldiers and sailors influenced others to overthrow the Russian government (Anonymous 1939). *No* revolution can succeed against a modern state without "turning" the military; otherwise revolution is suicidal. Turning the military requires that young communists be inside it.

Where class struggle culminates in communist-led insurrection, this occurs because out of the individual struggles, a large number of workers, youth, and soldiers have developed a long-term communist commitment and, through their bonds with other workers, laid the basis for yet further recruitment. When a revolutionary situation arises, when many workers have contempt for death, when ruling factions draw workers into political activity to try to gain advantage over rivals, communist revolution may occur if a large communist segment of the workers has deep ties with the rest. The process of expanding communist understanding and commitment would have to continue under workers' dictatorship. When there are strong bonds between the non-communist workers of the spontaneous movement and the more conscious communist element, there is development toward communism.

If Marxist views are right, then we can expect more frequent struggles and more engagement with a communist vision of a society without class exploitation and racism. If revolutionary situations arise and there is a large communist segment of the working class, it should be able to lead other workers in a fight for communism. I am not saying skepticism is unreasonable. The future is impossible to predict, and both hope of communism and skepticism can be reasonable.

Communism and workers' empowerment

"Paul, your ideal seems to harbor a contradiction or at least two ideals that may well not coincide and probably are conflicting ideals. On the one hand, your ideal is a communist society where we contribute labor not for a paycheck to support our families (there is neither money nor wages) but for the good of helping others, which we experience as part of our own good. On the other hand your ideal is a dictatorship of the *proletariat*, the working class, not a dictatorship of a relatively small Leninist party committed to moneyless communism. You assume you can realize both ideals simultaneously, that you can have a society where the masses of working-class people exercise initiative and control in organizing production and distribution of the things we need and have a society where there is no money and people work because they find labor to be a central good in their lives. But why think that these ideals can be realized simultaneously? What if, as seems likely, most workers don't aspire to communist social organization but aspire to be able to run their own small business? What is the source of a reasonable hope that these two ideals will coincide?

In response, parents commonly face a parallel problem; it is only weakly analogous because the relations of parents to their offspring is not at all the same as that of communists to non-communist workers. Parents ideally aim to raise children who as adults are competently self-governing and make decisions as other competent adults do, evaluating information in consultation with others but not routinely subordinating their will to that of another. At the same time parents ideally strive to raise children who, as adults, make *good* decisions, ones that properly show regard for the needs and feelings of others without slighting their own. These two goals may not coincide. Our adult children may make their own decisions, but they might not be very good ones, either showing insufficient regard for others or being wildly imprudent. The fact that these two goals may not coincide does not show that, as parents, we ought not reasonably aim at both.

It is the last point which is, I think, analogous in the relations between communists and non-communists. Communists may reasonably aim at a society governed by the working class *and* at a society based on communist social relations. This is true even if, in the event, workers in power do not opt for communist organization of production and distribution of goods, or a communist party in power (controlling a decisive military force) does not have the active participation of a large mass of workers. To explain why I believe there is reasonable hope that these two goals coincide I will review recent Chinese history. I address why the Chinese revolution failed to lead to communism and whether the faults can be corrected.

This section is organized as follows: first, I review activists in the Cultural Revolution who asserted that the Chinese Communist Party (CCP) had become a privileged bourgeois class; second, I go back to the commune movement in the Great Leap Forward (GLF) of 1958–61 and its successes and collapse; third, I trace the tendency for membership in the CCP and the government to be avenues to economic and social advantage. Finally, I draw these together to argue that it is reasonable to believe that, if communists take care to ensure that party members and government cadre display communism in their lives and do *not* live better than others, egalitarian collectivist ideals can inspire workers in building communist social relationships. The brief argument here is not a thorough study of these issues and arguments; that thorough study is beyond the scope of the present book. My argument does not have to settle everything but must give reasonable hope. We also need further investigation.

When the CCP took control of rural villages before and after 1949 they classified villagers by class—landlord, rich peasant, middle peasant, poor peasant, landless laborer, etc.—and organized the lower classes, poor peasants and landless laborers, to make revolution, particularly against the landlords. Those lower classes were recruited as village leaders in the new order (Hinton 1983, Potter and Potter 1990, Wu 2014). Some joined the Communist Party. A similar process was occurring in the cities, but there the party line was to cooperate with bourgeois and petit-bourgeois elements which had not been aligned with the Guomindang. Soon, however, former Guomindang officials were recruited into government and party.

In late August and September of 1966 Red Guard youth in Beijing, largely from the families of government and party elites, attacked people who were from more educated or elite backgrounds *purely on the basis of family ancestry*; they organized around a line of "good blood," elevating people from proletarian or poor peasant backgrounds. But in January 1967 Yu Luoke's widely read essay "On Class Origins" defended equal rights for all citizens regardless of class origin. The direction of struggle shifted. More people asserted that the dispossessed must struggle against a "new ruling elite" for a redistribution of property and power (Wu 2014: 93).

Shengwulian, a group in Hunan province, said that the enemy is a new privileged red bourgeoisie, that 90 percent of senior cadre are capitalist roaders who must be overthrown. Emerging in fall 1967 as an alliance of 20–25 activist groups, Shengwulian was crushed by the CCP in January and February of 1968. Still immersed in the cult of Mao, they found out that he would not attack the CCP. While (as I will argue) Shengwulian was correct that the CCP had become a "red bourgeoisie," it did not have a communist social program. Peasant demands included *protecting and honoring* the products of peasants' private gardens (Wu 2014: 177).

Shengwulian was branded "ultra-left" by the CCP leadership, but Progressive Labor Party (PLP), based in the US, was following events in China. Soon PLP (1971a) published "The Great Proletarian Cultural Revolution and the Reversal of Workers' Power in China." That essay defended Shenwulian's assertion that CCP senior leaders had become a "red bourgeoisie," a new privileged ruling class, and advocated a more radical social program than Shengwulian, including a defense of the people's communes in China's Great Leap Forward (GLF).

The commune movement had begun in winter and spring 1957–8 in several provinces to mobilize labor for water control projects which could be quite large, requiring cooperation of more people than any village could supply. What came to be called the people's communes grew out of these efforts.

By the end of 1958 the leadership of the CCP encouraged people's communes as part of the GLF. The communes went well beyond cooperative water projects. They could be huge, often 50,000 people, encompassing a fairly large region of a county. They were centrally administered. They typically had village dining halls where food was provided free, where sharing of food across a larger group would equalize the lives of peasants on poorer and better land. Several things, depending on the commune, might be taken out of the money economy for free distribution: nurseries for infants and group homes for the elderly, education for children, health care, entertainment, clothing, housing, and so forth.

Agricultural peoples often have time during the winter which is spent less productively or even unproductively. While water control is one example of projects that could make permanent improvements in land productivity, other projects could be undertaken from local resources to provide better tools for agriculture and other local needs. The push to expand iron and steel production led to many blast furnaces being built in villages, but much steel produced was of poor quality and hence relatively useless.

Was the purpose of the GLF to expand production or to create communist relations and labor motivation? How were these two goals to be evaluated? Was the purpose of free communist distribution to increase production? Or was increased production meant to enable free distribution? Or were they independent goals? In the early 1970s, as part of its evaluation of the Chinese experience, Progressive Labor Party (1971b) addressed these questions:

> Fighting for socialism ... means ... carrying out political struggles that advance an equalitarian, collectivist, anti-individualist way of life. The production of ever-increasing masses of people who struggle for this type of world is the main thing that socialist society must accomplish. The production of goods is secondary to this, must serve this, and must not obstruct this.

For the CCP, expansion of production was the essential thing.

The GLF contributed to the famine of 1959–1961. Certainly relevant is what Mark Selden (1979: 97) calls "some of the worst weather of the century." The famine undermined the great experiment in egalitarian collectivism represented by the people's communes. The CCP preached that anything was possible, that agricultural productivity could be hugely expanded, increasing food available for urban workers. They did some crazy stuff. Commune leaders *ignored the wisdom of the peasants* in the fields. If a lower level leader pointed out that production goals were impossible to reach, he would be called a "right opportunist" who lacked confidence in the people. Top-downism was extreme: instructions were given from the center—influenced by Lysenkoism (Friedman and others 1991: 222)—about how to plant crops; peasants knew that, if followed, they would retard production. Some followed them; many did not (Hinton 1983: 239; Potter and Potter 1990: 71–2).

People were pulled from agricultural production to other tasks. Roderick MacFarquhar tells of visiting Soviets who were struck by "the absence of peasants from the rice fields" during spring planting season. They saw "the thousands of smoking chimneys ... each day, and ... fires that were visible every night," evidence of peasants leaving planting to produce metals locally (MacFarquhar 1983: 119). This testifies not only to the drive for greater production but to excessive optimism about things they could not control. In the preceding years weather had been favorable and crops abundant. They assumed this would continue. Communists must never do that. They must *assume the worst* about things (weather) they cannot control.

Most important, however, few would have perished but for the lying. People were encouraged to lie about agricultural production, and the lies were passed up the chain to the center. Those who lied were honored for their "productive achievements" while those who told the truth were vilified. To show how well they were doing, commune, district, and provincial leaders exported grain to the cities. The peasants often lacked enough grain to survive and died (Hinton 1983: 233–57; see Li 2009: Chapter 4 for how the horror played out in one village and region). The central leadership had been misled and thought everything was fine.

All of this raises further questions: where did the top-downism, where did the lying, where did the contempt for ordinary peasants come from? Could the individualism which led to people wasting food or shirking work have been overcome? I believe these problems are related and go back to a culture that had developed within the CCP and within government cadre, a culture of careerism and individual advancement.

One of the people Hinton interviewed, a lower level communist leader Ch'en Yung-kuei, insisted that the pressure to lie came from higher up the chain of command:

> The exaggeration wind could not have started from down below among the peasants. ... [When reports of huge grain outputs were heard] [p]eople down below said, "Don't you believe it." But some people above said, "We watched the harvest and took part in it. How can the reports be false?" ...
>
> People from above came down to more advanced brigades fanning up the wind pushing for more and more exaggeration. Those people in the brigades who were more slavish followed their lead and did whatever they were told to do.
>
> 238

He told Hinton, "Communists can't tell lies. I can't do that" (235).

Communes inspired many ordinary people, inspiration which is important to the argument for reasonable hope. The water conservation and control projects of 1957–1958 relied on local initiative for design and implementation; they mobilized thousands, some over 100,000. They strengthened levees, built irrigations canals, drained swamps, created fish ponds (providing protein for people), built dams, and even transported water for irrigation across considerable distances. People could see collective efforts improving their lives (Hinton 1983, Potter and Potter 1990). Collective efforts took them beyond family-selfishness and even village-selfishness to think in terms of the common interests of a much larger group.

To get a sense of how broader motives can catch hold of us, let me quote a colleague who grew up in China. He described (in an email) a bit of his experiences as a child, emphasizing the communist culture that motivated many (edited slightly):

> When I was growing up, whenever there was a *difficult task* in the village, the leadership would say, the *communist party members go first*. Whenever, there was *not enough of something* to go around, the leadership would say the *communist party members would take this the last*.
>
> Young people like myself [were] very much inspired by that kind of spirit. We all have role models in our community, in our county and in our country. These were the people who made the sacrifice first when there was a need for it. People respect these people.
>
> My classmates and I would go to school earlier in winter to start a fire before everybody else. Nobody told us to do it, but we did it without telling anybody. When villagers went to work on the reservoirs, my classmates and I got up one hour earlier to fetch water for those families whose men were working on the irrigation sites. My father told me to do it. He said that that was how I could contribute to it. We were not paid to do these at all. But it was the culture of the time.
>
> ... We all had selfish ideas within ourselves. We need to fight against that. In a socialist society, it was possible to do it. But in the capitalist society, which was built on human selfishness, it is simply impossible. If you were not selfish, you would starve.
>
> emphasis added

While my colleague was writing about the culture he experienced as a child during the Cultural Revolution, it also describes the motivations of many during the GLF.

The free provision of food, infant and elderly care, education, health care, clothing, and other needs expresses the equal worth and dignity of each member of the commune. We get these things because we need them. We are worthy. In contrast, when important needs are available to us unequally because they depend on access to money of which some have much more than others, it is easily understood to express an attitude that the poor "ain't shit" (Gomberg 2016). Analogous to the bourgeois-liberal argument that the status of equal citizen confers equal dignity on all, the provision of material goods and services essential to our flourishing expresses the same idea but far more forcefully. Thus free provision (to each according to need) is an essential element of communist social organization. Many in the communes were attached to the collective dining halls and other elements of collective life for the reason that they expressed political and social equality (Hinton 1983).

Nonetheless, sharing created problems of motivation. Potter and Potter (1990:73) and Hinton (1983: 232) report that people would overeat or waste food that was in free supply. Some shirked labor, individual incentive having been removed. More than one explanation is possible. We could say, with Marx, that people weren't ready yet, that the springs of productive wealth had to bring forth more abundantly, but this connection between abundance and the possibility of communist distribution and contribution doesn't hold up to scrutiny (Gomberg 2016). Or we could say, with many skeptical of the possibility of communism, that it is just contrary to human nature to be motivated by collective incentives, at least absent very special and temporary situations. Egalitarian forager societies tell us otherwise (Gomberg 1997). We could say that communism works in small groups but that once human societies reach a certain size, communist incentives fail (Taylor 1982). I explore another alternative: that *inegalitarian* practices fundamental to socialism, including in its Chinese variant, defeated the GLF.

Generally Friedman and others' (1991) *Chinese Village, Socialist State* is quite skeptical of egalitarianism, arguing that early reforms (land redistribution, small scale cooperatives) worked within established peasant norms and were quite popular. In contrast, they say, radical egalitarianism was disruptive of peasant expectations and unpopular. At the end of their book, however, they express a view which contains the kernel of what I argue. They write, "Rulers praised self-reliance and common prosperity" but "bestowed rewards on a favored few" who "obtained the newest, best, and scarcest." People outside the "favored few" were "told that sharing and leveling brought wealth," but their experience was the opposite, and exposed the state's hypocrisy (Friedman and others 1991: 275). Note the contrast between the *inequality* that Friedman and others describe here and the communist principles that were the life experience of my colleague who grew up in China. Capitalist and communist principles battled *inside* the CCP: in many places communist principles prevailed, in others privilege.

Where did privilege come from? Edgar Snow (1968 [1938]) described shared austerity practiced by Yan'an revolutionaries when he visited them in 1936. How did the egalitarianism and the idealism of 1936 become something else? In answering that question we get a better understanding why twentieth-century communist revolutions did not lead to communism. At the same time, in identifying some correctible *sources* of that failure, we get a basis for reasonable hope of communism.

Marxists and Marxists-Leninists accepted a mechanical view of historical stages and the social relationships predominant at each stage. For Marx socialism (as it came to be called) or "the first phase of communist society" (as he called it) retained material incentives for workers to contribute and retained inequality among workers: a worker's access to resources (what came to be wages) was proportional to labor contribution, leading to inequality. Socialism was based on bourgeois right. Only when people had become more morally developed and production more abundant could workers move to the higher phase of communism based on "from each according to ability to each according to need" (Marx 1974b [1875]). No twentieth-century revolution following this Marxist model ever made it to communism. Why not?

Communists followed Marx in using a wage system in the socialist societies they created, retaining "bourgeois right" (material reward proportional to labor contribution). These revolutions entrenched inequality; they interpreted government service and membership in the Communist Party as making a *greater* contribution meriting *greater benefits*. Government service and party membership became avenues to social and economic advancement.

If we want a communist society—a society where we flourish together—we must never allow this to happen. Communist parties and government leadership drew people who wanted more material goods, even if many others were motivated by communist ideals. People motivated by self-advancement cannot administer egalitarian communist social policy.

How, in China, did the party and government become dominated by self-serving careerists? In a 1928 report to the CCP central committee on the party's military work and peasant organizing in the border area of Hunan and Jiangxi, Mao Zedong (Mao 1995 [1928]: 97–8) described the system of supplying the Red Army troops he led:

> ... everybody puts up with the same hardship: from the army commander to the cook everyone has five cents for food. And when pocket money is dispensed, no one gets more than the other: everyone has his twenty or forty cents.

Later the report amplifies on this egalitarianism:

> ... the reason why the Red Army can hold out despite such miserable material conditions and continuous fierce battles lies in its thorough implementation of democracy. The officers do not beat the soldiers; officers and men have the same food and clothing and receive equal treatment; soldiers enjoy freedom of assembly and speech ...

The report stresses how egalitarian relations can motivate people. The Red Army captured soldiers from the Guomindang army; many joined the Red Army. The report says

> The newly captured soldiers in particular feel that the camp of today and the camp of yesterday are worlds apart. They feel that, although materially they are worse off in the Red Army than in the White army, spiritually they have been liberated. *Therefore, they are reasonably content.* The fact that the same soldier fights more bravely in the Red Army today than he did for the enemy army yesterday reflects the influence of this democracy.
>
> emphasis in original

In essays that appeared around the time of the GLF Mao returned to the early communist practice of the CCP. He said, "Through several decades of battle, [the CCP] always practiced communism" (Mao 1989 [1958]: 436–7). In "Opinion on the Free Supply System" Mao (1960) wrote that for "a long time [the CCP] has implemented the free supply system" while the party grew to several million. Comrades "lived an egalitarian life ... and [t]here was *absolutely no reliance on material incentives*" (my emphasis). Yang Kuisong's research shows that up to 1937 in the Yan'an base area the only distinctions of supply were between front line troops and those in the rear, fighting troops getting more. "The gap of salary could only be embodied between the front line and the rear rather than on ranks" (Yang 2008: 447). According to both Mao and Yang in these early days, the party, when under Mao's leadership, established and lived by the principle *leaders do not get more or better.*

Something changed. In 1937 while food rations were the same for officers and soldiers, differences in allowances existed, high officials receiving 5 yuan, lower officials 3 yuan, ranging down to 1.5 yuan as the minimum (447). While the differences are probably quite small and modest (perhaps like the difference between getting five dollars and a dollar), they establish a principle of preferential treatment of leaders. After Ren Bishi, a CCP leader, returned from the Soviet Union in 1940, the "mess hall produced food divided into an ordinary dining room and a special dining room" (Anonymous n.d.: 3). Thus Soviet influence amplified distinctions between leaders and rank-and-file. The new line was that, until the stage of full-blown communism, the supply system needed to be graded according to people's ranks. Clothes were "divided into three colors and food divided into five grades" (3). These distinctions crossed a line and violated a fundamental communist principle of equality which, until then, had been CCP practice. The new principle was *leaders get more and better*.

After seizure of state power throughout China in 1949, the CCP gradually replaced the ranked supply system with a wage system. About this change Mao wrote, "Party and government organizations and enterprises recruit many members in a short time. They are heavily influenced by bourgeois ideology.... Therefore, we have to give in and let it be" (Yang 2008: 445). But then you are not building a party of communists. You are building a party of careerists. People like Mao hoped to remold them into communists in time, but that never happened. In retrospect we can see why: when you recruit people on the basis that they will *get more* as a communist, then that is the basis of their commitment, not communism. You will not remold them. They remolded the party. This is obvious in retrospect, not so easy for communists to see at the time.

Although the degree of inequality was subject to struggle and change, it was significant enough to give careerists a stake in rising up in the party and the government. It gave an additional incentive—besides the CCP's vigorous military opposition to the Japanese invasion—to induce Chinese nationalists who were not communists to join the party. In addition to the differences in salaries the "higher ups" had other perks as "supplies": servants, secretaries, chefs, private cars, fancy houses, etc. (489). What grew into fairly large and systematic inequalities started as very small inequalities that were instituted during the struggle for liberation. Small seeds produce giant trees.

This transformation of the party explains the failure of the GLF to advance egalitarian communism: in the communes communist leaders were living better than the people whom they were encouraging to share and live as equals (see the quotes above from Friedman and others). When production faltered, they lied to protect their careers. They shipped grain from areas short on grain to cities to advance their careers while peasants in their area (but not the officials!) were destined to die from the food shortages. People charged with leadership (with exceptions) were committed to self-advancement.

The principle *leadership gets more* also explains the top-downism of the GLF and contempt for the wisdom of workers whose hands were in the dirt and who knew what worked and what didn't. If we accept the principle leaders get more, then we tend to rationalize it. Why should leaders get more? The obvious rationalization is *leadership knows better*. Many peasants became passive, just obeyed instructions, even though they knew better. Wrong agricultural practices ensued. These combined with horrible weather, overemphasis on producing metals locally, and lying and maldistribution of what was produced. Famine was the result.

The fault was *capitalist principles* not communist ones, not egalitarianism and sharing but careerism, lying, and contempt for the wisdom of workers. We should ask ourselves what happened to the "implementation of democracy" and the "freedom of assembly and speech" that Mao praised in his army in 1928. Had these principles held, had peasants freely expressed their knowledge and experience and leaders attended to their wisdom, these incorrect top-down agricultural practices would not have been followed. People would not have lied to advance their careers. Famine and death would have been largely avoided. But the distributive inequality of the late 1930s had replaced democracy and respect for workers with a view that leaders knew better, a consequence of rationalizing their having more.

Communist ideals existed both inside and outside the CCP. The CCP leadership—Mao and those around him that had control of the Red Army—while aspiring to communist equality, thought that the CCP could and would gradually impose that equality (Wu 2014: 210). However, Friedman and others had it right: "The more the state preached ascetic equality, the more it exposed itself as hypocritical to the many excluded." CCP leaders who "manifestly profited from the entrenched system" could not impose communist norms on others (Friedman and others 1991: 275). Moreover, most CCP leaders wanted to protect their own privilege, not set the communist example of being the first to do difficult things and the last to take desirable things.

It didn't have to be this way! Another path that was missed: build a communist party of people committed to living by communist principles. There is surely reasonable hope that masses of workers can be inspired by communist ideals, *provided that communists live by them.*

"But, Paul, this is some crazy stuff. The CCP was successful precisely because it was flexible and pragmatic, willing to recruit educated and experienced people into the party, to encourage nationalists and even bourgeois forces to align themselves with the party. A party like that could deliver the goods to non-communist masses and win their support for the CCP. That flexibility and pragmatism is precisely the source of their success. Your party of principled communists is just bound to remain a small, isolated sect."

Two replies: (1) The experience of communist revolutions in the twentieth century tells us where such practices lead. The amplification of inequality after Ren Bishi returned from the Soviet Union was driven not by pragmatism but by a mechanical ideology that said that equality was premature given the low development of productive forces. Hierarchical social organization was introduced by communists wedded to incorrect theory. (2) When the CCP did practice egalitarian communist forms of life it built the loyalty of hundreds of thousands, even millions. Even if many or most peasants and workers were not ready initially to practice communist egalitarianism, they could be won to that way of life by communists who lived and thrived as equals. We can see evidence of that in the testimony of my colleague who grew up in China. Careerists can't win anyone to a communist way of life.

Nevertheless, we should not underestimate the difficulty of my proposed strategy for communist revolution. The Bolsheviks organized for "peace, land, and bread," not for communism. Chinese communists initially won support among poor peasants and landless workers by redistributing land and organizing cooperatives, not by fighting for communism. We cannot know now how popular the struggle for immediate communism might be among workers. What we do know, however, is that unless communists themselves are willing to live a communist life and set communist examples, there is no hope whatsoever of communism.

These, then, are my reasons for believing that it is reasonable for communists to aim at both a society run by the working class and a society based on egalitarian communist social organization.

Revolution and state power

"But a revolution to seize state power would involve so many casualties that the prospect of a communist society—especially because such an outcome is, at best, far from certain—cannot justify the suffering and death that a fight for power would cause." In reply: the existence of a state—concentrated overwhelming force under central command—makes it possible for a minority to create and enforce laws independently of consensus on those laws (Gomberg 1997). A state controlled by a capitalist minority must be crushed in the process of creating a society based on egalitarian communist norms (Lenin 1964d [1917], Marx 1974a [1871]). Can such a struggle succeed, and at what cost?

It is helpful to remind ourselves of what Lenin wrote about revolutionary situations. The revolutions in Russia and China occurred in the midst or aftermath of invasions by foreign armies. The ruling classes were divided and could no longer rule in the old way. People were experiencing war or its aftermath and were open to social change. While no revolution is bloodless, they can be, relatively at least, less bloody than revolutionary attempts against a more-or-less undivided ruling class, as in Syria recently. (Here the rebels were divided, the Syrian ruling class and military less so.) The point of these reminders is twofold: (1) revolution typically occurs in a context where the brutality of the old society—its destruction and degradation of human life—is manifest; (2) while revolutions are violent and involve loss of life, they are much less so than would be a frontal assault on an undivided ruling class.

It is hard to predict the future. We could not predict with any certainty the recent corona virus pandemic. Earlier I discussed whether capitalist ruling classes could avoid major war which would create conditions of instability and possibilities of revolution. There is another variable in these estimations: how will climate change or pandemics affect food availability and consequences of military conflict, particularly among the great powers? Apocalyptic predictions are very "iffy"; still we should be aware that the combination of climate change, pandemics, and inter-imperialist conflict creates potential of disaster for the world's workers. Objections to communist revolution based on the cost to human life should also consider the current and potential cost to human lives—different lives, the lives of the poor—of the current order.

We should prefer reasonable hope to reasonable despair

I have argued for a reasonable hope of communist society, that it is reasonable to believe that the struggle against racism can succeed, that capitalist society can be replaced by a communist world where we flourish by enabling others to flourish. I also believe despair of communism is reasonable, that it is reasonable to think this will never happen. If this is right, if both hope and despair of communism are reasonable, is there any reason to prefer one?

The vision of a communist society—where our social labor is devoted to advancing the good of others and is motivated by that purpose not by self-advancement—imagines human beings as fulfilling their best potential. That vision, that ideal, is one that can also inspire us in our day to day lives as we strive to live in a way that contributes positively to human good (see Gomberg 1989, 2007: Chapter 13). We strive for the best in ourselves and in others; this striving can inform all of our interactions, with family, with friends, with co-workers, with strangers on the street. We strive to live by ideals that, in a communist society, would prevail for everyone, live by what Engels called (in *Anti-Dühring*) a "really human morality."

Conversely, despair of communism, despair of a world without racism or any comparable injustice is likely to have consequences as well. I am not arguing that only communists can live morally; I don't believe that. Still, as the arguments of this book about the impossibility of ending racism within the limits created by capitalist society, as these arguments are assimilated and accepted, despair of a solution to racism becomes more dangerous to someone's moral integrity. Pessimism about the future can breed cynicism about moral ideals. It needn't, but it could undermine moral behavior: since social arrangements are pervasively unjust, I need not strive to be just in my relations with others.

So even if both despair of and hope of communism are reasonable, there are reasons to pursue a life devoted to ending racism and bringing about a communist world where we flourish by promoting one another's flourishing: living that way tends, here and now, to develop the best in us and in our relations with others.

References

Alexander, Michelle. 2010. *The New Jim Crow: Mass Incarceration in the Age of Colorblindness*. New York: The New Press.
Allen, Theodore W. 1997. *The Invention of the White Race: The Origins of Racial Oppression in Anglo-America*, vol. 2. London: Verso.
Anderson, Elizabeth. 2010. *The Imperative of Integration*. Princeton: Princeton University Press.
Anonymous ("A Fictitious Old Man") n.d. "The Wage Grade System—Breeding Ground of Revisionism." Available at http://marxistphilosophy.org/Fictious.pdf.
Anonymous. 1939. *The History of the Communist Party of the Soviet Union* Short Course. New York: International Publishers.
Anonymous. 1971. "Imperialists at Each Other's Throats." *Progressive Labor* 8(2): 58–88.
Anonymous. 1979. "John Brown's Raid: Guns against Slavery." *Progressive Labor* 12(4): 14–53.
Aptheker, Herbert. 1993. *American Negro Slave Revolts* (50th Anniversary Edition). New York: International Publishers.
Armstrong, Philip, Andrew Glyn, and John Harrison. 1991. *Capitalism since 1945*. Oxford: Blackwell.
Arrighi, Giovanni. 2003. "The Social and Political Economy of Global Turbulence." *New Left Review* 20: 5–71.
Bakke, E. Wight. 1966. *Mutual Survival: The Goal of Unions and Management* (second edition). Hamden, CT: Archon Books.
Baptist, Edward E. 2014. *The Half Has Never Been Told: Slavery and the Making of American Capitalism*. New York: Basic Books.
Barenberg, Mark. 1993. "The Political Economy of the Wagner Act: Power, Symbol, and Workplace Cooperation." *106 Harvard Law Review 1381*.
Barrett, James R. 1987. *Work and Community in the Jungle: Chicago's Packinghouse Workers 1894–1922*. Urbana, IL: University of Illinois Press.
Beckert, Sven. 2014. *Empire of Cotton: A Global History*. New York: Vintage.
Beinin, Joel. 2016. *Workers and Thieves: Labor Movements and Popular Uprisings in Tunisia and Egypt*. Stanford, CA: Stanford University Press.
Bellah, Robert N., Richard Madsen, William M. Sullivan, Ann Swidler, and Steven M. Tipton. 2008. *Habits of the Heart: Individualism and Commitment in American Life*. Berkeley, CA: University of California Press.
Bennett, Lerone Jr. 1993. *The Shaping of Black America*. New York: Penguin Books.
Bennett, Lerone Jr. 2000. *Forced into Glory: Abraham Lincoln's White Dream*. Chicago: Johnson Publishing.
Berlin, Ira. 1998. *Many Thousands Gone: The First Two Centuries of Slavery in North America*. Cambridge, MA: Harvard University Press.
Biden, Joe. 2022. https://www.whitehouse.gov/briefing-room/speeches-remarks/2022/08/30/remarks-by-president-biden-on-the-safer-america-plan/
Blackburn, Robin. 1997. *The Making of New World Slavery: From the Baroque to the Modern 1492–1800*. London: Verso.

Blackmon, Douglas A. 2008. *Slavery by Another Name: The Re-Enslavement of Black Americans from the Civil War to World War II*. New York: Doubleday.

Blum, Lawrence. 2002. *"I'm Not a Racist, But...": The Moral Quandary of Race*. Ithaca, NY: Cornell University Press.

Bolton, Charles C. 1996. *Poor Whites of the Antebellum South: Tenants and Laborers in Central North Carolina and Northeast Mississippi*. Durham, NC: Duke University Press.

Bonosky, Phillip. 2000 [1953]. *Brother Bill McKie: Building the Union at Ford*. New York: International Publishers.

Bowles, Samuel, David M. Gordon, and Thomas E. Weisskopf. 1990. *After the Waste Land: A Democratic Economics for the Year 2000*. Armonk, NY: M.E. Sharpe.

Boyer, Brian D. 1973. *Cities Destroyed for Cash: The FHA Scandal at HUD*. Chicago: Follett Publishing.

Braden, Anne. 1999 [1958]. *The Wall Between*. Knoxville, TN: University of Tennessee Press.

Brandmeir, Kathrin, Michaela Grimm, Michael Heise, and Arne Holzhausen. 2016. "Allianz Global Wealth Watch Report 2016." Allianz SE Economic Research. Online at https://www.allianz.com/v_1474281539000/media/economic_research/publications/specials/en/AGWR2016e.pdf.

Brecher, Jeremy. 2014. *Strike!* Revised, Expanded and Updated Edition. Oakland, CA: PM Press.

Breen, T. H. and Stephen Innes. 2005. *"Myne Owne Ground": Race and Freedom on Virginia's Eastern Shore, 1640–1676*. New York: Oxford University Press.

Brenner, Robert. 2006. *The Economics of Global Turbulence*. London: Verso.

Brier, Stephen. 1977. "Interracial Organizing in the West Virginia Coal Industry: The Participation of Black Mine Workers in the Knights of Labor and the United Mine Workers, 1880–1894." In *Essays in Southern Labor History*. Westport, CT: Greenwood Press.

Brier, Stephen. 1989. "In Defense of Gutman; The Union's Case." *Politics, Culture, and Society* 2: 383–95.

Brody, David. 1993. *Workers in Industrial America* (second edition). New York: Oxford University Press.

Brumbach, Kate and Ray Henry. 2011. "Georgia Officials Put Probationers to Work Harvesting Crops." Associated Press June 22, 2011. Available at http://www.nola.com/business/index.ssf/2011/06/georgia_officials_put_probatio.html.

Bunche, Ralph. 1935. "Reconstruction Reinterpreted: Book Review of W. E. B. Du Bois, Black Reconstruction" *Journal of Negro Education* 4: 568–70.

Bynum, Victoria E. 2016. *The Free State of Jones: Mississippi's Longest Civil War*. Chapel Hill, NC: University of North Carolina Press.

Callender, Guy Stevens (editor). 1909. *Selections From the Economic History of the United States, 1765–1860: With Introductory Essays*. Boston: Ginn and Company.

Campbell, Stanley W. 1972. *The Slave Catchers: Enforcement of the Fugitive Slave Law 1850–1860*. New York: W. W. Norton.

Capeci, Dominic. 1984. *Race Relations in Wartime Detroit: The Sojourner Truth Housing Controversy of 1942*. Philadelphia: Temple University Press.

Carter, Dan T. 1979. *Scottsboro: A Tragedy of the American South* (revised edition). Baton Rouge, LA: Louisiana State University Press.

Cashin, Sheryll. 2004. *The Failures of Integration: How Race and Class are Undermining the American Dream*. New York: Public Affairs.

Chamberlain, Neil W. 1948. *The Union Challenge to Management Control*. New York: Harper and Brothers.

Choi, Jung, Jun Zhu, Laurie Goodman, Bhargavi Ganesh, and Sarah Strochak. 2018. "Millennial Homeownership: Why Is it so Low, and How Can we Increase it? Urban Institute. Available at: https://www.urban.org/sites/default/files/publication/98729/2019_01_11_millennial_homeownership_finalizedv2_0.pdf.

Collins, James W. Jr, Richard J. David, Arden Handler, Stephen Wall, and Steven Andes. 2004. "Very Low Birthweight in African American Infants: The Role of Maternal Exposure to Interpersonal Racial Discrimination." *American Journal of Public Health* 94: 2132–8.

Collins, James W. Jr. and Richard J. David. 2009. "Racial Disparities in Low Birth Weight and Infant Mortality." *Clinical Perinatology* 36: 63–73.

Collins, Jane L. and Victoria Mayer. 2010. *Both Hands Tied: Welfare Reform and the Race to the Bottom in the Low-Wage Labor Market*. Chicago: The University of Chicago Press.

Combahee River Collective. 2000 [1977]. In Barbara Smith ed. *Home Girls*. New Brunswick, NJ: Rutgers University Press.

Communist Party U.S.A. 1931. *Race Hatred on Trial*. New York: Workers Library.

Congressional Record. 1904. Congressional Record Fifty-Eighth Congress, Second Session, Volume XXXVIII, Part V. Washington, D. C. Government Printing Office.

Cosby, Bill. 2004. "Speech at the NAACP on the 50th Anniversary of Brown vs. Board of Education." Available at: https://www.americanrhetoric.com/speeches/billcosbypoundcakespeech.htm.

Cox, Oliver Cromwell. 1970 [1948]. *Caste, Class, & Race: A Study in Social Dynamics*. New York: Monthly Review Press.

Cox, Oliver Cromwell. 2000. *Race: A Study in Social Dynamics* Adolph Reed (editor). New York: Monthly Review.

Crenshaw, Kimberlé. 1989. "Demarginalizing the Intersection of Race and Sex: A Black Feminist Critique of Antidiscrimination Doctrine, Feminist Theory and Antiracist Politics." *University of Chicago Legal Forum* 1: 139–67.

Daniel, Cletus E. 1981. *Bitter Harvest: A History of California Farmworkers 1870–1941*. Berkeley, CA: University of California Press.

Daniel, Pete. 1985. *Breaking the Land: The Transformation of Cotton, Tobacco, and Rice Cultures since 1880*. Urbana, IL: University of Illinois Press.

Dattel, Gene. 2009. *Cotton and Race in the Making of America: The Human Costs of Economic Power*. Lanham, MD: Ivan R. Dee.

David, Richard J. and James W. Collins. 2014. "Layers of Inequality: Power, Policy, and Health." *American Journal of Public Health* 104 S1(February 1, 2014): S8–S10.

Davis, David Brion. 1975. *The Problem of Slavery in the Age of Revolution*. Ithaca, NY: Cornell University Press.

Dean, Jodi. 2019. *Comrade: An Essay on Political Belonging*. London: Verso.

Dimitroff, Georgi. 1975 [1935]. "The Fascist Offensive and the Tasks of the Communist International." In Dimitroff, *The United Front: The Struggle against Fascism and War*. San Francisco: Proletarian Publishers.

Doppen, Frans H. 2016. *Richard L. Davis and the Color Line in Ohio Coal: A Hocking Valley Mine Labor Organizer, 1862–1900*. Jefferson, North Carolina: McFarland & Company, Inc.

Drake, St. Clair and Horace R. Cayton. 1945. *Black Metropolis: A Study of Negro Life in a Northern City*. New York: Harcourt, Brace and Company.

Du Bois, W.E.B. 1962 [1909]. *John Brown*. New York: International Publishers.

Du Bois, W.E.B. 1962 [1935]. *Black Reconstruction in America 1860–1880*. New York: Atheneum.

Du Bois, W.E.B. 2007 [1903]. *The Souls of Black Folk*. Oxford: Oxford University Press.

Dunbar-Ortiz, Roxanne. 2018. *Loaded: A Disarming History of the Second Amendment.* San Francisco: City Lights Books.

Dutt, R. Palme. 1974 [1934]. *Fascism and Social Revolution: How and Why Fascism Came to Power in Europe.* San Francisco: Proletarian Publishers.

Edin, Kathryn and Laura Lein. 1997. *Making Ends Meet: How Single Mothers Survive Welfare and Low-Wage Work.* New York: Russell Sage Foundation.

Ervin, Keona K. 2017. *Gateway to Equality: Black Women and the Struggle for Economic Justice in St. Louis.* Lexington, KY: University Press of Kentucky.

Evans, Joe. 1933. "15,000 Cotton Pickers On Strike!" *Labor Unity* 8(6): 8–9.

Evans, William McKee. 2009. *Open Wound: The Long View of Race in America.* Urbana, IL: University of Illinois Press.

Fannin, Mark. 2003. *The Promised Land: Radical Visions of Gender, Race, and Religion in the South.* Knoxville, TE: The University of Tennessee Press.

Fausz, J. Frederick. 1990. "'Abundance of Blood Shed on Both Sides': England's First Indian War, 1609–1614." *The Virginia Magazine of History and Biography* 98: 3–56.

Feagin, Joe R. 2006. *Systemic Racism: A Theory of Oppression.* New York: Routledge.

Feurer, Rosemary. 1996. "The Nutpickers' Union, 1933–34: Crossing the Boundaries of Community and Workplace." In Staughton Lynd ed., *"We Are All Leaders": The Alternative Unionism of the Early 1930s.* Urbana, IL: University of Illinois Press.

Fichtenbaum, Myrna. 1991. *The Funsten Nut Strike.* New York: International Publishers.

Fields, Barbara Jeanne. 1990. "Slavery, Race, and Ideology in the United States of America." *New Left Review* 181: 95–118.

Foley, Neil. 1997. *The White Scourge: Mexicans, Blacks, and Poor Whites in Texas Cotton Culture.* Berkeley, CA: University of California Press.

Foner, Eric. 1993. "Thaddeus Stevens and the Imperfect Republic." *Pennsylvania History: A Journal of Mid-Atlantic Studies*: 60: 140–52.

Foner, Eric. 2015. *Gateway to Freedom: The Hidden History of the Underground Railroad.* New York: W.W. Norton.

Foner, Philip S. 1981. *Organized Labor and the Black Worker, 1619–1981.* New York: International Publishers.

Foote, Thelma Wills. 2004. *Black and White Manhattan: The History of Racial Formation in Colonial New York City.* Oxford: Oxford University Press.

Forret, Jeff. 2006. *Race Relations at the Margins: Slaves and Poor Whites in the Antebellum Southern Countryside.* Baton Rouge, LA: Louisiana State University Press.

Foster, William Z. 1952. *History of the Communist Party of the United States.* New York: International Publishers.

Franklin, John Hope and Loren Schweninger. 1999. *Runaway Slaves: Rebels on the Plantation.* New York: Oxford University Press.

Fredrickson, George M. 1981. *White Supremacy: A Comparative Study in American and South African History.* Oxford: Oxford University Press.

Friedman, Edward, Paul G. Pickowicz, and Mark Selden. 1991. *Chinese Village, Socialist State.* New Haven, CT: Yale University Press.

Gebert, Bill. 1933. "The St. Louis Strike and the Chicago Needle Trades Strike." *The Communist: A Magazine of the Theory and Practice of Marxism-Leninism* 8: 800–9.

Genovese, Eugene D. 1979. *From Rebellion to Revolution: Afro-American Slave Revolts in the Making of the Modern World.* New York: Vintage.

Gerteis, Joseph. 2007. *Class and the Color Line: Interracial Class Coalition in the Knights of Labor and the Populist Movement.* Durham, NC: Duke University Press.

Gibson, Campbell and Kay Jung. 2002. Historical Census Statistics on Population Totals by Race, 1790 TO 1990, and by Hispanic Origin, 1970 TO 1990, for the United States, Regions, Divisions, and States. Working Paper No. 56. Washington, DC: US Census Bureau. Available at https://census.gov/content/dam/Census/library/working-papers/2002/demo/POP-twps0056.pdf.
Gilbert, Alan. 2012. *Black Patriots and Loyalists: Fighting for Emancipation in the War for Independence*. Chicago: University of Chicago Press.
Gilpin, Toni. 1992. *Left by Themselves: A History of the United Farm Equipment and Metal Workers Union, 1938–1955*. Ph.D. dissertation, Yale University.
Gilpin, Toni. 2020. *The Long Deep Grudge: A Story of Big Capital, Radical Labor, and Class War in the American Heartland*. Chicago: Haymarket Books.
Glyn, Andrew. 2006. *Capitalism Unleashed: Finance, Globalization, and Welfare*. Oxford: Oxford University Press.
Gomberg, Paul. 1989. "Consequentialism and History." *Canadian Journal of Philosophy* 19: 383–403.
Gomberg, Paul. 1990. "Can a Partisan be a Moralist?" *American Philosophical Quarterly* 27: 71–9.
Gomberg, Paul. 1994. "How Racial Identities Contribute to Racism." American Philosophical Association Central Division Meeting, Kansas City May 7, 1994. Available at: https://www.academia.edu/56650526/HOW_RACIAL_IDENTITIES_CONTRIBUTE_TO_RACISM.
Gomberg, Paul. 1997. "How Morality Works and Why it Fails: On Political Philosophy and Moral Consensus." *The Journal of Social Philosophy* 28: 43–70.
Gomberg, Paul. 2007. *How to Make Opportunity Equal: Race and Contributive Justice*. Oxford: Blackwell.
Gomberg, Paul. 2016. "Why Distributive Justice is Impossible but Contributive Justice Would Work," *Science and Society* 80: 31–55.
Gomberg, Paul. 2018. "Against Patriotism, for Internationalism: A Marxist Critique of Patriotism." In M. Sardoc (ed), *Handbook of Patriotism*. Cham: Springer.
Gomberg-Muñoz, Ruth. 2011. *Labor and Legality: An Ethnography of a Mexican Immigrant Network*. New York: Oxford University Press.
Gould, Stephen J. 1981. *The Mismeasure of Man*. New York: W. W. Norton.
Gourevitch, Alex. 2015. *From Slavery to the Cooperative Commonwealth: Labor and Republican Liberty in the Nineteenth Century*. New York: Cambridge University Press.
Green, James R. 1980. *The World of the Worker: Labor in Twentieth-Century America*. New York: Hill and Wang.
Green, James R. 2015. *The Devil is Here in These Hills: West Virginia's Coal Miners and Their Battle for Freedom*. New York: Atlantic Monthly Press.
Grusky, David B., Charles Varner, and Marybeth Mattingly. 2017. "Executive Summary." In "State of the Union: The Poverty and Inequality Report," ed. Stanford Center on Poverty and Inequality, special issue, *Pathways Magazine*.
Gutman, Herbert. 1977 [1968]. "The Negro and the United Mine Workers of America: The Career and Letters of Richard L. Davis and Something of their Meaning" in *Work Culture and Society in Industrializing America: Essays in America's Working Class and Social History*. New York: Vintage.
Halpern, Rick. 1997. *Down on the Killing Floor: Black and White Workers in Chicago's Packinghouses, 1904–1954*. Urbana, IL: University of Illinois Press.

Halpern, Rick and Roger Horowitz. 1996. *Meatpackers: An Oral History of Black Packinghouse Workers and Their Struggle for Racial and Economic Equality*. New York: Twayne Publishers.

Harris, Abram Harris. 1989 [1935]. "Reconstruction and the Negro," in *Race, Radicalism, and Reform: Selected Papers of Abram L. Harris*, ed. William A. Darity, Jr. New Brunswick, NJ: Transaction Publishers.

Harris, Leslie M. 2003. *In the Shadow of Slavery: African Americans in New York City, 1626–1863*. Chicago: University of Chicago Press.

Haslanger, Sally. 2000. "Gender and Race: (What) Are They? (What) Do We Want Them To Be." *Noûs* 34(1): 31–55.

Haywood, Harry. 1978. *Black Bolshevik: Autobiography of an Afro-American Communist*. Chicago: Liberator Press.

Healey, Dorothy and Maurice Isserman. 1990. *Dorothy Healey Remembers: A Life in the American Communist Party*. New York: Oxford University Press. In 1993 reissued by University of Illinois Press under the title *California Red*.

Hening, William W. 1823 [1809–1823]. The Statutes at Large: Being a Collection of All the Laws of Virginia, from the First Session of the Legislature, in the year 1619. New York: R. & W. & G. Bartow. Available at: http://vagenweb.org/hening/.

Henrici, Jane editor. 2006. *Doing Without: Women and Work after Welfare Reform*. Tucson, AZ: University of Arizona Press.

Herrnstein, Richard J. 1971. "IQ." *The Atlantic* 228(3): 43–64.

Hinton, Elizabeth. 2016. *From the War on Poverty to the War on Crime: The making of Mass Incarceration in America*. Cambridge, MA: Harvard University Press.

Hinton, William. 1983. *Shenfan*. New York: Random House.

Honey, Michael. 1993. *Southern Labor and Black Civil Rights: Organizing Memphis Workers*. Urbana, IL: University of Illinois Press.

Horne, Gerald. 1988. *Communist Front? The Civil Rights Congress, 1946–1956*. Rutherford, NJ: Farleigh Dickinson University Press.

Horne, Gerald. 1997. *Powell v. Alabama: The Scottsboro Boys and American Justice*. New York: Franklin Watts.

Horne, Gerald. 2014. *The Counter-revolution of 1776: Slave Resistance and the Origin of the United States of America*. New York: New York University Press.

Horne, Gerald. 2018. *The Apocalypse of Settler Colonialism: The Roots of Slavery, White Supremacy, and Capitalism in Seventeenth-Century North America and the Caribbean*. New York: Monthly Review Press.

Horowitz, Roger. 1997. *"Negro and White, Unite and Fight!" A Social History of Industrial Unionism in Meatpacking, 1930–90*. Urbana, IL: University of Illinois Press.

Howard, Walter T. (ed.). 2008. *Black Communists Speak on Scottsboro: A Documentary History*. Philadelphia: Temple University Press.

Hudson, Hosea. 1972. *Black Worker in the Deep South*. New York: International Publishers.

Hughes, Langston. 1992. *Good Morning Revolution: Uncollected Writings of Social Protest*. Edited by Faith Berry. New York: Citadel Press.

Human Rights Watch. 2004. *Blood, Sweat, and Fear: Workers' Rights in US Meat and Poultry Plants*. New York: Human Rights Watch. Available at: https://www.hrw.org/sites/default/files/reports/usa0105.pdf.

Jackson, Kenneth T. 1985. *Crabgrass Frontier: The Suburbanization of the United States*. New York: Oxford University Press.

Jefferson, Thomas. 1954 [1787]. *Notes on the State of Virginia*. Chapel Hill, NC: University of North Carolina Press, 1954.

Jenkins, Sally and John Stauffer. 2009. *The State of Jones: The Small Southern County That Seceded from the Confederacy*. New York: Doubleday.

Johnson, Jenna. 2015. "One of the last in, Scott Walker enters 2016 presidential race near the top of the GOP field." *Washington Post*, July 13, 2015. Available at: https://www.washingtonpost.com/news/post-politics/wp/2015/07/13/one-of-the-last-in-scott-walker-enters-2016-presidential-race-near-the-top-of-the-gop-field/.

Jones, Claudia. 1949. "An End to the Neglect of the Problems of Negro Women!" *Political Affairs* June.

Jones, Jacqueline. 1992. *The Dispossessed: America's Underclasses from the Civil War to the Present*. New York: Basic Books.

Jones, Jacqueline. 1998. *American Work: Four Centuries of Black and White Labor*. New York: W. W. Norton and Company.

Jordan, Don and Michael Walsh. 2007. *White Cargo: The Forgotten History of Britain's White Slaves in America*. New York: New York University Press.

Jordan, Winthrop. 1968. *White over Black: American Attitudes toward the Negro*. Chapel Hill, NC: University of North Carolina Press.

Kandel, William. 2009. "Recent Trends in Rural-based Meat Processing." Conference on Immigration Reform: Implications for Farmers, Farm Workers, and Communities. Washington DC, May 21–22, 2009.

Katznelson, Ira. 2005. *When Affirmative Action Was White: The Untold History of Racial Inequality in Twentieth-Century America*. New York: W. W. Norton.

Keeran, Roger. 1980. *The Communist Party and the Auto Workers' Unions*. New York: International Publishers.

Kelley, Robin D. G. 1990. *Hammer and Hoe: Alabama Communists during the Great Depression*. Chapel Hill, NC: University of North Carolina Press.

Kelly, Brian. 2001. *Race, Class, and Power in the Alabama Coalfields, 1908–21*. Urbana, IL: University of Illinois Press.

Kessler, David. 2009. "Free to Leave? An Empirical Look at the Fourth Amendment's Seizure Standard." *The Journal of Criminal Law and Criminology* 99(1): 51–88.

Kimeldorf, Howard. 1988. *Reds or Rackets? The Making of Radical and Conservative Unions on the Waterfront*. Berkeley, CA: University of California Press.

Kirby, Jack Temple. 1987. *Rural Worlds Lost: The American South 1920–1960*. Baton Rouge: Louisiana State University Press.

Kirschenman, Joleen and Kathryn M. Neckerman. 1999. "'Wed Love to Hire Them, But . . . The Meaning of Race for Employers." In *Race and Ethnic Conflict: Contending Views on Prejudice, Discrimination, and Ethnoviolence*. Boulder, CO: Westview Press.

Klinkner, Philip A. and Rogers M. Smith. 1999. *The Unsteady March: The Rise and Decline of Racial Equality in America*. Chicago: University of Chicago Press.

Kolchin, Peter. 2003. *American Slavery 1619–1877* (revised edition). New York: Hill and Wang.

Korstad, Karl. 1992. "Black and White Together: Organizing in the South with the Food, Tobacco, Agricultural & Allied Workers Union (FTA-CIO), 1946–1952" in Rosswurm.

Korstad, Robert Rodgers. 2003. *Civil Rights Unionism: Tobacco Workers and the Struggle for Democracy in the Mid-Twentieth-Century South*. Chapel Hill, NC: University of North Carolina Press.

Krysan, Maria and Sarah Moberg. 2016. *Trends in Racial Attitudes*. University of Illinois Institute of Government and Public Affairs. Available at: http://igpa.uillinois.edu/programs/racial-attitudes.

Kulikoff, Allen. 1986. *Tobacco and Slaves: The Development of Southern Cultures in the Chesapeake, 1680–1800*. Chapel Hill, NC: University of North Carolina Press.
Lamont, Michelle. 2000. *The Dignity of Working Men: Morality and the Boundaries of Race, Class, and Immigration*. New York: Russell Sage Foundation.
Lassiter, Luke Eric. 2009. *Invitation to Anthropology* (third edition). Lanham, MD: Alta Mira Press.
Lenin, Vladimir Ilyich. 1962 [1906]. "Lessons of the Moscow Uprising." In Lenin, *Collected Works* Volume 11. Moscow: Progress Publishers.
Lenin, Vladimir Ilyich. 1964a [1914]. "The Right of Nations to Self-Determination." In Lenin, *Collected Works* Volume 20. Moscow: Progress Publishers.
Lenin, Vladimir Ilyich. 1964b [1915]. "The Collapse of the Second International." In Lenin, *Collected Works* Volume 21. Moscow: Progress Publishers.
Lenin, Vladimir Ilyich. 1964c [1916]. "Imperialism, The Highest Stage of Capitalism." In Lenin, *Collected Works* Volume 22. Moscow: Progress Publishers.
Lenin, Vladimir Ilyich. 1964d [1917]. "The State and Revolution." In Lenin, *Collected Works* Volume 25. Moscow: Progress Publishers.
Lenin, Vladimir Ilyich. 1966 [1920]. "'Left-Wing' Communism: An Infantile Disorder." In Lenin, *Collected Works* Volume 31. Moscow: Progress Publishers.
Letwin, Daniel. 1998. *The Challenge of Interracial Unionism: Alabama Coal Miners, 1878–1921*. Chapel Hill, NC: The University of North Carolina Press.
Levenstein, Harvey A. 1981. *Communism, Anticommunism, and the CIO*. Westport, CT: Greenwood Press.
Lewis, Ronald L. 1987. *Black Coal Miners in America: Race, Class, and Community Conflict 1780-1980*. Lexington, KY: The University Press of Kentucky.
Li, Huaiyin. 2009. *Village China Under Socialism and Reform: A Micro-History, 1948–2008*. Stanford: Stanford University Press.
Linebaugh, Peter and Marcus Rediker. 2012. *The Many-Headed Hydra: The Hidden History of the Revolutionary Atlantic* (second edition). London: Verso.
Litwack, Leon F. 1961. *North of Slavery: The Negro in the Free States 1790–1860*. Chicago: University of Chicago Press.
Lyons, David. 2013. *Confronting Injustice: Moral History and Political Theory*. Oxford: Oxford University Press.
MacFarquhar, Roderick. 1983. *The Origins of the Cultural Revolution: 2 The Great Leap Forward 1958–1960*. Oxford: Oxford University Press.
Mann, Charles C. 2005. *1491: New Revelations of the Americas before Columbus*. New York: Alfred A. Knopf.
Mao, Zedong. 1960. "Opinion on the Free Supply System." Available at: https://www.marxists.org/reference/archive/mao/selected-works/volume-8/mswv8_55.htm.
Mao, Zedong. 1989 [1958]. "On Communism and Laziness" Remarks by Mao Zedong at the Beidaihe Conference, 30 August, 1958. In Mao, *The Secret Speeches of Chairman Mao*. Roderick MacFarquhar, Eugene Wu, and Timothy Cheek eds. Cambridge, MA: Harvard University Press.
Mao, Zedong. 1995 [1928]. "Report of the Jinggangshan Front Committee to the Central Committee." In Mao, *Mao's Road to Power: Revolutionary Writings 1912–1949*, volume 3, ed. Stuart R. Schram. Armonk, NY: M. E. Sharpe.
March, Richard. 2017. *A Great Vision: A Militant Family's Journey through the 20th Century*. Brooklyn, NY: Hardball Press.
Marx, Karl. 1973 [1852]. "The Eighteenth Brumaire of Louis Bonaparte." In Marx, *Surveys from Exile*, ed. David Fernbach. Harmondsworth, UK: Penguin.

Marx, Karl. 1974a [1871] "The Civil War in France." In Marx, *The First International and After*, ed. David Fernbach. Harmondsworth, UK: Penguin.

Marx, Karl. 1974b [1875]. "Critique of the Gotha Programme." In Marx, *The First International and After*, ed. David Fernbach. Harmondsworth, UK: Penguin.

Marx, Karl. 1975 [1852]. "Letter to Weydemeyer March 5, 1852." In Marx and Friedrich Engels.

Marx, Karl. 1976 [1867]. *Capital*, vol. 1. Harmondsworth, UK: Penguin.

Marx, Karl. 2010 [1851]. "Revelations concerning the Communist Trial in Cologne." In *Marx-Engels Collected Works* Volume 11. London: Lawrence and Wishart. Available at: http://www.hekmatist.com/Marx%20Engles/Marx%20%20Engels%20Collected%20Works%20Volume%2011_%20Ka%20-%20Karl%20Marx.pdf.

Marx, Karl and Frederick Engels. 1974 [1848]. "The Communist Manifesto." In Marx, *The Revolutions of 1848*, ed. David Fernbach. Harmondsworth, UK: Penguin.

Marx, Karl and Frederick Engels. 1975. *Selected Correspondence* (third revised edition). Moscow: Progress Publishers

Massey, Douglas S. and Nancy A. Denton. 1993. *American Apartheid: Segregation and the Making of the Underclass*. Cambridge, MA: Harvard University Press.

Massey, Douglas S., Jorge Durand, and Nolan J. Malone. 2002. *Beyond Smoke and Mirrors: Mexican Immigration in an Era of Economic Integration*. New York: Russell Sage Foundation.

Mayer, Gerald. 2004. *Union membership trends in the United States*. Washington, DC: Congressional Research Service.

McPherson, James M. 1965. *The Negro's Civil War: How American Blacks Feld and Acted during the War for the Union*. New York: Vintage, 2003.

Meier, August and Elliott Rudwick. 1973. *CORE: A Study in the Civil Rights Movement 1942–1968*. Urbana, IL: University of Illinois Press.

Meisner, Maurice. 1999. *Mao's China and After: A History of the People's Republic* (third edition). New York: The Free Press.

Merali, Zeeya. 2010. "Physics: The Large Human Collider." *Nature* 464: 482–4.

Merritt, Keri Leigh. 2017. *Masterless Men: Poor Whites and Slavery in the Antebellum South*. Cambridge: Cambridge University Press.

Metzl, Jonathan M. 2019. *Dying of Whiteness: How the Politics of Racial Resentment is Killing America's Heartland*. New York: Basic Books.

Miller, Loren. 1935, "Let My People Go!," *New Masses* October 29: 23–4.

Mills, Charles W. 1997. *The Racial Contract*. Ithaca, NY: Cornell University Press.

Mills, Charles W. 2003. *From Class to Race: Essays in White Marxism and Black Radicalism*. Lanham, MD: Rowman and Littlefield.

Mills, Charles W. 2004. "Racial Exploitation and the Wages of Whiteness," In George Yancy, ed., *What White Looks Like: African-American Philosophers on the Whiteness Question*. New York: Routledge.

Morgan, Edmund S. 1975. *American Slavery American Freedom: The Ordeal of Colonial Virginia*. New York: W. W. Norton.

Morgenson, Gretchen and Joshua Rosner. 2011. *Reckless Endangerment: How Outsize Ambition, Greed, and Corruption Led to Economic Armageddon*. New York: Times Books.

Murray, Charles. 1984. *Losing Ground: American Social Policy 1950–1980*. New York: Basic Books.

Naison, Mark. 1983. *Communists in Harlem During the Depression*. Urbana, IL: University of Illinois Press.

Nash, Gary B. 2005. *The Unknown American Revolution: The Unruly Birth of Democracy and the Struggle to Create America*. New York: Penguin.
Nelson, Bruce. 1988. *Workers on the Waterfront: Seamen, Longshoremen, and Unionism in the 1930s*. Urbana, IL: University of Illinois Press.
Nelson, Bruce. 2001. *Divided We Stand: American Workers and the Struggle for Black Equality*. Princeton, NJ: Princeton University Press.
Nelson, Truman. 1960. *The Surveyor*. New York: Doubleday.
Nelson, Truman. 1973. *The Old Man*. New York: Holt, Rinehart, and Winston.
Northwestern University Center for Public Safety. 2007. "Illinois Traffic Stop Study." Available at: https://idot.illinois.gov/Assets/uploads/files/Transportation-System/Reports/Safety/Traffic-Stop-Studies/2007/2007%20Illinois%20Traffic%20Stop%20Summary.pdf.
Oakes, James. 1982. *The Ruling Race: A History of American Slaveholders*. New York: Vintage Books.
Olmsted, Kathryn. 2011. "Quelling Dissent: The Sacramento Conspiracy Trial and the Birth of the New Right." *Boom: A Journal of California* 1(2): 59–74.
Oxfam America. 2018. "No Relief: Denial of Bathroom Breaks in the Poultry Industry." Available at: https://s3.amazonaws.com/oxfam-us/www/static/media/files/No_Relief_Embargo.pdf.
Pager, Devah, Bart Bonikowski, and Bruce Western. 2009. "Discrimination in a Low-Wage Labor Market: A Field Experiment." *American Sociological Review* 74(5): 777–99.
Pager, Devah. 2007. *Marked: Race, Crime, and Finding Work in an Era of Mass Incarceration*. Chicago: University of Chicago Press.
Painter, Nell Irvin. 1977. *The Exodusters: Black Migration to Kansas after Reconstruction*. New York: Alfred A. Knopf.
Painter, Nell Irvin. 1979. *The Narrative of Hosea Hudson: His Life as a Negro Communist in the South*. Cambridge, MA: Harvard University Press.
Painter, Nell Irvin. 2010. *The History of White People*. New York: W. W. Norton.
Parenti, Christian. 1999. *Lockdown America: Police and Prisons in the Age of Crisis*. London: Verso.
Parkinson, Robert G. 2016. *The Common Cause: Creating Race and Nation in the American Revolution*. Chapel Hill, NC: The University of North Carolina Press.
Passel, Jeffrey and D'Vera Cohn. 2009. *A Portrait of Unauthorized Immigrants in the United States*. Washington, DC: Pew Research Center. Available at: http://www.pewhispanic.org/2009/04/14/a-portrait-of-unauthorized-immigrants-in-the-united-states/.
Payne, Charles M. 1995. *I've Got the Light of Freedom: The Organizing Tradition and the Mississippi Freedom Struggle*. Berkeley, CA: University of California Press.
Perelman, Michael. 2002. *The Pathology of the US Economy Revisited: The Intractable Contradictions of Economic Policy*. New York: Palgrave.
Pew Research Center. 2016. "On Views of Race and Inequality, Blacks and Whites Are Worlds Apart." Available at: https://www.pewsocialtrends.org/2016/06/27/on-views-of-race-and-inequality-blacks-and-whites-are-worlds-apart/.
Potter, Sulamith Heins and Jack M. Potter. 1990. *China's Peasants: The Anthropology of a Revolution*. Cambridge: Cambridge University Press.
Progressive Labor Party. 1971a. "The Great Proletarian Cultural Revolution and the Reversal of Workers' Power in China." *Progressive Labor* 8 (3), November. Available at: https://www.marxists.org/history/erol/1960-1970/plpculturalrevolution.htm.
Progressive Labor Party. 1971b. "Strengths and Weaknesses in the Line of the International Communist Movement." *Progressive Labor* 8 (3), November. Available at: https://www.marxists.org/history/erol/ncm-8/pl-int.htm.

Progressive Labor Party. 1982. "Road to Revolution 4." New York: Progressive Labor Party.
Quarles, Benjamin (editor). 1972. *Blacks on John Brown*. Urbana, IL: University of Illinois Press.
Quin, Mike. 1979. *The Big Strike*. New York: International Publishers.
Rabinowitch, Alexander. 2007. *The Bolsheviks in Power: The First Year of Soviet Rule in Petrograd*. Bloomington, IN: Indiana University Press.
Rabinowitch, Alexander. 2014. *The Bolsheviks Come to Power: The Revolution of 1917 in Petrograd* (new edition). London: Pluto Press.
Ransom, Roger and Richard Sutch. 1988. "Capitalists without Capital: The Burden of Slavery and the Impact of Emancipation." *Agricultural History* 62: 133–60.
Reich, Michael. 1981. *Racial Inequality: A Political-Economic Analysis*. Princeton, NJ: Princeton University Press.
Reynolds, David S. 2005. *John Brown, Abolitionist: The Man Who Killed Slavery, Sparked the Civil War, and Seeded Civil Rights*. New York: Vintage.
Reynolds, Katherine J., Benjamin M. Jones, Kerry O'Brien, and Emina Subasic. 2013. "Theories of Socio-Political Change and the Dynamics of Sub-Group Versus Superordinate Interests." *European Psychologist* 18: 235–44.
Rivers, Larry Eugene. 2012. *Rebels and Runaways: Slave Resistance in Nineteenth-Century Florida*. Urbana, IL: University of Illinois Press.
Robinson, Cedric J. 2000 [1983]. *Black Marxism: The Making of the Black Radical Tradition*. Chapel Hill, NC: The University of North Carolina Press.
Robinson, Cyril. 2011. *Marching with Dr. King: Ralph Helstein and the United Packinghouse Workers of America*. Santa Barbara, CA: Praeger.
Roediger, David. 1991. *The Wages of Whiteness: Race and the Making of the American Working Class*. London: Verso.
Rosswurm, Steve. 1992. *The CIO's Left-Led Unions*. New Brunswick, NJ: Rutgers University Press.
Ruchames, Louis (editor). 1969. *John Brown: The Making of a Revolutionary*. New York: Grosset and Dunlap.
Rutman, Darrett B. and Anita H. Rutman. 1984a. *A Place in Time: Explicatus*. New York: W. W. Norton.
Rutman, Darrett B. and Anita H. Rutman. 1984b. *A Place in Time: Middlesex County, Virginia 1650–1750*. New York: W. W. Norton.
Satter, Beryl. 2009. *Family Properties: How the Struggle over Race and Real Estate Transformed Chicago and Urban America*. New York: Metropolitan Books.
Schrecker, Ellen W. 1992. "McCarthyism and the Labor Movement: The Role of the State" in Rosswurm 1992.
Schrecker, Ellen W. 1998. *Many Are the Crimes: McCarthyism in America*. Princeton, NJ: Princeton University Press.
Schultz, Mark. 2005. *The Rural Face of White Supremacy: Beyond Jim Crow*. Urbana, IL: University of Illinois Press.
Schwartz, Michael. 1976. *Radical Protest and Social Structure: The Southern Farmers' Alliance and Cotton Tenancy, 1880–1890*. Chicago: The University of Chicago Press.
Selden, Mark (editor). 1979. *The People's Republic of China: A Documentary History of Revolutionary Change*. New York: Monthly Review Press.
Self, Robert O. 2003. *American Babylon: Race and the Struggle for Postwar Oakland*. Princeton, NJ: Princeton University Press.

Sherif, Muzafer, O. J. Harvey, B. Jack White, William R. Hood, and Carolyn W. Sherif. 1988 [1961]. *The Robbers Cave Experiment: Intergroup Conflict and Cooperation*. Middletown, CT: Wesleyan University Press.

Sherman, Jennifer. 2009. *Those Who Work, Those Who Don't: Poverty, Morality, and Family in Rural America*. Minneapolis: University of Minnesota Press.

Smith, Barbara. 1979 [originally 1977]. "Toward a Black Feminist Criticism." *Women's Studies International Quarterly* 2: 183–94.

Snow, Edgar. 1968 [1938]. *Red Star over China*, First Revised and Enlarged Edition. New York: Grove Press.

Solnit, Rebecca. 2009. *A Paradise Built in Hell: The Extraordinary Communities That Arise in Disaster*. New York: Viking.

Solomon, Mark. 1998. *The Cry Was Unity: Communists and African Americans, 1917–1936*. Jackson, MS: University Press of Mississippi.

Stalin J. 1975 [1913]. "Marxism and the National Question" In Stalin J. *Marxism and the National-Colonial Question*. San Francisco: Proletarian Publishers.

Starobin, Robert S. 1970a. "The Economics of Industrial Slavery in the Old South." *Business History Review* 64: 131–74.

Starobin, Robert S. 1970b. *Industrial Slavery in the Old South*. New York: Oxford University Press.

State of Virginia. 1906. *Report of the proceedings and debates of the Constitutional Convention, state of Virginia*. Volume II. Richmond: Hermitage Press. Available at: https://babel.hathitrust.org/cgi/pt?id=dul1.ark:/13960/t84j42d9t;view=1up;seq=5.

Steinberg, Stephen. 2001. *The Ethnic Myth: Race, Ethnicity, and Class in America* (third edition). Boston: Beacon Press.

Steinberg, Stephen. 2007. *Race Relations: A Critique*. Stanford, CA: Stanford University Press.

Stepan-Norris, Judith and Maurice Zeitlin. 1996. *Talking Union*. Urbana, IL: University of Illinois Press.

Stepan-Norris, Judith and Maurice Zeitlin. 2003. *Left Out: Reds and America's Industrial Unions*. Cambridge: Cambridge University Press.

Stevens, Margaret. 2017. *Red International and Black Caribbean: Communists in New York City, Mexico, and the West Indies, 1919–1939*. London: Pluto Press.

Storch, Randi. 2007. *Red Chicago: American Communist at Its Grassroots, 1928-35*. Urbana, IL: University of Illinois Press.

Stuesse, Angela. 2008. *Globalization "Southern Style": Transnational Migration, the Poultry Industry, and Implications for Organizing Workers across Difference*. Ph.D. dissertation, University of Texas.

Stuesse, Angela. 2016. *Scratching out a Living: Latinos, Race, and Work in the Deep South*. Oakland, CA: University of California Press.

Sugrue, Thomas J. 2008. *Sweet Land of Liberty: The Forgotten Struggle for Civil Rights in the North*. New York: Random House.

Sumner, Charles. 1875. *The Works of Charles Sumner, Vol. IX*. Boston: Lee and Shepard. Available at: https://books.google.com/books?id=S48sAAAAIAAJ&pg=PA437&source=gbs_toc_r&cad=4#v=onepage&q&f=false

Sweet, James H. 1997. "The Iberian Roots of American Racist Thought." *The William and Mary Quarterly* 54(1): 143–66.

Tajfel, Henri and John Turner. 1979. "An Integrative Theory of Intergroup Conflict." Reprinted in Michael A. Hogg and Dominic Abrams, eds., *Intergroup Relations: Essential Readings*. Philadelphia: Psychology Press.

Tajfel, Henri. 1981. *Human Groups and Social Categories*. Cambridge: Cambridge University Press.
Takaki, Ronald. 1979. *Iron Cages: Race and Culture in 19th-Century America*. New York: Oxford University Press.
Taylor, Keeanga-Yamahtta. 2017. *How We Get Free: Black Feminism and the Combahee River Collective*. Chicago: Haymarket Books.
Taylor, Michael. 1982. *Community, Anarchy and Liberty*. Cambridge: Cambridge University Press.
Thomas, Laurence. 1990. "In My Next Life I'll Be White." *Ebony*, December.
Thomas-Lycklama a Nijeholt, Geertje. 1980. *On the Road for Work: Migratory Workers on the East Coast of the United States*. Boston: Martinus Nijhoff.
Tilly, Charles. 1988. *Durable Inequality*. Berkeley, CA: University of California Press.
Tolnay, Stewart E. and E. M. Beck. 1995. *A Festival of Violence: An Analysis of Southern Lynchings 1882–1930*. Urbana, IL: University of Illinois Press.
Trice, Dawn Turner. 2006. "Immigration Issues Real in Delta." *Chicago Tribune* June 11, 2006. Available at: http://articles.chicagotribune.com/2006-06-11/news/0606110290_1_catfish-workers-catfish-industry-sarah-claree-white.
Uggen, Christopher, Jeff Manza, and Melissa Thompson. 2006. "Citizenship, Democracy, and the Civic Reintegration of Criminal Offenders." *Annals of the American Academy of Political and Social Science* 605(1): 281–310.
United for a Fair Economy. 2008. "Foreclosed: State of the Dream 2008." Boston: United for a Fair Economy.
United States Bureau of Justice Statistics. 1982. "Prisoners 1925–1981." Available at: https://www.bjs.gov/content/pub/pdf/p2581.pdf.
United States Bureau of Justice Statistics. 2020. "Correctional Populations in the United States, 2017–2018." Available at: https://www.bjs.gov/content/pub/pdf/cpus1718.pdf.
United States Census Bureau. 2012. *Statistical Abstract of the United States*. Available at: https://www.census.gov/library/publications/2011/compendia/statab/131ed.html.
United States Department of Agriculture, Economic Research Service. 2016. "Percent of consumer expenditures spent on food, alcoholic beverages, and tobacco that were consumed at home, by selected countries." Available at: https://www.ers.usda.gov/data-products/food-expenditures/.
United States Department of Labor, Bureau of Labor Statistics. 2016. "Major Work Stoppages in 2015." News Release February 10, 2016. Available at: https://www.bls.gov/news.release/pdf/wkstp.pdf.
United States Department of Labor, Bureau of Labor Statistics. 2017a. "Table 1. Union affiliation of employed wage and salary workers by selected characteristics." Available at: https://www.bls.gov/news.release/union2.t01.htm.
United States Department of Labor, Bureau of Labor Statistics. 2017b. "Table 3. Union affiliation of employed wage and salary workers by occupation and industry." Available at: https://www.bls.gov/news.release/union2.t03.htm.
United States Department of State. 1801. *Return of the Whole Number of Persons within the Several Districts of the United States*. Available at: https://www2.census.gov/prod2/decennial/documents/1800-return-whole-number-of-persons.pdf.
United States Immigration and Customs Enforcement. 2016. "Fiscal Year 2016 ICE Enforcement and Removal Operations Report." Available at: https://www.ice.gov/sites/default/files/documents/Report/2016/removal-stats-2016.pdf.
Wallerstein, Immanuel. 1974. *The Modern World-System: Capitalist Agriculture and the origins of the European World-Economy in the Sixteenth Century*. New York: Academic Press.

Wallerstein, Immanuel. 2011 [1980]. *The Modern World-System II: Mercantilism and the Consolidation of the European World-Economy, 1600–1750*. Berkeley, CA: University of California Press.

Warren, Wendy. 2016. *New England Bound: Slavery and Colonization in Early America*. New York: Liveright Publishing Corporation.

Watson, Hilbourne. 2014. "Oliver Cromwell Cox's understanding of capitalism and the problem of his materialist perspective." *Canadian Journal of Latin American and Caribbean Studies* 39: 382–402.

Weatherford, Jack. 1988. *Indian Givers: How the Indians of the Americas Transformed the World*. New York: Fawcett Columbine.

Wertenbaker, Thomas J. 1959. *The Planters of Colonial Virginia*. New York: Russell and Russell.

Western, Bruce. 2006. *Punishment and Inequality in America*. New York: Russell Sage Foundation.

Williams, David. 2008. *Bitterly Divided: The South's Inner Civil War*. New York: The New Press.

Williams, Eric. 1944. *Capitalism and Slavery*. Chapell Hill, NC: The University of North Carolina Press.

Williams, Patricia J. 2008. "Movin' On Down." *The Nation*: June 26, 2008. Available at: https://www.thenation.com/article/archive/movin-down/.

Williamson, Kevin D. 2016. "Chaos in the Family, Chaos in the State: The White Working Class's Dysfunction." *National Review* 28. Available at: https://www.nationalreview.com/2016/03/donald-trump-white-working-class-dysfunction-real-opportunity-needed-not-trump/

Wilson, William Julius. 1987. *The Truly Disadvantaged: The Inner City, the Underclass, and Public Policy*. Chicago: University of Chicago Press.

Wolfe, Patrick. 2016. *Traces of History: Elementary Structures of Race*. London: Verso.

Woodrum, Robert H. 2007. *"Everybody Was Black Down There" Race and Industrial Change in the Alabama Coalfields*. Athens, GA: University of Georgia Press.

Woodward, C. Vann. 1971 [1951]. *Origins of the New South 1877–1913*. Baton Rouge, LA: Louisiana State University Press.

Woodward, C. Vann. 1974. *The Strange Career of Jim Crow* (third revised edition). New York: Oxford University Press.

Wu, Yiching. 2014. *The Cultural Revolution at the Margins: Chinese Socialism in Crisis*. Cambridge, MA: Harvard University Press.

Yang, Kuisong. 2008. "From the Supply System to the Duty-graded Salary System: Evolution of Income Distribution System of Government Officials around the Founding of the People's Republic of China." *Frontiers of History in China* 3: 444-97.

Zinn, Howard. 2003. *A People's History of the United States: 1492–Present*. New York: HarperCollins.

Index

Note: References in *italic* refer to figures. References followed by "n" refer to notes.

abolitionism 30, 37
Acciacca, Archie 102
"acolytes" of white people 147
activism 45, 46, 48, 58, 108, 113, 123, 214
   anti-racist 1, 7, 197, 199, 209
ADC. *See* Aid to Families with Dependent Children
AFDC. *See* Aid to Families with Dependent Children
agriculture 45, 55–6
   Arkansas Wheel 51
   Black Codes 47
   capitalism and 58–9
   Colored Farmers' Alliance 51
   cotton production 49–54
   Freedmen's Bureau 47–8
   Jim Crow laws 50, 54–8
   scalawags 48–9
   Southern Farmers' Alliance 51–2
   "tenantization" of yeomen 50–1
Aid to Families with Dependent Children (AFDC) 130
Alabama communists 76–84
Alexander, Michelle 134, 135, 137
alienating race 169–75
alliance 54, 165, 219
   of black maroon communities 39
   of capitalists with southern planter class 48, 178
   communists 84
   electoral 53
   between enslaved and free black people 29
   role in banning of the slave trade 34
   in uniting indigenous, black, and white opponents 49
   white-black 53
allostatic load 190–1
American Civil War 17, 29, 40, 183
   aftermath of 50, 128, 151, 178
   black fighters in 40–3
   black labor and US economy 36, 62
   expansion of racist society 33–6
   racism in Northern cities 36–8
   racist rationalizations of social inequality 36
   resistance to slavery and racism 38–40
   "Underground Railroad" 39–40
American identity 171–2
American Railway Union (ARU) 63
American Revolution 29
   English abolitionism 30
   manumission laws 31
   racial foundations of 31–3
   rationalization of race 32
   republicanism 31–2
   slavery and economic interests in Virginia 33–4
   suffrage laws 38
Anderson, Elizabeth 146, 153, 157
   integrationism 199–201
Anderson, John W. 113
Anderson, William A. 54
anti-black
   capitalist society 190
   mass incarceration 136
   material racism 191
   oppression 6, 186, 190
   propaganda in politics 53
   racial injustice 4, 5, 21, 85, 86, 107, 121, 147, 151, 153, 167, 169
   racism 4, 5, 25, 26, 36–9, 40, 145, 152, 160–1, 168, 172, 182, 185, 190, 191, 202, 204
   racist psychology 147
   riots 37
   stereotypes 33, 36, 41, 139, 147, 162, 169, 182
   terror 21

anti-busing 125, 150
anti-discrimination 106, 108
antisemitism 170–1
anti-sexism 187
anti-war demonstration Washington, DC 188
Arbery, Ahmaud 141
Arkansas Wheel 51
ARU. *See* American Railway Union
Ashby, William 122
"asian" 2–3, 118, 141, 155, 159, 162, 169, 184, 216
Atlantic creoles" 15, 20, 24
atrocities against indigenous people 12
axes-of-oppression analysis 190, 193

Bacon, Don 72, 110
Bacon, Nathaniel 17, 18, 24
Bakke, E. Wight 110
Baptist, Edward 34, 49
Barenberg, Mark 114
Bartnick, Bruno 98
Beidel, John 80
Bellah, Robert 191
Bennett, Jr., Lerone 14, 19
Berkeley, George 181
Berkeley, Sir William 17
Berlin, Ira 23
Beverly, Leon 106
Biden, Joe 141
bigotry 3, 20, 25, 105, 108, 113, 114
Bishi, Ren 224
Black Belt 84, 179
black identity 92, 155, 164, 169, 171, 174, 180, 184
blackness 2–3, 23, 163, 166, 169, 174, 182, 193
black separatism 61, 64–5
black soldiers 29, 39, 41–2, 46, 49, 122
    in Civil War 40–3
black/white disparity in infant mortality 190–1
black workers 3, 38, 45–59, 61, 85, 90, 101, 104, 113, 115, 121, 128, 137, 138, 180, 194
    agriculture under Jim Crow 55–8
    barred in ILWU dockworkers 95–6
    cotton production 49–54
    disadvantaged 167

economy growth in US from 36
excluded from social benefit 118
exploitation of 48, 50, 85, 86, 88, 108, 179
"harsh treatment" 69
hired in auto industry 124
Jim Crow laws 54–5
mass incarceration 133
negative stereotype 70, 91, 125
racial injustice 49–54
Reconstruction and its aftermath in South 45–9
Blum, Lawrence 146
Boatin, Paul 102, 103
bondspeople 23–4
Bonner, Pamela 165
Braden, Anne 100, 101
Briggs, Aaron 30
Briggs, Cyril 85
Brody, David 110, 113
Brown, John 30, 40, 42
Burns, Milt 96
Burt, Robert 108, 109
Bynum, Virginia 43

Capeci, Dominic 104
capitalism 3, 5, 27, 49, 54, 73, 75, 128, 136, 182, 193–4, 198, 211
    black workers and 58–9
    in Europe 28, 180
    industrial 62
    opposition to 170
    racial categories of 184
    against racial injustice 91
    radical rejection of 72
    relative surplus population 136
    society 26–8, 128, 197
    in United States 4, 29, 40, 50, 92, 180, 184
Carter, Jimmy 129
Cashin, Sheryll 122
CCP. *See* Chinese Communist Party
Chamberlain, Neil 110
Chambers, Pat 91
checkweighman 65, 65n3
Ch'en Yung-kuei 221
Chinese Communist Party (CCP) 218–20
    egalitarianism and privilege in Chinese society 223

Great Leap Forward 218, 219, 220, 225
  leadership 226
  transformation of 224–5
CIO unions, 75n1, 94, 152
  International Longshore and
    Warehouse Union 95–6
  UCAPAWA-FTA 94–5
  United Auto Workers Local 600, 101–5
  United Farm Equipment and Metal
    Workers of America 96–101
  United Packinghouse Workers of
    America 105–9
civil rights 122–6
class consciousness 213
classless communism 193
coal miners 35, 49, 61–74, 90, 110, 151
  anti-racist lessons from battles of
    Alabama 66–7
  communist lessons 73–4
  industrial slavery 61–2
  lessons from the life 62–6
  United Mine Workers of America
    (UMWA) 67–73
Cobb, Ned 56
Cohn, D'Vera 133
Collins, James W. Jr. 190
"Colord Union Woman" 69–70
Colored Farmers' Alliance 51
Combahee River Collective (CRC) 186–7, 189
communism/communists. *See also*
    Chinese Communist Party;
    Communist Party
  Alabama communists 76–84
  anti-racism 112–15, 177
  cultivating sizeable community of
    communists 214–15
  inspirational spirit of 221–2
  moral imperative of pursuing 227–8
  as path to raceless society 197, 209
  revolution 215–18
  role in ending racism 206–8
  society 4, 152, 177, 185, 197, 211, 223, 228
  transformation through struggle 211–14
  urban uprisings and revolutionary
    situations 209–11
  workers' empowerment and 218–27

Communist International (Comintern) 84
Communist Party (CP) 75–115
  in 1930s 91–2
  Alabama communists 76–84
  anti-racism of red-led CIO unions 94–109
  as anti-racist/anti-racism 84–6, 90–1, 92–3, 112–15
  Congress of Industrial Organizations
    (CIO) and 93–4
  Food, Tobacco, and Agricultural (FTA)
    and 94–5
  "Good Morning, Revolution" 93, 113
  International Labor Defense (ILD) and 88–9
  International Longshore and
    Warehouse Union (ILWU) and 95–6
  repression and 109–12
  Scottsboro Campaign and 88–9
  Unemployed Councils (UCs) and 86–8
  United Auto Workers Local 600 and 101–5
  United Cannery, Agricultural, Packing
    and Allied Workers of America
    (UCAPAWA) 94–5
  United Farm Equipment and Metal
    Workers of America (FE) and 96–101
  United Packinghouse Workers of
    America (UPWA) and 105–9
  Yokinen trial 85–6
Congress of Industrial Organizations
    (CIO) 83, 94–109
Congress of Racial Equality (CORE) 123
contemporary racism
  civil rights 122–6
  "color blind" racism 126
  'ghetto lending' practices 120
  housing segregation 119–20, 121, 122, 203
  New Deal legislation 117–22
  poultry industry 138–9
  recreating racial injustice 126–7
  recreation of state-centered racial
    injustice 130–7
  red-lining practices 119, 120
  school segregation 125–6
  social change 127–8

Index

systemic racism 119–20, 141–2
   in US food industry 137–40
   workers' rights and 140–1
   workers without rights 126–7, 138
CORE. *See* Congress of Racial Equality
Cosby, Bill 148
cotton production 49–54, 57, 58, 203
cotton strike organizers 91
Cox, Oliver Cromwell 177, 180–3, 184, 195, 214
Cramer, Deborah 166
Crenshaw, Kimberle 186
criminal syndicalism 91
crop lien laws 50

Daniel, Pete 56
David, Richard J. 190
Davis, Henderson 95
Davis, Richard L. 61, 62. *See also* industrial slavery
   in Alabama coalfields 65
   black separatism 64
   racial segregation of miners 63
   struggle against racism 62–3
Decker, Caroline 91
Declaration of Independence 30
"deindustrialization" 124
Democratic Party 45–6, 52–5
Democratic-Republican 36, 40
demonstration Los Angeles, California *188*
"dictatorship of the proletariat" 82–3, 177, 179, 185, 218
Dorosh, Walter 102
"double-consciousness" 174
Douglass, Frederick 42
"Driving while black" (DWB) 135
dual unions 86
Du Bois, W. E. B. 21, 152, 174, 177–80, 207
Dyson, John Mack 95

Edin, Kathryn 131
egalitarianism 224–6
   idealism and 223
   racial 66, 73, 77, 80
   radical anti-racist 204–6
ego-defense 155–6
Emancipation Proclamation 40, 41, 45, 65
Engels, Frederick 228
enslaved Africans 5, 11–20, 22–4, 28

enslaved black people 22, 24, 30–1, 35, 40
European invasion 11–12

Fair Employment Practices Commission (FEPC) 124
Farmers Alliances 6, 117, 154, 193
Farrakhan, Louis 148
"fatigue duty" 42
FE. *See* United Farm Equipment and Metal Workers of America
Feagin, Joe 147
Federal Housing Administration (FHA) 119–120
FEPC. *See* Fair Employment Practices Commission
FHA. *See* Federal Housing Administration
Fielde, Gerald 96
Fields, Barbara 14, 32
Floyd, George 141
Flynn, Elizabeth Gurley 110
Food, Tobacco, and Agricultural, and Allied Workers Union (FTA) 94–5
Ford, James 78
Foster, William Z. 87, 94
Franklin, Benjamin 33
Fredrickson, George 37
Freedmen's Bureau 47–8
freed people 39, 45, 49, 55
   Freedmen's Bureau 47–8
   returning to plantations 47
   as source of wealth 46
Free State of Jones 42–3
Friedman, Edward 223, 226
FTA. *See* Food, Tobacco, and Agricultural, and Allied Workers Union
Fusion Party 53, 55

Gates, Henry Louis 166
General Motors (GM) 111, 186
Gilpin, DeWitt 96
Gilpin, Toni 97, 98, 111
Gini score 192
GLF. *See* Great Leap Forward
GLP. *See* Greenback Labor Party
Gomberg-Munoz, Ruth 113, 133
Gooch, William 20
"Good Morning, Revolution" 93, 113
Grantham, Thomas 17
grassroots activism 123

Grbac, Jane 105
Great Depression 58
Great Leap Forward (GLF) 218, 219, 220, 225
Greenback Labor Party (GLP) 67
Griffith, D. W. 177
Gray, Jim 78
group identity 159
    Rationalization Principle 161
    realistic group conflict theory 160
    social identity theory 160
    social psychology of 159–62
    thinking of racism as interracial 162
Gutman, Herbert 62, 63, 71

Haldeman, H. R. 134
Halpern, Rick 106, 108
Haslanger, Sally 25n4, 170n2
Hathaway, Clarence 85
Haywood, Harry 84–5
Healey, Dorothy 87, 113
Helstein, Ralph 107, 111
Henry, Patrick 30
Herrnstein, Richard 181
Hicks, William 70
Higginson, Thomas Wentworth 41
Hinton, Elizabeth 134, 221, 222
HOLC. *See* Home Owners Loan Corporation
home ownership, racial disparity 121
Home Owners Loan Corporation (HOLC) 119
Horowitz, Roger 106
Housing and Urban Development Act 120
housing segregation 119–20, 121, 122, 203
Howard, Samuel 164–6, 173
Hudson, Hosea 75. *See also* Communist Party
    activism 80
    city-wide leaflet distribution 82
    in communist training school 78
    confronting white chauvinism 78–9
    devotion to party 77
    as leader of party work at Stockham 76
Hughes, Langston 113
Hunger March 102

ILA. *See* International Longshoremen's Association

ILD. *See* International Labor Defense
ILWU. *See* International Longshore and Warehouse Union
Immigration Act (1924) 132
immigration 47, 142
    illegal 132
    Mexican 132
    reform 130
    undocumented 154
indigenous people 3, 24, 34, 180
    atrocities against 12
    conflict of frontier farmers with 17
    as savages and heathens 13
individualism 37, 155, 191–2, 198, 221
industrial slavery 61–2
    Alabama coal miners 66–7
    "Colord Union Woman" 69–70
    operators 72–3
    racial egalitarianism in Rendville 66
    racial segregation of miners 63
    radical rejection of capitalism 71–2
    Richard L. Davis and 62–6
    southern iron industry 66
    UMWA in Alabama 67–73
    white miners 65
Industrial Workers of the World (IWW) 59
infant mortality 50, 153
    black/white disparity in 190–1
    racial and international differences in 192
institutional racism 167
integrationism 199–201
intergroup phenomenon 145
International Labor Defense (ILD) 76, 88–89
International Longshore and Warehouse Union (ILWU) 95–96
International Longshoremen's Association (ILA) 90, 96
International Workers Order (IWO) 102
interracial model of racism 146–53, 199
    "acolytes" of white people 147
    anti-black thought in black people 148
    intergroup phenomenon 145
    opportunity hoarding 146–7
    race relations model 148–9
    white benefit 151–3
Isserman, Maurice 113

IWO. *See* International Workers Order
IWW. *See* Industrial Workers of the World

Jackson, Andrew 34, 36
Jackson, Reginald 164
Jefferson, Thomas 12, 18, 30, 32–3
Jesup, Thomas Sidney 39
jewish identity 170–1
Jim Crow laws 6, 25, 45, 49–50, 54–5, 58, 68, 123
   agriculture under 55–8
   contacts between workers 56
   CP fighting against 75–8, 84
"John Brown's Body" 42
Johnson, Lyndon 134
Jones, Jacqueline 152

Kalm, Peter 24
Kamarczyk, Gertie 112
Katznelson, Ira 119
Kelly, Brian 68, 69, 70, 72
Kennedy, John Fitzgerald 134
Kimeldorf, Howard 96
Klinkner, Philip 33
Knights of Labor 57, 58, 65
Korstad, Karl 94, 95
Kuisong, Yang 224
Ku Klux Klan 45, 47, 177, 179
Kulikoff, Allan 22, 23

Lease, Mary Ellen 52
Lein, Laura 131
Lenin, Vladimir Ilych 84, 210–1, 215, 227
Leonard, Mary 77
Letwin, Daniel 68, 69, 71
Levenstein, Harvey 94
Lightfoot, Claude 88
Lincoln, Abraham 41
Linnaeus, Carl 32
Lyons, David 204–6

MacFarquhar, Roderick 220–1
Madison, James 12, 33
manumission laws 31
Manza, Jeff 136
Mao Zedong 224
March, Herb 113, 114
March on Washington Movement (MOWM) 124

maroon communities 6, 21, 24, 30, 39
Marrero, Frederick 99
Marx, Karl 27, 38, 436, 183, 215, 222–3
   dictatorship of the proletariat 82–3, 177, 179, 185, 218
Marxism, race-centered 177–83, 195–6
   allostatic load 190–1
   axes-of-oppression analysis 190, 193
   black/white disparity in infant mortality 190–1, 192
   challenging oppression and building working-class solidarity 193–5
   Cox on 180–3
   CRC 186–7
   dehumanization of worker 181–2
   Du Bois on 177–80
   oppression 180, 186–93
   race-centered aracial Marxism 183–5
   race prejudice 182–3
   racism and individualism 191
   Revolutionary Marxism 194
   superficial anti-racism 179–80
   working-class unity 179, 185, 192–3
mass incarceration 130, 133–7, 141, 150, 153, 156, 194, 210
McGurty, Lawrence 95
McNeil, Charlie 1, 172
Merritt, Keri Leigh 35
Mexican-American War 132
Mindel, Jacob "Pop" 78–9
Miller, Calvin 78–9, 164–6, 167, 173
Mills, Charles 146, 149, 181n2
   on reparations 201–4
"minimal group" experiments 160
Monroe, James 12
Montgomery Bus Boycott 123
Moore, Dave 102, 111
Moore, Richard 85
Morgan, Edmund S. 20, 21
Morgan, J. P. 53
Murphy, Al 76
Murray, Charles 131
Murray, John 30

Nasanov, Charles 84
National Association for the Advancement of Colored People (NAACP) 83, 88, 89, 109, 122, 123, 148, 161, 16

National Labor Relations Act (1935) 94, 114
National Labor Relations Board (NLRB) 94, 98, 99, 102, 111, 211
National Rectification Project 204
Needle Trade Workers Industrial Union (NTWIU) 85
New Deal 56, 117–22
Nixon, Richard 134
NLRB. *See* National Labor Relations Board
non-black people 168–9
non-communists revolution 215–18
NTWIU. *See* Needle Trade Workers Industrial Union

Oakes, Grant 96
Obama, Barack 148
"othering" people 163–4
outward migration 22

Packing House Workers Industrial Union (PHWIU) 105, 106
Packinghouse Workers Organizing Committee (PWOC) 105, 108
Painter, Nell Irvin 81
Parenti, Christian 134, 135
Parkinson, Robert 30
Passel, Jeffrey 133
Pearson, Charles 108
People's Party. *See* Populists
Perot, Ross 163
peremptory refusal 174
"perpetual Brand" 20
Phillips, James 164–5
PHWIU. *See* Packing House Workers Industrial Union
plantation agriculture 12–4, 49–54
PLP. *See* Progressive Labor Party
Populists 52–4, 55, 154, 178
Porter, Jimmy 109
Potter, Jack M. 222
Potter, Sulamith Heins 222
poor white people 21, 23, 35, 47–9, 54, 151, 154, 165, 179, 203
poultry industry 138–9
Progressive Labor Party (PLP) 219, 220
prosecutorial racism *189*
Punch, John 16

PWOC. *See* Packinghouse Workers Organizing Committee

race/racism 26–8, 145–57. *See also* contemporary racism
alienating 169–75
amalgamation 37
anti-black racism 1, 4, 5, 25, 33, 39, 40, 172, 182, 190–1, 202
of black people 164–8
communism role in ending 206–8
definition of 25–6, 153–4
division of workers by 18
egalitarianism 66, 125
fighting 164–9
interracial model of 146–53
materialist history 5
meaning of 153–4
models of 145–6
prejudice 182–3
proposed remedy to 199–206
rationalization of 32
relations 148–9
resistance to slavery 38–40
Revolution of 1776 and 29–31
superficial anti-racism 179–80
systemic racism 119–20, 141–2
transfers 26
two models of 145–6, 157
race-centered Marxism 177–83, 195–6
raceless society
anti-racists 197–9
communism role in ending racism 206–8
integrationism 199–201
proposed remedy to racism 199–206
radical anti-racist egalitarianism 204–6
reparations 201–4
racial harms model of racism 153–7
definition of race 153–4
ego-defense 155–6
racial perceptions and differential experiences 156–7
racist social thought 154–5
Rationalization Principle 154, 156
racial identity alienation 159, 169, 175
American identity and 171–2
confronting racism and building cross-racial relationships 172

"double-consciousness" 174
jewish identity and 170–1
white identity vs. black identity 174
racial inequality 117–22
racial injustice 1, 32, 86, 126–7, 146, 199
   anti-black 21
   black workers 49–54
   recreating 126–7
   state-centered 130–7
   transformed and recreated 117
   racial injustice 86, 126–7, 146
   reparations for 204
   state-centered racial injustice 130–7
   white public opinion 124–5
racial oppression 6, 149, 180, 182
racial slavery 21–3, 25, 27, 28, 35, 126, 151
racial superiority 18–19, 37
racist social thought 154–6, 163–4
radical anti-racist egalitarianism 204–6
Radical Reconstruction 47, 48, 178
Randolph, A. Phillip 124
Raspberry, William 112
Rationalization Principle 154, 156, 161, 166
realistic group conflict theory 160
"Redemption" governments 45, 49
red-lining practices 119, 120
Reed, Jr., Adolph 48
Reich, Michael 152
reparations 201–4
republicanism 31–33
Republican Party 40, 45, 48, 49, 52, 53, 55, 134
Restore Our Alienated Rights (ROAR) 150
Reuther, Walter 104, 111
Revolutionary Marxism 194
ROAR. *See* Restore Our Alienated Rights
Rolfe, John 13
Rutman, Anita 23
Rutman, Darrett 23

scalawags 48–9
school segregation 125–6, 203
Schrecker, Ellen 110
Schultz, Mark 54, 55
Schwartz, Michael 50
scientific racists 36
Scottsboro Campaign 76, 88–9
SCU. *See* Share Croppers Union

segregation 38, 63, 90, 92, 119, 123, 172, 175, 203. *See also* Jim Crow laws
   housing segregation 119–20, 121, 122, 203
   residential 125, 126
Selden, Mark 220
Self, Robert O. 121
separatism 61, 64–5
Seven Years War 30
sexism and racism 5, 101, 216
Share Croppers Union (SCU) 58, 83
sharecropping 6, 45–6, 48, 76, 117, 154, 202–3
Shengwulian 219
Simmons, Marian 108
Singleton, John 148
slave economy 21–5, 30, 34, 180
slave labor 34–5, 45, 61, 183
slavery 6, 11, 26–8. *See also* industrial slavery
   in colonial Virginia 12–21
   conflicts concerning expansion and 30
   of Deep South 35
   and economic interests in Virginia 33–4
   European slavery 11
   medieval worldview 31
   resistance to 38–40
   southern racial slavery 35
Smalls, Robert 41
Smith, Barbara 186
Smith, Carmelita 165–6
Smith, Moranda 94
Smith, Rogers 33
Smith, William 33
Snow, Edgar 223
social change 127–8
social identity theory 155, 160–1
social order 19, 35, 38, 67, 75, 125, 162, 203
social psychology 159–62
Socialization Principle 205
Somerset, James 30
Southern Farmers' Alliance 51–2
Southern Tenant Farmers Union (STFU) 58
stagflation 129, 137
state-centered racial injustice 130–7
   mass incarceration and workers without rights 133–7

undocumented migration 132–3
  welfare reform 130–1
Steinberg, Stephen 45, 48, 148–9, 150
Stepan-Norris, Judith 98, 104, 112
Stevens, Thaddeus 47
STFU. *See* Southern Tenant Farmers Union
Stuesse, Angela 138
suffrage laws 38, 54
Sumner, Charles 46
superficial anti-racism 179–80
systems of oppression 186–93

Taft-Hartley amendment 75, 111, 113, 118
Tajfel, Henri 160
Taney, Roger Brooke 40
TANF. *See* Temporary Assistance for Needy Families
Tappes, Shelton 103
Taylor, Breonna 141
Taylor, Keeanga-Yamahtta 187
TCI. *See* Tennessee Coal and Iron
Temple, William 181
Temporary Assistance for Needy Families (TANF) 130, 131, 138, 140
Tennessee Coal and Iron (TCI) 67, 68, 70, 72
Thomas, Laurence 168
Thompson, Melissa 136
Tillman, William 41
Tilly, Charles 146
top-downism 75, 83, 220, 221, 225, 226
Tractor Works 96–7
Trade Union Unity League (TUUL) 105
Tubman, Harriett 40
Tucker, William 12
Turner, Terence 165
TUUL. *See* Trade Union Unity League

UCAPAWA. *See* United Cannery, Agricultural, Packing and Allied Workers of America
UCs. *See* Unemployed Councils
Uggen, Christopher 136
UIC. *See* University of Illinois at Chicago
UMWA. *See* United Mine Workers of America
"Underground Railroad" 39–40
undocumented migration 132–3

Unemployed Councils (UCs) 86–8
United Auto Workers Local (600) 101–5
  CP-led International Workers Order 102
  Hunger March 102
  racial integration and worker defense 104–5
  struggles for equality and solidarity 103
United Cannery, Agricultural, Packing and Allied Workers of America (UCAPAWA) 94–5
United Farm Equipment and Metal Workers of America (FE) 96–101
  challenging racial attitudes in union hall 100–1
  Local 236's struggles at Harvester Plant 99–100
  shop stewards and worker solidarity 97–8
  Tractor Works activists 96–7
  transformative effects of workplace militancy on racial attitudes 101
United Mine Workers of America (UMWA) 62–6, 90
  in Alabama 67–73
United Packinghouse Workers of America (UPWA) 105–9
  challenging racism and building unity 106
  housing shortage 108
United Steel Workers of America (USWA) 83
University of Illinois at Chicago (UIC) 165
University of the Toilers of the East (KUTV) 84, 89
UPWA. *See* United Packinghouse Workers of America
urban uprisings 124, 128, 134, 135, 209–11, 215
USWA. *See* United Steel Workers of America

Veterans Administration (VA) 119
Virginia, colonial 12–21, 33–4
  Bacon's Rebellion 17, 18, 24
  English groupcentrism 15
  enslavement to resistance 20–1
  group-centrism 13

    racial superiority 18–19
    slave economy 21
    status of slave-for-life 17–18
    tobacco plantation 13–15
Volcker, Paul 129

"wages of whiteness" 179
Walker, Scott 141
Wallace, George 125
Wallerstein, Immanuel 27, 28
War on Drugs 135, 141
War on Poverty 134
Washington, George 12, 33
Washington, Lowell 86, 88
Watson, Tom 52
Weatherford, Jack 12, 26
Weems, Anna Mae 107, 109
welfare reform 130–1
Western, Bruce 134
white benefit 21–3, 151–3
"white chauvinism" 77, 78–9
white corporate agency 149–51
white identity 24, 126, 155, 163, 169, 174–5
white labor 22–3, 36–7, 45, 57, 66–7, 151–2, 178–9
White, Maude 85, 86
white privilege 6, 21, 122, 145, 153
white supremacy 145, 146
Williams, Cleophas 96
Williams, David 42, 43
Williams, Eric 27

Williams, L. C. 107, 109
Williamson, Kevin 181
Williams, Patricia J. 120
Wilson, Charles 110
Wilson, Henry 178
Winant, Howard 150
Wolfe, Patrick 25
white workers 23, 46, 98, 100–1, 107, 115, 121
    anti-black stereotypes 139
    miners 63, 65, 68, 69, 72
    racism among 64, 178, 190
    stereotypes of 36
    white identity among 126
    white-over-black induced 56
workers' empowerment 114, 218–27
Workingman, Honest 71
Works, McCormick 98
Wormley bargain 49
Wright, James 99, 100
Wright, Jim 115
Wyatt, Addie 106

YCL. *See* Young Communist League
yeoman 36, 52, 57
    "tenantization" of 50–1
Yokinen, August 84
    trial 85–6
Young Communist League (YCL) 105

Zeitlin, Maurice 98, 104, 112